Counterparty Credit Risk

For other titles in the Wiley Finance series
please see www.wiley.com/finance

Counterparty Credit Risk

The New Challenge for Global Financial Markets

Jon Gregory

A John Wiley and Sons, Ltd, Publication

ISBN 978-0-470-68576-1 (H/B)

A catalogue record for this book is available from the British Library.

Project Management by OPS Ltd, Gt Yarmouth, Norfolk
Typeset in 10/12pt Times
Printed in Great Britain by CPI Antony Rowe, Chippenham, Wiltshire

Contents

Acknowledgements

I would first like to acknowledge Michael Pykhtin and Dan Rosen who initially had the idea for this book, which they discussed with me in Geneva in December 2008. I would like to further thank Michael Pykhtin for reading and providing invaluable comments on initial chapters and for collaborating on the writing of Chapter 11. I have been lucky to be able to call on informal referees for draft chapters, namely Kirk Buckley, Darrell Duffie, Alex Gu, Andrew Green, Jean-Paul Laurent, Matthew Leeming, John Ovens, Vladimir Piterbarg, David Rowe, Lutz Schloegl and Tom Wilde. I am very grateful to these people for reading early drafts of chapters and putting up with the spelling mistakes and bad grammar to provide some invaluable suggestions. Needless to say, I take responsibility for any remaining errors.

I would like to thank Pete Baker, Aimee Dibbens and Viv Wickham at John Wiley & Sons for their excellent support during this project and to Neil Shuttlewood at OPS for working so quickly and efficiently at the copy-editing stage.

Thanks finally to my daughter Christy, son George and wife Ginnie for putting up with me during the writing process.

Jon Gregory
December 2009

Spreadsheets

The following spreadsheets have been prepared to allow the reader to gain some simple insight into some of the quantitative aspects discussed in the main text. The spreadsheets can be downloaded freely from my website *www.oftraining.com* under the counterparty risk section. Many of these examples have been used for training courses and have therefore evolved to be quite intuitive and user-friendly. New examples will be added over time. Any questions then please email me at *jon@oftraining.com*

Abbreviations

ABS	Asset-Backed Security
AIG	American International Group Inc.
AIGFP	AIG Financial Product
ASW	Asset SWap
ATE	Additional Termination Event
BCBS	Basel Committee on Banking Supervision
BCVA	Bilateral Credit Value Adjustment
BSM	Black–Scholes–Merton
CAPM	Capital Asset Pricing Model
CCDS	Contingent Credit Default Swap
CCF	Credit Conversion Factor
CCP	Central CounterParty
CDO	Collateralised Debt Obligation
CDPC	Credit Derivative Product Company
CDS	Credit Default Swap
CEM	Current Exposure Method
CF	CashFlow
CFTC	Commodity Futures Trading Commission
CLN	Credit-Linked Note
CPPI	Constant Proportion Portfolio Insurance
CPU	Central Processing Unit
CRG	Counterparty Risk Group
CSA	Credit Support Amount
CSO	Collateralised Synthetic Obligation
CVA	Credit Value Adjustment
DBL	Drexel–Burnham–Lambert
DC	Determination Committee
DD	Distance to Default
DPC	Derivatives Product Company (or Corporation)
EAD	Exposure At Default
EDF	Expected Default Frequency
EE	Expected Exposure

EEPE	Effective Expected Positive Exposure
EPE	Expected Positive Exposure
ERM	Enterprise Risk Management
ETO	Early Termination Option
EVT	Extreme Value Theory
FX	Foreign eXchange
G10	Group of Ten
GCM	General Clearing Member
ICM	Individual Clearing Member
IMM	Internal Model Method; International Monetary Market
IRB	Internal Ratings Based
IRS	Interest Rate Swap
ISDA	International Swaps and Derivatives Association
LGD	Loss Given Default
LHP	Large Homogeneous Pool
LIBOR	London Inter-Bank Offer Rate
LSS	Leveraged Super Senior
LTCM	Long Term Capital Management
MA	Maturity Adjustment
MBS	Mortgage-Backed Security
MMR	Modified Modified Restructuring
MR	Modified Restructuring
MTA	Minimum Transfer Amount
MtM	Mark-to-Market
NA	North American
NAV	Net Asset Value
NCM	Non-Clearing Member
NGR	Ratio of current Net exposure to current GRoss exposure
NN	No Netting
NS	Netting Set
OTC	Over The Counter
PD	Probability of Default
PFE	Potential Future Exposure
PWC	PriceWaterhouseCooper
RC	Regulatory Capital
RED	Reference Entity Database
S&P	Standard & Poor
SFAS	Standards of Financial Accounting Statement
SFT	Structured Finance Transaction
SIV	Structured Investment Vehicle
SM	Standardised Method
SPAN	Standard Portfolio Analysis of Risk
SPE	Special Purpose Entity
SPV	Special Purpose Vehicle
TRS	Total Return Swap
VAR	Value-at-Risk
WR	Withdrawn Rating

Introduction

THE NEW CHALLENGE FOR GLOBAL FINANCIAL MARKETS

In 2007 we started to experience what would be the worst financial crisis since the 1930s. The crisis spread from origins in the United States to become a global crisis. It also spread rapidly from the financial markets to have a significant impact on the real economy. Some financial institutions failed including the extremely high profile bankruptcy of the investment bank Lehman Brothers founded in 1850. Even more financial institutions would have failed were it not for government bailouts.

The first decade of the 21st century has been disastrous for derivatives and financial risk management. One area that needs special attention is that of counterparty credit risk, often known simply as counterparty risk. Counterparty risk arises from the credit risk in securities financing transactions such as repos and the vast and often complex OTC (over-the-counter) derivatives market. For example, Lehman Brothers had a notional amount of $800 billion of OTC derivatives at the point of bankruptcy. In addition, the complex web of transactions, collateral positions and structures such as SPVs (special purpose vehicles) needing to be unwound during the Lehman's bankruptcy has provided a reminder of the presence and complexity of counterparty risks within the financial system.

The use of derivatives among companies is widespread although the majority of the risk is centralised among financial institutions and further concentrated amongst the largest banks or "dealers". Non-financial users of derivatives tend to apply them only for hedging specific risks. Banking institutions did not fail because of unprofitable OTC derivatives-trading activities. However, derivatives do have the potential to create a complex web of transactions and also allow much of the leverage that can bring about major market disturbances. Furthermore, the complexity and bilateral nature of derivatives, together with the rapidly moving financial markets, means that the financial instability of a large institution can easily cause major shockwaves through the entire highly connected financial system.

Whilst Lehman Brothers was the only high-profile default of the credit crisis, many other large financial institutions (for example, Bear Stearns, AIG, Fannie Mae, Freddie Mac, Merrill Lynch, Royal Bank of Scotland) needed external support (mainly government) to avoid their failure. The "too big to fail" mentality that seemingly existed in the market has been thoroughly discredited and the failure or financial instability of any institution large or small should be regarded as plausible. A key concern around the default of a large financial institution is the systemic risk arising from a cascade of events that could lead to a major crisis within the financial markets. Such systemic risk episodes are of great concern and therefore need to be strongly mitigated against.

A lack of proper assessment of credit exposure and default probability was a key driver of the credit crisis from 2007 onwards. The too-big-to-fail illusion meant that many counterparties were given (perhaps only implicitly) zero or close to zero default probability. Rating agencies were able to earn income from assessing securities that were potentially far riskier than indicated by their given rating which in many cases turned out to be inaccurate and of little value. Many years of laziness in assessing credit risk led to a major crisis. Lessons need to be learned, a key one being that all institutions must improve their understanding, quantification and management of their counterparty risks.

OVERVIEW OF THIS BOOK

This book is a comprehensive guide to the subject of counterparty risk for practitioners dealing with this or related topics. All aspects of counterparty risk and related areas are discussed. Whilst financial risk management has tended to be rather quantitative in recent years, there is a well-known danger in overuse of models and quantitative methods. We aim to strike a balance by including quantitative material in appendices for the book, which are not compulsory. The main text can be read freely by the non-quantitative reader whilst appendices may be consulted by those wishing to go into more detail on the underlying mathematical points. There are also spreadsheet examples accompanying the book that can be freely downloaded (see p. xviii).

We begin the book with two introductory chapters: *Chapter 1* sets the scene and describes counterparty risk in context with other financial risks (market, liquidity, operational, credit) and concepts such as VAR (value-at-risk). *Chapter 2* introduces and defines counterparty risk, explaining the product coverage, components and important terminology and discusses many of the key topics that will be covered in more detail in later chapters.

Netting and collateral reduces counterparty risk substantially with the overall exposure of firms reduced to a small fraction of their gross exposure. In *Chapter 3* we discuss these risk mitigation techniques together with others such as termination events and the use of default-remote entities that have been much utilised to limit counterparty risk. We also describe the importance of mitigation techniques in allowing the OTC derivatives market to grow exponentially in size and we consider the potential dangers of the benefits of risk mitigation being overestimated.

Derivatives can fluctuate from an asset to a liability position, hence both parties face credit exposure over time. An important consideration for many financial institutions for many years has been the modelling of credit exposure and its use, together with credit lines, to control counterparty risk. *Chapter 4* is dedicated to discussing the quantification of credit exposure and describing methodologies, models and systems requirements. *Chapter 5* follows on with a discussion on quantifying credit exposure in the presence of collateral agreements. With collateralisation becoming increasingly important and common, there is particular relevance to understand fully the extent to which collateral agreements change future credit exposure.

Between 2001 and 2007, the notional value of outstanding credit default swaps (CDSs) grew by a factor of 100. Due to the turbulence in the credit markets, the counterparty risk problem became critical for the financial industry and resulted in a dramatic shrinkage of the market. *Chapter 6* is an introduction to credit risk and credit derivatives for readers not experienced in this area and then covers more complex aspects of the credit derivatives market that will be useful knowledge for later chapters. We describe recent developments such as the "Big Bang Protocol" introduced to improve market transparency and liquidity and agreed to by the majority of banks, hedge funds and asset managers trading CDSs. We also describe some of the intricacies of portfolio credit derivatives and, in particular, super senior tranches that will be part of important discussions in later chapters regarding monoline insurers and so-called wrong-way risk.

There has been substantial interest recently for banks and other financial institutions to price dynamically their counterparty risk and so to fairly charge all future counterparty risk losses at the point of origin (e.g. an individual trader). *Chapter 7* discusses the intricacies involved in computing credit value adjustment (CVA) as a means to price counterparty risk and the inclusion of all risk mitigants within the pricing. Also discussed is the practice of including one's own default in the assessment of counterparty risk, so-called bilateral CVA or DVA (debt value adjustment). This is an important and hotly debated theme at the current time for institutions with large counterparty risk exposures. Chapter 7 is the most complex chapter but, with the mathematical formulae in optional appendices, should be also accessible to less technically minded readers.

Chapter 8 continues the discussion on CVA but without the usual simplifying assumption that there is no wrong-way risk. Wrong-way risk causes CVA to increase substantially and we analyse specific cases of relevance such as interest rate, foreign exchange and commodity contracts. Extensive focus is given to credit derivatives since the counterparty risk inherent in these instruments has been blamed for playing a pivotal role in the collapse of Lehman Brothers and the failure of AIG. All this makes the evaluation and hedging of CVA for CDSs vital for the financial system as a whole.

As well as being driven by institutions wanting to value properly counterparty risk, the need for CVA is also strongly driven by accountancy regulations, which require the fair valuation of the counterparty risk of derivatives positions. Since CVA is necessarily driven by market-implied parameters, then it will be important for most firms to hedge or at least limit certain sensitivities, for example due to credit spreads. Failure to do this will lead to highly volatile CVA numbers and potentially severe mark-to-market losses due to counterparty risk. *Chapter 9* considers hedging aspects with the focus on practical strategies that are used by some large banks rather than theoretical ideas that cannot be put into practice.

Portfolio credit risk and associated economic capital concepts have been an important topic for well over a decade. In *Chapter 10* counterparty risk portfolio aspects are introduced from the two-name case, relevant for contracts known as contingent credit default swaps (CCDSs) to the multi-name case, relevant for quantification of unexpected losses and economic capital. We discuss the treatment of random exposures in a credit portfolio framework. The regulatory side of portfolio counterparty risk, largely in relation to Basel II, is discussed in *Chapter 11*, which covers aspects such as the double-default rules for hedged counterparty risks and the treatment of derivatives exposures under the IRB (internal rating based) approach of Basel II.

With the quantification, mitigation, pricing, hedging and regulation of counterparty risk increasing in focus, many institutions have or plan to create dedicated units for managing counterparty risk and related aspects. Such "CVA desks", as they are sometimes known, perform a key role for an organisation, centralising the management of all counterparty risk and ensuring that all new business is priced appropriately and competitively. *Chapter 12* tackles the important topic of how to manage counterparty risk within a financial institution considering responsibilities, organisational aspects, the mechanics of charging internal clients and the associated risk management of a firm's entire counterparty risk.

Chapter 13 explains in a historical context the concept of a default-remote or triple-A counterparty, a concept that has taken a number of guises, many of which are fundamentally flawed and may therefore in reality be nothing more than counterparty risk black holes. We describe derivative product companies (DPCs) that have had a long and successful existence and the more recent and specialised credit derivative product companies (CDPCs). We discuss in detail the monoline debacle that led to billions of dollars of losses for investment banks during the 2007–2008 period due to flawed assessment of triple-A credit quality.

For regulators, a perceived lack of transparency of OTC derivatives was a fundamental cause of the credit crisis. In 2009 the Obama Administration (through the US treasury) proposed a new framework for greater market regulation and oversight to the OTC derivatives market. One of the aims was to mandate centralised clearing of standardised CDS contracts. *Chapter 14* discusses central counterparties as a means of ultimately reducing counterparty risk within the financial markets and minimising the chance of future systemic risks and severe market disturbances. We try to give a balanced view of the positive and negative points of central clearing and define the situations in which it can have a beneficial impact on financial markets.

There has been much recent interest in counterparty risk and related aspects such as collateral management, credit value adjustments, wrong-way risk, credit default swaps and central clearing. In *Chapter 15* we consider briefly what the future might hold and put in context the current initiative aimed at controlling counterparty risk – the new challenge for global financial markets.

There are likely to be many changes and innovations in the counterparty risk area, please visit my website, *www.oftraining.com*, to check on up-to-date information on training courses, new initiatives and updates to the topics covered in this book.

1

Setting the Scene

"If history repeats itself, and the unexpected always happens, how incapable must Man be of learning from experience."

George Bernard Shaw (1856–1950)

1.1 FINANCIAL RISK MANAGEMENT

Financial risk management has experienced a revolution over the last two decades. This has been driven by infamous financial disasters due to the collapse of large financial institutions such as Barings (1995), Long Term Capital Management (1998), Enron (2001), Worldcom (2002), Parmalat (2003) and Lehman Brothers (2008). Such disasters have proved that huge losses can arise from insufficient management of financial risk and cause negative waves throughout the global financial markets.

Corporations need to manage risk carefully. This may be achieved rather passively by simply attempting to avoid exposure to risk factors that could be potentially damaging. More commonly, a firm may see the ability to understand risks and take exposure to particular areas as offering a strong competitive advantage. Quantitative approaches to risk management have been widely adopted in recent times, in particular with the popularity of the value-at-risk concept. Whilst strong quantitative risk management and reliance on financial models can be a useful part of the risk management armoury, overreliance on mathematics can be counterproductive.

Financial risk is broken down into many areas, of which counterparty risk is one. Counterparty risk is arguably one of the more complex areas to deal with since it is driven by the intersection of different risk types (for example, market and credit) and is highly sensitive to systemic traits, such as the failure of large institutions. Counterparty risk also involves the most complex financial instruments, derivatives. Derivatives can be extremely powerful and useful for corporations and have aided the growth of global financial markets. However, as almost every average person now knows, derivatives can be highly toxic and cause massive losses and financial catastrophes if misused.

Counterparty risk should be considered and understood in the context of other financial risks, which we briefly review next.

1.1.1 Market risk

Market risk arises from the (short-term) movement of market prices. It can be a linear risk, arising from an exposure to the direction of movement of underlying variables such as stock prices, interest rates, foreign exchange rates, commodity prices or credit spreads. Alternatively, it may be a non-linear risk arising from the exposure to market volatility as might arise in a hedged position. Market risk has been the most studied financial risk of the past two decades, with quantitative risk management techniques widely applied in its measurement and management. This was catalysed by some serious market risk related losses in the 1990s (Barings, Orange County) and the amendments to the Basel I capital accord in 1995 that allowed financial institutions to use proprietary mathematical models to compute their capital requirements for market risk. Indeed, market risk has led to the birth of the value-at-risk (described later) approach to risk quantification.

1.1.2   Liquidity risk

Liquidity risk is normally characterised in two forms. Asset liquidity risk represents the risk that a transaction cannot be executed at market prices, perhaps due to the size of the position and/or relative illiquidity of the underlying. Funding liquidity risk refers to the inability to fund payments, potentially forcing an early liquidation of assets and crystallisation of losses. Since such losses may lead to further funding issues, funding liquidity risk can manifest itself via a "death spiral" caused by the negative feedback between losses and cash requirements. It is extremely important in leveraged positions, which are subject to margin calls.

1.1.3   Operational risk

Operational risk arises from people, systems, internal and external events. It includes human error (such as trade entry mistakes), failed processes (such as settlement of trades), model risk (inaccurate or badly calibrated models), fraud (such as rogue traders) and legal risk (such as the inability to enforce legal agreements). Whilst some operational risk losses may be moderate and common (incorrectly booked trades, for example), the most significant losses are likely to be a result of highly improbable scenarios or even a "perfect storm" combination of events. Operational risk is therefore extremely hard to quantify, although quantitative techniques are increasingly being applied.

1.1.4   Credit risk

Credit risk is the risk that a counterparty may be unable or unwilling to make a payment or fulfil contractual obligations. This may be characterised in terms of an actual default or, less severely, by deterioration in a counterparty's credit quality. The former case may result in an actual and immediate loss whereas, in the latter case, future losses become more likely leading to a mark-to-market impact. When characterising credit risk, the probability of the counterparty defaulting is clearly a key aspect. However, the potential exposure at default and associated recovery value are also important quantities to consider.

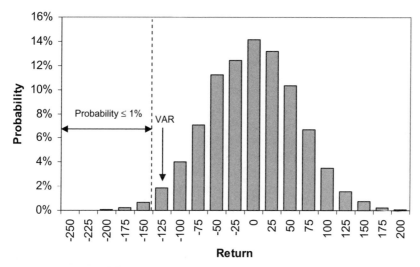

Figure 1.1. Illustration of the value-at-risk (VAR) concept at the 99% confidence level. The VAR is 125, since the chance of a loss greater than this amount is no more than 1%.

1.1.5 Value-at-risk

Value-at-risk (VAR) has been a key risk management measure over the last two decades. Initially designed as a metric for market risk, it has been subsequently used across many financial areas as a means for efficiently summarising risk via a single quantity. VAR is most simply a quantile of the relevant (continuous) distribution. A quantile gives a value on a probability distribution where a given fraction of the probability falls below that level. Therefore, for example, the 1% quantile of a distribution gives a value such that there is 1% probability of being below and 99% of being above that value. The only slight complexity in the definition of VAR is that the distribution defining the risk might not be *continuous*. This means that the distribution is discrete and cannot be divided into areas of arbitrary probability.

VAR is defined as the worst loss over a target horizon that will not be exceeded with a certain confidence level. The VAR at the α% confidence level gives a loss value that will be exceeded with *no more* than $(1 - \alpha)$% of probability. An example of the computation of VAR is shown in Figure 1.1. The VAR at the 99% confidence level is 125 (by convention the "worst loss" is expressed as a positive number) since the probability that this will be exceeded is no more than 1% (it is actually 0.92% due to the discrete nature of the distribution). To find the VAR, we look for the *minimum* loss that will be exceeded with the specified probability.

1.1.6 Disadvantages of value-at-risk

VAR is a very useful way in which to summarise the risk of an entire distribution in a single number that can be easily understood. It also makes no assumption as to the nature of distribution itself, such as that it is normal (Gaussian).[1] It is, however, open

---

[1] Certain implementations of a VAR model (notably the so-called variance–covariance approach) may make normal distributions assumptions but these are done for reasons of simplification and the VAR idea itself does not require them.

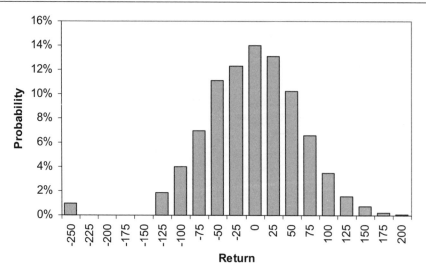

Figure 1.2. Distribution with the same VAR as Figure 1.1.

to problems of misinterpretation since VAR says nothing at all about what lies beyond the defined (1% in above example) threshold. In Figure 1.2, we show a slightly different distribution with the same VAR. In this case, the probability of losing 250 is 1% and hence the 99% VAR is indeed 125 (since there is zero probability of other losses in-between). We can see that changing the loss of 250 does not change the VAR since it is only the *probability* of this loss that is relevant. Hence, VAR does not give an indication of the possible loss outside the confidence level chosen. A certain VAR number does not mean that a loss of 10 times this amount is impossible (as it would be for a normal distribution). Overreliance of VAR numbers can be counterproductive as it may lead to false confidence.

1.2   THE FAILURE OF MODELS

1.2.1   Why models?

The use of metrics such as VAR encourages a reliance on quantitative models in order to derive the distribution of returns from which a VAR number can be calculated. Models are useful for making quick pricing calculations to assess the value of transactions and the inherent risk. The use of complicated models facilitates combining many complex market characteristics such as volatility and dependence into one or more simple numbers that can represent the benefits and risks of a new trade. Models can compare different trades and quantify which is better, at least according to certain pre-defined metrics. All of these things can be done in minutes or even seconds to allow institutions to make fast decisions in rapidly moving financial markets.

   However, the financial markets have a somewhat love–hate relationship with mathematical models and the "quants" who develop them. In good times, models tend to be regarded as invaluable, facilitating the growth in complex derivatives products and highly dynamic approaches to risk management adopted by many large financial institutions. Only in bad times, and often after significant financial losses, is the realisation that models are only simple approximations to the reality of financial markets fully appreciated. Most recently, following the credit crisis beginning in 2007, mathematical models have been heavily criticised for the incorrect modelling of mortgage-backed securities and other structured credit products that led to significant losses (see Chapter 6).

1.2.2   Good model, bad model

The potential for "blowups" in financial markets, especially derivatives, has led to models being either loved or berated depending on the underlying market conditions. Take the most famous model of them all, the Black Scholes Merton (BSM) option-pricing formula (Black and Scholes, 1973) as an example. The financial markets took a while to warm to this approach, but by around 1977 traders were treating the formula as gospel. On Black Monday (19th October 1987), US stocks collapsed by 23%, wiping out $1 trillion in capital, and this was partly due to dynamic-hedging strategies like CPPI (constant proportion portfolio insurance) made possible by the BSM theory. Nevertheless, in 1995, Myron Scholes and Robert Merton were awarded the Nobel Prize for Economic Sciences.[2] The danger is that models tend to be either viewed as "good" or "bad" depending on the underlying market conditions. Whereas, in reality, models can be good or bad depending on how they are used. An excellent description of the intricate relationship between models and financial markets can be found in MacKenzie (2006).

The reasons for the changing and inconsistent view of quantitative models within finance also arises from the fact that models are applied to many different problems, some of which are reasonable to model and some of which are not. The rating agencies' willingness to rate highly complex structured credit products (see Chapter 6) with sophisticated new models is an example of the latter category. In this case, the data available was so scarce that no statistical model should have ever be applied, no matter how good the underlying theory.

VAR provides another good example of the application-of-models dilemma. A 99% VAR over 10 days is potentially a "modellable" quantity[3] since a one in a hundred 10-day event is not particularly extreme. On the other hand, consider 99.9% annual VAR, a one of a thousand probability event in a given year. Such an event is in the realm of a market meltdown or crash. Such events are almost impossible to model quantitatively and institutions should rely more on experience, intuition and methods such as stress testing to quantity such risks.

Therefore, whilst models are useful tools for any financial risk manager, they must not be overused. In this book, we will certainly use models where relevant, but we have endeavoured to keep this to a minimum and to keep all mathematical descriptions outside the main text.

---

[2] Fischer Black had died in 1995.
[3] Some debate even this aspect but our point is that more extreme events become less easy to model.

1.3   THE DERIVATIVES MARKET

1.3.1   What is a derivative?

Derivatives contracts represent agreements either to make payments or to buy or sell an underlying contract at a time or times in the future. The times may range from a few weeks or months (for example, futures contracts) to many years (for example, long-dated foreign exchange products). The value of derivatives contracts will change with the level of one of more underlying assets or indices and possibly also decisions made by the parties to the contract. In many cases, the initial value of a derivative traded will be contractually configured to be zero for both parties at inception.

In many ways, derivatives are no different from the underlying cash instruments. They simply allow one to take a very similar position in a synthetic way. For example, an airline wanting to reduce their exposure to a potentially rising oil price can buy oil futures, which are cash-settled and therefore represent a very simple way to go "long oil" (with no storage or transport costs). An institution wanting to reduce their exposure to a certain asset can do so via a derivative contract, which means they do not have to sell the asset directly in the market, which would essentially "advertise" their trade (which they may not want clients or competitors to know).

The use of derivatives as synthetic versions of cash assets is not particularly worrying. However, a key difference of derivatives instruments is *leverage*. Since most derivatives are executed with only a small (with respect to the notional value of the contract) or no upfront payment made, they allow significant leverage. If an institution has the view that US interest rates will be going down, they may buy US treasury bonds.[4] There is natural limitation to the size of this trade, which is the cash that the institution can raise in order to invest in bonds. However, entering into a receiver interest rate swap in US dollars will provide approximately the same exposure to interest rates but with no initial investment.[5] Hence, the size of the trade, and the effective leverage, must be limited by the institution themselves, their counterparty in the swap transaction or a regulator. Inevitably, it will be significantly bigger than that in the previous case of buying bonds outright.

1.3.2   Market structure

The derivatives market has grown exponentially over the last two decades. Derivatives have been shown to have many uses and have fuelled an increase in the efficiency of financial markets. However, derivatives have been repeatedly shown to be capable of creating major market disturbances. They have been given such labels as "financial weapons of mass destruction". The fact is that, as any invention that offers significant advantages such as commercial aircraft or nuclear power, derivatives can be extremely dangerous. However, that does not mean they should be outlawed, but just that they should be used with caution and regulated with extreme care and pessimism.

Within the derivatives markets, many of the simplest products are traded through exchanges. An exchange has the benefit of facilitating liquidity and therefore making trading and unwinding of positions easy. An exchange also mitigates all credit risk

---

[4] This may not be the most effective way to act on this view but is simply an example.
[5] Aside from initial margin requirements and capital requirements.

concerns since the default of a member of the exchange would be absorbed by the exchange (in theory at least, this point is discussed in depth in Chapter 14). Products traded on an exchange must be well standardised to facilitate liquidity and transparent trading. Non-standard products are traded in the so-called over-the-counter (OTC) derivatives market.

OTC derivatives often tend to be less standard structures and are typically traded *bilaterally*, i.e. between two parties. In a bilateral contract, each party should have credit risk concerns with respect to the other party. This is very different from a traditional view of credit risk where one party lends another money and consequently takes credit risk (which they will charge for in the lending agreement) whilst the other party (the borrower) takes no such risk.

In 1986, OTC derivatives fell slightly behind exchange-traded instruments with $500 billion notional outstanding.[6] By 1995, OTC derivatives' notional exceeded that of exchange-traded instruments by a ratio of more than 5 to 1, a ratio maintained in 2005.[7] The OTC interest rate market is by far the largest component, having grown since the early 1980s to $284 trillion in notional value. OTC derivatives are significant in other asset classes such as foreign exchange, equities and commodities. Credit derivatives products were first developed to supplement the cash bond market but in many ways are now even more significant than cash bonds. The current notional of value of credit derivatives is around $26 trillion.[8] Credit derivatives can on the one hand be very efficient at transferring credit risk but, if not used correctly, can be counterproductive and highly toxic.

1.4 RISKS OF DERIVATIVES

The pace of growth and constant development of new derivatives instruments, not surprisingly, has led to many questions being raised on the efficiency and stability of derivatives markets. Operational, liquidity and credit aspects have all been of concern. The question of risks posed by derivatives has for many years been a valid one. This has been clear since the derivatives market reached a size where any serious problems could threaten the stability of financial markets in general.

1.4.1 Too big to fail

There is a key but subtle problem that serves as a threat to the stability of derivatives. OTC derivatives have evolved into a market dominated by a relatively small number of financial intermediaries (often referred to as dealers). These financial intermediaries act as common counterparties to large numbers of end-users of derivatives and also actively trade with each other to manage their positions. The centralisation of OTC derivatives with a small number of high-quality counterparties may have been perceived to be adding stability – after all, surely none of these counterparties would ever fail or at least be allowed to fail?

---

[6] Source: ISDA survey 1986 covering only swaps.
[7] Source: BIS reports 1995 and 2005.
[8] Source: ISDA.

It seems to have been a widely held view for many years that large firms would not fail, since they could hire the best staff and have the best risk management practices. Such a view ignores the political, regional and management challenges within a large institution that can lead to opaque representation and communication of risks, especially at a senior level. Recent events have taught the financial markets that the "too big to fail" (or even the slightly more subtle "too big to be allowed to fail") concept is a fundamentally flawed one. A stable derivatives market is not one heavily dominated by a few large institutions (all of which are wrongly assumed to be too big to fail) but rather a market with smaller institutions who can and will fail, but with less dramatic consequences. The failure of these small institutions may also be anticipated and acted upon.

The problem of the "too big to fail" mentality is illustrated by American International Group Inc. (AIG) which had written[9] CDS protection on around half a trillion of notional of debt. AIG did not have to set aside capital or reserves and was able to sell CDS protection without any margin (collateral) requirements. Counterparties were presumably happy to transact with AIG on this basis due to their excellent credit quality. However, AIG suffered a \$99.3 billion loss in 2008 and failed in September 2008 due to liquidity problems[10] causing the US Department of the Treasury and Federal Reserve Bank of New York to arrange loans as support. AIG required over \$100 billion of US taxpayers' money to cover losses due to the excessive risk taking.

AIG was, unfortunately, not "too big to fail" but was, even more unfortunately, "too big to be allowed to fail".

1.4.2 Systemic risk

Systemic risk in financial terms concerns the potential failure of one institution that creates a chain reaction or domino effect on other institutions and consequently threatens the stability of the entire financial markets and even the global economy. Systemic risk may not only be triggered by actual losses; just a heightened perception of risk and resulting "flight to quality" away from more risky assets may cause serious disruptions. Derivatives have always been strongly linked to systemic risk due to the relatively large number of dominant counterparties, the leverage in the market together, unfortunately, with the shortsighted greed of many of the participants within these markets.

1.4.3 Compensation culture

In banks, hedge funds and other financial institutions, profits are rewarded with big bonuses. There is no obvious problem with this, since a corporation must retain high-performing staff in order to continue to make good profits and failure to pay good bonuses will give the initiative to competitors. The problem with compensation is that bonuses are normally paid annually (or even more frequently), with all or a substantial portion being paid immediately in cash. This is perverse since the profits that fuel bonuses are made against financial risks that usually exist for many more years (and

---

[9] Through AIG Financial Products (AIGFP), a subsidiary that was able to command the strong reputation of its parent AIG.
[10] The downgrade of AIG's bonds triggered collateral calls that the insurer was unable to make.

sometimes even decades). Hence, annual bonuses encourage excessive risk taking in order to maximise short-term returns with little regard to long-term risks. They also encourage "copycat" behaviour amongst firms (to replicate profits made by competitors) which exposes them to the same risks and ultimately creates more systemic risk in the market.

A firm has no recourse against a monumental error made by an employee that is discovered only after the bonus is paid. Attempts to reduce financial risk are futile without an important shift in compensation culture. Deferments or clawbacks in bonuses, which result in payments being withheld or potentially reclaimed later, force risk takers to take more prudent and sensible risks over the long run. Whilst these schemes have always existed, for example with a percentage of bonuses paid in stock which vests over a certain period, they have not been aggressive enough.

It could be argued that many of the key issues relating to counterparty risk such as the toxicity of derivatives and the nature of systemic risk are strongly linked to the bonus culture. At the time of writing, many firms are being more aggressive on the nature of bonus payments and regulators and governments are threatening to enforce this. It remains to be seen whether financial institutions can really move *en masse* to a completely new and fair compensation culture that will aid the long-term stability of derivatives markets.

1.4.4 Credit derivatives

The credit derivative market, whilst relatively young, has grown swiftly due to the need to transfer credit risk efficiently. The core credit derivative instrument, the credit default swap (CDS), is simple and has transformed the trading of credit risk. However, CDSs themselves can prove highly toxic since, whilst they can be used to hedge counterparty risk in other products, there is counterparty risk embedded within the CDS itself. The market has recently become all too aware of the dangers of CDSs and most participants are reducing their usage in line with this realisation. It is generally agreed that CDS counterparty risk poses a significant threat to global financial markets. That said, the underlying problems are not insurmountable and the CDS is still a very useful instrument whose use is likely to grow.

1.5 COUNTERPARTY RISK IN CONTEXT

1.5.1 What is counterparty risk?

Counterparty risk is traditionally thought of as credit risk between derivatives counterparties. Hence, in the context of financial risk, it is merely a subset of a single risk type. However, since the credit crisis of 2007 onwards and the failures of large prestigious institutions such as Bear Sterns, Lehman Brothers, Fannie Mae and Freddie Mac, counterparty risk has been considered by most market participants to be *the* key financial risk. We could indeed argue that the size and scale of counterparty risk has always been important but has for many years been obscured by the myth of the credit-worthiness of the "too big to fail" institutions such as those mentioned above.

1.5.2 Mitigation of counterparty risk

There are many ways to mitigate counterparty risk. These include netting, margining (or collateralisation) and hedging. All can reduce counterparty risk substantially but at additional operational cost. Central counterparties may act as intermediaries to reduce counterparty risk but create moral hazard issues and give rise to greater systemic risks linked to their own failure. Furthermore, the mitigation of counterparty risk creates other financial risks such as operational risk and liquidity risk. This means that the full understanding of counterparty risk involves the appreciation of all aspects of financial risks and the interplay between them.

1.5.3 Counterparty risk and integration of risk types

Not only is counterparty risk in itself such an important risk type but it also presents a challenge due to the fact that it is only manifested as a combination of credit risk with other risk types as described below:

- *Market risk.* Counterparty risk represents a combination of credit risk (the deterioration of the credit quality of the counterparty) together with market risk (the potential value of the contract(s) with that counterparty at the point at which the credit quality deteriorates). This interaction of market and credit risk has been long associated with counterparty risk and will be a key feature of much of this book.
- *Operational risk.* The management of counterparty risk relies on practices such as netting and collateralisation that themselves give rise to operational risks as will be discussed in more detail in Chapter 4.
- *Liquidity risk.* Collateralisation of counterparty risk may lead to liquidity risk if the collateral needs to be sold as some point due to a credit event. This may also be described as "gap risk". Such aspects are also tackled in Chapters 5 and 8. Rehypothecation of collateral (Chapter 3) is also an important consideration here.
- *Systemic risk.* Central counterparties (CCPs) act as intermediaries to centralise counterparty risk between market participants. Whilst offering advantages such as risk reduction and operational efficiencies, they potentially allow dangers such as moral hazard and asymmetric information to develop and flourish. CCPs may ultimately create greater systemic risk in the market due to the possibility that they themselves might fail. This is discussed at length in Chapter 14.

A strong focus in financial risk management is the combination of risk types in order to understand the overall risk as being more than just the conservative sum of the parts. The term enterprise risk management (ERM) has been much talked about although rarely used in practice. Due to its very nature, counterparty risk represents a combination of market and credit risks. Mitigating counterparty risk changes the nature of the underlying market risk component and creates other risks such as liquidity risk, operational risk and systemic risk. Hence, this is not just a book on counterparty risk; it is a book on market, credit, liquidity, operational and systemic risk. More importantly, it explores the linkages between different risk types as suggested by enterprise risk management.

1.5.4   Counterparty risk and today's derivatives market

Counterparty risk has been thrust into the fore of financial risk management since the events following the credit crisis in 2007. Concerns about counterparty risk have caused institutions to cut back on their use of CDSs and many have tightened margin (collateral) requirements since the outbreak of the global credit crisis. Banks hit hardest by the credit crisis have been the most aggressive when it comes to tightening up on counterparty risk but even those institutions that have been relatively immune to the problems have recognised the need to better understand and better manage counterparty risk. This has, temporarily at least, reduced trading activity. The need for better counterparty risk management is therefore clear, in that it can allow such trading activity to increase whilst also reducing the chance of significant future losses and systemic market crashes.

Historically, many financial institutions limited their counterparty risk by only trading with the most sound counterparties. Market participants tended to under-estimate its magnitude as a result of the implicit "too big to fail" assumption. Only a few large dealers invested heavily in assessed counterparty risk. Counterparty risk has rapidly become the problem of all financial institutions, big or small.

There are many solutions to the current counterparty risk problems, all of which help to mitigate the risk. Most institutions believe that a centralised CDS clearing system will reduce counterparty risk in the credit default swap market. Whilst such quick-fix solutions will inevitably be attractive, the best mechanism for controlling counterparty risk will be a full understanding of all aspects, including the many possible risk mitigants and hedging possibilities. Only as more market participants become knowledgeable will the control of this new dimension of financial risk management become achievable.

2

Defining Counterparty Credit Risk

> *"An expert is a person who has made all the mistakes that can be made in a very narrow field."*
>
> Niels Bohr (1885–1962)

2.1 INTRODUCING COUNTERPARTY RISK

"... probably the single most important variable in determining whether and with what speed financial disturbances become financial shocks, with potential systemic traits"

Counterparty Risk Management Policy Group (2005)

Counterparty risk is in one sense a specific form of credit risk, yet its significance is far greater than such a description might suggest. The understanding of counterparty risk requires knowledge of all financial risks, such as market risk, credit risk, operational risk and liquidity risk. Furthermore, the interaction of different financial risks is critical in defining the nature of counterparty risk. As has been shown in the market events of the last few years, counterparty risk is the most complex form of credit risk with systemic traits and the potential to cause, catalyse or magnify serious disturbances in the financial markets. Hence, the need to understand, quantify and manage counterparty risk is crucial. Without this, the future health, development and growth of derivatives products and financial markets in general will be greatly compromised.

2.1.1 Origins of counterparty risk

All corporate treasurers will generate substantial exposures to banks through deposits and investments as well as via derivatives products. Whilst they will try to have an even spread of business with counterparties, the need to manage counterparty risk will be key. Positions giving rise to counterparty risk such as repos, financing and lending transactions, and OTC derivatives contain certain generic characteristics. First, they create credit exposure, which is defined as the cost of replacing the transaction if the counterparty defaults (assuming zero recovery value). Second, the credit exposure depends on one or more underlying market factors, and instruments with counterparty risk often involve exchanges of payments such as in a swap. Counterparty risk is typically defined as arising from two broad classes of financial products:

- OTC (over the counter) derivatives, some well-known examples being:
  - interest rate swaps;
  - FX forwards;
  - credit default swaps.

- Securities financing transactions, for example
  - ○ repos and reverse repos;
  - ○ securities borrowing and lending.

The former category is the more significant due to the size of the market and diversity of OTC derivatives instruments together with other technical factors.

2.1.2 Repos

Many institutions use standard sale and repurchase agreements, or repos for short, as a liquidity management tool to swap cash against collateral for a pre-defined period. The lender of cash is paid a repo rate, which represents an interest rate on the transaction plus any counterparty risk charge. The collateral used tends to be liquid securities, of stable value, with a haircut applied to mitigate the counterparty risk arising due to the chance the borrower will fail to pay back the cash *and* the value of the collateral will fall. Repos are of great importance in international money markets and the repo market has been growing substantially in recent years.

2.1.3 Exchange-traded derivatives

Some derivatives are exchange-traded where the exchange usually guarantees the contract performance and eliminates counterparty risk (since the exchange will normally have a clearing entity with such a role attached to it). When trading a futures contract (a typical exchange-traded derivative), the actual counterparty to the contract is typically the exchange. Derivatives traded on an exchange are normally considered to have no counterparty risk since the only aspect of concern is the solvency of the exchange itself. Due to the need for customisation, a much greater notional amount of derivatives are traded OTC. OTC derivatives are traded bilaterally between two parties and each party takes counterparty risk to the other.

2.1.4 OTC derivatives

The market for OTC (over the counter) derivatives has grown dramatically in the last decade and this is illustrated graphically in Figure 2.1. The expansion has been driven primarily by interest rate products and then foreign exchange instruments with new markets such as credit derivatives (credit default swaps) contributing also (the credit default swap market increased by a factor of 10 between the end of 2003 and end of 2008). The total notional amount of all derivatives outstanding was $450.4 trillion at 2008 year-end, a decline of 15% compared with $531.2 trillion at mid-year 2008. Such a decrease is due partially to compression exercises that seek to reduce counterparty risk via removing offsetting and redundant positions. However, the decline can be mainly attributed to the market environment resulting in firms shrinking their balance sheets, re-allocating capital and looking to increase operational efficiency in the midst of a credit crisis. These aspects might be considered temporary and it could be argued that the global OTC derivatives market will continue to develop strongly (with a few inevitable hiccups along the way). Such a view is also fiercely debated by some, arguing that derivatives should be wholly exchange-traded or even, in some cases, outlawed (for

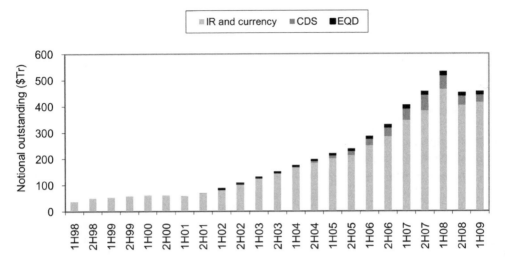

Figure 2.1. Total outstanding notional (in trillions of U.S. dollars) of derivatives transactions in the last decade. The figures cover interest rate and currency products, credit default swaps (from 2001 onwards) and equity derivatives (from 2002 onwards).
Source: ISDA.

example, see Soros, 2009). Whilst OTC derivatives clearly need careful regulation, we would suggest that their popularity is unlikely to fall dramatically and may well continue to grow.

The split of OTC derivatives by product type is shown in Figure 2.2. Interest rate products contribute the lion's share of the outstanding notional. With foreign exchange and credit default swaps coming a seemingly rather poor second and third place. However, it is important to consider that foreign exchange products can constitute large risks due to the joint impact of long-dated maturities and exchange of notional

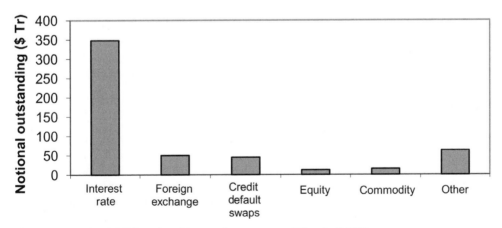

Figure 2.2. Split of OTC notional by product type as of first half 2008.
Source: ISDA.

(for example, on cross-currency swaps). Furthermore, credit default swaps have not only a large volatility component but also constitute significant "wrong-way risk" (discussed in detail in Chapter 8). So, whilst interest rate products make up a significant proportion of the counterparty risk in the market (and indeed are most commonly used in practical examples), one must not underestimate the other important (and sometimes more subtle) contributions.

A key aspect of derivatives products is that their exposure is substantially smaller than that of a loan or bond with a similar maturity. Consider an interest rate swap as an example; this contract involves the exchange of floating against fixed coupons and has no principal risk because only cashflows are exchanged. Furthermore, even the coupons are not fully at risk because at coupons dates only the difference in fixed and floating coupons or *net* payment will be exchanged. If a counterparty fails to perform then an institution will have no obligation to continue to make coupons payments. Instead, the swap will be unwound based on independent quotations as to its current market value. If the swap has a negative value for an institution then they stand to lose nothing if their counterparty defaults.

2.1.5   Counterparty risk

OTC derivatives, whilst being very powerful, can lead to significant risks, many of which have been well-documented over the years. However, one risk that has gained particular emphasis in recent times, largely due to the credit crisis that started in 2007, is counterparty risk. Counterparty risk is the risk that a counterparty in a derivatives transaction will default prior to expiration of a trade and will not therefore make the current and future payments required by the contract. The high-profile bankruptcies of Barings, Long Term Capital Management, Enron, WorldCom and Parmalat were in the 2008–2009 period joined by Lehman Brothers and some pseudo-bankruptcies (only saving by last-ditch rescues) during the credit crisis (Bear Stearns, AIG, Fannie Mae, Freddie Mac, Merrill Lynch, Royal Bank of Scotland). This has brought counterparty risk even more to the fore as market participants face the realisation that the concept of a "too big to fail" financial institution has been forever shattered.

Whilst the above statement might look rather odd (and obvious), the concept that certain counterparties would never fail (or be allowed to fail) had for many years created an illusion that the prevalence of counterparty risk in the market was modest at most. The historical negligence over counterparty risk can be broken down into the following flawed notions that have been widespread amongst institutions trading OTC derivatives:

- the counterparty will never default;
- the counterparty will never be allowed to default;
- by the time our counterparty has defaulted, much worse things will already have happened.

None of the above are acceptable arguments but have been commonly used to justify "risky" trades that have provided short-term returns, boosted bonuses and led to severe medium and long-term counterparty risk. Events such as the bankruptcy of Lehman Brothers have shattered these illusions and given derivatives markets a much needed wake-up call. The key point is

> No matter who you trade with (triple-A entities, large global investment banks, sovereigns, central counterparties) you take counterparty and related risks. This book is about understanding, quantifying and being in control of those risks.

2.1.6 Counterparty risk versus lending risk

Traditionally, credit risk can generally be thought of as lending risk. One party owes an amount of money to another party and may fail to pay some or all of this amount back due to insolvency. This can apply to loans, bonds, mortgages, credit cards and so on. Lending risk is characterised by two key aspects:

- The notional amount at risk at any time during the lending period is usually known with a degree of certainty. Market variables such as interest rates will typically create only moderate uncertainty in this amount. For example, in buying a fixed coupon bond with a par value of $1,000, the notional amount at risk for the life of the bond is close to $1,000. A repayment mortgage will amortise over time (the notional drops due to the repayments) but one can predict with good accuracy the outstanding balance at some future date. A loan or credit card may have a certain maximum usage facility, which may reasonably be assumed to be fully drawn[1] for the purpose of credit risk.
- Only one party takes lending risk. A bondholder takes considerable credit risk but an issuer of a bond does not face a loss if the buyer of the bond defaults. This point does not follow for most derivatives contracts.

With counterparty risk, as with all credit risk, the cause of a loss is the obligor being unable or unwilling to meet contractual obligations. However, two aspects differentiate counterparty risk from traditional credit risk:

- The value of a derivatives contract in the future is uncertain, in most cases significantly so. The value of a derivative at a potential default date will be the net value of all future cashflows to be made under that contract. This future value can be positive or negative and is typically highly uncertain (as seen from today).
- Since the value of a derivatives contract can be positive or negative, counterparty risk is typically *bilateral*. In other words, in a derivatives transaction, each counterparty has risk to the other. This bilateral nature of counterparty risk has been a particularly important feature of the recent credit crisis.

The primary distinguishing feature of counterparty risk compared with other forms of credit risk is that the value of the underlying contract in the future is uncertain, both in magnitude and in sign!

---

[1] On the basis that an individual unable to pay their credit card bill is likely to be close to their maximum limit.

2.1.7 Mitigating counterparty risk

Counterparty credit risk can be reduced by various means. Netting and collateralisation have been common ways to achieve this. They have the advantage that they can reduce the risk of both parties trading with one another. In the event of default, netting gives derivatives creditors additional benefits at the expense of other creditors. Aside from this point and the associated operational costs, the benefits of netting are essentially "free". However, the impact of netting is finite and heavily dependent on the type of underlying transactions involved. Collateralisation can reduce counterparty risk more significantly and, in theory, eliminate it entirely but it carries significant associated operational costs and gives rise to other risks, such as liquidity risk and legal risk.

Furthermore, the growth of the credit derivatives market has made hedging of counterparty risk a viable option, albeit at a cost. Credit derivatives products called contingent credit default swaps (CCDSs) have even been developed specifically for this purpose. Credit derivatives also create the opportunity to diversify counterparty risk by reducing counterparty exposure to the clients of a firm and taking instead exposure to other parties who may be clients only of a competitor.

Central counterparties, such as exchanges and clearing houses, can allow the centralisation of counterparty risk and mutualisation of losses. This at first seems like a simple solution to the problem raised by significant bilateral risks in the market, which can lead to a systemic crisis since the default of one institution creates a "domino effect". However, central counterparties can create moral hazard problems and asymmetric information problems by eliminating the incentive for market participants to monitor carefully the counterparty risks of one another. In Chapter 14 we will argue that central counterparties can potentially be counterproductive in mitigating counterparty risk.

We emphasise strongly that *any* mitigation of counterparty risk is a double-edged sword since it will reduce overall risks but could potentially allow financial markets to develop too quickly or to reach a dangerous size. This can be understood with a very simple example. Suppose there are 100 units of risk in a market dominated by 10 dealers. The market cannot develop further since the 10 dealers are unable or unwilling to increase their positions and further market participants are unable or simply do not see it as being profitable for them to enter the market. Now, suppose some form of risk mitigation is developed, and allowed by regulators, which reduces the total amount of risk to 25 units. The market is now likely to develop strongly due to existing dealers increasing their exposures and new entrants to the market. Eventually, the market may increase in size and again return to the situation of 100 units of risk. The risk mitigation has been extremely efficient since the market size (in terms of risk taken) has quadrupled. However, suppose the risk mitigation has some weaknesses and its impact has been therefore overstated, either due to dealers' overoptimistic assessments of their risks and/or regulators allowing too aggressive a reduction of capital. In this case, the overall risk in the market has actually increased due to the risk mitigation. Worse still, market participants and regulatory bodies are blind to these risks.

Understanding the balance between good and bad risk mitigation has not been easy for markets exposed to counterparty risk. We will devote separate chapters to understanding the full impact of collateralisation and netting (Chapter 3), hedging (Chapter 8), regulatory aspects (Chapter 11) and centralisation of counterparty risk (Chapter 14).

2.1.8 Counterparty risk players

The range of institutions that take significant counterparty risk has changed dramatically over the past 2–3 years (or more to the point institutions now fully appreciate the extent of counterparty risk they may face). Let us characterise these institutions generally:

- Large derivatives player
  - typically a large bank;
  - will have a vast number of OTC derivatives trades on their books;
  - will trade with each other and have many other clients;
  - coverage of all or many different asset classes (interest rate, foreign exchange, equity, commodities, credit derivatives).
- Medium derivatives player
  - typically a smaller bank or other financial institution such as a hedge fund or pension fund;
  - will have many OTC derivatives trades on their books;
  - will trade with a relatively large number of clients;
  - will cover several asset classes although may not be active in all of them (may, for example, not trade credit derivatives or commodities and will probably not deal with the more exotic derivatives).
- Small derivatives player
  - typically a large corporate with significant derivatives requirements (for example, for hedging needs) or a small financial institution;
  - will have a few OTC derivatives trades on their books;
  - will trade with potentially only a few different clients;
  - may be specialised to a single asset class (for example, some corporates trade only foreign exchange products, an airline may trade only oil futures, a pension fund may be only active in interest rate and inflation products).

Historically, the large derivatives players have had much stronger credit quality than the other participants. Hence, a large derivative player trading with a medium or small derivatives player would call the shots due to the assumed almost zero possibility that they would ever be bankrupt. This would mean that they would define the terms of any transaction in relation to counterparty risk. The difficulty caused by the bilateral nature of counterparty risk was "solved" merely by the fact that the large derivatives players were almost default-free. In derivatives trades between the large derivatives players (interbank trades) then, there is no dominant party and both parties carry risk to one another. This creates a potential impasse which in good markets has not proved to be a problem since the parties again consider one another to be risk-free (the credit spreads of large, highly rated, financial institutions prior to 2007 amounted to just a few basis points per annum[2]).

However, the above has ceased to be true (the myth has been destroyed) since 2007 and hence the bilateral nature of counterparty risk is ever-present. The impasse between derivatives counterparties caused by the bilateral nature of the risk has caused signifi-

---

[2] Meaning that the market priced their debt as being of very high quality and practically risk-free.

cant problems with previously liquid-trading activity becoming log-jammed (we discuss the quantification of bilateral counterparty risk in Chapter 7). Now, all institutions facing counterparty risk *must* take it seriously and build their abilities in quantification, pricing and hedging aspects. No institution has either such poor credit quality that they need not concern themselves with counterparty risk and no institution has such strong credit quality that their potential bankruptcy at some future date can be ignored.

Aside from the parties taking counterparty risk through their trading activities, other major players in the market are third parties. Third parties offer, for example, collateral management services, software, trade compression and clearing services. They allow market participants to reduce counterparty risk, the risks associated with counterparty risk (such as legal ones) and improve overall operational efficiency with respect to these aspects.

2.2   COMPONENTS AND TERMINOLOGY

2.2.1   Credit exposure

Credit exposure (hereafter often simply known as exposure) defines the loss in the event of a counterparty defaulting. Exposure is characterised by the fact that a positive value of a financial instrument corresponds to a claim on a defaulted counterparty, whereas in the event of negative value an institution cannot walk away. This means that if an institution is owed money and their counterparty defaults then they will incur a loss, whilst in the reverse situation they cannot gain[3] from the default by being somehow released from their liability.

Exposure is clearly a very time-sensitive measure since a counterparty can default at any time in the future and one must consider the impact of such an event many years from now. Exposure is needed in the analysis of counterparty risk since, for many financial instruments, notably derivatives, the creditor is not at risk for the full principal amount of the trade but only the *replacement cost*. A measure of exposure should encompass the risk arising from actual claims (current claims and those a financial institution is committed to provide), potential claims (possible future claims) as well as contingent liabilities. Essentially, characterising exposure involves answering the following two questions:

- What is the current exposure (the maximum loss if the counterparty defaults now)?
- What is the exposure in the future (what could be the loss if the counterparty defaults at some point in the future)?

The second point above is naturally far more complex to answer than the first, except in some simple cases. We emphasise that all exposure calculations, by convention, will ignore any recovery value in the event of a default. Hence, the exposure is the loss, as defined by the value or replacement cost that would be incurred assuming zero recovery value.

Finally, a very important point:

> Exposure is conditional on counterparty default.

---

[3] Except in some special and non-standard cases that we will consider later.

Exposure is relevant only if the counterparty defaults and hence the quantification of exposure should be "conditioned" upon this event, i.e.

- What is the exposure in 1 year assuming the counterparty will default in 1 year?
- What is the exposure in 2 years assuming the counterparty will default in 2 years?
- And so on.

Having said this, we will often consider exposure independently of any default event and so assume implicitly no "wrong-way risk". Such an assumption is reasonable for most products subject to counterparty risk. We will then address wrong-way risk, which defines the relationship between exposure and counterparty default, in more detail in Chapter 8.

2.2.2 Default probability and credit migration

When assessing counterparty risk, one must consider the credit quality of a counterparty over the entire lifetime of the transactions with that counterparty. Such time horizons can be extremely long. Ultimately, there are two aspects to consider:

- What is the probability of the counterparty defaulting[4] in a certain time horizon?
- What is the probability of the counterparty suffering a decline in credit quality over a certain time horizon (for example, a ratings downgrade)?

Credit migrations or discrete changes in credit quality, such as due to ratings changes, are crucial since they influence the *term structure* of default probability. They also should be considered since they may cause issues even when a counterparty is not yet in default. Suppose the probability of default of a counterparty between the current time and a future date of (say) 1 year is known. It is also important to consider what the same annual default rate might be in 4 years, in other words the probability of default between 4 and 5 years in the future. There are three important aspects to consider:

- Future default probability as defined above will have a tendency to decrease due to the chance that the default may occur before the start of the period in question. The probability of a counterparty defaulting between 20 and 21 years in the future may be very small. Not because they are very credit-worthy but – potentially quite the reverse – because they are unlikely to survive to 20 years!
- A counterparty with an expectation of deterioration in credit quality will have an increasing probability of default over time (although at some point the above phenomenon will reverse this).
- A counterparty with an expectation of improvement in credit quality will have a decreasing probability of default over time, which will be accelerated by the first point above.

There is a well-known empirical mean reversion in credit quality as evidenced by historical credit ratings changes. This means that good (above-average) credit quality firms tend to deteriorate and vice versa. Hence, a counterparty of good credit quality will

---

[4] We will for now use the term default to refer to any "credit event" that could impact the counterparty. Such credit events will be described in greater depth in Chapter 6.

tend to have an increasing default probability over time whilst a poor credit quality counterparty will be more likely to default in the short term and less likely to do so in the longer term. The term structure of default is very important to consider as the following example demonstrates:

A trader has to assess the expected loss on a new FX forward trade due to counterparty risk. The potential loss at the maturity of the trade is estimated to be 10% whilst the default probability of the counterparty over the 5-year period is also 10%. The trader argues that since the current exposure of the trade is zero, then the average loss over the life of the trade will be half the final value and hence the expected loss will be:

$$10\% \times 50\% \times 10\% = 0.5\%$$

This is a poor calculation. First, the estimate of average exposure is not 50% of the final value because the exposure does not increase linearly. Worse than this, there is an implicit assumption that the default probability is homogeneous through time. If the default probability actually increases through time, the actual expected loss might be more in the region of 0.8%. The counterparty may be more likely to default closer to the 5-year point (where the loss is 10%) than today (when the loss is zero).

We note finally that default probability may be computed under the real (historical) or risk-neutral (market-implied) measure. In the former case, we ask ourselves what is the *actual* default probability of the counterparty, whilst in the latter case we calculate the *market-implied* probability. The latter case is relevant when hedging the default component of the counterparty risk and the former otherwise. This point is discussed in detail in Chapters 9 and 12.

Spreadsheet 2.1. Counterparty risk for an FX forward trade

2.2.3 Recovery

In the event of a bankruptcy, the holders of OTC derivatives contracts with the counterparty in default would normally be *pari passu* with the senior bondholders. Hence, recovery rates (a percentage of the outstanding claim recovered) can sometimes be reasonably high. For example, a recovery of 60% will result in only half the loss compared with a recovery of 20%. Credit exposure is traditionally measured gross of any recovery (and hence is a worst case estimate). Recovery rates play a critical role in the estimation and pricing of credit risk although this has been a neglected area – in terms of both financial modelling and empirical research.

An associated variable to recovery is *loss given default* which is linked to recovery rate on a unit amount by the simple formula *loss given default = one − recovery rate*.

2.2.4 Mark-to-market

The mark-to-market (MtM) with respect to a particular counterparty defines what could be potentially lost today. It is therefore the sum of the MtM of all the contracts with the counterparty in question. However, this is dependent on the ability to net the trades in the event the counterparty was to default (Chapter 3). Furthermore, other aspects that will reduce the exposure in the event of default, such as collateral legally held against the contracts and possibly hedges, must be considered.

Current MtM does not constitute an *immediate* liability by one party to the other but rather is the present value of all the payments an institution is expecting to receive less those it is obliged to make. These payments may be scheduled to occur many years in the future and may have values that are strongly dependent on market variables. MtM may therefore be positive or negative, depending on whether a transaction is in an institution's favour or not. MtM represents *replacement cost*, which defines the entry point into an equivalent transaction(s) with another counterparty, under the assumption of no trading costs.

2.2.5 Replacement cost

The current replacement cost of a transaction, whilst closely coupled to the MtM value of the transaction, will not be the same as the MtM value of the transaction. To replace a transaction, one must consider costs such as bid–offer spreads, which may be significant for highly illiquid securities. However, such additional costs are probably more appropriately treated as liquidity risk. Hence, from the counterparty risk point of view, it is reasonable and standard practice to base exposure on the current MtM value of a transaction or transactions.

2.2.6 Exposure

A key feature of counterparty risk arises from the asymmetry of potential losses with respect to MtM. In the event that a counterparty has defaulted, an institution may close out the position and is not obliged to make future contractual payments (reasonably, since payments are unlikely to be received). However, the underlying contracts must be settled depending on the MtM value at the time of default. Consider the impact of positive or negative MtM with a counterparty in default:

- *Positive MtM.* When a counterparty defaults, they will be unable to make future commitments and hence an institution will have a claim on the positive MtM at the time of the default. The amount of this MtM less any recovery value will represent the loss due to the default.
- *Negative MtM.* In this case, an institution owes its counterparty through negative MtM and is still legally obliged to settle this amount (they cannot walk away from the transaction or transactions except in specifically agreed cases – see Section 2.3.5). Hence, from a valuation perspective, the position is essentially unchanged. An institution does not gain or lose from their counterparty's default in this case.

The above feature – an institution loses if their MtM is positive and does not gain if it is negative – is a defining characteristic of counterparty risk. We can define exposure as:

$$\text{Exposure} = \text{Max}(\text{MtM}, 0) = \text{MtM}^+ \qquad (2.1)$$

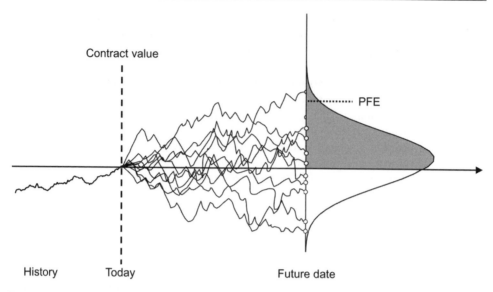

Figure 2.3. Illustration of potential future exposure (PFE). Any of the points in the shaded area at the future date represent a PFE with different underlying probabilities. A PFE will normally be defined with respect to a high confidence level (worst case) as shown.

2.2.7   Exposure as a short option position

Counterparty risk creates an asymmetric risk profile as shown by equation (2.1). When a counterparty defaults, an institution loses if the MtM is positive but does not gain if it is negative. The profile can be likened to a short[5] option position. Familiarity with basic options-pricing theory would lead to two obvious conclusions about the quantification of exposure:

- Since exposure is similar to an option payoff, a key aspect will be *volatility* (of the MtM).
- Options are relatively complex to price (compared with the underlying instruments at least). Hence, to quantify credit exposure even for a simple instrument may be quite complex.

2.2.8   Potential future exposure (PFE)

The concept of potential future exposure (PFE) arises from the need to characterise what the MtM might be at some point in the future. The PFE concept is illustrated in Figure 2.3, which can be considered to represent a single trade or a set of netted trades. PFE defines a possible exposure to a given confidence level, normally according to a worst case scenario. PFE over a given time horizon is analogous to the traditional value-at-risk measure introduced in Chapter 1.

PFE is characterised by the fact that the MtM of the contract(s) is known both at the current time and at any time in the past. However, there is uncertainty over the future

---

[5] The short option position arises since exposure constitutes a loss.

exposure that might take any one of many possible paths as shown. At some point in the future, one will attempt to characterise PFE via some probability distribution as shown in Figure 2.3. Finally, we can note that the shaded portion in Figure 2.3 corresponds to the exposure (positive MtM) and is therefore the main area of interest.

Characterisation of exposure builds on some of the definitions and risk management concepts discussed in Chapter 1. Quantifying exposure involves characterising a probability distribution at some future date and choosing metrics to most appropriately represent that distribution. The different metrics introduced will be appropriate for different applications.

2.3 CONTROLLING COUNTERPARTY CREDIT RISK

There are many ways to mitigate or limit counterparty risk. Some are relatively simple contractual risk mitigants, whilst other methods are more complex and costly to implement. The most common method historically for managing counterparty risk has been to trade only with the most financially sound banks and broker dealers. Whilst this is fairly simple and obvious, we will discuss many times the danger of taking the view that a counterparty can never fail (or be allowed to fail). Other forms of risk mitigation focus on controlling credit exposure with the most important being:

- *Diversification.* Spreading exposure across different counterparties.
- *Netting.* Being legally able to offset positive and negative contract values with the same counterparty in the event of their default.
- *Collateralisation.* Holding cash or securities against an exposure.
- *Hedging.* Trading instruments such as credit derivatives to reduce exposure and counterparty risk.

When quantifying exposure, it is important to account for all forms of risk mitigation as discussed in Chapters 4 and 5. We review below the basic ways of mitigating counterparty risk, which will be addressed in more detail in Chapter 3.

2.3.1 Trading with high-quality counterparties

For many years, the simplest and most obvious way to mitigate counterparty risk was to trade only with entities of very strong credit quality. Larger dealers within the derivatives market have needed strong credit ratings and some institutions, such as monoline insurers, have made use of triple-A ratings to argue that they represent a negligible counterparty risk and furthermore avoid the need to post collateral. Institutions have set up bankruptcy-remote entities (swap subsidiaries) and special purpose vehicles (SPVs) that can attain triple-A ratings better than the institution itself. This has been achieved by the entity pledging assets to a counterparty in the event that the parent institution defaults although the legal foundations critical for the integrity of SPVs has been recently shown to be highly questionable. High-quality counterparties and bankruptcy-remote entities will be covered in more detail in Chapter 13.

2.3.2 Cross-product netting

Cross-product netting (often known simply as netting) is a critical way to control the exposure to a counterparty across two or more transactions. It is specific to transactions that can have both positive and negative value (such as derivatives) and is typically not allowed for other product types. Without netting, the loss in the event of default of a counterparty is the sum of the value of the transactions with that counterparty that have *positive MtM value*. This means that derivatives with a negative value have to be settled (money paid to the defaulted counterparty) whilst those with a positive value will represent a claim in the bankruptcy process. Perfectly offsetting derivatives transactions or mirror trades with the same counterparty (as arises due to cancellation of a trade) will *not* have zero value if the counterparty is in default. The argument that the purpose of a trade was to cancel a previous one does not justify the netting of their values in the case the counterparty is in default.

A netting agreement is a legally binding contract that allows *aggregation* of transactions. This means, for example, that perfectly offsetting transactions may be netted against one another. Hence, they will always have zero value (one will always have the negative value of the other) in the event of default of a counterparty. Consider a counterparty with which there are many derivatives transactions. The sum of those with positive values (the counterparty owes money on a mark-to-market basis) is +$10m. The sum of those with negative values (the counterparty is owed money on a mark-to-market basis) is −$9m. The loss (without accounting for recovery) will then be $10m without netting and $1m with netting (Table 2.1). Furthermore, consider the position from the counterparty's point of view. The sum of trades with positive values is +$9m and of those with negative values is −$10m. The loss (without accounting for recovery) will then be $9m with no netting and zero with netting. Netting is very useful in reducing counterparty risk for both parties.

Table 2.1. Simple illustration of the impact of bilateral netting (MtM values are from the institution's point of view).

	Institution	Counterparty
Trades with positive MtM	+$10m	−$10m
Trades with negative MtM	−$9m	+$9m
Exposure (no netting)	+$10m	+$9m
Exposure (netting)	+$1m	Zero

Hence, netting allows counterparties to reduce the risk to each other via signing a legal agreement that becomes active if either of them defaults. However, it should also be noted that netting gives preferential benefit to derivatives counterparties at the expense of other creditors (for example, bondholders and shareholders) of an institution. Whilst this can be easily justified to be "fair" in a simple case such as a trade unwind, the strong risk-mitigating benefits of netting have surely been a catalyst for the significant notional amount of OTC derivatives traded. Shareholders and bondholders could argue that this adversely influences their position due to the increase in default probability and reduction of recovery potentially caused by sizeable derivatives exposure.

Some institutions trade many financial products (such as loans and repos as well as interest rate, foreign exchange, commodity, equity and credit products). The ability to apply netting to most or all of these products is desirable in order to reduce exposure. However, legal issues regarding the enforceability of netting arise due to trades being booked with various different legal entities across different regions. The legal and other operational risks introduced by netting should not be ignored.

2.3.3 Close-out

Consider a holder of a debt security of a bankrupt company. Not only do they expect to make a substantial loss due to the default, but they also must expect it to be some time (often years) before they will receive any recovery value linked to the notional amount of their claim. Whilst this is problematic, it has not been considered to be a major problem, for example, in the predominantly buy-to-hold, long only, cash bond market.

Derivatives markets are fast-moving, with participants regularly changing their positions and with many instruments constituting (partial) hedges for one another. Close-out, which permits the immediate termination of all contracts between an institution and a defaulted counterparty with netting of MtM values, is crucial in this context. Combined with netting, so-called close-out netting allows an institution to offset the amount it owes a counterparty against the amount it is owed to arrive at a net payment. If the institution owes money then it makes this payment whilst if it is owed money then it makes a bankruptcy claim for that amount. Close-out netting allows the surviving institution to *immediately* realise gains on transactions against losses on other transactions and effectively jump the bankruptcy queue for all but its net exposure. This offers strong protection to the institution at the expense of the defaulted counterparty and its other creditors.

2.3.4 Collateralisation

Collateralisation (also known as margining) provides a further means to reduce credit exposure beyond the benefit achieved with netting. Suppose that a netted exposure (sum of all the values of transactions with the counterparty) is large and positive. There is clearly a strong risk if the counterparty is to default. A collateral agreement limits this exposure by specifying that collateral must be posted by one counterparty to the other to support such an exposure. Like netting agreements, collateral arrangements may be two-way which means that either counterparty would be required to post collateral against a negative mark-to-market value (from their point of view).

Suppose two counterparties have many trades with one another where the netted value of all trades happens to be zero. Neither counterparty has any current exposure to the other. However, as soon as this netted value changes, the counterparty with positive value will have exposure to the other. Hence, the counterparties agree to collateralisation to mitigate the risk. If the collateralisation were bilateral (two-way), then either counterparty would be required to post collateral. Both counterparties will periodically mark all positions to market and check the net value. If this is positive then they will check the terms of the collateral agreement to calculate if they are owed collateral. To keep operational costs under control, posting of collateral will not be continuous and will occur in blocks according to pre-defined rules.

When collateral is posted against an exposure, it can essentially be regarded as reducing that exposure in the event of counterparty default, i.e. it is not required to give back the collateral in this case. Collateral in the form of securities involves transfer of ownership, although the collateral giver remains the owner of the security for economic purposes (such as payments of coupons and dividends).

Derivatives collateral is fundamentally different in both type and nature from the use of physical assets as security for debts. Secured creditors have a claim on particular assets but their ability to realise the value of the assets is subject to delays in the bankruptcy process. It is possible for secured creditors to petition the bankruptcy court to release their security but this is a complicated process (for example, see Baird, 2001). In contrast, collateral posted against derivatives positions is, in most cases, under the control of the counterparty and may be liquidated immediately upon an "event of default". This arises due to the laws governing derivatives contracts and the nature of the collateral (cash or liquid securities under the immediate control of the institution in question). Exposure, in theory, can be completely neutralised as long as a sufficient amount of collateral is held against it. However, there are legal obstacles to this and aspects such as rehypothecation (or re-lending, discussed in detail in Chapter 3). This was a significant issue in the Lehman Brothers' bankruptcy of 2008.

Whilst collateralisation is a very powerful mitigation tool against counterparty risk, it does give rise to other risks such as market risk, operational risk and legal risk. Hence, collateralisation needs to be implemented carefully and represents a significant work-load for an institution. However, it is increasingly common that many counterparties will simply not trade on an uncollateralised basis.

By the end of 2008 the total amount of collateral used in all OTC derivatives transactions was reported as being $4 trillion, an 86% increase.[6] Large US Commercial Banks have collateral covering 30–40% of net credit exposures. Collateralisation, although common, has been arguably still underused as a mechanism for reducing counterparty risk. Many market participants have been reticent to enter into stringent collateral agreements due to the need to post cash or high-quality securities and the operational workload associated with maintaining regular margining.

2.3.5 Walkaway features

Although standard OTC derivatives documentation dictates that exposure is as defined as in Section 2.2.6, in certain cases transactions may have "walkaway" or "tear-up" features. Such a clause effectively allows an institution to cancel transactions in the event that their counterparty defaults. They would clearly only choose to do this in case their overall MtM was negative (otherwise they would have a recovery claim on their exposure). Hence, a walkaway agreement means an institution can cease payments and will not be obliged to settle money owed to a counterparty on a mark-to-market basis. An institution can then gain in the event a counterparty defaults and may factor in this gain when assessing the counterparty risk (this will be assessed in Chapter 7).

In terms of defining exposure with a walkaway feature, we could write it simply as:

$$\text{Exposure}_{\text{walkaway}} = \text{MtM}, \qquad (2.2)$$

---

[6] ISDA Margin Survey 2008, see *http://www.isda.org/c_and_a/pdf/ISDA-Margin-Survey-2008.pdf*

so that positive MtM represents exposure as before but negative MtM represents "negative exposure" meaning that an institution would gain if their counterparty were to default.

2.3.6   Monolines

An obvious way to control counterparty risk is to limit or reduce credit exposure. However, an alternative solution is to simply only trade with counterparties with very strong credit quality. This is essentially the route taken by monoline insurance companies, who have provided guarantees[7] on various credit products to banks. A bank can have a significant credit exposure to a monoline but this potential risk issue is "solved" by the monoline gaining a triple-A rating (since a triple-A institution will almost surely not default). The triple-A ratings granted to monolines are interesting in that they are typically achieved thanks to the monoline *not* being obliged to post collateral against transactions. Hence, an institution trading with a monoline is critically relying on this triple-A rating to minimise their counterparty risk. One might reasonably ask the question as to why an institution's credit quality is somehow improved by the fact that they do *not* post collateral (monolines would typically be unable to gain triple-A ratings if they entered into collateral agreements). Indeed, this point is a first clue to the fundamental flaw in the triple-A ratings granted to monolines as discussed in more detail in Chapters 8 and 13.

A credit derivative product company (CDPC) is a simpler version of a monoline, essentially entering into the same business with a similar business model. The credit crisis has caused serious problems for monolines and CDPCs[8] and shown their business model to be fundamentally flawed. The rating agencies, who assigned the much-coveted triple-A ratings awarded to these institutions, have also been heavily criticised. We will argue in Chapter 8 that monolines and CDPCs represent an extreme case of wrong-way risk and, far from minimising counterparty risk, that they create more of it in a particularly toxic and systemic form.

2.3.7   Diversification of counterparty risk

The basic idea of diversification is to avoid putting all your eggs in one basket. Market participants can achieve this by limiting credit exposure to any given counterparty, in line with the default probability of that counterparty. This is the basic principle of credit limits discussed in Chapter 3. By trading with a greater number of counterparties, an institution is not so exposed to the failure of any one of them. Diversification is not always practical due to the relationship benefits from trading with certain key clients. In such cases, credit exposures can become excessively large and must be mitigated by other means.

2.3.8   Exchanges and centralised clearing houses

The credit crisis of 2007 onwards triggered grave concerns regarding counterparty risk, catalysed by events such as Lehman Brothers, the failure of monoline insurers (with

---

[7] Monolines are not allowed to trade derivatives but are allowed to enter into insurance contracts which essentially achieve the same goal.
[8] Although some CDPCs have escaped due to a late entry into the market.

triple-A ratings), bankruptcy of Icelandic banks (more triple-A ratings) and losses arising from some (yes, you've guessed it, triple-A) structured products. Whilst there are many ways to control and quantify counterparty risk better, in times of crisis it is natural to look for the silver bullet solution also. A centralised clearing house offers such a solution since counterparties would simply trade with one another through the clearing house that would effectively act as guarantor to all trades. All OTC derivatives traded through a clearing house would then be free of counterparty risk. The only issue is to ensure the default-remoteness of the clearing house itself.

Whilst clearing houses certainly constitute one of many ways to control and reduce counterparty risk, it is unlikely that they will offer a complete solution to the problem. We will discuss this in more detail in Chapter 14 but for now we just emphasise that it is rather easy to pass counterparty risk around (like a hot potato) but very difficult to actually get rid of it. Indeed, attempts to reduce counterparty risk have often led to a redistribution of the risk in another, potentially more toxic, form. Monolines represent a classic example of this mistake and it is important to ensure that similar errors are not made. Clearing houses also create moral hazard problems that may lead to the creation of subtle long-term risks whilst appearing to reduce the obvious short-term risks.

2.4   QUANTIFYING COUNTERPARTY RISK

Whilst counterparty risk can be strongly reduced via some combination of the methods described above, it certainly cannot be eradicated completely. Hence, it is important for an institution to correctly quantify the remaining counterparty risk and ensure that they are correctly compensated for taking it. Broadly speaking, there are three levels to assessing the counterparty risk of a single transaction:

- *Trade level*. Incorporating all characteristics of the trade and associated risk factors.
- *Counterparty level*. Incorporating risk mitigants such as netting and collateral for each counterparty individually.
- *Portfolio level*. Consideration of the risk to all counterparties knowing that only a small fraction may default in a given time period.

It is important to evaluate also the benefit of hedging counterparty risk with credit derivative transactions as this is another mechanism for reducing risk and should be considered alongside pricing aspects.

2.4.1   Credit lines

Throughout the rest of book, we will see many cases where the characterisation of exposure is important for pricing, risk management and regulatory purposes. For now though let us consider the first and most basic use of exposure, which is as a means to control the amount of risk to a given counterparty over time. This is achieved via attributing a credit line or credit limit to each specific counterparty as illustrated in Figure 2.4. The idea is to characterise the potential future exposure (PFE) to a counterparty over time and ensure that this does not exceed a certain value (the credit line). The credit line will be set arbitrarily according to the risk appetite of the institution in

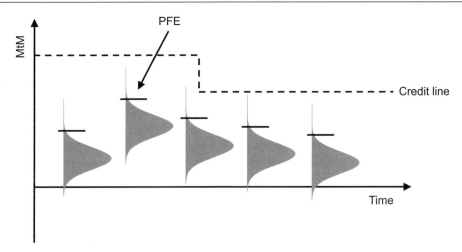

Figure 2.4. Illustration of the use of potential future exposure to control counterparty risk.

question. It will be time-dependent, reflecting the fact that exposures at different times in the future may be considered differently.

Credit lines allow a consolidated view of exposure with each counterparty and represent a first step in portfolio credit risk management. If a new trade will breach a credit line at any point in the future, it is likely to be refused. Credit lines will often be reduced over time, effectively favouring short-term exposures over long-term ones. This is due to the chance a counterparty's credit quality is more likely to have deteriorated over a longer horizon. Indeed, empirical and market-implied default probabilities for good quality (investment grade) institutions tend to increase over time (see Chapter 6 for more detail). Such an increase in default probability justifies the reduction of a credit line. The credit line of a counterparty with poor credit quality (sub investment grade) arguably should increase over time since, if the counterparty does not default, then its credit quality will be expected to improve eventually.

When assessing PFE against credit lines, no consideration will be made to possible future transactions. On the other hand, it is possible for changing market conditions (spot rates and volatilities, for example) to increase PFEs and cause credit lines to be breached. An institution must have not only a policy regarding credit lines, which defines the ability to transact further, but also a rule as to under what circumstances existing positions must be adjusted when a credit line is breached due to market moves. For example, a credit line of $10m might restrict trades that cause an increase in PFE above this value and may allow the PFE to move up to $12m as a result of changes in market conditions. In the event of the higher limit being triggered, then the PFE may need to be reduced to within the original $10m limit by adjusting positions or using credit derivatives to hedge the exposure.

A credit line controls exposure in a rather binary way without any dynamic reference to the relevant variables below:

- default probability of counterparty;
- expected recovery rate of counterparty;

- downgrade probability (worsening credit quality) of counterparty;
- correlation between counterparties.

All of the above variables are likely to be built into the defined credit line in some way. For example, a low default probability or high recovery may lead to a larger line, whilst a significant chance of downgrade may mean the credit line is decreased over time (as is the case in Figure 2.4). Finally, a counterparty that is highly correlated to others should have a lower credit line than a counterparty of the same credit quality but lower correlation. However, such decisions are made in a qualitative fashion and the nature of credit lines leads to either accepting or rejecting a new transaction with reference to exposure alone and not the actual profitability of the transaction. This is a key motivation for the pricing of counterparty risk.

2.4.2 Pricing counterparty risk

Traditional counterparty risk management, as described above, works in a binary fashion. The use of credit lines, for example, gives an institution the ability to decide whether to enter into a new transaction with a given counterparty. If the credit line would be breached then a transaction may be refused (unless it was made a special case). The problem with this is that the risk of a new transaction is the only consideration whereas the return (profit) should surely be a consideration also.

By pricing counterparty risk, one can move beyond a binary decision-making process. The question of whether to do a transaction becomes simply whether or not it is profitable once the counterparty risk component has been "priced in". As we will show in Chapter 7, the risky price of a derivative can be thought of as the risk-free price (the price assuming no counterparty risk) less a component to correct for counterparty risk. The latter component is often called CVA (credit value adjustment). As long as one can make more profit than the CVA, then the transaction is a good one. This counterparty risk charge should be calculated in a sophisticated way to account for all the aspects that will define the CVA:

- the default probability of the counterparty;
- the default probability of the institution (in the case of bilateral pricing covered in Chapter 7);
- the transaction in question;
- netting of existing transactions with the same counterparty;
- collateralisation;
- hedging aspects.

No transaction will be refused directly but an institution needs to make a return that more than covers the incremental counterparty risk of the transaction, i.e. the increase in risk taking into account netting effects due to any existing trades with the counterparty. Other aspects such as collateralisation should also be considered. Pricing aspects are considered in detail in Chapters 7 and 8.

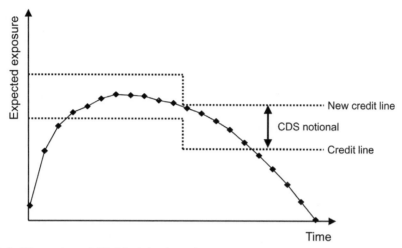

Figure 2.5. Illustration of CDS hedging in order to increase a credit line.

2.4.3 Hedging counterparty risk

The growth of the credit derivatives market has facilitated hedging of counterparty credit risk. Suppose an institution has a $10m netted exposure (uncollateralised) which is causing concern and furthermore preventing any further trading activity with the counterparty. Buying $10m notional of credit default swap (CDS) protection referenced to this counterparty will hedge this credit exposure. The hedging depends on the ability to trade CDS on the counterparty in question and comes at a cost. However, hedging enables one to reduce the exposure to zero and hence provides a means to transact further with the counterparty. CDS hedging can be considered to therefore increase a credit line by the notional of the CDS protection purchased.[9] This provides a means to use CDS protection to hedge the extent to which a transaction exceeds a credit line. The combination of hedging some portion of the exposure may be considered the most economically viable solution to trading with some counterparties. This is illustrated in Figure 2.5.

More tailored credit derivative products such as CCDSs (contingent credit default swaps) have been designed to hedge counterparty risk even more directly. CCDSs are essentially CDSs but with the notional of protection indexed to the exposure on a contractually specified derivative. They allow the synthetic transfer (to a third party) of counterparty risk related to a specific trade and counterparty. Suppose institution A trades a contract with party X and has counterparty risk. If A now buys CCDS protection from a party Y referencing both counterparty X and the underlying contract involved, then it has effectively passed the counterparty risk to Y (without X needing to be involved in the arrangement). Institution A now has risk to only the joint default or "double-default" of counterparties X and Y. This concept of mitigating counterparty risk will be discussed in more detail in Chapter 10.

---

[9] There are some technical factors that should be considered here, which may mean that the hedge is not effective. These will be discussed in detail in Chapters 6 and 9.

Since counterparty risk has a price (CVA as defined in Chapter 7) then an immediate question is what defines this price. The price of a financial instrument can generally be defined in one of two ways:

- The price represents an expected value of future cashflows, incorporating some adjustment for the risk that is being taken (the risk premium). We will call this the *actuarial price*.
- The price is the cost of an associated hedging strategy. This is the *risk-neutral* price.

A price defined by hedging arguments may often differ dramatically from one based on expected value + risk premium. Hence, it is natural to ask ourselves into which camp CVA falls. The answer is, unfortunately, both since CVA can be partially but not perfectly hedged. In the above example, we considered hedging a current exposure of $10m, but in this case future changes in exposure would not be hedged. Hence, one must account for any hedging possibilities or requirements when assessing counterparty risk but realise that pricing counterparty risk is not a totally "risk-neutral problem". An institution must also assess the residual risk that will always exist and ensure that this is correctly understood, managed and priced (i.e. the return of a transaction provides adequate compensation for the risk it ultimately creates). Hedging aspects in relation to counterparty risk are discussed in Chapter 9.

2.4.4 Capital requirements and counterparty risk

The concept of assigning capital against financial risks is done in recognition of the fact that unexpected losses are best understood at the portfolio level, rather than the transaction level. Capital requirements may be economic (calculated by the institution in question for accurate quantification of risk) or regulatory (imposed by regulators). Either way, the role of capital is to act as a buffer against unexpected losses. Hence, while pricing counterparty risk involves assessment of expected losses at the counterparty level, the concept of capital allows one to make decisions at the portfolio level (for example, all counterparties an institution trades with) and consider unexpected as well as expected losses.

The computation of capital for a credit portfolio is a rather complex issue since the correlation (or more generally dependency) between the defaults of different counterparties must be quantified. A high positive correlation (strong dependency) means that multiple defaults are possible which will therefore increase the unexpected loss and associated capital numbers. Assessment of capital for counterparty risk is even more important due to the asymmetric nature of exposure. One must not only understand the correlation between counterparty default events, but also the correlation between the resulting exposures. For example, suppose an institution has a transaction with counterparty *A* and hedges that transaction with counterparty *B*. This means the MtM positions with the two counterparties will always offset one another and *cannot* therefore be both positive. Hence, default of both counterparties *A* and *B* will create only a single loss in relation to whichever counterparty the institution has exposure to at the default time. Essentially, the negative correlation of the exposures reduces the overall risk. In case the MtM values of transaction with counterparty *A* and *B* were positively correlated then joint default would be expected to give rise to a greater loss. These ideas will be covered in more detail in Chapter 10.

2.5 METRICS FOR CREDIT EXPOSURE

In this section, we define the measures commonly used to quantify exposure. There is no standard nomenclature used and some terms may be used in other contexts elsewhere. We follow the Basel Committee on Banking Supervision (2005) definitions, which are probably the most commonly used although, unfortunately, not the most intuitively named.

In mainstream financial risk management, value-at-risk (VAR) has proved to be a popular single metric to characterise risk. However, the characterisation of future exposure for counterparty risk will require the definition and use of several metrics. There are several reasons for the increased complexity of definition:

- Unlike tradition single-horizon risk measures such as VAR, credit exposure needs to be defined over multiple time horizons to fully understand the impact of the time and specifics of the underlying contracts.
- Counterparty risk is looked at from both a pricing and risk management viewpoint, which require different metrics.
- In looking at counterparty risk at a portfolio level (many counterparties), it is important to understand the effective exposure or "loan equivalent" exposure with respect to each counterparty.

We begin by defining exposure metrics for a given time horizon.

2.5.1 Expected MtM

This component represents the forward or expected value of a transaction at some point in the future. Due to the relatively long time horizons involved in measuring counterparty risk, the expected MtM can be an important component, whereas for market risk VAR assessment (involving only a time horizon of 10 days), it is typically not. Expected MtM may vary significantly from current MtM due to the specifics of cash flows. Forward rates are also a key factor when measuring exposure under the risk-neutral measure (discussed in more detail in Chapter 3).

2.5.2 Expected exposure

Due to the asymmetry of losses described above, an institution typically cares only about positive MtM values since these represent the cases where they will make a loss if their counterparty defaults. Hence, it is natural to ask what the expected exposure (EE) is since this will represent the amount expected to be lost if the counterparty defaults. By definition, the EE will be greater than the expected MtM since it concerns only the positive MtM values.

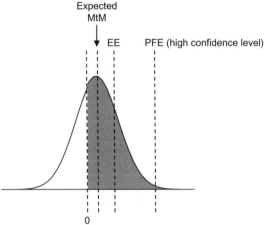

Figure 2.6. Illustration of the exposure metrics EE and PFE. The grey area represents positive MtM values or exposure.

2.5.3   Potential future exposure

In risk management, it is natural to ask ourselves *what is the worse exposure we could have at a certain time in the future?* A PFE will answer this question with reference to a certain confidence level. For example, the PFE at a confidence level of 99% will define an exposure that would be exceeded with a probability of no more than 1% (one minus the confidence level). We see that the definition of PFE is exactly the same as the traditional measure of value-at-risk (VAR) with two notable exceptions:

- PFE may be defined at a point far in the future (e.g. several years) whereas VAR typically refers to a short (e.g. 10-day) horizon.
- PFE refers to a number that will normally be associated with a gain (exposure) whereas traditional VAR refers to a loss.

This last point is important; VAR is trying to predict a worst-case *loss* whereas PFE is actually predicting a worst-case *gain*[10] since this is the amount at risk if the counterparty defaults.

The three exposure metrics discussed so far are illustrated in Figure 2.6.

2.5.4   EE and PFE for a normal distribution

In Appendix 2.A we give simple formulas for the EE and PFE for a normal distribution. These formulas are reasonably simple to compute and will be useful for some examples used throughout this book.

> **Spreadsheet 2.2.** EE and PFE for a normal distribution.

2.5.5   Overview of exposure metrics

In Figure 2.6, we illustrated the EE and PFE exposure metrics with respect to a

---

[10] Unless in an extreme case the expected MtM is very negative so even the worst case exposure is zero.

probability distribution representing future exposure. In this case, the mean of the distribution is positive and all exposures are represented by the grey area. Hence, the EE represents the expected value conditional on being within this (grey) region.

Example. Suppose a MtM is defined by a normal distribution with mean 1% and standard deviation 4%. As given by the formulae in Appendix 2.A, the EE and PFE (at the 99% confidence level) are:

$$EE = 2.15\%$$

$$PFE = 7.58\%$$

These values correspond approximately to the representation of PFE in Figure 2.6. Suppose the mean is changed to −1%, then we would obtain:

$$EE = 1.15\%$$

$$PFE = 5.58\%$$

In order to characterise an exposure evolving over time, one must look at many measures of EE and PFE. The final two exposure metrics represent some attempt to "collapse" such term structure into a single value.

2.5.6 Expected positive exposure

The previous exposure metrics are concerned with a given time horizon and we now consider the characterisation of exposure through time. Expected positive exposure (EPE) is defined as the average EE through time and hence can be a useful single number representation of exposure. We will see later that EPE has a strong theoretical basis for pricing (Chapter 7) and assessing portfolio counterparty risk (Chapter 10). EPE is illustrated in Figure 2.7.

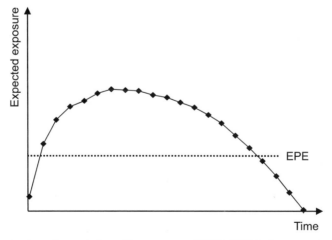

Figure 2.7. Illustration of expected positive exposure (EPE). EPE is the average of the EE profile shown.

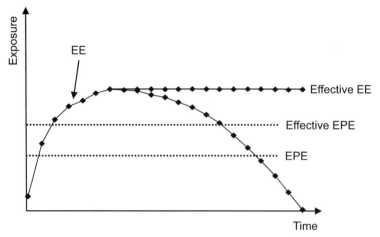

Figure 2.8. Illustration of effective EE and effective EPE assuming a time horizon of no more than 1-year.

2.5.7 Effective EPE

Measures such as EE and EPE may underestimate exposure for short-dated transactions (since capital measurement horizons are typically 1-year) and not capture properly rollover risk (Chapter 3). For these reasons, the terms effective EE and effective EPE were introduced by the Basel Committee on Banking Supervision (2005). Effective EE is simply a non-decreasing EE. Effective EPE is the average of the effective EE. These terms are shown in comparison with EE and EPE in Figure 2.8.

The role and definition of effective EPE is discussed in more detail in Chapter 10.

> **Spreadsheet 2.3.** EPE and effective EPE example

2.5.8 Maximum PFE

Maximum PFE simply represents the highest (peak) PFE value over a given time interval. Such a definition could be applied to any exposure metric but since it is a measure that would be used for risk management purposes, it is more likely to apply to PFE. This is illustrated in Figure 2.9.

We emphasise that some of the exposure metrics defined above, whilst the most common definitions, are not completely standard. Indeed, it could be argued that the naming of EE and EPE is rather confusing and, not surprisingly, some authors will replace EE with EPE and EPE with average EPE. PFE may be described as peak exposure or worst-case exposure. However, the definitions we use above are the most common naming conventions and will be used consistently throughout this book.

2.6 SUMMARY

In this chapter we have defined counterparty risk, introducing the key components of credit exposure, default probability and recovery, and outlining the risk mitigation

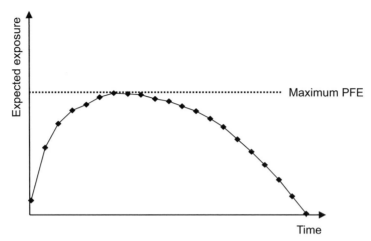

Figure 2.9. Illustration of maximum PFE.

approaches of netting and collateralisation. We have discussed various ways of quantifying and managing counterparty risk from the traditional approach of credit lines to the more sophisticated approaches of pricing and capital allocation. The concept of hedging as applied to counterparty risk has been introduced. Finally, some key definitions of potential future exposure (PFE), expected exposure (EE) and expected positive exposure (EPE) have been given. All of these aspects will be expanded upon heavily in the forthcoming chapters. Chapter 3 will deal in depth with the mitigation of counterparty risk.

APPENDIX 2.A: CHARACTERISING EXPOSURE FOR A NORMAL DISTRIBUTION

Consider a normal distribution with mean μ (expected MtM) and standard deviation (of the MtM) σ. Let us calculate analytically the two different exposure metrics discussed. Under the normal distribution assumption, the MtM value of the portfolio in question (for an arbitrary time horizon) is given by:

$$V = \mu + \sigma Z,$$

where Z is a standard normal variable.

(1) Potential future exposure (PFE)

This measure is exactly the same as that used for value-at-risk calculations. The PFE at a given confidence level α, PFE_α, tells us an exposure that will be only exceeded with a probability given by no more than $1 - \alpha$. For a normal distribution, it is defined by a point a certain number of standard deviations away from the mean:

$$\text{PFE}_\alpha = \mu + \sigma \Phi^{-1}(\alpha),$$

where $\Phi^{-1}(.)$ represents the inverse of a cumulative normal distribution function (this is the function NORMSINV(.) in Microsoft Excel^{TM}). For example, with a confidence level of $\alpha = 99\%$, we have $\Phi^{-1}(99\%) = +2.33$ and the worst case exposure is 2.33 standard deviations above the expected MtM.

(2) Expected exposure (EE)

Exposure is given by:

$$E = \max(V, 0) = \max(\mu + \sigma Z, 0)$$

The EE defines the expected value knowing the MtM is positive so it represents the average of only the positive MtM values in the future. The expected exposure is therefore:

$$EE = \int_{-\mu/\sigma}^{\infty} (\mu + \sigma x)\varphi(x)\, dx = \mu\Phi(\mu/\sigma) + \sigma\varphi(\mu/\sigma),$$

where $\varphi(.)$ represents a normal distribution function (this is the function NORMDIST(.) in Microsoft Excel^{TM} with additional parameters 0, 1 and "false") and $\Phi(.)$ represents the cumulative normal distribution function (this is the function NORMSDIST(.) in Microsoft Excel^{TM}). We see that EE depends on both the mean and the standard deviation; as the standard deviation increases so will the EE. In the special case of $\mu = 0$ we have:

$$EE_0 = \sigma\varphi(0) = \sigma/\sqrt{2\pi} \approx 0.40\sigma.$$

(3) Expected positive exposure

The above analysis is valid only for a single point in time. Suppose we are looking at the whole profile of exposure defined by $V(t) = \mu + \sigma\sqrt{t}Z$. Now we re-define σ to be an annual standard deviation (volatility). The EPE, assuming a zero mean as above and integrating over time, would be:

$$EPE_0 = \frac{1}{\sqrt{2\pi}}\sigma \int_0^T \sqrt{t}\, dt/T = \frac{2}{3\sqrt{2\pi}}\sigma T^{1/2} = 0.27\sigma T^{1/2}.$$

All of these calculations are demonstrated in Spreadsheet 2.2.

3
Mitigating Counterparty Credit Risk

> *"One ought never to turn one's back on a threatened danger and try to run away from it. If you do that, you will double the danger. But if you meet it promptly and without flinching, you will reduce the danger by half."*
>
> Sir Winston Churchill (1874–1965)

3.1 INTRODUCTION

In this chapter, we discuss ways of mitigating counterparty credit risk. The methods for doing this predominantly focus on reducing current credit exposure and potential future exposure. They often do not change the probability of suffering a loss but do reduce the resulting exposure (for example, by increasing the amount that would be recovered in the event of default). The main methods discussed will be:

- *Default-remote entities.* Whilst this has become a rather laughable concept in recent years, the most simple and commonly used method of mitigating counterparty risk has always been to trade with an institution or vehicle with an underlying default probability that is very small. The "too big to fail" mentality discussed in Chapter 1 has somewhat fuelled this practice and led to clear problems which will be discussed in later chapters.
- *Termination events.* This represents the opportunity to terminate a transaction at some point(s) between inception and the maturity date. It may exist as an option or be conditional on certain conditions being met (ratings downgrade, for example).
- *Netting.* This refers to the ability to offset all transactions (both in an institution's favour and against it) when a counterparty is in default.
- *Close-out.* This allows the termination of all contracts between the insolvent and a solvent counterparty without waiting for the bankruptcy to be finalised (which can take many years).
- *Collateralisation.* The agreement that cash or securities will be "posted" as a guarantee against an exposure according to pre-defined parameters.

3.1.1 Two-way or one-way agreements

The above methods are rather distinct but, with the exception of default-remote entities, share one commonality in that they might be applied to one or both parties to a transaction. Hence, it may be worthwhile for both parties to agree to these mitigation methods, bilaterally. Such bilateral arrangements can be extremely useful in allowing both parties to mitigate current and potential future exposure.

Risk mitigation is not always a two-way street though. In the case of a large difference in credit quality of two parties, the better quality party may demand strong mitigants highly skewed in their favour such as one-way collateral agreements and independent amounts (defined later). Historically, banks have always taken this stance when trading with hedge funds, for example. Monoline insurers have based their entire business model on skewed risk mitigation in that their triple-A status supports the fact that they will not agree to post collateral (covered in more detail in Chapters 8 and 13). However, events such as the bankruptcy of Lehman Brothers and failure of monoline insurers are reminders that the justification for one-way risk mitigation may not be always valid.

3.1.2 Standardisation

A key high-level aspect of risk mitigation is standardisation. Many OTC derivatives contracts have become standardised in their contractual terms, which reduces transaction costs and improves liquidity. Likewise, the standardisation of collateralisation has reduced the costs related to managing collateral. Organisations such as ISDA have also worked to reduce legal uncertainty through the use of standardised contract language and terms. It is standard practice for financial institutions to enter derivatives contracts documented using ISDA Master Agreements. ISDA contract holders are ranked *pari passu* to senior debt in terms of potential claims on the defaulted counterparty. The credit support annexes (CSAs) cover in detail the risk mitigation features and aspects such as bilateral marking to market of contracts.

3.2   DEFAULT-REMOTE ENTITIES

3.2.1   High-quality counterparties

The concept of high-quality, "too big to fail" counterparties for years created an illusion in financial markets that counterparty risk was not particularly prevalent. This was particularly the case with smaller institutions trading with bigger and, supposedly, less risky counterparties. Triple-A ratings given to some institutions exaggerated this problem since triple-A was perceived by many market participants to be almost default-free. Unfortunately, triple-A entities have included Icelandic banks, monoline insurance companies, Fannie Mae and Freddie Mac. The failure (or bailout) of these and other high-quality institutions such as Lehman Brothers has very much pulled the rug out from under those who relied on the "our counterparty will never fail" (or perhaps the "our counterparty will not fail before us") style of counterparty risk mitigation.

3.2.2   Special purpose vehicles

A special purpose vehicle (SPV), sometimes called a special purpose entity (SPE), is a legal entity (for example, a company or limited partnership) created typically to isolate a firm from financial risk. A company will transfer assets to the SPV for management or use the SPV to finance a large project without putting the entire firm or a counterparty at risk. Jurisdictions may require that an SPV is not owned by the entity on whose behalf it is being set up.

SPVs essentially change bankruptcy rules so that, if a derivative counterparty is insolvent, a client can still receive their full investment prior to any other claims being paid out. SPVs are most commonly used in structured notes where they use this mechanism to guarantee the counterparty risk on the principal of the note to a very high level (triple-A typically), better than that of the issuer. The credit-worthiness of the SPV will be assessed by rating agencies who will look in detail at the mechanics and legal specifics before granting a rating.

Unfortunately, legal documentation often evolves through experience and the enforceability of the legal structure of SPVs was not tested for many years. When it was recently tested in the case of Lehman Brothers, there was a significant question mark over the enforceability under US bankruptcy laws of prohibiting the surrender of assets. This means that the right of Lehman Brothers to a priority share of the SPV's assets in insolvency was called into question. Far from receiving money immediately as was the intention, many clients of Lehman Brothers have been waiting many months to receive cash they believed was guaranteed by the existence of a SPV. In July 2009 lawyers of the bankrupt Lehman Brothers filed in English courts a request to overturn the concept of bankruptcy-remoteness for SPVs. A ruling in favour, as seems likely, would be the final nail in the coffin of the, in retrospect, highly flawed SPV concept.

3.2.3 Central counterparties

The current section on "default-remote entities" is thus far looking rather bleak for mitigating counterparty risk given the myths of high-quality counterparties and SPVs having been fully exposed with recent market events. However, the concept of centralised counterparties will provide some slightly more positive news, albeit with significant warnings.

As mentioned in Chapter 2, exchange-traded derivatives are rather standardised, transparent products with no counterparty risk (since the exchange or a third party normally guarantees the contract). The reason why many derivatives do not already trade on an exchange is that OTC derivatives have higher profit margins and wider bid–ask spreads and are often transacted in situations where only one party has a good knowledge of their actual value. However, this is not a strong argument to allow the majority of derivatives to exist OTC. In the last couple of years, there has been strong interest to increase centralised trading of derivatives on exchanges in order to mitigate counterparty risk, especially with the more dangerous products such as credit default swaps. This is not surprising as a reaction to some of the problems and failures during the global credit crisis that started in 2007.

The disadvantages of exchanges are that products must be relatively standardised and go through rigorous regulatory scrutiny before being launched. However, having a central counterparty, such as an exchange, allows counterparty risk to be homogenised amongst market participants. The central counterparty can minimise the chance of a single institution failing and, even were this event to happen, they can ensure that the losses are shared by all counterparties. This loss sharing mitigates the possibility of systemic problems due to the failure of one institution creating a domino effect where other highly exposed institutions also fail.

Whilst the idea of a centralised counterparty sounds like a great idea, there are some arguments against it. OTC derivatives can be highly customised and new products can be developed and traded quickly. The standardisation required by an exchange can hinder this process. Furthermore, central counterparties may create moral hazard problems by, for example, disincentivising good counterparty risk management practice by market participants (since all the risk resides with the central counterparty itself). Institutions have no incentive to monitor each other's credit quality and act appropriately because a third party is taking all the risk. The failure of a central counterparty, whilst unlikely, would be a major and financially catastrophic event. The advantages of using central counterparties to mitigate OTC counterparty risk do not obviously outweigh the disadvantages. We will discuss the positive and negative impact of central counterparties in detail in Chapter 14.

The overall lesson of this section is that mitigating counterparty risk by trading with (or through) default-remote entities is highly suspect. As argued in Chapter 1, the "too big to fail" or "too big to be allowed to fail" concept is a fundamentally flawed one. The centralisation of counterparty risk is not obvious either. It is critical to have more sophisticated methods for mitigating counterparty risk.

3.3   TERMINATION AND WALKAWAY FEATURES

3.3.1   Termination events

Termination events are useful in giving the possibility that an institution can terminate a trade prior to their counterparty's credit-worthiness deteriorating to the point of bankruptcy. Some termination events may be freely exercisable. A break clause, also named a liquidity put or early termination option (ETO), is an agreement to terminate (break) a transaction at pre-specified dates in the future at market rates. Break clauses may often be bilateral in that either party may have the option to terminate the transaction. The point about terminating at market rates is that bid–offer and, probably more importantly, counterparty risk charges will not be incurred. Hence, a break clause provides the option to terminate without cost[1] a transaction with a significant exposure to a counterparty whose credit quality is in substantial decline.

A break clause may be particularly useful when trading with a relatively good credit quality counterparty on a long-maturity transaction (for example, 10 years or greater). Over such a time horizon, there is ample time for both the MtM of the transaction to become significantly positive and for the credit quality of the counterparty to decline. A *bilateral* break clause will often be relevant since both parties to the transaction may be in the same situation. The break clause will typically be only possible after a certain period (for example, 3 years) and possibly at pre-specified dates (for example, annually) thereafter.

Break clauses have not proved particularly popular in mitigating counterparty risk except in the case of specific transactions. This partially arises due to the banker's paradox; for a break clause to be useful, it should be exercised early before a counterparty's credit quality declines significantly.[2] Yet, such actions will often be avoided for the good of the relationship with the counterparty in question. Hence, many bilateral break clauses have been gimmicks, which have not been utilised when they should have been. A second reason for the lack of popularity of break clauses is collateralisation of credit exposure, which we discuss later in this chapter. Indeed a break clause can be

---

[1] Aside from the bid–offer cost of executing a new transaction with another counterparty.

[2] We will show in Chapter 7 that the choice to terminate a transaction will depend on the exposure, our counterparty's credit spread and, possibly, our own credit spread. As a general rule, we might consider it will be optimal to terminate when our counterparty's credit spread has increased beyond the level where the transaction was initiated.

thought of as an extreme and discrete form of collateralisation, which can be made more subtle via a more continuous posting of collateral.

More recently, with the advent of bilateral counterparty risk pricing, break clauses have an interesting role in mitigating possible severe costs in unwinding transactions with a counterparty with an impaired credit quality, with the unwind cost being a recognition of mark-to-market losses due to this impairment (CVA as it is known). We discuss this point in more detail in Chapter 7.

3.3.2   Additional termination events

Break clauses are often linked to specific events, normally termed additional termination events (ATEs) which enable an institution to terminate and close out a particular transaction or transactions with the counterparty only if the ATE event occurs. There is no ISDA standard ATE and events are therefore a result of negotiations between the parties concerned. Some common ATE events include:

- ratings triggers (the ATE is often then referred to as a credit trigger);
- merger;
- change of management;
- net asset value (NAV) declines (in the case of funds);
- a key person event (again in the case of funds where a key person ceases to make investment decisions for the fund).

Whilst ATEs of this type have been popular and might seem a useful risk mitigation feature, consider the case of American International Group Inc. (AIG), which failed in September 2008 due to liquidity problems. The liquidity problems stemmed from the requirement for AIG to post an additional \$20 billion[3] of collateral (relating to CDS trades) as a result of its bonds being downgraded. An institution trading with AIG may have thought the requirement for AIG to post collateral as a result of a downgrade would provide a safety net. However, since the downgrade was linked to the extremely poor performance of AIG's positions and collateral would be required to be posted to many institutions, in retrospect it in unlikely that a feature such as this would do anything more than catalyse a counterparty's demise.

3.3.3   Walkaway features

Walkaway clauses (also called limited two-way payments and one-way payments) allow a surviving institution to avoid (walk away) from net liabilities to a counterparty in default whilst still claiming in the event of a positive MtM (exposure). A walkaway clause therefore allows an institution to benefit from the default of a counterparty. They were common prior to the 1992 ISDA Master Agreement, have been less common since and are not part of standardised ISDA documentation. However, they have sometimes been used in transactions since 1992. Whilst walkaway features do not mitigate counterparty risk per se, they do result in potential gains due to counterparty risk aspects.

Walkaway agreements were seen in the Drexel Burnham Lambert (DBL) bankruptcy of 1990. Interestingly, in this case the counterparties of DBL decided not to walk away and chose to settle negative MtMs. This was largely due to relatively small gains

---

[3] AIG 2008 Form 10-K.

compared with the potential legal cost of having to defend the validity of the walkaway agreements, although the reputational cost of being seen as taking advantage of the DBL default may have also been an issue.

Another interesting case is that between Enron Australia (Enron) and TXU Electricity that traded a number of electricity swaps which were against TXU when Enron went into liquidation in early 2002. Although the swaps were not traded with a walkaway feature, TXU was able to avoid paying the MtM owed to Enron by not terminating the transaction (close-out) but also not making payments to their defaulted counterparty. The Enron liquidator went to court to try and force TXU effectively to settle the swaps but the court found in favour of TXU.

Walkaway features seem to have been present in some Lehman Brothers transactions following their bankruptcy in 2008 but seem more limited and at risk from litigation and reputational aspects. There has been criticism of these features by market participants and bankruptcy litigants since they cause additional problems for a bankrupt party. Walkaway features are rather unpleasant and should be avoided (and possibly legislated against) for the following reasons:

- They create an additional cost for a counterparty in the event of default.
- They create *moral hazard* since an institution is given the incentive to contribute to their counterparty's default due to the financial gain they can make.
- A walkaway feature may be "priced in" to a transaction. The possible gains in counterparty default will then offset the negative component due to potential losses that may ultimately "hide" some of the risk (see Section 7.3.8).

3.4   NETTING AND CLOSE-OUT

In most business relations, netting (or set-off as it is sometimes called) is not a significant issue. Generally, an institution either buys from or sells to another firm, but rarely does both simultaneously. Therefore, in the event of bankruptcy, few if any contracts could be netted or set off. However, derivatives markets often generate large numbers of bi-directional transactions between counterparties. Close-out and netting consist of two separate but related rights, often combined into a single contract:

(1) The right of a counterparty to terminate contracts unilaterally under certain specified conditions (close-out).
(2) The right to offset amounts due at termination of individual contracts between the same counterparties when determining the final obligation.

Bankruptcy proceedings are by their nature long and unpredictable processes. During such proceedings, likely counterparty risk losses are compounded by the uncertainty regarding the termination of proceedings. A creditor who holds an insolvent firm's debt has a known exposure, and while the eventual recovery is uncertain, it can be estimated and capped. However, this is not the case for derivatives where constant rebalancing is typically required to maintain hedged positions. Once a counterparty is in default, cashflows will cease and an institution will be likely to want or need to execute new replacement contracts. Furthermore, netted positions are inherently more volatile than their underlying gross positions and require continuous monitoring and management.

3.4.1 Close-out

Certain debt contracts may contain an *acceleration* clause that permits the creditor to accelerate future payments (for example, repayment of principal) in the event of a rating agency downgrade, default or other adverse credit event. Acceleration features are clearly aimed at protecting creditors. However, the acceleration of required payments can precipitate financial difficulties and catalyse the insolvency of a firm which may make it difficult to arrange refinancing or otherwise resolve matters in an orderly manner.

Rather than an acceleration, close-out involves the termination of all contracts between the solvent and insolvent counterparty. Termination cancels the contract and creates a claim for compensation based on the cost of replacing the contract on identical terms with another (solvent) counterparty. Upon default or a contractually agreed event, the net value due is determined by marking to market the contracts and calculating the total netted value. If the solvent party has a negative MtM, they are in debt to their counterparty and the full payment is made to the insolvent counterparty or their trustee (assuming there is no walkaway-type agreement). If, on the other hand, the party has an overall exposure then they become a creditor for this net amount. The calculations made by the surviving party may be later disputed via litigation. However, the prospect of a valuation dispute does not affect the ability of the surviving party to immediately terminate and replace the contracts with a different counterparty.

Close-out is clearly aimed at protecting surviving institutions rather than the counterparty in financial distress. Like acceleration, termination changes the payment amounts immediately due to and from the solvent counterparty, which may catalyse financial difficulties. For this reason, some jurisdictions limit the rights of counterparties to enforce the termination clauses in their contracts. The court can impose a stay, which does not invalidate termination clauses in contracts but rather overrides them, perhaps temporarily, at the discretion of the court. Staying contracts establishes a "time-out" while keeping the contracts in force with normal payments being still due.

Close-out also limits the uncertainty that an institution has with respect to the value of their positions with a defaulted counterparty. Suppose an institution has offsetting trades with different counterparties, one of whom is in default. Without close-out, it would not know to what extent the positions offset one another since it would not be clear what fraction of the exposure to the defaulted counterparty would be recovered. Hence, the percentage of the transaction that needs to be re-hedged is unclear. Even if the counterparty were eventually to make good on its contracts, the institution would still face cashflow mismatches during the bankruptcy process.[4] Close-out means that the institution can fully re-hedge the transaction with the defaulted counterparty and wait to receive a claim on their exposure at the default time. There is likely to be a counterparty risk loss (unless recovery is 100%), but there will not be additional market risk and trading uncertainty on top of this.

Close-out permits derivatives market participants to freeze their exposures in the event of the failure of a counterparty or other event of default stipulated in their Master Agreement. Without the ability to close out their positions at the time a counterparty becomes insolvent, market participants would find themselves locked into contracts

---

[4] The bankruptcy administrator might allow payment on existing contracts.

that fluctuate in value and are impossible to hedge (due to the uncertainty of future recovery).

3.4.2 Payment and close-out netting

The case of KfW Bankengruppe

As the problems surrounding Lehman Brothers grew ever-more apparent, most of Lehman's counterparties stopped doing business with the company. However, government-owned German bank KfW Bankengruppe made what they described as an "automated transfer" of €300 million to Lehman Brothers literally hours before the latter's bankruptcy. This provoked an outcry with one German newspaper calling KfW "Germany's dumbest bank". Two of the bank's managing directors and the head of the risk control department were suspended in the aftermath of the mistake. Since the bank was government-owned, the transfer would have cost each German citizen around €4 each. The bank's total loss, including other deals with Lehman Brothers, was calculated to be nearer €600m.

There are two distinct types of netting used widely in the derivatives market:

- *Payment netting*. This covers a situation when an institution will have to make and receive more than one payment during a given day. Payment netting means that they agree to combine those cashflows into a single net payment. Payment netting reduces settlement risk and enhances operational efficiency.
- *Close-out netting*. This form of netting is most relevant to counterparty risk since it reduces pre-settlement risk. It covers the netting of the value of contracts in the event of a counterparty defaulting at some date in the future.

Payment netting is important as the KfW example illustrates. For example, if a $305m floating swap payment is to be made and a $300m fixed payment received (on the same day) then the institution in question would simply make a net payment of $5m with the $300m payment having no counterparty risk. Payment netting is therefore quite simple to implement. Most of the following discussions will be based on the more complex topic of close-out netting.

3.4.3 The need for close-out netting

It is not uncommon to have many different trades with an individual counterparty. Such trades may be simple or complex and may cover a small or wider range of products across different asset classes. Furthermore, trades may fall into one of the two following categories:

- Trades may constitute hedges (or partial hedges) so that their values should naturally move in opposite directions.
- Trades may constitute unwinds in that, rather than cancelling a transaction, the

reverse (or mirror) trade may have been executed. Hence two trades with a counterparty may always have equal and opposite values, to reflect the fact that the original trade has been cancelled. Without compression exercises, which are only now becoming common, such trades will be live for potentially many years.

In light of the above points, it is rather worrying that from a legal point of view the loss on a counterparty defaulting is the *sum* of the exposures. Consider the case of a trade (trade 1) cancelled via executing the reverse transaction (trade 2). Suppose there are two scenarios in that trade 1 and trade 2 can take the values +10 and −10, respectively, or vice versa. Table 3.1 shows the possible outcomes.

Table 3.1. Illustration of the exposure of two equal and opposite trades with and without netting.

	Scenario 1	Scenario 2
Trade 1 MtM	+10	−10
Trade 2 MtM	−10	+10
Total MtM	*0*	*0*
Trade 1 exposure	+10	0
Trade 2 exposure	0	+10
Total exposure (without netting)	*+10*	*+10*

We see that, whilst the total value of the two trades is zero (as it should be since the aim was to cancel the original trade), the total exposure is +10 in both scenarios. This means that if the counterparty defaults, in either scenario there would be a loss due to having to settle the trade with the negative MtM but not being unable to claim (either directly or via offsetting) the trade that has a positive MtM. This is a rather perverse situation since any valuation system would show the above position as having zero MtM value and furthermore a market risk system would show the position as having zero market risk. Yet the counterparty credit exposure of the position is far from zero. We note also the following point:

> Without netting, one can analyse the different transactions with a counterparty independently since the overall exposures will be additive.

Netting means that individual exposures of transactions are non-additive which is beneficial since the overall risk is likely to be reduced substantially. However, this lack of additivity does make the pricing of counterparty risk more complex as we shall discuss in Chapter 7.

3.4.4 The birth of netting

Of all risk mitigation methods, netting has had the greatest impact on the structure of the derivatives markets. Without netting, the current size and liquidity of the derivatives markets would be unlikely to exist. Netting means that the overall credit exposure in the market grows at a lower rate than the notional growth of the market itself. This has historically allowed dealers to build a large book on a limited capital base. The expansion and greater concentration of derivatives markets has increased the extent of netting from around 50% in the mid-1990s to close to 100% today.

3.4.5 Netting agreements

A netting agreement is a legal agreement that comes into force in the event of a bankruptcy. It enables one to net the value of trades with a defaulted counterparty before settling the claims. As such, netting agreements are crucial in order to recognise the benefit of offsetting trades with a defaulted counterparty. We will use the concept of a "netting set" which will correspond to a set of trades that can be legally netted together in the event of a default. A netting set may be a single trade and there may be more than one netting set for a given counterparty. Across netting sets, exposure will then always be additive, whereas within a netting set MtM values can be added.

Example. Suppose we have five different transactions with a certain counterparty with current MtM values given by $+7$, -4, $+5$, $+2$, -4. The total exposure is:

$$+ 14 \text{ (without netting)}$$
$$+ 6 \quad \text{(with netting)}$$

Spreadsheet 3.1. Simple netting calculation

3.4.6 The ISDA Master Agreement

Central to the ISDA approach to netting is the concept of a Master Agreement that governs transactions between counterparties. The Master Agreement is designed to eliminate legal uncertainties and to provide mechanisms for mitigating counterparty risk. It specifies the general terms of the agreement between counterparties with respect to general questions such as netting, collateral, definition of default and other termination events, documentation and so on. Multiple individual transactions can be subsumed under this general Master Agreement to form a single legal contract of indefinite term, under which the counterparties trade with one another. Individual transactions are incorporated by reference in the trade confirmation to the relevant Master Agreement. Placing individual transactions under a single Master Agreement that provides for netting is intended to avoid any problems netting agreements may encounter under differing treatments of bankruptcy. Netting legislation covering derivatives has been adopted in most countries with major financial markets. ISDA has obtained legal opinions supporting their Master Agreements in most relevant jurisdictions.

3.4.7 Product coverage

Bilateral netting is generally recognised for OTC derivatives, repo-style transactions and on-balance-sheet loans and deposits. However, netting across these product categories is often not allowed and may not be recognised for regulatory capital purposes (Chapter 11).

3.4.8 Netting and exposure

We illustrate the impact of netting on exposure in Figure 3.1 with exactly opposite transactions. When there is no legal agreement to allow netting then exposures must be considered additive. This means that the positions do not offset one another. With netting allowable (and enforceable), one can add MtM values at the netting set level before calculating the exposure and therefore the profiles shown give a zero exposure at all points in the future.

3.4.9 Advantages and disadvantages of netting

Netting has many complex economic implications, which can be disadvantageous as well as representing mechanisms for risk reduction:

- *Exposure reduction.* By combining two offsetting contracts under the same Master Agreement, the two parties need only manage their net positions. Since positions may often offset one another to some degree (especially hedges), this reduces risk and saves on operational aspects. Whilst netting reduces exposure dramatically, it means that resulting exposures may be highly volatile (on a relative basis[5]) making the control of exposure more complex.
- *Unwinding positions.* Suppose an institution wants to trade out of a position. OTC derivatives are often not liquid and readily tradable. If the institution executes an offsetting position with another market participant, whilst removing the market risk as required, they will have counterparty risk with respect to the original and the new counterparty. Collateral may need to be posted to one counterparty and, although it may be received from the other, mismatches and operation burden will be present. Netting means that executing the reverse position with the original counterparty offsets not only the market risk but also the counterparty risk. Hence, any risk should be completely eradicated and collateral associated with the initial position is no longer required. However, this point can have negative consequences since a counterparty knowing that an institution is heavily incentivised to trade out of the position with them may offer unfavourable terms to extract the maximum financial gain. The institution can either accept these unfavourable terms or trade with another counterparty and accept the resulting counterparty risk.
- *Multiple positions.* The above point extends to establishing multiple positions with different risk exposures. Suppose an institution wants both interest rate and foreign exchange hedges. Since these trades are imperfectly correlated, by executing the hedges with the same counterparty, the overall counterparty risk generated is

---

[5] Meaning that the net exposure will be typically reduced by a greater amount than the overall volatility. Whilst a netted position will be less volatile, the fact that netting allows an institution to trade a greater notional value means that the overall volatility of their positions is likely to be increased.

(a) No netting

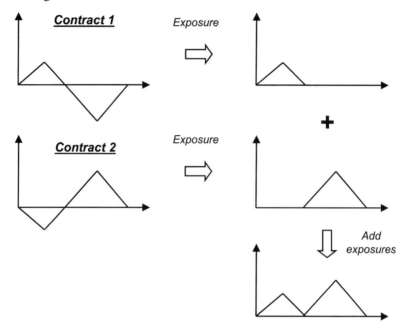

(b) With netting

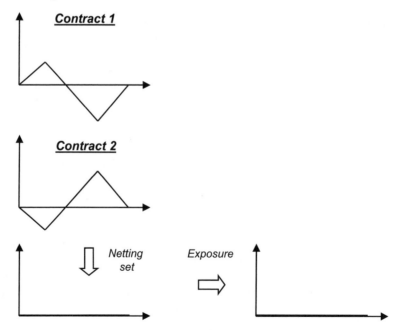

Figure 3.1. Illustration of the impact of netting on exposure. Possible MtM scenarios are shown on the left-hand side with the exposures on the right.

reduced. This institution may obtain more favourable terms and reduced collateral requirements.

- *Stability*. An additional implication of netting is the effect of incentives on the way market participants react to perceptions of increasing risk of a particular counter-party. If credit exposures were driven by gross positions then all those trading with the troubled counterparty would have strong incentives to attempt to terminate existing positions and stop any new trading. Such actions would likely result in even more financial distress for the troubled counterparty. With netting, an institution will be far less worried if there is no current exposure (MtM is negative). Whilst they will be concerned about potential future exposure and may require collateral, netting reduces the concern when a counterparty is in distress and may mean that a workout is more achievable.

Netting is widespread in derivatives markets. For example, at the end of 2008 netting was estimated to reduce OTC derivatives exposure of US commercial banks by 88.7%.[6]

3.4.10 Multilateral netting

All of the netting arrangements described above are assumed to be undertaken *bilaterally*, i.e. between two institutions only. Whilst bilateral netting has a significant impact on reducing overall credit exposure, it is limited to pairs of institutions within the market. Suppose that institution A has an exposure to institution B, whilst B has the same exposure to a third institution C that has another identical exposure to the original institution A. Even using bilateral netting, all three institutions have exposure (A has exposure to B, B to C and C to A). Some form of trilateral netting between the three institutions would allow the exposures to be netted further. This would give rise to questions such as how losses would be allocated between institutions A and B if institution C were to default. Problems such as this mean that some membership organisation needs to be at the centre of multilateral netting. Typically, such an entity will be an exchange or clearing house that will handle many aspects of the netting process such as valuation, settlement and collateralisation. A disadvantage of multi-lateral netting it that it tends to mutualise and homogenise counterparty risk, creating a reduced incentive for institutions to scrutinise the credit quality of their counterparties.

Other innovations have been developed to facilitate multilateral netting. Redundant positions can easily be built up across networks of participants and increase adminis-trative burdens, especially in the event of an actual counterparty default. A reduction of this is offered by, for example, TriOptima[7], which runs algorithms to detect redundant positions and notifies subscribers of early termination trades that eliminate redundan-cies and therefore reduce operational costs and minimise the overall exposure in the market. In 2008, TriOptima was reported to have offset trades to eliminate $30.2 trillion of notional value using its compression service.[8] Multilateral netting requires knowledge of all the positions of all members in the network. However, this may include proprie-tary information that the institutions involved may wish to keep secret. Disclosure is a partial hurdle for multilateral netting.

---

[6] IMF Global Financial Stability Report: *Responding to the Financial Crisis and Measuring Systemic Risks*, see *http://www.imf.org/external/pubs/ft/gfsr/2009/01/index.htm*
[7] See *www.trioptima.com* TriOptima reported on 9 July 2009 that tear-ups cut CDS notional by $9 trillion in notional outstanding from the credit default swap (CDS) market in the first half of 2009.
[8] "CDS dealers compress $30 trillion in trades in 2008", *Reuters*, 12 January 2009.

The topic of having a centralised clearing house for OTC derivatives transactions, particularly those such as CDS which are perceived to be the most sensitive to counterparty risk, has been a hot topic since the credit crisis of 2007 onwards. For this reason, we will dedicate a large portion of Chapter 14 to considering the impact of centralised clearing to facilitate multilateral netting and underwriting of derivatives transactions.

3.5 NETTING AND EXPOSURE

It should be obvious from the above discussion that netting can never increase the exposure to a given counterparty (for the sceptical or mathematically inclined reader this is presented more formally in Chapter 4). We now consider in more depth the impact of netting on exposure. Since netting allows the MtM of trades to offset each other then one must consider all individual MtM values with a given counterparty together. As we shall see, there are several different aspects to contemplate before understanding the full netting impact on overall exposure with respect to a particular counterparty. Below we will describe the general points to consider. In Chapter 4 we will look at them in more rigour and detail when considering the incremental and marginal impacts of combining exposures.

3.5.1 Negativity of MtM

For an instrument to give any benefit from netting then there must be *some chance* of it having a negative MtM at some point in its lifetime. If the MtM of an instrument can only be positive, then it can never have a beneficial impact on the overall exposure (although other trades may be considered to reduce *its* own exposure). The most obvious instruments that fall into this category are long option positions where the entire premium is paid upfront. This can cover a wide range of products across asset classes. Some examples are:

- equity options;
- swaptions;
- caps and floors;
- FX options.

In addition to instruments that cannot have a negative MtM, we should consider instruments that can have a negative MtM but where this is less likely than a positive MtM. Such instruments would give some netting benefit but it would be less significant. Examples include:

- long option position without an upfront premium;
- payer interest rate swap with an upwards-sloping yield curve (as discussed in Chapter 7);
- receiver interest rate swap with a downwards-sloping yield curve (as discussed in Chapter 7);
- FX forwards and cross-currency swaps paying the currency with the lower interest rates (see Chapter 9);
- off-market instruments (e.g. swaps with a large upfront payment);
- wrong-way risk exposures (see Chapter 7).

We could ask ourselves why one would bother to put a long option with an upfront premium under a netting agreement when it can never have a negative MtM. However, this would be beneficial since the exposure of the option could be offset by a negative MtM of other instruments within the same netting set at some point in the future.

Suppose all trade(s) with a given counterparty can only have positive MtM values. Would it still be worth putting them under a netting agreement? There are at least three reasons why an institution would do this:

1.   They may do trades in the future that may have negative MtM values and provide some offsetting of the current trades.
2.   They must be able to include all positions for effective collateralisation as discussed later in this chapter. Indeed, for a collateralised counterparty the impact of netting and collateral are closely linked and must be considered together.
3.   Furthermore, if the option position needs to be unwound at some point in the future then netting will be required in order to execute the mirror trade and have no residual counterparty risk.

3.5.2   Impact of correlation

When considering the netting benefit of two of more trades, the most obvious and probably important consideration is the correlation between the MtM values (and therefore exposures also). A high positive correlation means that MtMs are likely to be of the same sign. This means that the netting benefit will be small or even zero. We illustrate this in Table 3.2 where we can see that the two sets of MtM values create very little netting benefit. Netting will only help in cases where the MtM values of the trades have opposite signs, which occurs only in scenario 3. The EE is reduced only marginally.

Table 3.2. Illustration of the impact of netting when there is positive correlation between MtM values. The expected exposure (EE) is shown assuming each scenario has an equal weight.

	MtM		Total exposure		
	Trade 1	Trade 2	No netting	Netting	Netting benefit
Scenario 1	25	15	40	40	0
Scenario 2	15	5	20	20	0
Scenario 3	5	−5	5	0	5
Scenario 4	−5	−15	0	0	0
Scenario 5	−15	−25	0	0	0
EE			13	12	1

Perfectly correlated MtM values (as in Table 3.2) will provide the least netting benefit and, in the case of identical distributions (add 10 to each scenario for trade 2 to see this effect), this simply corresponds to increasing the size of a given transaction, in which case there will be clearly no netting benefit at all.

In the case of negative correlations, MtM values are much more likely to have opposite signs and hence the netting benefit will be stronger. We illustrate this in Table 3.3 where we see that netting is beneficial in four out of the five scenarios. Indeed, one can consider that either trade 1 or trade 2 adds little exposure to the overall risk. The EE is almost half the value without netting.

Table 3.3. Illustration of the impact of netting when there is negative correlation between MtM values. The expected exposure (EE) is shown assuming each scenario has an equal weight.

	MtM		*Total exposure*		
	Trade 1	*Trade 2*	*No netting*	*Netting*	*Netting benefit*
Scenario 1	25	−15	25	10	15
Scenario 2	15	−5	15	10	5
Scenario 3	5	5	10	10	0
Scenario 4	−5	15	15	10	5
Scenario 5	−15	25	25	10	15
EE			18	10	8

The extreme case of perfect negative correlation (as in Table 3.3) will provide the maximum netting benefit. In the case of identical distributions (subtract 10 from each scenario for trade 2 to see this effect) this simply corresponds to perfectly offsetting transactions (perhaps due to a cancellation via executing the opposite trade) in which case the netting benefit is 100% since there is no overall risk.

A majority of netting may occur across instruments of different asset classes which may be considered to have only a small correlation. One should note that this would still create a positive benefit. Indeed, for a simple example in Appendix 3.A we show the reduction corresponding to the case of normal variables with zero mean and equal variance. We derive the following formula for the "netting factor" with respect to exposure under the assumption of jointly normally distributed random variables:

$$\text{netting factor} = \frac{\sqrt{n + n(n-1)\bar{\rho}}}{n},\tag{3.1}$$

where n represents the number of exposures and $\bar{\rho}$ is the average correlation. The above measure will be +100% if there is no netting benefit ($\bar{\rho} = 100\%$) and 0% if the netting benefit is maximum ($\bar{\rho} = -(n-1)^{-1}$).[9] We illustrate the above expression in Figure 3.2 where we can see that the benefit improves for a large number of exposures and low correlation as one would expect since these conditions maximise the diversification benefit. We do note that this is a highly stylised example assuming zero mean and equal volatilities but it shows the general impact of correlation and the size of the netting set.

With no correlation, the simple formula tells us that the overall netting factor for n exposure is $1/\sqrt{n}$. This means, for example, that two independent exposures with zero

---

[9] Note that there is a restriction on the correlation level that ensures that the term inside the square root in equation (3.1) does not become negative. This is explained in Appendix 3.A.

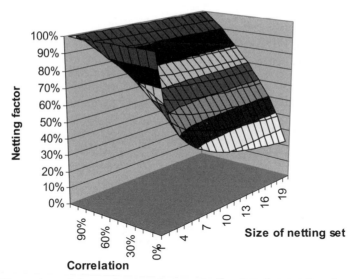

Figure 3.2. Illustration of the netting benefit in a simple example as a function of the size of the netting set (number of trades) and correlation as derived in Appendix 3.A. Only positive correlations are shown.

mean and equal volatility have a netted exposure reduced to 71% of the exposure without netting. For five exposures, the netting factor decreases to 45%.

3.5.3 Negative MtM of a netting set

Netting not only depends on the correlation between the MtMs of the different transactions, but also on the initial MtM. Consider the results shown in Table 3.4. trade 1 has a strongly negative MtM in all scenarios and therefore offsets the positive MtM of trade 2 in scenarios 1–3. This is a result of the negative MtM of trade 1 and not linked to a correlation of MtMs (indeed the MtM values in Table 3.4 have been constructed to have zero correlation). The EE is reduced from nine to just one.

Table 3.4. Illustration of the impact of netting when there is an initial negative MtM. The expected exposure (EE) is shown assuming each scenario has an equal weight.

	MtM		Total exposure		
	Trade 1	Trade 2	No netting	Netting	Netting benefit
Scenario 1	−20	25	25	5	20
Scenario 2	−25	15	15	0	15
Scenario 3	−15	5	5	0	5
Scenario 4	−15	−5	0	0	0
Scenario 5	−25	−15	0	0	0
EE			9	1	8

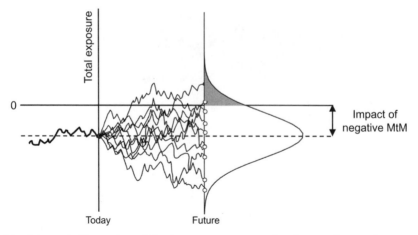

Figure 3.3. Schematic illustration of the impact on a new trade of a negative mark-to-market of existing trades in a netting set. The negative MtM will provide a cushion against the exposure of a new trade.

An illustration of the impact of negative MtM of a netting set is shown in Figure 3.3.

3.5.4 Positive MtM of a netting set

A positive initial MtM can also have a beneficial impact with respect to netting. Consider the results shown in Table 3.5. Trade 1 has a strongly positive exposure, which nets with the negative exposure of trade 2 in scenarios 4 and 5. This can also be considered to result from an imperfect correlation of exposures between instrument 1 and instrument 2 (the MtM values in Table 3.4 have zero correlation). The EE is reduced from 29 to 25. Alternatively, we can consider that the netting benefit means we add only the expected MtM of trade 2 (5) rather than the EE (9).

Table 3.5. Illustration of the impact of netting when there is an initial positive MtM. The expected exposure (EE) is shown assuming each scenario has an equal weight.

	MtM		*Total exposure*		
	Trade 1	*Trade 2*	*No netting*	*Netting*	*Netting benefit*
Scenario 1	20	25	45	45	0
Scenario 2	25	15	40	40	0
Scenario 3	15	5	20	20	0
Scenario 4	15	−5	15	10	5
Scenario 5	25	−15	25	10	15
EE			29	25	4

An illustration of the impact of positive MtM of a netting set is shown in Figure 3.4. It

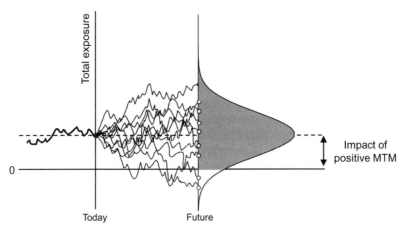

Figure 3.4. Schematic illustration of the impact on a new trade of a positive mark-to-market of existing trades in a netting set. The negative MtM of the new trade will offset some of the existing exposure.

can be seen that the expected MtM, rather than the larger EE value, of the new trade is more important in determining the increase in exposure.

We emphasise that the results of this and the previous section will be no longer relevant in the case of collateralisation (discussed next). However, for an un-collateralised (or only partially collateralised) counterparty, they remain important considerations.

3.6 COLLATERAL

Collateral management has been a key way in which to control counterparty risk over the last two decades and has been recently thrust still further into the limelight. Collateral management began in the 1980s, with Bankers Trust and Salomon Brothers taking collateral against credit exposures. There were no legal standards, and most calculations were performed manually on spreadsheets. Collateralisation of derivatives exposures became widespread in the early 1990s, with collateral typically in the form of cash or government securities. Standardisation began in 1994 via the first ISDA documentation. In the 1997/1998 period, collateral management had a greater focus with the default of Russia, the Asian crisis and the failure of the large hedge fund Long Term Capital Management (LTCM). These events resulted in tighter credit controls and a greater interest in mitigation techniques such as collateralisation.

Managing credit exposures to individual counterparties depends either on limiting the notional amount of business or for the business needs of the counterparty generating demand for offsetting positions (the notional of contracts may be high but the netting effect decreases the overall exposure). Netting significantly reduces counterparty risk but can still limit trading activities with certain counterparties. The use of collateral has enabled the further mitigation of credit risk and the expansion of the market to include less credit-worthy counterparties. Collateral use has increased substantially since 2003 and at the current time around half of OTC derivatives exposures are collateralised. This proportion increases for more counterparty risk-sensitive products such as CDSs (two-thirds of CDS exposures are collateralised[10]). The impact of collateralisation reduces overall exposure by around four-fifths (Ghosh et al., 2008). Incorporating the fact that credit exposures are first decreased through netting and the remaining net exposures are further mitigated by the pledging of collateral reduces total market exposure by nearly 93% (Bliss and Kaufman, 2005).

The motivation for collateral management is clearly to reduce counterparty risk but can be summarised in more detail as follows:

- Reduce credit exposure so as to be able to do more business. To maintain exposures within credit lines and overcome the bankers paradox.
- Enable one to trade with a particular counterparty. For example, ratings restrictions may not allow uncollateralised credit lines to certain counterparties.
- To reduce capital requirements. For example, as discussed in Chapter 11, Basel II gives capital relief for collateralised exposures.
- To give more competitive pricing of counterparty credit risk (see Section 7.2.1 for an example).

The fundamental idea of collateral management is very simple in that cash or securities are passed from one counterparty to another as security for a credit exposure. However, effective collateral management is much harder than one might initially think, and there are many pitfalls along the way, which we will aim to expose thoroughly. It is also important to note that, whilst collateralisation can be used to reduce credit exposure, it gives rise to new risks, such as market risk, operational risk and liquidity risk. All of these risks must be correctly understood, quantified and managed.

3.6.1   The basics of collateralisation

The basic idea of collateralisation is very simple; it is illustrated in Figure 3.5. In a swap transaction between parties A and B, party A makes a mark-to-market (MtM) profit whilst party B makes a corresponding MtM loss. Party B then posts some form of collateral to party A to mitigate the credit exposure that arises due to the positive MtM. The collateral may be in cash or other securities, the characteristics of which have been agreed before initiation of the contract.

> Collateral is an asset supporting a risk in a legally enforceable way.

Note that, since collateral agreements are often bilateral, collateral must be returned or posted in the opposite direction when exposure decreases. Hence in the case of a positive MtM, an institution will call for collateral and in the case of a negative MtM they will have to post collateral.

---

[10] ISDA Margin Study 2009.

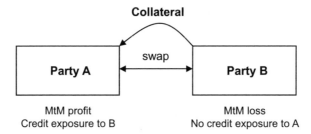

Figure 3.5. Illustration of the basic principle of collateralisation.

3.6.2 Analogy with mortgages

A collateralised position is analogous to a mortgaged house in many ways. As such, it is useful to consider the risks that a mortgage provider faces when making such a loan for their client to purchase a property. The risk that the mortgagee is unable or fails to make future mortgage payments is *default risk*. This risk is mitigated by the house being pledged as collateral for the mortgage but this will in turn create other risks as outlined below:

- The risk that the value of the property in question falls below the outstanding value of the loan or mortgage. This is often known as the situation of "negative equity" and corresponds to *market risk*. Note that this depends on both the value of the property (collateral) and the value of the mortgage (exposure).
- The risk that the mortgage giver is unable, or faces legal obstacles, to take ownership of the property in the event of the failure to make mortgage payments and faces costs in order to evict the owners and sell the property. This corresponds to *operational risk*.
- The risk that the property cannot be sold immediately in the open market and will have a falling value if property values are in decline. To achieve a sale, the property may then have to be sold at a discount to its fair value[11] if there is a shortage of buyers. This is *liquidity risk*.
- The risk that there is a strong dependence between the value of the property and the default of the mortgagee. For example, in an economic downturn, high unemployment and falling property prices make this rather likely. This is a form of *correlation* (or even *wrong-way*) risk.

3.6.3 Setting up a collateral agreement

The process by which two counterparties will agree to collateralise their exposures can be summarised as follows:

- Parties negotiate and sign a collateral support document, containing the terms and conditions under which they will operate.
- Trades subject to collateral are regularly marked-to-market, and the overall valuation including netting is agreed (unless this amount is disputed as discussed later).

---

[11] Although we might point out to any estate agents that fair value is indeed the price at which the property can be sold.

- The party with negative MtM delivers collateral (subject to minimum transfer amounts and thresholds as discussed later).
- The collateral position is updated to reflect the transfer of cash or securities.
- (Periodic reconciliations should also be performed to reduce the risk of disputes.)

The collateral agreement should cover all possible parameters defining the nature of the collateral agreement in all possible scenarios. Important points to be covered are:

- base currency;
- type of agreement (one-way or two-way);
- quantification of parameters such as independent amounts, minimum transfer amounts and rounding (defined later);
- eligible collateral that may be posted by each counterparty and the quantification of haircuts that act to discount the value of various forms of collateral with price volatility;
- timings regarding the delivery of collateral (margin call frequency, notification times and delivery periods);
- interest rates payable for cash collateral.

3.6.4 Valuation agent

The valuation agency is normally the party calling for delivery or return of collateral and thus must handle all calculations. Large counterparties trading with smaller counterparties may insist to be valuation agents for all purposes. In such a case, the "smaller" counterparty is not obligated to return or post collateral if they do not receive the expected notification whilst the valuation agent is under obligation to make returns where relevant.

The role of the valuation agent in a collateral calculation is as follows:

- calculate credit exposure under the impact of netting;
- calculate the market value of collateral previously posted;
- calculate the credit support amount (CSA) which represents the amount of uncollateralised exposure;
- calculate the delivery or return amount (the amount of collateral to be posted by either counterparty). This is likely to differ from the CSA due to the discrete nature of collateral agreements, which means that collateral is transferred in blocks.

The fact that counterparty risk has become more widely dispersed across various institutions means that in many transactions there is not obviously a "large" and "small" counterparty. In such a case, both counterparties may be valuation agent and each will call for collateral when they have an exposure. This is obviously more likely to lead to disputes, which can delay the process of collateralisation considerably. Third-party valuation agents may be used for this reason and can be useful when the counterparties involved are relatively small (and it may therefore not be worthwhile for them to have their own collateral management functions).

Responsibilities of third parties in a collateralisation agreement will involve:

- receiving and processing exposure figures;
- valuing and checking the eligibility of collateral;
- making interest and coupon payments;
- processing substitutions (collateral exchange in order to receive back securities previously posted as collateral);
- resolving disputes;
- producing daily valuation reports.

3.6.5   Types of collateral

There exists a wide range of possible collateral used to collateralise credit exposure with varying degrees of riskiness. Below are some common forms of collateral used historically:

- cash;
- government securities;
- government agency securities (e.g. Fannie Mae/Freddie Mac);
- mortgage-backed securities (MBSs);
- corporate bonds/commercial paper;
- letters of credit and guarantees;
- equity.

Cash collateral is the most common form (in 2005 ISDA reported that US dollar and euro-denominated collateral accounted for 73% of collateralised assets) and is increasing. The ability to post other forms of collateral is often highly preferable for liquidity reasons but the credit crisis has shown that even government agency securities (for example, Fannie Mae and Freddie Mac) and triple-A MBS securities are far from the high-quality assets with minimal price volatility that they were once assumed to be. Non-cash collateral also creates the problems of reuse of collateral or rehypothecation (discussed later) and additional volatility arising from the price uncertainty of collateral posted and its correlation to the original exposure (discussed in Chapter 5). On the other hand, in extreme market conditions, when cash collateralisation is highly preferred, cash tends to be in limited supply.

3.6.6   Coverage of collateralisation

Collateral agreements will reference the netted value of some or all trades with a specific counterparty. From a risk mitigation point of view, one should include the maximum number of trades but this should be balanced against the need to effectively value all such trades. Having just a single trade that, for whatever reason, cannot be valued correctly in a timely manner can impede calling collateral from a given counterparty covering many more trades. Hence, it may be optimal to focus a collateral agreement on a particular subset of trades constituting the majority of the total credit exposure. The issues to consider are:

- *Product considerations*. In the case of trading across many asset classes, if there are certain contracts that it will be hard to value in a timely manner due to either their

complexity (e.g. exotic options) or illiquidity (e.g. credit derivatives) then it may be beneficial to leave them out of a collateral agreement altogether.
- *Global considerations*. In the case of trading with a counterparty over many centres and across multiple time zones, one must agree on market close times and be able to value all products in a timely manner across the various centres. If a particular region might prove problematic and constitutes only a small portion of the credit exposure then it might be handled separately.

One should have in mind that the above issues should be considered from an institution's own point of view and from their counterparty's point of view. For example, an institution may know or expect that their counterparty will struggle to value certain products, even if they themselves have no such problem. It may then be preferable to leave that small subset of products uncollateralised rather than risk frequent disputes because of either or both parties having valuation issues. Such disputes would result in the inability to agree collateral transfer for a much larger trade population. Collateral agreements do normally require the transfer of the undisputed amount immediately, which means that the majority of products should still be collateralised even when there are disputes regarding a minority. However, the cleaner approach of leaving such products outside a collateral agreement is sometimes favoured.

3.6.7 Disputes and reconciliations

A dispute over a collateral call is common and can arise due to one or more of a number of factors:

- trade population;
- trade valuation;
- application of netting rules;
- market data and market close time;
- valuation of previously posted collateral.

If the difference in valuation or disputed amount is within a certain tolerance specified in the collateral agreement, then the counterparties may "split the difference". Otherwise, it will be necessary to find the cause of the discrepancy. Obviously, such a situation is not ideal and will mean that one party will have a partially uncollateralised exposure at least until the origin of the disputed amount can be traced, agreed upon and corrected. The following steps are normally followed in the case of a dispute:

- The disputing party is required to notify its counterparty (or the third-party valuation agent) that it wishes to dispute the exposure or collateral calculation no later than the close of business on the day following the collateral call.
- The disputing party agrees to transfer the undisputed amount and the parties will attempt to resolve the dispute within a certain timeframe (the "resolution time"). The reason for the dispute will be identified (e.g. which transactions have material differences in valuation).
- If the parties fail to resolve the dispute with the resolution time, they will obtain MtM quotations from several market makers (typically four) for the components of the

disputed exposure (or value of existing collateral in case this component is under dispute).

Reconciliations aim to minimise the chance of a later valuation dispute by agreeing on valuation figures even though the resulting netted exposure may not lead to any collateral changing hands. They can even be performed using dummy trades before two counterparties even trade with one another. It is good practice to perform reconciliations at periodic intervals (for example, weekly or monthly) so as to minimise differences in valuation between counterparties. Such reconciliations can pre-empt later problems that might arise during more sensitive periods. Reconciliations may be rather detailed and will therefore highlight differences that otherwise may be within the dispute tolerance or that by chance offset one another. Hence, problems that may otherwise appear only transiently should be captured in a thorough reconciliation.

3.7 THE MECHANICS OF COLLATERALISATION

Collateral or margin agreements are normally negotiated prior to any trading activity between counterparties or may be agreed or updated prior to an increase in trading volume. They must define explicitly all the parameters of the collateralisation and account for all possible scenarios. The choice of parameters will often come down to a balance between the workload of calling and returning collateral versus the risk mitigation benefit of doing so. We will look at methods to evaluate such a balance in Chapter 5. Failure to define appropriately the collateral terms and cover possible future scenarios can strongly compromise the ability to mitigate counterparty risk and may create in some cases far greater risks. We will define below the key parameters that define a collateral agreement. The reader should note that all the definitions might be applied differently to each counterparty in a transaction, often in a very asymmetrical manner. We will give specific examples of such asymmetries below.

3.7.1 Linkage of collateral parameters to credit quality

It is quite common to attempt to link the precise terms of a collateral agreement to the credit quality of one or both counterparties. The motivation for doing this is to minimise the operational workload whilst a counterparty has strong credit quality but have the ability to tighten up the terms of collateralisation when their credit quality deteriorates. The quantities to which collateral terms can obviously be linked are:

- credit ratings;
- traded credit spread;
- market value of equity;
- net asset value (sometimes used in the case of hedge funds).

The most commonly used of the above have been credit ratings, and examples will be given in the next sub-sections. Linking a tightening of collateral terms to a credit rating (for example, a downgrade to sub-investment grade) might seem a rather easy and obvious method of mitigating an increase in counterparty risk. However, this type of agreement can lead to rather unpleasant discontinuities since a downgrade of a counter-party's credit rating can occur rather late and then cause further credit issues due to the requirement to post collateral. An institution with similar agreements with many of its counterparties can be forced into a "death spiral", a concept we discuss in more detail in Chapters 8 and 13 in relation to monoline insurers. Hence, it may be more relevant to link collateral terms to more continuous quantities such as the second to fourth on the above list. This should be more beneficial in being able to tighten terms immediately a counterparty is in trouble rather than having to wait for a more delayed and discrete credit-rating change.

3.7.2   Margin call frequency

Margin call frequency refers to the periodic timescale with which collateral may be called and returned. Intra-day margining is common for vanilla products such as repos but other instruments such as swaps may require at least a daily margin call frequency in order for the relevant valuations to be carried out. A longer margin call frequency may be agreed upon, most probably to reduce operational workload. Whist a margin call frequency longer than daily might be practical for asset classes and markets that are not so volatile, daily margining is becoming a market standard. Some smaller institutions may struggle with the operational and funding requirements in relation to the daily margin calls required by larger counterparties.

3.7.3   Threshold

A threshold is a level of exposure below which collateral will not be called. The threshold therefore represents an amount of uncollateralised exposure. If the exposure is above the threshold, only the incremental exposure will be collateralised. In return for taking the risk of a moderate uncollateralised exposure, the operational burden of calling and returning collateral will be reduced. Put another way, many counterparties may only consider collateralisation important when the exposure exceeds a certain level, the threshold. A threshold of zero implies that any exposure is collateralised whilst a threshold of infinity is used to specify that a counterparty will not post collateral under any circumstance. An example of thresholds and their linkage to credit rating is shown in Table 3.6.

Table 3.6. Illustration of linkage of threshold to credit rating. The threshold will be the minimum based on the two rating scales shown, so, for example, a counterparty rated BBB−/Ba1 would have a threshold of zero.

S&P rating	Moody's rating	Threshold
AAA to BBB−	Aaa to Baa3	$1,000,000
BB+ and below	Ba1 and below	Zero

The above case corresponds to a simple case of a reasonable threshold when a counterparty is rated investment-grade by both ratings agencies and a threshold of zero otherwise. A downgrade of the counterparty to sub-investment grade may trigger an immediate collateral call of up to $1,000,000. As discussed previously, if such an agreement is in place with many counterparties then it may cause cashflow issues at precisely the worst time.

3.7.4 Independent amount

An independent amount (sometimes referred to as initial margin) corresponds typically to a quantity of collateral (very commonly in the form of cash) that is posted upfront and is independent of any subsequent collateralisation. It therefore corresponds to a desired level of overcollateralisation and will often be required by the "stronger" credit quality counterparty. It may also be posted to account for the fact that one counterparty is much more likely to have an exposure than the other. Independent amounts are common in credit or equity transactions to mitigate a widening of credit spreads or decline in equity value. There is a linkage between independent amount and credit lines (see Section 2.4.1) since an independent amount may not be charged to a better quality counterparty for which some unutilised credit line still exists.

An illustration of an independent amount is shown in Table 3.7. In this case, there is no independent amount as long the counterparty is rated investment-grade but substantial collateral must be posted if they are downgraded to below investment-grade by either rating agency. Such an amount would be additive with respect to any collateral already posted or received.

Table 3.7. Illustration of linkage of independent amount to credit rating. The value will be the maximum based on the two rating scales shown, so, for example, a counterparty rated BB+/Baa3 would have to post an independent amount of $5,000,000.

S&P rating	Moody's rating	Independent amount
AAA to BBB−	Aaa to Baa3	Zero
BB+ and below	Ba1 and below	$5,000,000

We can think of an independent amount as transforming counterparty risk into "gap risk". A transaction with a risky counterparty might be collateralised with both frequent margin calls and additionally an independent amount. The aim is then that the transaction is always overcollateralised by the independent amount so that even if the counterparty defaults, it is highly unlikely that any loss will be suffered. The residual risk is that, when the counterparty defaults, the value of the transactions will move dramatically or "gap" before it can be unwound. The independent amount is often considered large enough to make such a gap event in the relevant time horizon highly unlikely.

Independent amounts are often specific to a particular trade and are common for counterparties considered to be of relatively poor credit quality (such as hedge funds). Indeed, OTC derivatives dealers' exposures to hedge funds have traditionally been small since they are usually overcollateralised via independent amounts. An example of the structuring of deals with independent amounts is given in more detail in Chapter 6 when describing the mechanics of a total return swap (TRS) and the conversion of counterparty risk into "gap risk".

3.7.5 Minimum transfer amount

A minimum transfer amount is the smallest amount of collateral that can be transferred. It is used to avoid the workload associated with a frequent transfer of insignificant amounts of collateral. The size of the minimum transfer amount again represents a balance between risk mitigation versus operational workload. The minimum transfer amount and threshold are additive in the sense that the exposure must exceed the sum of the two before any collateral can be called. We note this additively does not mean that the minimum transfer amount can be incorporated into the threshold – this would be correct in defining the point at which the collateral call can be made but not in terms of the collateral due.[12] In Table 3.8 we illustrate an example of minimum transfer amount linked to rating. When the counterparty has a weaker credit rating then the additional operational workload required to make a larger number of smaller collateral calls is a reasonable price to pay for being able to reduce the amount of uncollateralised exposure.

Table 3.8. Illustration of the linkage of minimum transfer amount to credit rating. The amount will be the minimum based on the two rating scales shown, so, for example, a counterparty rated BBB+/Ba3 would correspond to a minimum transfer amount of $100,000.

S&P rating	Moody's rating	Minimum transfer amount
AAA to A−	Aaa to A3	$1,000,000
BBB+ to BB	Baa1 to Ba2	$250,000
BB− and below	Ba3 and below	$100,000

3.7.6 Rounding

A collateral call or return amount will always be rounded to a certain lot size to avoid unnecessarily small amounts. The rounding may be always up (or down) or might always be to the favour of one counterparty (i.e. up when they call for collateral and down when they return collateral).

3.7.7 Haircuts

A haircut is a discount applied to the value of collateral to account for the fact that its value may deteriorate over time. Cash collateral will require no haircut but other

---

[12] For example, for a minimum transfer amount (MTA) and threshold (K), the collateral call can be made when the (potentially already collateralised) exposure (E) exceeds MTA + K but the collateralisation required is $E - K$. If we used the approximation of adding MTA and K we would be conservative since we would model the collateralisation required as $E - K -$ MTA.

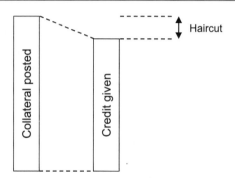

Figure 3.6. Illustration of a haircut applied to collateral.

securities will have pre-specified haircuts depending on their individual characteristics. A haircut of $x\%$ means that for every unit of that security posted as collateral, only $(1 - x)\%$ of credit (or "valuation percentage") will be given, as illustrated in Figure 3.6. The collateral giver must account for the haircut when posting collateral.

Some examples of haircuts together with eligible collateral types are shown in Table 3.9.

Table 3.9. Example of haircuts in a collateral agreement.

	Party A	*Party B*	*Valuation percentage*	*Haircut*
Cash in eligible currency	✓	✓	100%	0%
Debt obligations issued by the governments of the USA, UK or Germany with a maturity less than 1 year	✓	✓	98%	2%
Debt obligations issued by the governments of the USA, UK or Germany with a maturity between 1 and 10 years	✓	✓	95%	5%
Debt obligations issued by the governments of the USA, UK or Germany with a maturity greater than 10 years	✓		90%	10%

The important points to consider before assigning a haircut are:

- time taken to liquidate the collateral;
- volatility of the underlying market variable(s) defining the value of the collateral;
- default risk of the security;
- maturity of the security;
- liquidity of the security.

Example. Consider a security attracts a haircut of 5% and is being posted to cover a collateral call of $100,000. Only 95% of the value of this security is credited for collateral purposes and so the actual amount of collateral posted must be

        Market value of collateral = $105,263
        Haircut   = $5,263 (5% of $105,000)
        Credit given   = $100,000 (difference between the above)

It is the collateral giver's responsibility to account for haircuts when posting collateral so that if a collateral call is made as above then (assuming they do not dispute the amount) the counterparty could post $100,000 in cash but $105,263 in terms of the market value of a security attracting a 5% haircut.

For example, a high-quality 10-year government security has significant interest rate volatility due to the long maturity although default and liquidity risk will be probably not of great concern. Such a security might therefore attract a haircut of around a few percent. A triple-A corporate bond might be thought of in similar terms except that it may be considered to have additionally some credit spread volatility risk. Triple-A structured products should be considered additionally to have liquidity risk (and of course in hindsight much more default risk but that is another matter). Finally, securities such as equity and commodities (for example, gold) have substantial price volatility and possible liquidity risk and may attract substantial haircuts. In Chapter 11 we will make a more quantitative analysis of haircuts to illustrate the above points.

In particular, for risky assets it is important that haircuts can be dependent on current market conditions and also reviewed periodically. Like independent amounts, haircuts may sometimes by driven by a more complex formula involving many variables which may be driven by some type of value-at-risk (VAR) approach. This style of approach will also be discussed in more detail in Chapter 11.

3.7.8 Coupons and interest payments

Interest will be typically paid on cash collateral at an overnight rate (for example, EONIA in Europe, Fed Funds in the US). A development seen in light of the credit crisis in 2007 has been for some institutions to offer to pay in excess of such a rate in order to incentivise the collateral giver to post cash rather than other more risky and volatile securities. This would seem to make sense, especially in a highly volatile and illiquid market. Indeed, there is an argument that paying the overnight risk-free rate plus a spread in line with the collateral giver's credit quality would be reasonable. We discuss this point alongside bilateral counterparty risk in more detail in Chapter 7.

As long as the giver of collateral is not in default then they remain the owner from an economic point of view. Hence, the receiver of collateral must pass on coupon payments, dividends and any other cashflows. The only exception to this rule is in the case where an immediate margin call would be triggered. In this case, the collateral receiver may typically keep the minimum component of the cashflow in order to remain appropriately collateralised.

3.7.9   Substitution, reuse of collateral and rehypothecation

Sometimes, a counterparty may require or want securities posted as collateral returned (for example. to meet delivery commitments). In this case, they can make a substitution request and post an alternative amount of eligible collateral with the relevant haircut applied. The requested collateral does not need to be released until the substitutable collateral has been received. A substitution request will be reasonably refused if the substitutable collateral is not valid but *cannot* be refused on the grounds that the original collateral has been repoed, posted to another counterparty, sold or is otherwise inaccessible.

Non-cash collateral may be sold (although the equivalent security may need to be purchased later if the counterparty makes a substitution request), be used in repos or, more commonly, passed on as collateral to other counterparties. This process is known as *rehypothecation* and can lead to securities being posted in a chain across several different counterparties. The question arises as to whether rehypothecating a security in this way creates additional risk due to a loss of control of collateral. An institution faces two possible risks in this respect:

- Collateral pledged in a collateral agreement against a negative MtM to another counterparty may be rehypothecated and consequently not be returned (in the event of a default of the counterparty coupled to an increase in the MtM).
- Collateral received from party A and then rehypothecated to party B. This may not be retrieved in the event that party B defaults, creating a liability to party A.

Prior to the credit crisis in 2007, the pledging, reuse and rehypothecation of collateral was strongly encouraged. This was viewed as being critical to the entire financial system (Segoviano and Singh, 2008). However, the practice of rehypothecation probably became too widespread, especially in the inter-bank market (presumably, since there was little concern of actual bank defaults). The bankruptcy of Lehman Brothers has illustrated the potential problems with rehypothecation. One example is that customers of Lehman Brothers Inc. (US) could be potentially treated more favourably than the UK customers of Lehman Brothers International (Europe) in terms of the return of rehypothecated assets (due to differences in customer protection between the UK and the US). The liquidator of Lehman (PWC) stated in October 2008, shortly after the bankruptcy, that certain assets provided to Lehman Brothers International (Europe) had been rehypothecated and may not be returned.

Singh and Aitken (2009) have reported a significant drop in rehypothecation, which can be seen as a good thing, although it does lead to an increase in funding costs. Hedge funds are tending to be unwilling to allow rehypothecation, which will surely lead to an increase in prime broker fees. The problems with rehypothecation is another driving force behind cash collateralisation becoming increasingly the standard and, in many cases, the only option that most institutions are willing to adopt.

3.7.10   Call-and-return example

A simple example of collateral transfer calculations is given in Table 3.10. This assumes that there is no dispute over the portfolio MtMs so that party B has exactly the reverse

MtM as party *A*. This shows a case where party *A* has an exposure and therefore calls collateral from party *B*. Note the convention used in the calculation with respect to rounding in that a positive number will mean that any collateral posted is rounded up and a negative number means that it will be rounded down. Hence, in the situation shown below, party *A* is able to round up and down in their favour and the rounding will always be against party *B*.

Spreadsheet 3.2. Call-and-return collateral example with logic relating to independent amounts, thresholds, collateral held, minimum transfer amount and rounding

---

Table 3.10. Example of collateral calculation.

	Party A point of view	*Party B point of view*
Portfolio MtM	371,628	−371,628
Independent amount	—	—
Threshold	—	—
Collateral held	—	—
Minimum transfer amount	100,000	100,000
Rounding	50,000	−50,000
Credit support amount	371,628	−371,628
Less collateral held	371,628	−371,628
Call or return amount	400,000	−400,000

In Table 3.11, the situation has changed since the exposure of party *B* has decreased. Hence, party *B* expects collateral to be returned.

Table 3.11. Example of collateral calculation.

	Party A point of view	*Party B point of view*
Portfolio MtM	254,234	−254,234
Independent amount	—	—
Threshold	—	—
Collateral held	400,000	−400,000
Minimum transfer amount	100,000	100,000
Rounding	50,000	−50,000
Credit support amount	254,234	−254,234
Less collateral held	−145,766	145,766
Call or return amount	−100,000	100,000

In Chapter 5 we provide a more detailed discussion on the calculation of collateral call-and-return amounts.

3.8   IS RISK MITIGATION ALWAYS A GOOD THING?

It might seem odd to question the overall benefits resulting from risk mitigation, but when viewed outside the OTC derivatives markets some objections can be raised. Most creditors are unable to enforce their rights when a firm is in bankruptcy whereas derivatives contracts give such additional rights. They allow netting, close-out and prompt access to collateral without being subject to prolonged legal proceedings. Netting, close-out and collateralisation allow large derivatives dealers to control their risk and are available in normal markets, not just financial crises. The main arguments used as to why derivatives creditors require special protection outside the normal bankruptcy process applied to other creditors are:

- Derivatives markets are critical to the smooth functioning of the financial system, so that their operation deserves special protection.
- Derivatives markets are particularly susceptible to systemic failures due to the volatile nature of the value of derivatives contracts.

Derivatives markets have long been viewed as a major source of systemic risk and require measures to limit the possibility of severe systemic damage to financial markets and economies. Does this mean that the special provisions discussed in this chapter are valid regardless of the costs to other market participants and creditors of a failed institution?

An alternative way to look at the above question is posed by Bliss and Kaufman (2005) who turn the argument on its head somewhat. Netting, close-out and collateralisation have facilitated counterparty risk management to the extent that they have allowed a massive expansion of the OTC derivatives market, with major dealers having massive notional risks (for example, Lehman Brothers had a total notional amount of $800bn of OTC derivatives at the time of their bankruptcy). Without such risk mitigants, the size, liquidity and concentrations seen in the derivatives dealer network would simply not exist. Increasing the capital required to engage in derivatives dealing by a significant factor (for example, due to the lack of netting) would materially alter the economics of derivatives markets.

Market participants are likely to overestimate the benefit of risk mitigation. Since counterparty risk acts to reduce profits on transactions, it would not be surprising that the reduction in risk offered by a risk mitigant would be over-stated (consciously or unconsciously) in order to maximise the profitability of such transactions. Regulators may overestimate risk reduction in this way, either through a lack of complete understanding of all aspects or pressure from market participants, or both. We are left, therefore, with a dilemma. Are netting, close-out and collateral critical elements in reducing counterparty risk in the derivatives market? Alternatively, is the massive global OTC derivatives market and its associated counterparty risk actually an artefact of these mechanisms being granted to derivatives counterparties?

Netting and collateral may increase systemic risk by allowing a concentration of dealers to develop. Close-out is potentially a source of systemic risk by making it more difficult to manage insolvency of a major dealer as its counterparties choose to terminate all transactions. Together these mechanisms may make it more difficult to avoid the failure of a distressed but still financially viable (in the long run) major dealer.

In assessing the benefits of risk mitigation, the transformation of counterparty risk into others risks must be carefully considered. Whilst collateralisation reduces counterparty risk, it can cause significant funding liquidity risk since counterparties need to provide collateral at short notice as market conditions become volatile. If rehypothecation is reduced then such funding costs will be increased. A shortage of high-quality collateral at times of market stress can cause additional problems.

We must end on a note of caution then. After a credit crisis, firms will – not surprisingly – focus in more depth on mitigation of counterparty risk, which is surely beneficial for the market as a whole. However, when markets return to normality, this may lead to a naive increase in trading activity and risk which may not be fully appreciated until the next crisis.

3.9   SUMMARY

In this chapter we have described ways of mitigating counterparty risk or, more specifically, mitigating credit exposure. Early termination events (or break clauses) allow the mid-market termination of a transaction to mitigate an exposure combined with a deterioration of the credit quality of a counterparty, possibly linked to some event such as a credit ratings downgrade. Netting agreements are a crucial way to control credit exposure by being legally able to offset transactions with positive and negative mark-to-market values in the event a counterparty does default. Finally, we have discussed in detail the use of collateral management in controlling credit exposure, which is a crucial method when trading involving large positions and/or relatively risky counterparties. We note that, together, netting and collateralisation decrease the amount of counterparty risk in the market by at least an order of magnitude. We end, however, on a word of caution with the argument that risk mitigation techniques may actually be counterproductive due to allowing the size, concentration and systemic risk of derivatives markets to develop to an extent so as to negate the overall impact of risk mitigation.

In the next two chapters we will discuss ways of modelling, quantifying and measuring credit exposure both with and without the various risk mitigation techniques described above. This will give a more concrete assessment of the benefits of mitigating counterparty risk. We shall also assess the gains in risk reduction versus the associated increases in operational workload together with the associated risks.

APPENDIX 3.A: EE OF INDEPENDENT NORMAL VARIABLES

We have already shown in Appendix 2.A that the EE of a normally distributed random variable is:

$$\mathrm{EE}_i = \mu_i \Phi(\mu_i/\sigma_i) + \sigma_i \varphi(\mu_i/\sigma_i).$$

Consider a series of independent normal variables representing transactions within a netting set (NS). They will have a mean and standard deviation given by:

$$\mu_{\mathrm{NS}} = \sum_{i=1}^{n} \mu_i \qquad \sigma_{\mathrm{NS}}^2 = \sum_{i=1}^{n} \sigma_i^2 + 2 \sum_{i=1,j>i}^{n} \rho_{ij}\sigma_i\sigma_j$$

where ρ_{ij} is the correlation between transaction MtM values. Assuming normal variables with zero mean and equal standard deviations, $\bar{\sigma}$, we have that the overall mean and standard deviation are given by:

$$\mu_{NS} = 0 \qquad \sigma^2_{NS} = (n + n(n-1)\bar{\rho})\bar{\sigma}^2,$$

where $\bar{\rho}$ is an average correlation value. Hence, since $\varphi(0) = 1/\sqrt{2\pi}$, the overall EE will be:

$$EE_{NS} = \bar{\sigma}\sqrt{n + n(n-1)\bar{\rho}}/\sqrt{2\pi}$$

The sum of the individual EEs gives the result in the case of no netting (NN):

$$EE_{NN} = \bar{\sigma}n/\sqrt{2\pi}$$

Hence the netting benefit will be:

$$EE_{NS}/EE_{NN} = \frac{\sqrt{n + n(n-1)\bar{\rho}}}{n}$$

In the case of perfect positive correlation, $\bar{\rho} = 100\%$, we have:

$$EE_{NS}/EE_{NN} = \frac{\sqrt{n + n(n-1)}}{n} = 100\%$$

The maximum negative correlation is bounded by $\bar{\rho} \geq -1/(n-1)$ and we therefore obtain:

$$EE_{NS}/EE_{NN} = \frac{\sqrt{n - n(n-1)/(n-1)}}{n} = 0\%$$

4

Quantifying Counterparty
Credit Exposure, I

> *"The trouble with our times is that the future is not what it used to be."*
>
> Paul Valery (1871–1945)

A key function of the risk management department of a financial institution is the quantification of counterparty credit exposure. In this chapter we characterise and explain how to quantify credit exposure, a key component in determining counterparty risk. Credit exposure is often considered a purely market risk component with no default-related aspects and indeed, as we shall explain, will often be calculated without any reference to the credit quality of the counterparty with which the exposure exists. We would furthermore expect the quantification of credit exposure to have many parallels to market risk as seen in traditional value-at-risk models. Whilst this is true, we will see that there is a key difference between quantifying market risk and credit exposure, which is that for the latter we must often consider a much longer time horizon.

4.1 QUANTIFYING CREDIT EXPOSURE

Quantifying exposure is important for the following reasons:

- trade approval by comparing against credit lines;
- pricing (and hedging) counterparty risk;
- calculating economic and regulatory capital.

We present an overview of the various methods to quantify exposure. These vary from the simple but crude to the more complex generic approach of Monte Carlo simulation. The practical calculation of exposure involves choosing a balance between sophistication and operational considerations.

At the heart of the problem of quantifying exposure lies a balance between the following two effects:

- As we look into the future, we become increasingly uncertain about market variables. Hence, risk increases as we move through time.
- Many financial instruments have cashflows that are paid over time and hence this tends to reduce the risk profiles as the instruments "amortise" through time.

> **Example.** An interest rate swap trader is discussing a 5-year swap with a new
> counterparty. They need to assess where the maximum exposure occurs. They think
> it is unlikely to occur in the first year since there is less uncertainty about the
> movement of interest rates in that period. However, they also think it is unlikely
> to be in the last year since most of the swap payments will have already have been
> made by then.
>
> We will see later that the maximum exposure will be probably between 2 and 3
> years from now (this depends on many aspects such as the contractual terms and
> slope of the yield curve). This represents a balance between the uncertainty of time
> and the remaining cashflows in the swap.

4.1.1   Mark-to-market + add-ons

The simplest approach to approximate future exposure is to take the current exposure
(positive mark-to-market) and add a component that represents the uncertainty of the
PFE in the future. This type of approach is highly simplistic and forms the basis of the
Basel I capital rules (discussed in Chapter 11). The "add-on" component should account
for:

- the time horizon in question;
- the volatility of the underlying asset class;
- the nature of the underlying transaction(s).

For example, longer time horizons will require larger add-ons, and volatile asset classes
such as FX and commodities should also attract larger add-ons. Add-on approaches are
fast and may be reasonably accurate for certain deal-based exposures. They also allow
exposures to be pre-calculated and distributed via simple "grids". An example grid for
vanilla interest rate swaps is shown in Table 4.1. Such grids allow a very quick look-up
of the PFE impact of a new trade. The exposure for these instruments is defined by
maturity and currency; a longer maturity instrument has more risk whilst the slightly
different add-ons per currency may reflect different yield curve shapes and/or interest
rate volatility.

Table 4.1. Example add-ons (percentage of notional value) for interest rate swaps as a function of currency and maturity.

	USD	EUR	GBP
0–1 years	0.25%	0.20%	0.30%
1–3 years	0.50%	0.45%	0.60%
3–5 years	1.00%	1.00%	1.20%
5–10 years	1.50%	1.40%	1.75%

However, ideally an add-on approach would also account for more subtle effects
including:

- the specifics of the transaction in question (cash flows, etc.);
- if the transaction has a mark-to-market very far from zero (other than the addition of this mark-to-market when it is positive);
- netting;
- collateral.

Such effects, however, will probably be largely ignored for reasons of simplicity. For example, two interest rate swaps of the same maturity will probably have the same add-on, whereas there are many reasons why they may have rather different PFE profiles:

- currencies;
- payer versus receiver swaps;
- payment frequencies (quarterly, semi-annual, annual) on each leg;
- floating reference rates.

More sophisticated add-on methodologies have been developed (for example, Rowe, 1995 and Rowe and Mulholland, 1999) although the increased complexity of such approaches must be balanced against the power afforded by a more generic method such as Monte Carlo simulation.

4.1.2 Semi-analytical methods

Semi-analytical methods are generally more sophisticated than the simple add-on approaches but still require some approximations. Their advantage is to avoid the time-consuming process of Monte Carlo simulation. A semi-analytical method will generally be based on:

- make some simple assumption regarding the risk factor(s) driving the exposure;
- find the distribution of the exposure as defined by the above risk factor(s);
- calculate a semi-analytical approximation to a risk metric for that exposure distribution.

A simple example of a semi-analytical approximation for a forward contract is shown in Appendix 4.A. The exposure metrics computed with such an approximation are shown in Figure 4.1.

> **Spreadsheet 4.1.** Exposure calculation for a forward contract

Whilst semi-analytical calculations can be useful for certain products, they have several drawbacks:

- Semi-analytical calculations depend on simplifying assumptions made with respect to the risk factors involved. Hence, complicated assumptions such as mean reversion cannot always be easily incorporated.
- Exposure calculations across time are made independently of one another. Hence, any path-dependent aspects, such as exercise decisions, may not be captured.
- Often semi-analytical calculations will give us just a single risk measure (such as PFE) rather than the full distribution.
- Such calculations typically ignore netting effects, which are hard to incorporate.
- The calculation of collateralised exposures is not easy to incorporate.

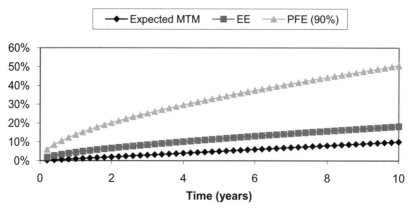

Figure 4.1. Exposure calculations using the normal approximation for a forward contract as described in Appendix 4.A. The relevant parameters are $\mu = 1\%$ and $\sigma = 10\%$ (volatility). The PFE is shown at the 90% confidence level.

There are exceptions to the above restrictions. For example, Sorensen and Bollier (1994) show that the EE of an interest rate swap can be accurately defined in terms of a series of interest rate swaptions. Arvanitis and Gregory extend this idea to consider a physically settled interest rate swaption (accounting for the exercise decision). Brigo and Masetti (2005b) consider the netting impact and derive formulas for portfolios of interest rate swaps in restricted cases. Whilst some useful analytical formulas exist, these are best used at the single-trade level whilst the generality implied by netting requires the use of more flexible simulation methods.

4.1.3 Monte Carlo simulation

Monte Carlo simulation, whilst the most complex and time-consuming method to assess exposure, is completely generic and copes with many of the complexities ignored by add-on and semi-analytic approaches such as transaction specifics, path dependency, netting and collateralisation. It is also required due to the high dimensionality involved in most netting sets due to the relatively large number of market variables (and their correlations) involved.

The generic Monte Carlo calculation of credit exposure can be described in the following steps.

(1) Factor choice

One must first consider what risk factors will influence the exposure of the transaction or transactions in question. This leads to a choice of model for the risk factors and consequently the PFE. Risk factors will typically be underlyings such as spot interest rates and spot FX rates or may be more complex such as implied volatilities. Model choice may be a simple one-factor model or a more complex multi-factor approach. We will give examples of specific models in Section 4.3 and discuss the trade-off between model sophistication and simplicity but for now we simply emphasise the characteristics that such a model should have:

- The model must provide a reasonable distribution of the possible risks of the transactions and thus account for a large fraction of future plausible scenarios.
- The model must calibrate to (match) today's market variables (for example, yield curves, FX rates, commodity prices).
- It must be possible and practical to simulate discrete scenarios of the risk factors using the model. Typically, many thousand scenarios will be required at several points in time and hence there must be an efficient way in which to generate this many scenarios quickly.

Regarding different asset classes, risk factor analysis and model choice will probably be made for each asset class individually and then some correlation between risk factors may be considered after such a choice.

(2) Scenario generation

Having made a choice of risk factors and model, it is necessary to generate scenarios via simulation of these risk factors. Each scenario is a joint realisation of risk factors at various points in time. One will first need to choose a grid for simulation, which we denote by:

$$[t_0, t_1, \ldots, t_{n-1}, t_n]. \tag{4.1}$$

The number of simulation dates must be reasonably large to capture the main details of the PFE but not so large as to make the computations unfeasible. A typical value for n might be in the region of 50–200. The final simulation date t_n must be greater than or equal to the longest maturity instrument under consideration. Note that the spacing of the above dates need not be uniform for reasons such as roll-off (discussed later). Furthermore, the ability to change grids for different counterparties is beneficial due to different maximum maturity dates and underlying instrument type.

(3) Revaluation

One the scenarios have been generated, it is necessary to revalue the individual positions at each point in time in the future. For example, to revalue an interest rate swap in a given scenario at a given point in time, one must calculate the corresponding risk factors (interest rates), and then use the standard pricing for the swap as a function of these interest rates (probably via a formula for reconstructing the yield curve at this particular point in time).

The revaluation step clearly requires the use of efficient valuation models and algorithms. Suppose the total population of trades and exposure calculation involves:

- 250 counterparties;
- on average, 40 trades with each counterparty;
- 100 simulation steps – n in equation (4.1);
- 10,000 scenarios.

Then the total number of instrument revaluations will be $250 \times 40 \times 100 \times 10,000 = 10,000,000,000$ (10 billion). This means that pricing functions for vanilla instruments must be highly optimised whilst exotic products will probably require approximations.

Exotic products are often priced via lattice-based or Monte Carlo methods that will typically be too slow to price in the many scenarios "on the fly". Examples of more efficient ways to handle this kind of problem can be found in Longstaff and Schwartz (2001), Glasserman and Yu (2004) or Gordy and Juneja (2008). Alternative, crude ad hoc approximations may be deemed of sufficient accuracy; for example, approximating a Bermudan swaption as a European swaption (which admits a closed-form formula).

(4) Aggregation

Once the revaluation step has been done, for each transaction there will be a matrix of values with respect to scenario number and point on the time grid. One must now aggregate these values up to the netting set. This requires knowledge of the relevant netting conditions for the counterparty in question. It might be informative to introduce some brief notion here. Suppose the cube $V_{i,j,k}$ represents the mark-to-market value of trade i at time point j in scenario k. Let us assume that trades $i = 1, m$ all belong to a single netting set. The exposure for this netting set is characterised by the matrix:

$$E_{j,k} = \max\left(\sum_{i=1}^{m} V_{i,j,k}, 0 \right). \tag{4.2}$$

Now $E_{j,k}$ defines the exposure of the netting set at time point j in scenario k.

(5) Post-processing

We now have the netted exposures with respect to scenario number and grid point for each counterparty. However, there may be post-processing required in order to account for effects such as collateral. In the case of collateral, as described later, we will go through each exposure path and apply logic to determine at each point how much of the exposure would be collateralised. This can be done independently of (but after) the previous steps under the assumption that the collateral parameters do not depend on any of the underlying market variables, only on the total exposure.

(6) Extraction of statistics

Finally, once all the above steps have been completed, one can extract any metrics desired (for example, for risk management, pricing or regulatory purposes). This is illustrated in Figure 4.2. Scenarios can be collapsed into metrics such as EE but in order to account for future trades then all of the $E_{j,k}$ values must be kept (this is discussed later).

4.1.4 Roll-off risk

Exposures will be calculated at only a number of discrete time points to minimise computational effort. However, when making the choice of such time points, it is crucial to attempt to avoid missing any key areas of risk or "hotspots". Representing exposure over a relatively compact number of time points will assume (perhaps only implicitly) that it is possible to interpolate to find intermediate exposures. However, exposure profiles can be highly discontinuous over time due to maturity dates, option exercise, cashflow payments and amortisation. The risk of missing jumps in exposure caused by

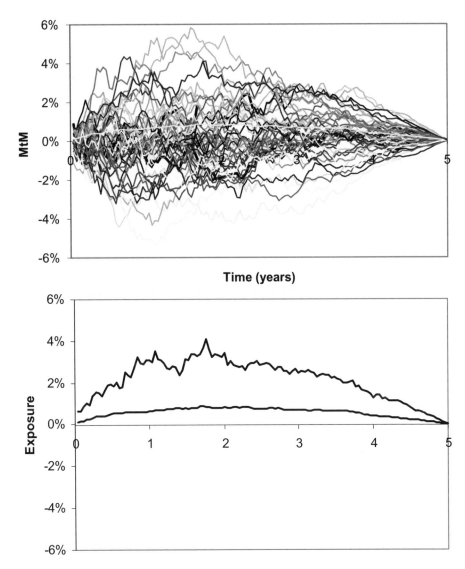

Figure 4.2. Illustration of calculation of EE and PFE from many scenarios. The EE and PFE are shown as solid black lines in the bottom chart.

these aspects is called "roll-off risk". Such jumps may be small in duration but large in magnitude. The impact of roll-off risk is shown in Figure 4.3.

Roll-off risk can be controlled by using non time-homogeneous time grids, at least providing a better definition as discrepancies become closer. On the other hand, this can mean that PFE may change significantly from day to day due to exposure jumps gradually becoming engulfed within the more granular short time grid. A better approach is to incorporate the critical points where exposure changes significantly (for example, due to maturity dates, settlement dates and cashflow payment dates) into

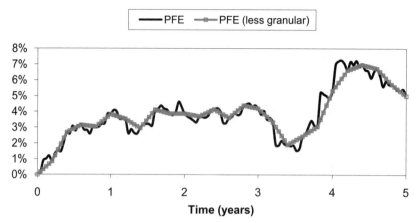

Figure 4.3. PFE for a counterparty calculated at different levels of granularity. In the normal case, the time intervals are spaced by 10 days, while in the less granular case, the interval is five times greater.

the time grid. This must, however, be done separately for each netting set. The ability to use different grids is important; for example, to provide more granularity for certain instrument types or shorter maturities.

4.2   TYPICAL CREDIT EXPOSURES

We now give some examples of actual exposure for various different product types and illustrate some important effects such as maturity, option exercise, payment frequencies, roll-off and default. In all cases, we show exposure profiles based on PFE (generally a 99th quantile has been used although the choice of confidence level does not change the qualitative behaviour and so is not so important) as a percentage of notional value.

4.2.1   Loans, bonds and repos

The exposures of bonds, loans and repos can usually be considered almost deterministic and approximately equal to the notional value. Bonds typically pay a fixed rate and therefore will have some additional uncertainty since, if interest rates decline, the exposure may increase. In the case of loans, they are typically floating rate instruments but the exposure may decline over time due to the possibility of prepayments (Figure 4.4).

4.2.2   Swaps

The most commonly shown exposure profile is that of a swap which is characterised by a peaked shape as shown in Figure 4.5. The shape arises from the balance between future uncertainties over payments, combined with the roll-off of swap payments over time. A swap with a longer maturity has much more risk due to both the increased lifetime and the greater number of payments due to be exchanged. An illustration of the swap cashflows is made below the graph in Figure 4.5 to illustrate this.

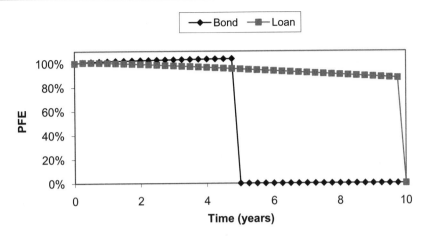

Figure 4.4. PFE for a 5-year bond and a 10-year loan.

In Figure 4.6 is shown the PFE for off-market interest rates swaps. The initial MtM being away from zero increases or decreases the PFE directly. However, this has the more subtle impact of changing the maximum exposure point. For example, when the MtM is negative, there is little chance of an exposure in the short term and it takes longer for the maximum exposure to occur. At later time horizons, the impact caused by the initial MtM is not so strong. This illustrates a difficulty of using a MtM + add-on approach to quantifying exposure since it is clearly not possible to separate completely the impact of initial MtM and future exposure uncertainty.

4.2.3 FX products

Foreign exchange exposures can be considerable due to the high FX volatility driving the risk coupled to the long maturities and final exchanges of notional required in most swap contracts. The risk of these instruments is driven by a large final payment and thus the profile increases monotonically until the maturity of the trade. There is some contribution from interest rates, but the major driver of the exposure is the FX risk from the notional exchange as shown in Figure 4.7.

In Figure 4.8 we illustrate PFE for cross-currency swaps of different maturities. The FX risk does not change but the longer maturity swaps have marginally more risk due to the greater number of interest rate payments on the swap.

4.2.4 Options

The general exposure profile of a long option position is shown in Figure 4.9. The exposure tends to increase until exercise due to the increased possibility that the option can be highly in the money. The precise shape of the graph can depend on whether the option is in, out or at the money but the basic shape is the same. Strips of options such as caps and floors and options that are physically settled will be discussed in Section 4.3.7.

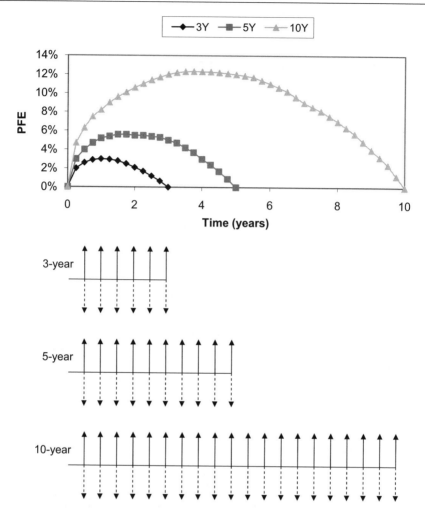

Figure 4.5. PFE for interest rate swaps of different maturities (top). Illustrative swap cashflows (fixed lines represent fixed cashflows and dotted lines floating cashflows) for the different maturities are shown (bottom) assuming semi-annual payment frequencies on both sides.

4.2.5 Credit derivatives

Credit derivatives represent a big problem for counterparty risk assessment due to wrong-way risk, which will be discussed extensively in Chapter 8. Even without this as a consideration, exposure profiles of credit derivatives are hard to characterise due to the discrete payoffs of the instruments. Consider the exposure profile of a long-protection credit default swap (CDS) as shown in Figure 4.10. The exposure increases in the early stages, which corresponds to scenarios in which the CDS premium (credit spread) will have widened. However, the maximum exposure on the CDS corresponds to the reference entity experiencing a credit event, which triggers an immediate payment of the notional less a recovery value. Hence, the exposure will be capped at this level (60% in the example assuming a 40% recovery value). This is a rather unnatural effect (see

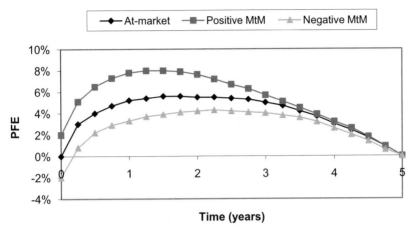

Figure 4.6. PFE behaviour for off-market interest rate swaps comparing swaps with initial mark-to-market values of +2% and −2% with an "at market" swap with zero initial MtM.

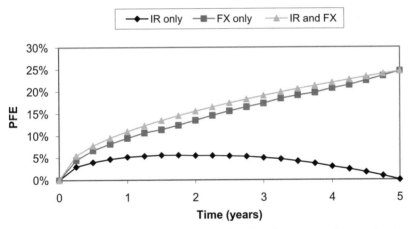

Figure 4.7. PFE for a 5-year cross-currency swap, showing the impact of interest rates and FX rates on the exposure. Shown are the PFE arising due to interest rate effects only (no exchange of notional), FX rates only (exchange of notional only) and for the cross-currency swap (IR and FX).

also Hille et al. (2005) as it means that PFE may or may not represent the credit event occurring and is sensitive to the confidence level used. In the example, at 3 years the 90% PFE is defined by a large credit spread widening whilst the 99% PFE is defined by the credit event. Using a measure such as expected shortfall[1] does partially solve this problem.

We comment that the above impact could be argued to be largely a facet of common modelling assumptions, which assume default as a sudden unanticipated jump event

---

[1] Expected shortfall is a measure used in preference to VAR in some cases since is has more mathematically convenient properties and, unlike VAR, is argued to be a "coherent risk measure". In this case, it corresponds to the expected exposure above the relevant PFE value.

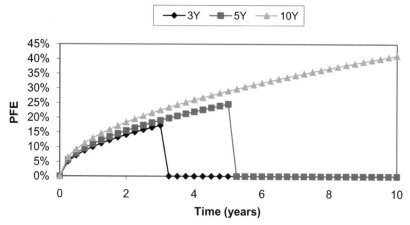

Figure 4.8. PFE for cross-currency swaps of different maturity.

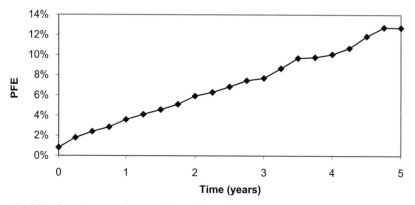

Figure 4.9. PFE for a long option product with upfront premium.

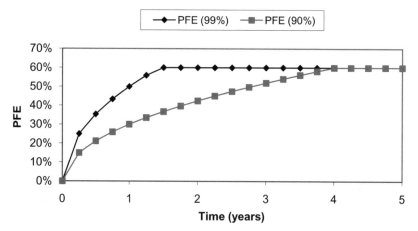

Figure 4.10. PFE for a long-protection credit default swap trade computed at confidence levels of 99% and 90%. A PFE of 60% arises from default with an assumed recovery rate of 40%.

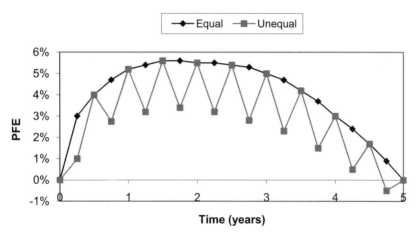

Figure 4.11. PFE for an interest rate swap with equal and unequal payment frequencies.

with a known recovery value (40%). Using a more realistic modelling of default and an unknown recovery value gives behaviour that is more continuous.

4.2.6 Payment frequencies

In Figure 4.11 we show exposure profiles for a 5-year interest rate with unequal payment frequencies (in this case semi-annual fixed payments are made and quarterly floating payments received). We can see that a risk profile can be substantially altered due to the specifics of the cash flows in a transaction. The unequal case has a reduced exposure since payments are received more frequently than they are made. This effect is similar to a simple version of collateralisation.

Clearly, a swap where the payments are made more frequently than they are received will then have more risk than the equivalent equal payment swap. Simplified methods (for example, add-ons) of computing exposure are typically unable to account for such details that can be easily handled by a full Monte Carlo simulation with enough time points to capture such granular effects.

4.2.7 Exercise dates

The impact of exercise decisions creates some complexities in exposure profiles. In Figure 4.12 we show the exposure for an interest rate swaption that is swap-settled (physical delivery) rather than cash-settled.[2] The underlying swap has different payment frequencies also. We compare it with the equivalent forward swap. Before the exercise point, the swaption must always have a greater exposure than the forward swap[3] but, thereafter, this trend will reverse since there will be scenarios where the forward swap has positive value but the swaption would not have been exercised. This point is illustrated in Figure 4.13, which shows a scenario that would give rise to exposure in the forward swap but not the swaption.

---

[2] The cash-settled swaption has an identical exposure until the exercise date and then zero exposure thereafter.
[3] The option to enter into a contract cannot be worth less than the equivalent obligation to enter into the same contract.

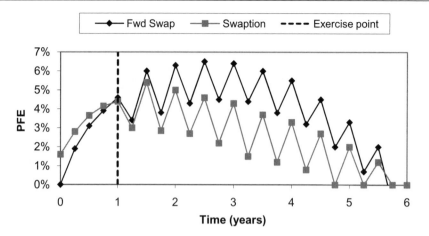

Figure 4.12. PFE for a swap-settled (physically settled) interest rate swaption and the equivalent forward swap. The option maturity is 1 year and the swap maturity 5 years.

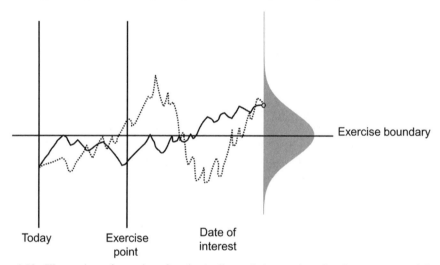

Figure 4.13. Illustration of exercise of a physically settled swaption showing two potential MtM scenarios of the underlying swap. The dotted line corresponds to a scenario where the swaption would be exercised, giving rise to an exposure at the date of interest (the swap would have the same exposure as the swaption). The solid line shows a scenario that *would* give rise to an exposure (in terms of the MtM of the underlying swap) but where the swaption would not have been exercised. The exercise boundary will in this case represent the point at which the underlying swap has zero MtM value and exercise will occur only when this value is positive (above the exercise boundary).

4.3   MODELS FOR CREDIT EXPOSURE

In this section, we give some details on models used for exposure simulation. We consider the calibration issues, the balance between complex and simple models and give some specific examples for various asset classes.

The good news for those with an allergy to complex mathematical models is that for the current purpose and especially in light of the credit crisis beginning in 2007, simple and transparent approaches with fewer parameters can justifiably be favoured over ones that are more complex. Consider analysing the risk of a single-currency portfolio. In a simple one-factor model, a single parameter drives the risk. If a risk manager is concerned with the risk of the portfolio, it is easy to make a sensitivity analysis with respect to this parameter whereas with a multi-factor model this process is far more involved. Now suppose a new currency is added to the netting set. In a single-factor model, it is clear that the correlation between the two currencies must be modelled, whereas in a multi-factor model the choice of dependency between currencies is more complex. In short, it is better to have a simple model that can be easily understood by risk managers and senior management than a more complex model that cannot.

4.3.1 Calibration

Whilst the choice of models for the underlying market variables is an important aspect, calibration of these models is just as important since future scenarios will be determined by this. Models calibrated using historical data predict future scenarios based on statistical patterns observed in the past and assume that this previous behaviour is a good indicator of the future; such models are slow to react to changes in market conditions. Models calibrated to market prices tend to be more forward-looking but contain components such as risk premiums and storage costs that introduce bias. The consideration of whether to use historical (real) or market-implied (risk-neutral) probabilities is an important one.

4.3.2 Risk-neutral or real?

Scenario generation for risk management purposes and arbitrage pricing are not the same thing. Arbitrage-based pricing uses the so-called risk-neutral measure, which is justified through hedging considerations and arbitrage. Parameters (and therefore to some extent probability distributions) such as drifts and volatilities are market-implied and need not correspond to real distributions (or even comply with common sense). For a risk management application, such as exposure generation, one does not need to use the risk-neutral measure and should be focused rather on the real measure, estimated using historical data and common sense.

Sometimes, risk-neutral parameters are used for risk management purposes and indeed some practitioners favour this style of approach. Take the example of volatility estimation. If one uses a historical estimate then the implicit assumption is that the past will be a good indication of the future. It is also necessary to decide what history of data to use; a short history will give poor statistics whereas a long history will give weight to "old" meaningless data. When markets suddenly become more volatile, the historical estimate will only gradually increase to reflect this as the window of data moves. Contrast this with using the implied volatility which will react immediately when the market becomes more uncertain and can be justified via the "market knows best" (or at least the market knows better than historical data). Any risk premium embedded in market-implied volatilities will lead to a conservative overestimate of the overall risk.

Whilst using market-implied volatilities for VAR calculations is reasonable for the above reasons, we would urge some caution when adopting other market-implied parameters for exposure modelling. Due to the nature of counterparty risk and the

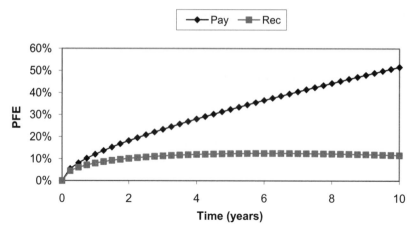

Figure 4.14. PFE for opposite cross-currency swaps, the first case (Pay) corresponds to paying the currency with higher interest rates while the second (Rec) is the reverse swap receiving the high interest rate currency. An exchange of notional at the swap maturity is assumed.

long time horizons also involved, drift is also an important parameter in determining exposure. Consider the exposure of the two cross-currency swaps calculated under the risk-neutral measure as shown in Figure 4.14. We assume the currencies involved have very different interest rate levels (as was the case, for example, with widely traded dollar versus yen swaps for many years before the dramatic US interest rate cuts of 2008/09). The swap paying the currency with higher interest rates has a much greater exposure than the opposite swap. The high interest rates paid will be offset by the gain on the notional exchange at the maturity of the contract[4] and this expected gain on exchange of notional leads to a significant exposure for the payer of the high interest rate. In the reverse swap, it is increasingly likely that there will be a negative MtM on the swap when paying the currency with the lower interest rates. This creates a "negative drift" on the exposure that means the PFE is much lower.

In the above example, we can also see that, in the long term, the drift dominates the volatility effect, effectively pulling the PFE back to zero. Mathematically, this occurs because the impact of volatility follows the "square of time" whereas the drift scales linearly with time – see Appendix 4.A) – so in the long run a strong drift will dominate.

The above example arises because forward FX rates are very far from spot rates. This is due to arbitrage considerations and the fact that the interest rates in the two currencies are different and should not necessarily be attributed to the "view of the market". Indeed, there has long been doubt regarding the ability of long-term forward rates to predict future spot rates, see, for example, Meese and Rogoff (1983) and a more recent review by Sarno and Taylor (2002). If we take the view that the forward rate is indeed the best expectation of the future spot rate then this may lead to a strong drift assumption. If this assumption is wrong then it will significantly overstate and understate, respectively, the risk on the pay and receive swaps in Figure 4.14.

In summary, exposure management should generally focus on real parameters, with market-implied parameters used when there are good reasons (such as in the example of

---

[4] In expectation under the risk-neutral measure.

using implied volatility above). Pricing should *generally* focus on (risk-neutral) market-implied parameters, especially in the case where counterparty risk is actively managed. However, if counterparty risk is priced in more of an actuarial sense,[5] then it may be appropriate to exercise caution over the use of risk-neutral drifts and other parameters (such as correlations) which might be better represented by their real-world values. We will return to this topic in Chapter 9 when we consider the hedging of counterparty risk.

In the subsections below, we will first describe the basic ideas with respect to modelling equity, FX, commodity and credit products. Sometimes the variables to be simulated will be single values, whereas in other cases a vector of variables must be generated. An example of the later case includes yield curves and forward curves. In such a situation, the model used must be sufficiently flexible to capture the majority of possible moves, without producing arbitrageable variables. Some values, such as interest rates, exhibit mean reversion, which is important to include since it suppresses volatility, especially for long-dated transactions. Failure to include mean reversion can lead to unrealistically large exposures at long time horizons. We will describe other specific features that need to be considered for one or more asset classes such as seasonality, jumps, credit migrations and defaults. Finally, we will discuss in some detail the issue of modelling interest rates both as a case study and since these products represent such a large fraction of the total counterparty risk in the market.

4.3.3   Equities

The standard model for equities is a geometric Brownian motion as defined by:

$$\frac{dS_t}{S_t} = \mu(t)\,dt + \sigma_E(t)\,dW_t, \tag{4.3}$$

where S_t represents the value of the equity in question at time t, $\mu(t)$ is the drift, $\sigma_E(t)$ is the volatility and dW_t is a standard Brownian motion. The approach assumes that the equity returns are normally distributed. The drift may be chosen to be positive or negative to reflect a conservative assumption based on the transactions involved or it may be set to the risk-free rate plus some risk premium (as defined by the capital asset pricing model). The volatility could also be either market-implied or determined from historical analysis.

For practical purposes, it may not be advisable to attempt to simulate every single underlying stock. Not only is this highly time-consuming but it also leads to a large correlation matrix that may not be of the appropriate form.[6] Rather, one may choose to simulate all major indices and then estimate the change in the individual stock price by using the beta[7] of that stock, assuming a correlation of 100% between the stock and index (this may often represent a conservative approximation).

---

[5] We will define what we mean here in more detail in Chapter 12.
[6] Such aspects can be solved; in particular, there are methods to regularise correlations, so as to obtain the closest possible valid (positive semi-definite) correlation matrix. However, this is time-consuming and may be viewed as being too complex with simpler methods preferred, especially if equity constitutes only a moderate portion of the overall exposure.
[7] As defined by the Capital Asset Pricing Model (CAPM) the beta represents the covariance of the stock and index returns divided by the standard deviation of both the stock and index returns.

4.3.4 FX

In a traditional model for FX rates, X_t is to assume a standard geometric Brownian motion as for equities:

$$\frac{dX_t}{X_t} = \mu(t)\,dt + \sigma_{FX}(t)\,dW_t. \tag{4.4}$$

This ensures that FX rates are always positive. The drift, $\mu(t)$, can be calibrated to the forward rates or determined via historical analysis as discussed above. One could also consider adding some mean reversion to avoid FX rates becoming unrealistically large or small, especially for long time horizons. The equation can then be re-written:

$$\frac{dX_t}{X_t} = k(\theta - \ln X_t)\,dt + \sigma_{FX}(t)\,dW_t \tag{4.5}$$

where k is the rate of mean reversion to a long-term mean level θ. This long-term mean may be set at the current spot level or set to a different level due to the view of a risk manager, historical analysis, forward rates or simply to be conservative. Whilst it is conservative to ignore mean reversion, in such a model long-term FX rates can arguably reach unrealistic levels.

In some circumstances it may be relevant to include jumps in FX rates that could occur due to a shock to the economy of a given currency or even a devaluation perhaps linked to a sovereign default. Jump–diffusion processes have often been used to characterise emerging markets or pegged currencies. The shorter the time horizon, the greater the importance of capturing such jumps (see, for example, Das and Sundaram, 1999). We will address these points in detail in Chapter 8 on wrong-way risk.

4.3.5 Commodities

Commodities tend to be highly mean reverting around a level, which represents the marginal cost of production (see, for example, Geman and Nguyen, 2005 and Pindyck, 2001). Furthermore, many commodities exhibit seasonality in prices due to harvesting cycles and changing consumption throughout the year. A simple and popular model (see Geman, 2005) is:

$$\ln S_t = f(t) + Z(t) \tag{4.6a}$$

$$dZ(t) = (\alpha - \beta Z(t))\,dt + \sigma_C(t)\,dW_t \tag{4.6b}$$

where $f(t)$ is a deterministic function, which may be expressed using sin or cos trigonometry functions to give the relevant periodicity and the parameters α and β are the mean reversion parameters. For commodities, the use of risk-neutral drift is particularly dangerous due to the strong backwardation and contango present for some underlyings. However, non-storable commodities (for example, electricity) do not have an arbitrage relationship between spot and forward prices and therefore the forward rates might be argued to contain relevant information about future expected prices.

4.3.6 Credit spreads

Credit products have significant wrong-way risk and so a naive modelling of their exposure without reference to counterparty default is dangerous. Whilst we return to this problem in detail in Chapter 8, for now we give an idea of a model representing the key aspects of credit spread behaviour. Credit spreads, like the above asset classes, require a model that prevents negative values. They also, more than any other asset class, might be expected to have jumps caused by a sudden and discrete change in credit quality (such as an earning announcement or ratings downgrade or upgrade). An approach that fits these requirements is the following model:

$$d\lambda_t = \theta(\eta - \lambda_t)\, dt + \sigma_\lambda \sqrt{\lambda_t}\, dW_t + j\, dN, \tag{4.7}$$

where λ_t is the intensity (or hazard rate) of default[8] and θ and η are mean reversion parameters. Additionally, dN represents a Poisson jump with jump size j. This jump size can itself be random such as following an exponential distribution.

4.3.7 Interest rates

Interest rates may be one asset class where we may be willing to allow negative rates to provide the benefit of tractability. The simplest interest rate model that meets the criteria presented in Section 4.1.3 is the one-factor Hull and White (or extended Vasicek) model (Hull and White, 1990) where the "short rate" (short-term interest rate) is assumed to follow the following process:

$$dr_t = [\theta(t) - ar_t]\, dt + \sigma_r\, dW_t. \tag{4.8}$$

In this model, the short rate follows a Brownian motion with mean reversion. Mean reversion dictates that when the rate is above some "mean" level, it is pulled back towards that level with a certain force according to the size of parameter α. The mean reversion level $\theta(t)$ is time-dependent which is what allows this model to be fitted to the initial yield curve. The parameters a and σ_r can then be calibrated to market data or estimated from historical data. Mean reversion has the effect of damping the standard deviation of discount factors, $B(t, T)$, written as:

$$\sigma(B(t, T)) = \sigma_r \left[\frac{1 - \exp(-a(T - t))}{a(T - t)} \right]. \tag{4.9}$$

If one can estimate the standard deviation (volatility) of zero-coupon bond prices of various maturities, then it is possible to estimate values for σ_r and a. If the zero-coupon bond price volatility is increasing, then mean reversion will be negative. This is not particularly pleasant since it implies that the interest rates are exploding. Although the yield curve is not modelling directly, it can be "reconstructed" at any point, given knowledge of the above parameters and the current short rate. Hence, using such an approach in a Monte Carlo simulation is relatively straightforward.

Criticisms of the above model are that it allows negative interest rates, which for risk management purposes are not especially objectionable. A more concerning point is that this one-factor approach is restrictive in the possible yield curve movements that it captures and hence can "miss" some of the risk.

A common alternative model used for simulation of interest rates is a multi-factor simulation of the principal factors in describing yield curve movements. Historically, a

---

[8] This means that the default probability in a period dt conditional on no default before time t is $\lambda_t\, dt$. The intensity of default is closely related to the credit spread as is explained in Chapter 6.

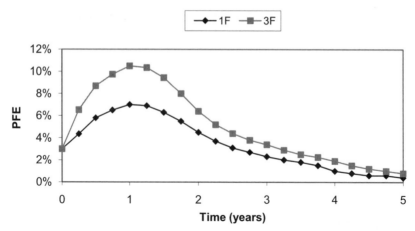

Figure 4.15. PFE for an interest rate cap with both one-factor and three-factor models.

substantial portion of the observed movements in yield curves can be explained in terms of three principal factors (e.g. see Rebonato, 1998). These factors correspond to parallel shifts, twists and butterfly movements. Such approaches have been described as more realistic models for interest rate risk modelling by Jamshidian and Zhu (1997) and Reimers and Zerbs (1999). To illustrate this difference between a more sophisticated approach and the simpler model, we show the PFE of an interest rate cap in Figure 4.15 with both one-factor and three-factor approaches calibrated against the same historical data.

> **Spreadsheet 4.2.** Simulation of an interest rate swap exposure with a one-factor Hull–White model

The explanation for the above results is that a one-factor model generally only captures parallel moves in the yield curve – in the approach as described by equation (4.8) there is some steepening and flattening created by the mean reversion parameter but this is limited. The more sophisticated three-factor approach, on the other hand, will produce much more complex changes in the shape of the yield curve. This leads to a significantly greater PFE for the interest rate cap, which has a strong sensitivity to changes in yield curve shape.

The disadvantages of a more complex multi-factor model are that implementation is more difficult since dimensionality is increased and calibration is more complex. Nevertheless, relatively complex approaches have been developed by market practitioners in the last decade.

4.3.8 Advanced models

In the above five sections, we have described the simplest realistic models that have been quite commonly applied to the various asset classes. We could of course consider extensions to all of these approaches to make them more realistic. As in the example for interest rates, a multi-factor model will capture a great range of future scenarios and therefore get closer to explaining the PFE, especially for more exotic products. One can add jump processes as discussed in the case of credit spreads to model the chance of sudden discontinuous moves. Finally, one might add stochastic volatility to any of the processes.

Whilst all of these additional components can represent a more flexible and realistic model, they may well be left out for reasons of simplicity and tractability. The simple approaches will be more straightforward and parsimonious to calibrate and easier to simulate numerically. Risk management remains as much an art as a science and hedging counterparty risk has not developed to a level to warrant more advanced models. We therefore believe the simpler, pragmatic and practical approaches offer the greater benefits over advanced but opaque techniques. Given the recent credit crisis, a flight to simplicity with regard to models may be appropriate.

4.3.9   Model validation

The modelling challenge to simulate the PFE for a typical derivatives portfolio is significant and every effort must be made in order to check and validate the modelling assumptions, involving both internal and external auditors. In particular, the following steps should be considered:

- *Source code control.* As is standard, source code must be fully documented and controlled for updates.
- *Implementation.* Model implementations should be checked against alternative implementations and periodically re-checked using regression tests covering at least the most significant population of trades.
- *Input reconciliation.* Market data should be checked against alternative sources and trade positions, collateral parameters and other static information should be checked.
- *Output checking.* Calculated quantities, such as EE and PFE, should be checked via simple formulas and full-scale manual calculations as well as stress scenarios.
- *Backtesting.* Like VAR models, exposure models should be backtested via, for example, observing the empirical exceedance of a PFE and comparing it with the underlying confidence level used for computing the PFE. Whilst VAR models work on a 1-day or 10-day horizon, PFE approaches involve much longer time horizons. This creates a problem for backtesting since the positions with a given counterparty may change significantly over the time horizon being backtested. Hence, for fair comparison, it is necessary to backtest using original positions and ignoring any subsequent trades or other changes to trade population.

4.3.10   Correlations

Another reason for choosing relatively simple single-factor approaches to modelling exposures is that in many cases the population of trades with a given counterparty will cover several different asset classes and hence the dependency between the different risk factors must be considered. Furthermore, this is usually a more important consideration than those defining complex one-dimensional representations of risk factors. For example, for two interest rate swaps in different currencies, the correlation between the rates may be more important than factors defining more subtle yield curve movements. Even for a single trade, dependency can be important: a cross-currency swap has risk to the FX rate and the two interest rates and hence these three risk factors and the three correlations between them must be accounted for. For cross-currency swaps involving n different currencies, there will be a total of $2n - 1$ rates to be modelled (n interest rates and $n - 1$ FX rates) and one therefore needs to estimate a correlation matrix of dimension $2n - 1$. For a typical counterparty there will be a wide range of assets resulting in many cross-asset correlations to be accounted for. Using more complex models for some asset classes will make such dependency between different transactions even more difficult to handle.

4.4 NETTING

In addition to being able to model all trade types individually, one needs to understand how netting influences the overall exposure and how the exposure will change when a new trade is added to a netting set. This is the focus of the next section.

4.4.1 Modelling netting

A netting agreement allows two parties to net a set of positions (explicitly covered by the netting agreement) in the event of default of one of them. This is a critical way to control exposure but can typically only be quantified effectively in a Monte Carlo framework. Netting benefits arise in scenarios where the MtM values of two trades are of opposite signs. Hence, to calculate the impact of netting one must aggregate (Step 4 in Section 4.1.3) at the individual transaction level.

> We cannot add exposure metrics (such as EE) to incorporate the impact of netting. Netting must be incorporated before calculating quantities such as EE.

To illustrate the above point, we recall Section 4.1.3 together with equation (4.2) and the related discussion showing the impact netted exposure $E_{j,k}$ for a netting set at time point j in simulation k. In order to calculate the new exposure of this netting set when a trade indexed by $m + 1$ has been added, one needs to calculate the expression:

$$E'_{j,k} = \max\left(\sum_{i=1}^{n} V_{i,j,k} + V_{m+1,j,k}, 0\right). \tag{4.10}$$

In order to do this, the values of $V_{j,k}^{\mathrm{NS}} = \sum_{i=1}^{n} V_{i,j,k}$, which represent the MtM of the netting set at time point j in simulation k must be preserved. From a systems point of view the total MtM of the original trades might be run in an overnight batch and then stored. However, we note that it is only necessary to store the matrix of netting set level data, $V_{j,k}^{\mathrm{NS}}$, and not the cube of trade level data represented by $V_{i,j,k}$ (which could be extremely costly). The simulations for a new trade, giving $V_{m+1,j,k}$, may then be generated "on the fly" as and when required. These quantities can then be re-aggregated to compute the new exposure and then $E'_{j,k} - E_{j,k}$ gives the change in exposure due to the new trade.

4.4.2   Netting factor

In Table 4.2, we give a very simple example of the impact of netting similar to those given in Chapter 3. We will work in terms of EE since this metric will be additive in the case of no netting. We also use the EPE to define a "netting factor" as:

$$\text{netting factor} = \frac{\text{EPE (no netting)}}{\text{EPE (netting)}} \tag{4.11}$$

The above measure will be +100% if there is no netting benefit and 0% if the netting benefit is maximum. Note that a single time horizon netting factor is defined by EE whereas a time-averaged value is defined using EPE.

Table 4.2. Simple illustration of the impact of netting showing example exposures for scenarios involving two trades with and without the impact of netting.

	Trade 1	Trade 2	No netting	Netting	Netting factor
Scenario 1	25	15	40	40	
Scenario 2	15	5	20	20	
Scenario 3	5	−5	5	0	
Scenario 4	−5	−15	0	0	
Scenario 5	−15	−25	0	0	
EE	9	4	13	12	92%

4.4.3   Examples

We now consider the netting benefit achieved in several examples. The starting trade is a 5-year interest rate swap paying fixed and receiving floating (IRS payer). We consider the impact on the exposure of adding this to three different trade types. All results were calculated with 100,000 Monte Carlo simulations using the models described in the previous section.

Spreadsheet 4.3. Illustration of the impact of netting for interest rate and cross-currency swaps

(i)   Case 1: 5-year IRS payer + 6-year IRS payer

These two instruments will be rather highly correlated since they differ only in maturity date. An example scenario showing their future mark-to-market values in a particular scenario is given in Figure 4.16.

In this scenario, there is a small chance the swap MtM values have opposite signs but most of the time the high structural correlation means that the netting benefit will be minimal. We show the EE values in Figure 4.17 which are almost additive: the netting factor is 98.4%.

(ii)   Case 2: 5-year IRS payer + 6-year IRS receiver

We now consider the netting impact with the reverse 6-year swap. Although the maturities do not match, we would expect a strong negative correlation between the mark-to-market values of the two instruments. This is the case, although the MtM

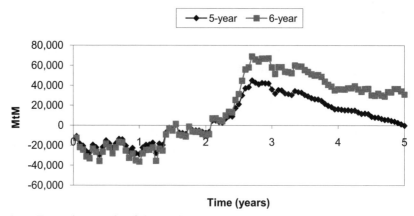

Figure 4.16. Example scenario of the mark-to-market values of the 5-year and 6-year interest rate swaps.

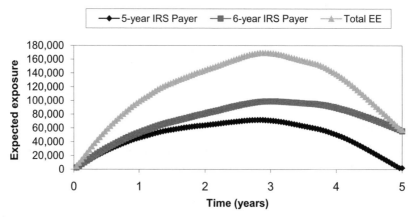

Figure 4.17. EE profiles for the 5-year pay fixed interest rate swap and a 6-year pay fixed interest rate swap. Also shown is the total EE with netting. The EE components are almost additive due to the very high correlation.

values can diverge over time.[9] Hence, not surprisingly the total netted EE (Figure 4.18) is much smaller than either of the individual EEs. The netting factor is 21.4%.

(iii) Case 3: 5-year IRS payer + cross-currency swap

Finally, we take the combination of our 5-year IRS with a cross-currency swap of the same maturity. In such a case, the overall correlation may be quite small and hence the netting benefit will be reasonably strong. The EE profiles are shown in Figure 4.19 and the netting factor is 76.5%. This is quite close to the simple approximation (assuming

---

[9] This is due to the fact that the longer maturity swap has a greater sensitivity to interest rates moves and also to the de-correlation as a result of changes in the shape of the interest rate curve.

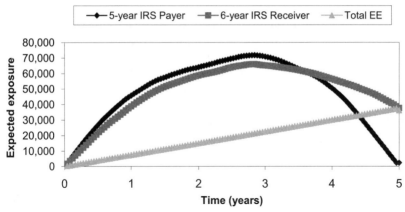

Figure 4.18. EE profiles for the 5-year pay fixed interest rate swap and the 6-year receive fixed interest rate swap. Also shown is the total EE with netting.

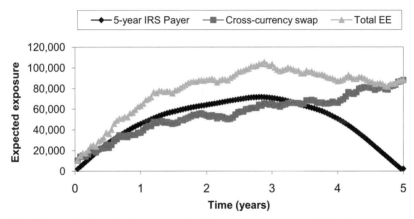

Figure 4.19. EE profiles for the 5-year pay fixed interest rate swap and the 5-year cross-currency swap. Also shown is the total EE with netting.

zero correlation and MtM distributions with zero mean and equal standard deviation) of $1/\sqrt{2} = 70.7\%$ as discussed in Section 3.5.2.

4.5   EXPOSURE CONTRIBUTIONS

At the netting set level, a measure such as EE or PFE is useful to characterise the total exposure with respect to a single counterparty. However, in risk management it is common and natural to ask the question of from where the underlying risk arises. Risk managers find it useful to be able to "drill down" from a number representing counterparty exposure and understand which trades are contributing most to the overall risk. This can be important information when considering whether to unwind transactions or enter into more business and allows the return on a transaction to be assessed against its contribution to the overall exposure. Consider the following problem.

Example. An exposure profile has caused an uncollateralised credit limit to be breached at a given point in time in the future, which is causing some concern. There are only two trades with the counterparty that are still alive at the time point in question. These trades have almost identical expected exposures of $7.7m and $7.6m, respectively. The total exposure is $10.7m, which is above the $10m credit limit.

Do these trades contribute almost equally to the overall expected exposure as their EE values suggest?

The answer to the above problem is possibly no. Just because trade level expected exposures are similar, it does not mean that the contributions to the total netted exposure are also similar. Suppose it is necessary to reduce one of the trades in the above example to reduce the overall exposure and comply with the credit line. All other things being equal, the trade contributing most to the overall EE should be considered.

4.5.1 Marginal EE

Suppose we have calculated a netted exposure for a set of trades under a single netting agreement. We would like to be able to write the total EE as a linear combination of EEs for each trade, i.e.:

$$\text{EE}_{\text{total}} = \sum_{i=1}^{n} \text{EE}_i^*. \tag{4.12}$$

If there is no netting then we know that the total EE will indeed be the sum of the individual components and hence the marginal EE will equal the EE, $\text{EE}_i^* = \text{EE}_i$. However, since the benefit of netting is to reduce the overall EE, we expect in the event of netting that $\text{EE}_i^* < \text{EE}_i$. In the case of perfectly offsetting exposures, the marginal EEs must sum to zero.

Marginal risk contributions are well-studied concepts due to the need to allocate risk measures back to individual constituents. For example, they have been described by Arvanitis and Gregory (2001) for credit portfolios and a discussion on marginal VAR can be found in Jorion (2007). In most situations, a marginal contribution can be readily calculated as the derivative of the risk measure with respect to its weight. Hence, we need numerically to calculate the derivative of the total EE with respect to each constitution exposure in order to know the marginal EEs. These marginals will then sum to the total EE as required by equation (4.12). The mathematical details are given in Appendix 4.B.

4.5.2 Simple two-trade marginal EE example

Suppose we have two trades with MtM distributions at a future date being normally distributed with the following parameters:

Trade 1	$\mu_1 = 6\%$	$\sigma_1 = 10\%$
Trade 2	$\mu_2 = -10\%$	$\sigma_2 = 30\%$

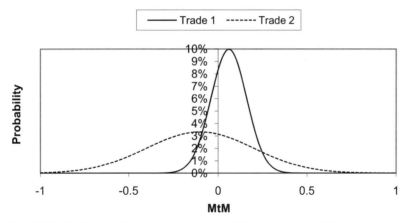

Figure 4.20. MtM distribution for the two trades used in the marginal EE example.

The expected MtM distributions of the trades are very different as illustrated in Figure 4.20. However, the EEs are similar at 7.69% and 7.63%[10] for trade 1 and trade 2, respectively.

We calculate the marginal EEs under the assumption of independence between the two exposure distributions and summarise the overall results in Table 4.3. In the case of normal distributions, the analytical expression makes the calculation of marginal EE quite easy without the need for simulation. We can see that the marginal EE of trade 2 is actually quite significantly higher than that of trade 1 even though the standard EE is lower. The trade with a smaller expected value and a larger volatility is more risky than the trade with the opposite characteristics. Note that these numbers correspond to the example given at the start of Section 4.5.

Table 4.3. Summary of marginal EE calculations assuming independence between exposures.

	No netting (EE)	Netting (marginal EE)	Reduction
Trade 1	7.69%	3.95%	49%
Trade 2	7.63%	6.77%	11%
Total	15.31%	10.72%	30%

Spreadsheet 4.4. Marginal exposure calculation

4.5.3   Marginal EE and correlation

We can repeat the calculations in the previous example for a whole range of correlation values as shown in Figure 4.21. The total EE is very small at low correlations and increases as the correlation increases since the overall netting benefit is reduced. The

---

[10] These EE numbers can be computed using the formula in Appendix 2.A.

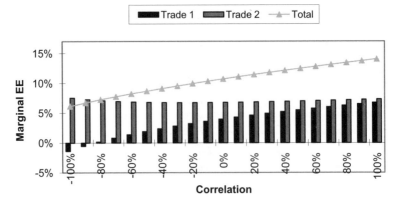

Figure 4.21. Marginal EEs for the simple two-trade example as described in the text as a function of the correlation between the trade values.

breakdown of total EE into marginal components depends very much on the correlation. At zero correlation, as we have already seen, trade 2 has a larger contribution to the overall EE. At negative correlation, the more "risky" trade 2 has a positive marginal EE that is partly cancelled out by trade 1 having a negative marginal EE. At high correlations, the marginal EEs are both positive and of almost equal magnitude (since there is little or no netting benefit).

We can therefore conclude that for trades that are not highly correlated or even negatively correlated, marginal EEs will be particularly important to understand which trades are driving the total EE. The marginal EE of a trade depends on the relationship of that trade to others in the netting set. A trade which is risk-reducing (negative marginal EE) in one netting set might not have the same characteristic in a different netting set.

4.5.4 General example

We now look at a general example of marginal EE calculation using the interest rate and cross-currency swap (Case 3) from Section 4.4.3. In the case of these exposures, the marginal EE can be calculated numerically from Monte Carlo simulation results and is shown in Figure 4.22. The total EE is the same as "Total EE" in Figure 4.19. From this figure, it should be clear that marginal EPE can be readily computed from marginal EE.

The marginal EE concept is useful since it makes it possible to drill down within a counterparty exposure and understand which trades are driving the risk at different points in time. We will again use this concept when we discuss pricing counterparty risk in Chapter 7.

4.6 SUMMARY

In this chapter, we have described the quantification of credit exposure by various methods, ranging from simple approximations to a more general simulation approach. We have shown exposure profiles for common instrument types and outlined the method for simulating exposure for different asset classes. We have also discussed

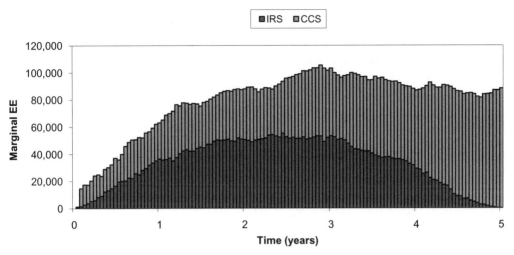

Figure 4.22. Illustration of the marginal EEs for a 5-year payer interest rate swap and a cross-currency swap.

the quantification of exposure in the presence of risk mitigants such as netting and collateral. We have discussed how to calculate marginal exposures and therefore drill down to understand the contribution of exposure within a netting set.

The quantification of credit exposure in the presence of collateral is an important topic, especially due to the increasing use of collateral to mitigate credit exposure. In Chapter 5 we will look at the topic of quantifying collateralised credit exposure in more detail.

APPENDIX 4.A: SEMI-ANALYTICAL FORMULA FOR EXPOSURE OF A FORWARD CONTRACT

Suppose we want to calculate the exposure on a forward contract and are willing to assume the following model for the evolution of the MtM value of the contract (V_t):

$$dV_t = \mu \, dt + \sigma \, dW_t,$$

where μ represents a drift and σ is the volatility of the exposure with dW_t representing a standard Brownian motion. Under such assumptions the MtM value at a given time s in the future will follow a normal distribution with known mean and standard deviation:

$$V_s \sim N(\mu(s - t), \sigma\sqrt{s - t})$$

We therefore have analytical expressions for the PFE and EE following from the formulas in Appendix 2.A:

$$\text{PFE}_\alpha = \mu(s - t) + \sigma\sqrt{s - t}\,\Phi^{-1}(\alpha)$$

$$\text{EE} = \mu(s - t)\Phi\left(\frac{\mu}{\sigma}\sqrt{s - t}\right) + \sigma\sqrt{s - t}\,\varphi\left(\frac{\mu}{\sigma}\sqrt{s - t}\right).$$

These formulas are illustrated in Spreadsheet 4.1.

APPENDIX 4.B: COMPUTING MARGINAL EE

The aim is to find allocations of EE that reflect a trade's contribution to the overall risk and sum up to the counterparty level EE, (EE_{total}):

$$EE_{total} = \sum_{i=1}^{n} EE_i^*.$$

For trades not subject to netting, the result is trivial since $EE_{total} = \sum_{i=1}^{n} EE_i$ and therefore $EE_i^* = EE_i$. For the case of netting, first assign a weight to each individual exposure:

$$\alpha_i MTM_i \equiv MTM_i(\alpha_i).$$

Now the total expected exposure is given by:

$$EE_{total}(\boldsymbol{\alpha}) = E\left[\max\left[\sum_{i=1}^{n} MTM_i(\alpha_i), 0\right]\right],$$

where n represents the number of trades under the given netting set and $\boldsymbol{\alpha} = [\alpha_1, \alpha_2, \ldots, \alpha_n]$ is the vector of weights. Since the exposure is a homogeneous function of the weights then from Euler's theorem we can define the marginal EE as:

$$EE_i^* = \frac{\partial EE_{total}(\boldsymbol{\alpha})}{\partial \alpha_i}.$$

These formulas are illustrated in Spreadsheet 4.3.

5

Quantifying Counterparty Credit Exposure, II – The Impact of Collateral

> *"There is no security on this earth, there is only opportunity."*
>
> General Douglas MacArthur (1880–1964)

5.1 INTRODUCTION

In this chapter we describe the quantification of credit exposure in the presence of collateral. The use of collateral has become so widespread that such considerations must be given a detailed assessment. Collateral typically reduces exposure but there are many sometimes subtle points that must be considered in order to properly assess the true extent of any risk reduction. To properly account for the real impact of collateral, parameters such as thresholds and minimum transfer amounts must be properly understood and represented appropriately. Furthermore, the margin period must be carefully analysed to determine the true period of risk with respect to collateral transfer.

As mentioned previously, whilst collateralisation is a risk mitigation technique, it gives rise to many potential new risks, which must be thoroughly appreciated. In the event of two-way collateral agreements, collateralisation can increase exposure due to effects such as rehypothecation (discussed in Chapter 3) or the inability to retrieve cash from a defaulted counterparty. Collateralisation also creates other risks, such as operational risk, FX risk and liquidity risk. Effective collateral management is only possible if all of these risks are well-understood and properly managed.

5.2 THE IMPACT OF COLLATERAL ON CREDIT EXPOSURE

5.2.1 Remargin period

Let us ask the question of what is the effective margin call frequency ("remargin period") or the period one should assume in a worst case scenario before being able to take delivery of collateral after a valid call (or alternatively to put the counterparty into default). Such a period is crucial since it defines the period of risk in the worst case scenario and should therefore be assumed in any assessment of the collateralised position. The worst case scenario is valid since one must base all calculations on the assumption that a counterparty *will* default as discussed in Chapter 1. In order to assess the remargin period, it is important to consider all of the following effects that may slow the collateral process:

- *Valuation/margin call*. This represents the time taken to compute current exposure and the current market value of collateral, working out if a valid call can be made and finally making that call. This should include the time delay due to the contractual period between margin calls.
- *Receiving collateral*. The delay caused due to a counterparty processing a collateral request from the point they receive the request (fax/email) to the point at which they release collateral.
- *Settlement*. Collateral will not be received immediately as there is a settlement period depending on the type of collateral. Cash collateral may settle on an intra-day basis whereas other securities will take longer. For example, governments and corporate bonds may be subject to 1-day and 3-day settlement periods, respectively.
- *Grace period*. In the event a valid collateral call is not followed by the receipt of the relevant collateral, there may be a relevant grace period before the counterparty would be deemed to be in default (due to a failure-to-pay credit event discussed in more detail in Chapter 6).
- *Liquidation/close-out and re-hedge*. Finally, it will be necessary to liquidate collateral and close out and re-hedge positions.

We consider a possible scenario relating to a daily margin call frequency in Table 5.1 (longer periods than daily should obviously increase the valuation/margin call step). We consider OTC derivatives and repo transactions separately since they are governed by different documentation. Collateralisation in repo markets is generally tighter due partly to the more complex nature of OTC derivatives which makes valuation more complex.

Table 5.1. Example timeline for the remargin period in a worst case scenario based on the assumption of a daily margin call. This does not consider the additional delay potentially caused by disputes. The Basel II minimum period (see Chapter 11 for more detail) is also shown.

	OTC derivatives (CSA[a])	Repo (GMRA[b])
Valuation/margin call	2 days	—
Receiving collateral	1 day	1 day
Settlement	2 days	1 day
Grace period	3 days	—
Liquidation/close-out and re-hedge	2 days	1 day
Total	*10 days*	*3 days*
Basel II minimum period	10 days	5 days

[a] Credit Support Annex.
[b] Global Master Repurchase Agreement.

The above periods could easily be argued to be different depending on the precise assumptions and legal interpretations. Longer remargin periods could be appropriate depending on the collateral agreement and counterparty in question as well as legal considerations and even the management structure of the institution concerned (institutions may be more lenient with certain counterparties to maintain good relations). In particular, Table 5.1 does not assess potential delays as a result of disputes or longer grace periods, which are likely in practice (especially when a counterparty is close to failing). An institution should decide carefully on the relevant remargin period with all of these considerations taken into account.

The main point above is to show that for risk assessment purposes, the remargin period (when collateral will be received in a worst case scenario) will be significantly longer than the actual legal margin call frequency. For the examples in subsequent chapters, we will use a period of 10 days (or multiples thereof) which we consider to be a reasonable assessment of the true risk period for daily margin calls. This period also corresponds to the time horizon for most VAR calculations and is the minimum period for assessment of collateral specified under Basel II (see Chapter 11 for more discussion).

5.2.2 Potential future exposure with collateral

Uncollateralised credit exposure should be considered over the full time horizon of the transaction or transactions in question. Long-term distributional assumptions, such as mean reversion and drift, are important and the specifics of the transactions, such as cashflow dates and exercise times, must also be considered. Strong collateralisation will change the above picture entirely by transforming a risk that should be considered usually over many years into one that needs only be considered over a much shorter period (the remargin frequency).

As illustrated in Figure 5.1, at some point far in the future it is known that a position is likely to be well-collateralised and hence the main concern is the relatively small amount of risk over the remargin period. It should be hopefully clear that in addition to assessing the length of the period of risk, the main additional parameter to concern ourselves with is the volatility of the exposure during this period. Hence, some of the intricacies of modelling potential future exposure can probably be ignored as long as the counterparty is well-collateralised (for example, the cashflows shown in Figure 5.1 are not important due to the length of the remargin period). The problem now becomes a short-term market risk issue and therefore shares many commonalities with market risk VAR methodologies. This point will become clearer in later examples in Section 5.4.

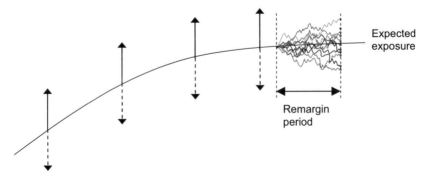

Figure 5.1. Schematic illustration of the impact of collateralisation on characterised potential future exposure.

5.2.3 Volatility of exposure

The first aspect to consider for a collateralised exposure is the uncertainty of the exposure over the remargin period. In Appendix 5.A, we give simple formulas for the PFE and EE based on normal distribution assumptions. For example, the PFE is given by:

$$\text{PFE}_\alpha = k \times \sigma_E \times \sqrt{T_M}, \tag{5.1}$$

where σ_E would represent the (annual) volatility for the collateralised exposure (all netted positions and the impact of current collateral held against the exposure where relevant), T_M the remargin frequency in years and k is a constant that depends on the confidence level required (e.g. $k = 2.33$ for 99% confidence).

Example. Suppose an exposure with an annual volatility of 4% is perfectly collateralised by a cash amount. Over a 10-day period, the worst case change in the value of this exposure (the uncollateralised portion) as estimated by the above formula would be:

$$-2.33 \times 4\% \times \sqrt{10/250} = -1.9\%$$

Such an analysis makes for a rather easy characterisation of a well-collateralised credit exposure. We would however draw attention to a few problems that would be overlooked in such a treatment:

- If a position is not "strongly" collateralised – for example, if there is a relatively large threshold or minimum transfer amount – then the above analysis is not appropriate since there will be many scenarios where collateral will not be held against exposure. This potentially represents the hardest case to quantify as it requires a combination of both long-term and short-term considerations to properly assess the risk. We will deal with these aspects in Section 5.4.7.
- This analysis ignores the uncertainty of any volatility of the collateral that is held against the position at the start of the period (discussed in Sections 5.2.4 and 5.2.5).
- The analysis ignores potential liquidity or liquidation risk (discussed in Section 5.5.4).
- The volatility parameter σ_C should be an estimate based on the assumption that the counterparty is in default and hence may differ strongly from the expected or implied volatility at the current time.
- The analysis ignores any wrong-way risk which may manifest itself via a jump in the exposure or value of collateral linked to the counterparty defaulting.

More detailed discussions on modelling both collateralised and uncollateralised credit exposures are presented in the next section.

5.2.4 Collateral volatility

Non-cash collateral will have a price volatility that should be considered since a decline in its value will potentially lead to an uncollateralised exposure (depending on the change in the exposure itself and the haircut applied to the collateral). The impact of collateral in different currencies (including cash) should also be accounted for. We can use a similar formula to that given in equation (5.1) to assess the worst case change in value of collateral (the only difference being that we need a minus sign to denote the fact that the risk arises from a decline in value). One could also use such a formula to assess the required haircuts against various forms of collateral. We will return to this subject in more detail in Chapter 11 when considering regulatory issues.

Example. Suppose an exposure is collateralised by a 15-year government bond with an effective price volatility of 6% (for example, this would correspond to an interest rate volatility of 0.5% and bond duration of 12 years, assuming zero credit spread volatility). Over a 10-day period, the worst case change in the value of the collateral is estimated as:

$$-2.33 \times 6\% \times \sqrt{10/250} = -2.8\%.$$

Suppose the volatility of the underlying exposure is 4%. Assuming no correlation between the exposure and collateral value, then the overall volatility is $\sqrt{6\%^2 + 4\%^2} = 7.2\%$. The worst case change in the value of this position (exposure + collateral) is then:

$$-2.33 \times 7.2\% \times \sqrt{10/250} = -3.4\%.$$

The presence of collateral, whilst mitigating the current exposure, increases the volatility of the position in the future.

5.2.5 Correlation between collateral and exposure

Consider a payer interest rate swap collateralised by a triple-A bond. Since the bond has little or no default risk surely the position is not a risky one? However, imagine the impact of interest rates going up: the value of the swap increases,[1] whilst the bond price goes down. This negative correlation between collateral and exposure is non-desirable. In the case of a receiver interest rate swap, the situation is reversed and we have a beneficial positive correlation.

The mathematical treatment of exposure and collateral is given in Appendix 5.B.

Example. Suppose a 10-year swap is collateralised by a 15-year government bond. The price volatilities are 4% and 6% (for example, this would correspond to an interest rate volatility of 0.5% and swap and bond durations of 8 years and 12 years, respectively, and assuming zero credit spread volatility). The effective volatility of this position is given by:

$$\sqrt{4\%^2 + 6\%^2 - 2 \times \text{correlation} \times 4\% \times 6\%}.$$

For correlations of -100%, 0% and $+100\%$, the effective volatility is 10%, 7.2% and 2%, respectively. Hence using a simple normal approximation to the PFE as

---

[1] In a payer interest rate swap, one pays the fixed rate and receives the floating rate. Hence an increase in interest rates will increase the value of the swap (exposure).

before, over a 10-day period, the worst case change in the value of the overall collateralised position is estimated as:

$$2.33 \times \text{effective volatility} \times \sqrt{10/250}.$$

Hence the overall risk of the position as a function of correlation is:

$$4.7\% \text{ (correlation} = -100\%),$$

$$3.4\% \text{ (correlation} = 0\%),$$

$$0.9\% \text{ (correlation} = +100\%).$$

The above correlations can be considered to *approximately* represent a payer swap, swap in a different (uncorrelated) currency and a receiver swap, respectively.

In certain circumstances, we can see that the assessment of collateral volatility and correlation between exposure and collateral value is critical to assess the overall risk. In the above example, the payer interest rate swap (similar to the 100% correlation case) is five times more risky than a corresponding receiver swap (−100% correlation case).

5.3 MODELLING COLLATERAL

We will now give some basic details and results on the modelling of collateral. As discussed in Chapter 4 (Section 4.1.3), collateral can be accounted for after the simulation of exposure, under the assumption that the collateral agreement depends only on exposure and not other market variables. There are situations where this assumption may not be entirely appropriate; for example, collateral parameters may be defined in different currencies from the deals to which they apply. In practice, this means some FX translations may be required when the collateral parameters are applied within the simulation. However, in the majority of situations the assumptions made will be valid and will greatly simplify the analysis of collateralised exposures.

Collateralisation of credit exposure can substantially reduce risk but to quantify the extent of the risk mitigation is not trivial and requires many, sometimes ad hoc, assumptions. Given an uncollateralised exposure at time u of E_u, the amount of collateral held against the position will be $C_{u-\Delta}$ where Δ represents the time since collateral was last received (remargin period). Overall, there are two sources of risk for a collateralised exposure:

- The risk of imperfect collateralisation at a given date due to the terms in the collateral agreement (threshold, minimum transfer amount and rounding) which will not permit a call for the full credit support amount. This corresponds to the fact that $E_{u-\Delta} > C_{u-\Delta}$.
- The risk that the exposure increases *in-between* margin calls and it is therefore not possible to collateralise that portion of the exposure. This corresponds to $X_u > X_{u-\Delta}$.

We also emphasise that the treatment of collateral is path-dependent since the amount of collateral called for at a given time depends on the amount of collateral called (or posted) in the past. This is even more important in the case of two-way collateral agreements. In this case, for example, the exposure (credit support amount) may be zero but there may be a need to call for the return of previously posted collateral.

5.3.1 Parameters

When working out the impact of collateral on a credit exposure, the factors that we must consider are listed below. The impact of these factors will be seen in examples in Section 5.4.

(i) Remargin period

As discussed in Section 5.2.1, one must first consider the remargin period since this is the effective time assumed between a collateral call and receiving the appropriate collateral (or in a worst case scenario putting the counterparty in default, closing out the trade, liquidating existing collateral and re-hedging the trade). Intervals between simulation time points are often significantly greater than the length of the remargin period. In such cases, extra "look-back" simulation points can be introduced for collateralised trades only.

(ii) Threshold

Collateral cannot be called below the threshold and hence any exposure level within the threshold will typically be uncollateralised (unless an amount of collateral is already held which does not need to be returned due to a minimum transfer amount).

(iii) Minimum transfer amount

Collateral cannot be transferred in blocks that are smaller than the minimum transfer amount and hence this must be considered when calculating the amount of collateral that could be called. This will typically mean that an increasing exposure will be slightly undercollateralised due to minimum transfer restrictions. On the other hand, a decreasing exposure will typically mean an institution has a small overcollateralisation since they do not need to return collateral continuously.

(iv) Independent amount

Any independent amount should be considered and will reduce the uncollateralised exposure. It is typically held as a cushion against "gap risk", the risk that the market value of a transaction(s) may gap substantially in a short space of time. An independent amount can be significant and reduce exposure to practically zero. Independent amounts and gap risk are discussed further in Chapter 6.

(v) Rounding

Rounding is typically a relatively small amount and will have a small effect on the impact of collateralisation. However, the impact of rounding can be considered alongside the other factors above and will cause minor but noticeable impacts on the overall exposure.

5.3.2 Collateral logic

In Section 4.1.3 we discussed the steps of generating credit exposure and described how the post-processing of exposures could be performed in order to calculate the impact of collateral. Post-processing for a collateralised exposure means going through each exposure path and applying the relevant logic to determine at each point how much of the exposure would be collateralised. This will require:

- Choice of remargin period. This can conveniently be set to be equal to the time step of the exposure simulation. For the examples in the rest of this chapter, we will use a time step of 10 days (discussed in Section 5.2.1) which assumes implicitly that the remargin period is also 10 days (2 weeks). This period corresponds to the typical conservative period that is often assumed by institutions, although shorter, more aggressive periods have often been assumed. We will assume (conservatively) that, whilst collateral called for will take 10 days to arrive, collateral will be returned immediately.
- Calculation of collateral called or returned at each point in time taking into account the relevant parameters.
- Calculation of collateralised exposure at each point in time, knowing that the collateral held will be all amounts called up to the current time less the remargin period. Note that the collateralised exposure may correspond to a single netting set or multiple netting sets,[2] but in the latter case it is simply a question of summing over the netting sets to find the relevant exposure.

The mathematics of the above calculation, whilst not complex, are rather tedious and are shown in Appendix 5.C.

5.4   FULL COLLATERALISATION

We will start by assessing the risk of a fully collateralised position by which we mean that the collateralisation is not subject to any threshold amount. We will see that in this case the characterisation of the exposure becomes relatively straightforward since the time horizon concerned is reduced significantly, generally from years to just days.

5.4.1 Parameters

We consider the impact of collateral on a $10m notional, 5-year maturity swap exposure and assume the base case parameters for the collateral agreement given in Table 5.2 (since we consider a single deal we use percentages rather than absolute amounts that would be used in practice). The base case parameters assume two-way collateralisation and equal collateral parameters so the discussion below can be assumed to be from the point of view of either party A or party B. We do not assume any volatility of collateral value relevant in the case of non-cash collateral which is increasingly less common. Other securities posted as collateral may increase the risk slightly depending on their precise characteristics although this is not usually an important consideration.

---

[2] This included the definition of single deals which are not under a netting agreement as a netting set.

Table 5.2. Base case parameters used for the collateral examples as percentage values. For example, for the $10m swap considered these would correspond to threshold = $0, minimum transfer amount = $25,000 and rounding = $5,000.

	Party A	*Party B*
Independent amount	0.00%	0.00%
Threshold	0.00%	0.00%
Minimum transfer amount	0.25%	0.25%
Rounding	0.05%	0.05%

Spreadsheet 5.1. Quantifying the impact of collateral on exposure

5.4.2 Scenarios

We first show some example scenarios and the corresponding collateral calculations. In Figure 5.2 is shown a scenario where there is significant positive MtM and therefore exposure on the swap, which is mitigated by collateral. In the first 2.5 years, the counterparty mainly posts collateral to cover the exposure. There is some residual risk ("Overall" profile is mostly positive) due to the minimum transfer amount of 0.25%. After 2.5 years, the MtM is decreasing and hence collateral is being returned to the counterparty. In this case, the minimum transfer amount means that there is generally a small overcollateralisation ("Overall" profile is mostly negative) of up to 0.25%.

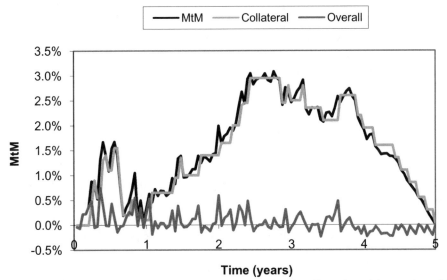

Figure 5.2. Swap MtM scenario together with the associated collateral position and resulting collateralised exposure. This scenario illustrates a case where the MtM increases substantially and collateralisation reduces the overall exposure.

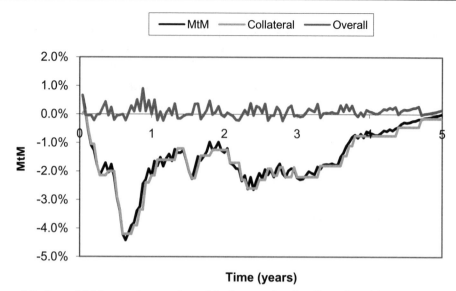

Figure 5.3. Swap MtM scenario together with the associated collateral position and resulting collateralised exposure. This scenario considers a case where the MtM decreases substantially and collateralisation can increase the overall exposure.

In Figure 5.3 we show an almost opposite scenario where the MtM is significantly negative and hence collateral must be posted to the counterparty. However, once the exposure starts increasing again then collateral should be returned. The minimum transfer amount means that there is some uncollateralised exposure in this region (although this will depend on whether it is possible to retrieve the collateral posted if the counterparty defaults, see discussion of rehypothecation in Section 3.7.9). In this scenario (but not all scenarios) it would therefore be better to have no collateral agreement in place. This illustrates an important point that collateralisation can increase as well as reduce risk.

In Figure 5.4 we show a final scenario where the MtM of the swap has both positive and negative values through the lifetime. Collateralisation increases the exposure (from zero) in the first 2.5 years but reduces it in the final 2.5 years. In this case whether or not collateralisation is beneficial is not so obvious.

5.4.3 Exposure distributions

We now look at the nature of the exposure distribution with and without the impact of collateral as shown in Figure 5.5. The MtM values are reduced substantially by the collateral agreement and the profile of the exposure over time also changes. This is asymmetry caused by the assumption that collateral will be posted immediately but only received after a 10-day period.

In addition to the reduction in risk due to collateralisation, the MtM distribution with collateral is now more homogeneous through time. The decay is caused by the shortening maturity of the swap which means that the impact of interest rate changes has a smaller impact on the change in swap MtM over a 10-day period. This illustrates the

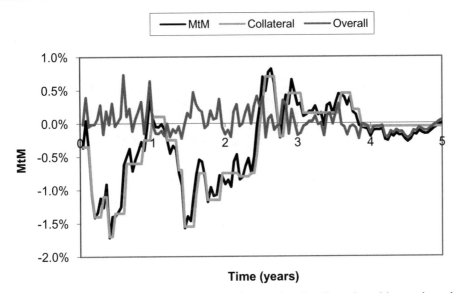

Figure 5.4. Swap MtM scenario together with the associated collateral position and resulting collateralised exposure. This scenario considers a case where the MtM is both positive and negative and the overall impact of collateralisation is not significant.

effect discussed early in Section 3.7.5 that collateralisation simplifies exposure modelling due to the long-term risk being transformed into a short-term risk. Indeed, in contrast to the uncollateralised case, we will illustrate that this collateralised exposure can be reproduced via some simple formulas.

5.4.4 Simple approximation – idealised case

It is possible to have quite simple approximations to the collateralised exposure presented in Figure 5.5 using the formulas given in Appendix 5.A. In such cases, a full simulation of the collateralised exposure might be deemed unnecessary due the ability to represent the EE and PFE via simple formulas. We will illustrate this with a simple example which will be explained in detail in the remainder of this section.

Example. Suppose a trader has a collateralised interest rate swap and needs to calculate the EPE of the trade. The collateral parameters are as defined by Table 5.2. The trader argues that the MtM volatility will be more significant than the minimum transfer amount and therefore uses a simple formula for the EPE based on an average volatility (σ) of the swap over time of 0.225% (this number will be explained below). Using the formulas of Appendix 2.A (and assuming an expected MtM of zero), the calculation gives:

$$EPE \approx 0.4\sigma = 0.090\%.$$

The actual EPE calculated from the scenarios shown in Figure 5.5 is 0.093%.

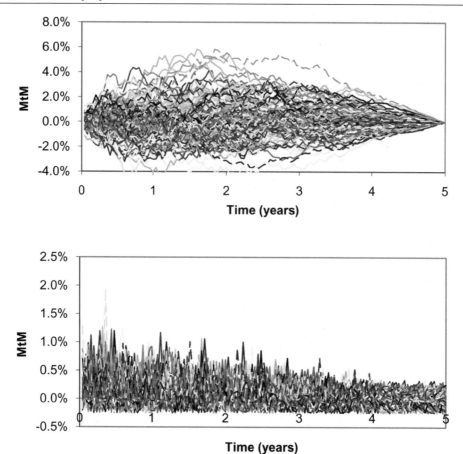

Figure 5.5. Graphs showing many MtM scenarios for the swap with (top) and without (bottom) the effect of collateralisation for 100 scenarios. Note that the y-axis is reduced in the bottom case to reflect the strong risk mitigation.

Assume an idealised case where all collateral parameters (threshold, minimum transfer amount, rounding) are zero. Hence, the exposure will be characterised by the variability of the MtM within the remargin period of 10 days. The MtM volatility of the swap will be given by the interest rate volatility multiplied by the remaining duration of the swap. Now the EE of the collateralised swap at a given time t can be approximated by:

$$\mathrm{EE}(t) \approx 0.4 \times \sigma_r \times (T - t) \times \sqrt{T_M}, \qquad (5.2)$$

where σ_r is the interest rate volatility, T is the maturity of the swap and T_M is the remargin frequency. In the above formula, it is assumed (conservatively) that the duration of the swap will be equal to the remaining maturity, $(T - t)$. The PFE is approximately defined in a similar way as:

$$\mathrm{PFE}_\alpha(t) \approx \Phi^{-1}(\alpha) \times \sigma_r \times (T - t) \times \sqrt{T_M}, \qquad (5.3)$$

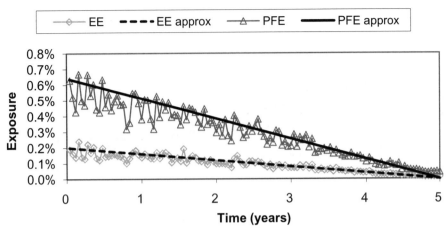

Figure 5.6. Illustration of the EE and PFE (at the 90% confidence level) for the collateralised 5-year maturity swap with no minimum transfer amount or rounding applied compared with the simple approximations given in equations (5.2) and (5.3). Note that the actual results are quite noisy due to only 100 scenarios being used.

where $\Phi^{-1}(\alpha)$ is the inverse cumulative normal distribution function for the confidence level of α. We illustrate the EE and PFE of the example interest rate swap in Figure 5.6 and compare the values obtained with simple approximations resulting in good agreement. The exposure transformation created by collateralisation therefore makes the calculation of collateralised exposure more straightforward as this example demonstrates.

5.4.5 Simple approximation – impact of minimum transfer amount

The above analysis ignored the presence of a minimum transfer amount, MTA. We now incorporate a potential MTA via the following simple rules:

- *Expected exposure.* In the case of expected exposure (EE), the underlying logic is that the MtM will be positive approximately half of the time and then the average exposure will be equal to half the minimum transfer amount. This would lead to an EE of $0.25 \times$ MTA. We then define the EE with a minimum transfer amount as $\text{EE}^{\text{MTA}}(t) = \max(\text{EE}(t), 0.25 \times \text{MTA})$.
- *Potential future exposure (PFE).* In the case of a PFE, assuming a reasonably high confidence level, then the worst case scenario will be that the exposure has moved by almost the full minimum transfer amount. We then define the PFE with a minimum transfer amount as $\text{PFE}^{\text{MTA}}(t) = \max(\text{PFE}(t), \text{MTA})$.

A question that might be asked is why we consider the maximum of the terms above rather than their sum. Consider the case of PFE; the worst case scenario is defined as *either* a significant MtM move – according to equation (5.3) – *or* the exposure being just below the minimum transfer amount with a collateral call being not possible. Adding

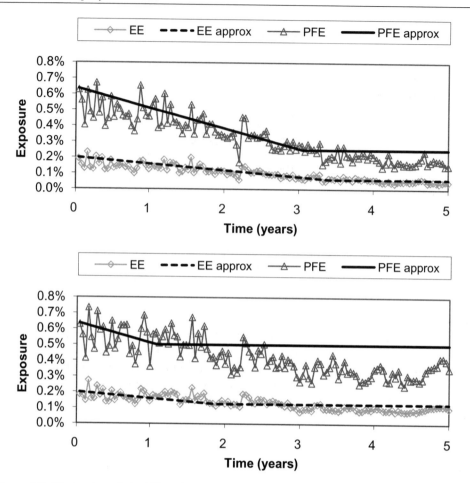

Figure 5.7. Illustration of the EE and PFE (at the 90% confidence level) for the collateralised 5-year maturity swap with a minimum transfer amount of 0.25% (top) and 0.5% (bottom) compared with the simple approximations given in the text. Note that the actual results are quite noisy due to only 100 scenarios being used.

these terms would assume that *both* these worst case events would occur and would therefore be expected to give a conservative estimate of the PFE.

We illustrate the EE and PFE of the example interest rate swap in Figure 5.7 together with the values obtained with the above simple approximations. We can see good agreement is achieved in the case of minimum transfer amounts of both 0.25% and 0.5%.

5.4.6   Impact of threshold

In the previous examples we have shown that full collateralisation reduces credit exposure substantially. Furthermore, it makes the quantification of exposure simpler due to the shortening of the risk horizon (to 10 days in the examples from several years).

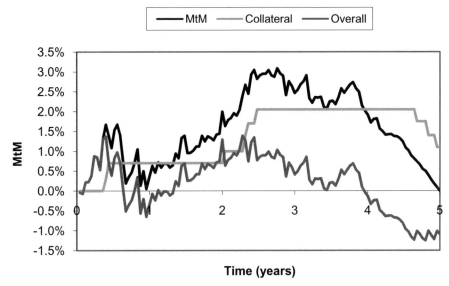

Figure 5.8. Swap MtM scenario together with the associated collateral position and resulting collateralised exposure. This scenario is the same as that shown in Figure 5.2 but assuming a collateral threshold of 1.0% for both parties.

However, all the previous examples assume a zero threshold for the collateral calculations. In reality, thresholds for both counterparties may be used so as to allow a tolerable amount of exposure and also reduce the operational workload in relation to collateral management.

Let us consider the previous example but with a threshold introduced for both parties to the transaction. In Figure 5.8 we illustrate the scenario shown earlier in Figure 5.2 but with a collateral threshold of 1.0% for both parties. This illustrates that the presence of a threshold results in far fewer collateral calls but also leaves a significant amount of residual risk.

5.4.7 Simple approximation – impact of threshold

The presence of a threshold significantly complicates the analysis and requires a more sophisticated approach. For example, Gibson (2005) derives a simple semi-analytical formula for a collateralised exposure incorporating collateral thresholds, which is shown to agree well with a full simulation approach. However, in keeping with our simple approach and for reasons that will become clear when we discuss Basel II in Chapter 11, we will look at a more simple and conservative approach in order to approximate the impact of a collateral threshold.

Consider that the EE is defined as being equal to the threshold plus the expected exposure with the latter quantity as defined by equation (5.2). This clearly represents a worst case scenario since the exposure may often be significantly below the threshold. The results for thresholds of 0.5% and 1.0% are shown in Figure 5.9. We see that the EE

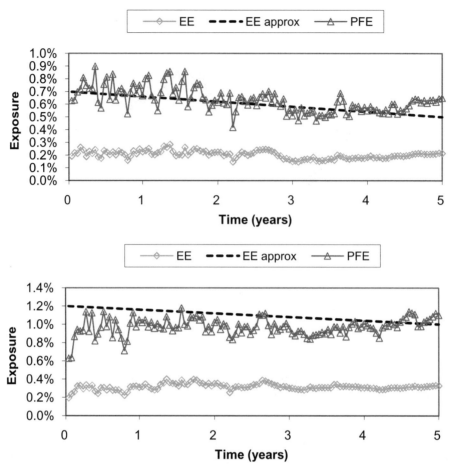

Figure 5.9. Illustration of the EE and PFE (at the 90% confidence level) for the collateralised 5-year maturity swap with a threshold of 0.5% (top) and 1.0% (bottom) compared with the simple approximation for PFE described in the text. Note that the actual results are quite noisy due to only 100 scenarios being used.

approximation is rather conservative, especially for a higher threshold and indeed is closer to the PFE.

5.4.8 Operational cost versus reduction of exposure

One important use of thresholds is to minimise the operational costs associated with exchanging collateral at the expense of increasing future exposure. In Figure 5.10 we show the expected number of collateral calls (or returns) per year together with the EPE of the collateralised exposure. We can see the balance between risk reduction and operational workload so critical in collateral management. A low threshold will reduce significantly the EPE with a high workload for the collateral management unit. On the other hand, decreasing the number of collateral calls can only be achieved by accepting a larger EPE.

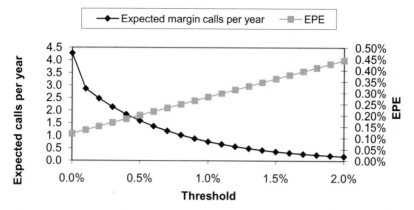

Figure 5.10. Illustration of the expected number of collateral calls per year against the EPE of the collateralised exposure.

5.5   THE RISKS OF COLLATERALISATION

Collateral management should be understood as a way to improve recovery in the event a counterparty actually defaults but it is certainly not a replacement for a proper ongoing assessment of credit quality and assessment of credit exposure. Furthermore, the use of collateral gives rise to many additional risks, some of which have been previously discussed (see Chapter 3). In this section we review the relevant risks that occur as a result of entering into collateral agreements.

5.5.1   Operational risk

The time-consuming and intensely dynamic nature of collateralisation means that operational risk is a very important aspect. The following are examples of specific operational risks:

- missed collateral calls;
- failed deliveries;
- computer error;
- human error;
- fraud.

There is clearly no point in having a collateral management program that reduces significantly many credit exposures only to find that, in the event of an actual default, losses are not mitigated due to some lack of control or error. The following is a non-exhaustive list of points to consider in relation to operational risk:

- Legal agreements must be accurate and enforceable.
- IT systems must be capable of automating the many daily tasks and checks that are required.
- The regular process of calls and returns of collateral is complex and can be extremely time-consuming with a workload that increases in more volatile markets.

- Timely accurate valuation of all products is absolutely key.
- Information on independent amounts, minimum transfer amounts, rounding, collateral types and currencies must be maintained accurately for each counterparty.
- Failure to deliver collateral is a potentially dangerous signal and must be followed up swiftly.

5.5.2 Default risk

Default relating to a security posted as collateral would clearly reduce the value of that collateral substantially and the haircut is very unlikely to cover such an event. For this reason, only high-quality debt securities are typically allowed to be used as collateral. If the credit rating of an underlying security held as collateral declines below that specified in the collateral agreement, then it will normally be required to be replaced immediately. Haircuts are designed to cover the price volatility of assets only and it is therefore crucial that every effort is made to mitigate default risk of the collateral.

5.5.3 FX risk

When two counterparties do not have the same local currency, one of them will have to take FX risk linked to the collateral posted, even when it is in the form of cash. Securities in various currencies may be specified as admissible collateral but may also attract larger haircuts due to the additional FX risk. FX risk from posted collateral can be hedged in the spot and forward FX markets but it must be done dynamically as the value of collateral changes.

5.5.4 Liquidity and liquidation risk

In addition to the market and operational risks collateral generates, there may be certain circumstances where liquidity risk will be a consideration. Indeed, sometimes, a concentration limit of 5–10% will be imposed to prevent severe liquidation risk in the event of a counterparty defaulting. When agreeing to collateral that may be posted and when receiving securities as collateral, important considerations are:

- What is the total issue size or market capitalisation posted as collateral?
- Is there a link between the collateral value and the credit quality of the counterparty? Such a link may not be obvious and predicted by looking at correlations between variables.[3]
- How is the relative liquidity of the security in question likely to change if the counterparty concerned is in default?

We distinguish between two forms of liquidity risk:

- *Liquidity risk*. The risk that we incur some transaction costs (bid–offer) when forced to issue a notice of default and liquidate collateral held.

---

[3] In the case of the Long Term Capital Management (LTCM) default, a very large proprietary position on Russian government bonds made these securities far from ideal as collateral.

- *Liquidation risk.* The risk that by liquidating an amount of a security that is large compared with the volume traded in that security, the price will be driven down and a potentially large loss incurred. If one chooses to liquidate the position more slowly in small blocks then there is exposure to market volatility for a longer period of time.

5.6 SUMMARY

In this chapter we have discussed the quantification of credit exposure in the presence of collateral. We introduced the concept of a "remargin period" which defines a worst case scenario for the time lag that should be considered before requested collateral is actually received. We have discussed how the presence of a collateral agreement changes the nature of future exposure. The impact of exposure and collateral volatility and correlation has been discussed and we have described simple formulas to define EE and PFE in the presence of collateral. This topic will be discussed again in Chapter 11 in relation to Basel II.

So far, this book has been concerned mainly with credit exposure. Whilst this is a critical component of counterparty risk, it is not the only component. Assessing the potential magnitude of a credit exposure is a useful step but is meaningless without an associated quantification of the probability that a counterparty will default. Having a potential credit exposure of $10m with a counterparty of very good credit quality is very different than facing an equivalent exposure with a counterparty much more likely to default. In Chapter 6, we will turn our attention to credit risk and default probability to understand fully this aspect. This will then lead us to more fully define counterparty risk as credit exposure coupled to the likelihood of an actual default event.

APPENDIX 5.A: CALCULATION OF COLLATERALISED PFE (CASH COLLATERAL)

Assuming that a netted set of trades is perfectly collateralised at a given time and the change in the netted exposure (and collateral value) follows a normal distribution with zero mean and volatility parameter σ_E, then using the results of Appendix 2.A, the potential future exposure at a given confidence level α is given by:

$$\text{PFE}_\alpha = \Phi^{-1}(\alpha) \times \sigma_E \times \sqrt{T_M},$$

where T_M denotes the remargin period of the risk. The above formula is analogous to a VAR formula under a normal distribution assumption of portfolio value. The EE is given by:

$$\text{EE} = \sigma_E \sqrt{T_M} \varphi(0) = \frac{1}{\sqrt{2\pi}} \times \sigma_E \times \sqrt{T_M} \approx 0.4\sigma_E \sqrt{T_M}.$$

Given the short period, it is unlikely that the drift of the distribution is likely to be an important consideration. The assessment of the volatility parameter is covered in Appendix 5.B.

In the case of a debt security, duration, D, must be considered in order to derive a price volatility, σ_E, from the volatility of the underlying variable (usually an interest rate), σ_r. As a first-order approximation, we then have $\sigma_E \approx \sigma_r \times D$.

APPENDIX 5.B: CALCULATION OF COLLATERALISED NETTED EXPOSURE WITH COLLATERAL VALUE UNCERTAINTY

Let us assume that a netted set of n trades is perfectly collateralised at a given time and the change in the MtM of each trade follows a normal distribution with zero mean and volatility parameter σ_i. The volatility of the MtM of the netting set required by the calculations in Appendix 5.A can then be calculated from:

$$\sigma_E^2 = \sum_{i=1}^{n} \sigma_E^2 + 2 \sum_{i=1, j>i}^{n} \rho_{ij}\sigma_i\sigma_j,$$

where ρ is the correlation between the MtM values of trades i and j within the netting set.

Assume the change in the value of the collateral follows a normal distribution with zero mean and volatility parameter σ_C (in the case of several different types of collateral then this may be calculated in a similar way to the exposure volatility above). The effective volatility of the position is then:

$$\sigma_{E,C}^2 = \sigma_E^2 + \sigma_C^2 - 2\rho_{E,C}\sigma_E\sigma_C,$$

where the correlation between exposure and collateral value is given by $\rho_{E,C}$. The minus sign in the above formula arises due to the nature of collateralisation since the exposure and collateral essentially have opposite signs. Once the above is calculated then the potential future exposure can be assessed using the formulas given in Appendix 5.A.

APPENDIX 5.C: MATHEMATICAL TREATMENT OF A COLLATERALISED EXPOSURE

This analysis will calculate whether a party can call for collateral from their counterparty. It does not account for negative collateral calls, i.e. those in the opposite direction. These require the same formula implemented from the counterparty's point of view.

We use the following definitions:

V_s – mark to market of portfolio at time s
K – collateral threshold
IA   – independent amount
A – collateral held at the current point in time
MTA – minimum transfer amount
R – rounding

The credit support amount is given by adding the independent amount and subtracting the threshold above which collateral will be taken (note that no more than one of these components will be used):

$$\text{CSA}_s = V_s + \text{IA} - K.$$

We have to also account for the current amount of collateral held which gives us the collateral required, CR_s:

$$CR_s = CSA_s - A.$$

However, we now need to account for the minimum transfer amount since a call can be made only if $CR_s > MTA$. This gives:

$$CR'_s = \frac{(CR_s - MTA)^+}{CR_s - MTA} CR_s.$$

Let us assume the amount will be rounded down to blocks of R:

Rounding down: $\quad CR''_s = CR'_s - (CR'_s \bmod R)$

Rounding up: $\quad CR''_s = CR'_s - (CR'_s \bmod R) + R.$

The full formula for collateral that can be called at the current time assuming rounding down will be:

$$CR''_s = C - C \bmod R, \qquad C = \frac{(CSA_s - A - MTA)^+}{CSA_s - A - MTA}(CSA_s - A)$$

with $CSA_s = V_s + IA - K$.

6

Overview of Credit Risk and Credit Derivatives

So far, this book has been largely concerned with credit exposure. Now we aim to describe the default component in more detail. We discuss the nature of default probability, recovery rates and associated credit spreads. The focus will be largely on corporate entities, which are most relevant from the point of view of counterparty risk. We will also review the range of credit derivatives products, which will be discussed in some later chapters. Hence, this chapter is a review of all the key credit risk and credit derivatives aspects and may be skipped by the reader experienced in these areas. However, many subtle questions can only be answered from a detailed knowledge of credit risk and credit derivatives products. For example:

Suppose an institution has an uncollateralised credit exposure of $10m to a defaulted counterparty but they also have $10m of credit default swap protection against the counterparty in question. Is this a perfect hedge?

The short answer to the above question is no but the long answer is much more complex, as we shall explore in both this chapter as well as Chapter 9.

6.1 DEFAULTS, RECOVERY RATES, CREDIT SPREADS AND CREDIT DERIVATIVES

Default probability and the associated recovery rate define the expected loss on an asset. Market credit spreads reflect the market price for such losses and hence a commonly used relationship is:

$$\text{credit spread} \cong \text{default probability} \times \text{loss given default}, \qquad (6.1)$$

where all quantities can be assumed to be percentages. This relationship is a useful guide but is not perfectly accurate for theoretical reasons and, more importantly, ignores many components such as liquidity risk premiums. It is important to understand fully the relationship defined by equation (6.1) in order to be able to price counterparty risk properly. We also note that, in assessing counterparty risk, we may define expected losses using either side of equation (6.1), the left-hand side reflecting market-implied probabilities and the right-hand side reflecting real probabilities.

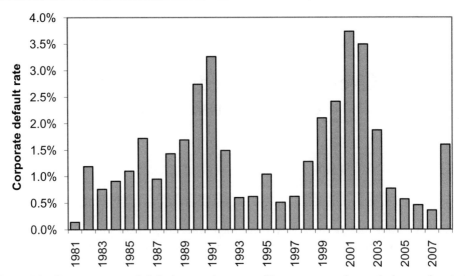

Figure 6.1. Corporate annual default rates (average of investment and speculative grade rates). Source: Standard & Poor's (2008).

6.1.1 Default rates

Whether credit-sensitive instruments are treated on a stand-alone basis or within a portfolio context, default probability plays a critical role in risk assessment and valuation. An example of historical default rates for investment and speculative-grade assets is shown in Figure 6.1. Default rates tend to vary substantially through the credit cycle, which poses an immediate problem for counterparty risk management. Knowing that some years will result in an unusually large number of counterparty defaults than others, how is it possible to quantify and manage counterparty risk in a reasonable way?

6.1.2 Recovery rates

Recovery rates define loss given default (LGD) and the two quantities can be used interchangeably. We will always discuss recovery rate (as a percentage of par value) which is related to the LGD via:

$$\text{loss given default} = (1 - \text{recovery rate}), \tag{6.2}$$

therefore, for example, a low recovery rate of 20% implies a high loss given default of 80%. Recovery values, like default probabilities, tend to show significant variation over time as illustrated in Figure 6.2. We can see further variation according to variables such as sector (Table 6.1) and debt seniority (Table 6.2). Recoveries also tend to be negatively correlated with default rates (for example, see Hamilton et al., 2001). This negative correlation means that a high default rate will give rise to lower recovery values. Hence, the random nature of default probability and recovery over time coupled to the negative correlation creates strong variability in default losses.

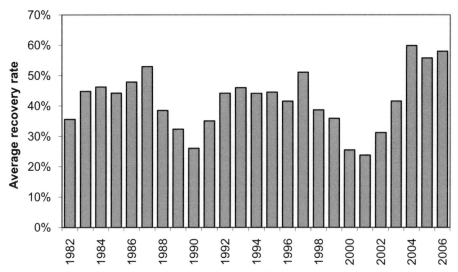

Figure 6.2. Average recovery values across all debt seniorities.
Source: Moody's Investors Service (2007).

Table 6.1. Recovery rates by sector.

Industry	Recovery rate average
Public utilities	70.5%
Chemicals, petroleum, rubber and plastic products	62.7%
Machinery, instruments and related products	48.7%
Services (business and personal)	46.2%
Food and kindred products	45.3%
Wholesale and retail trade	44.0%
Diversified manufacturing	42.3%
Casino, hotel and recreation	40.2%
Building material, metals and fabricated products	38.8%
Transportation and transportation equipment	38.4%
Communication, broadcasting, movie production, printing and publishing	37.1%
Financial institutions	35.7%
Construction and real estate	35.3%
General merchandise stores	33.2%
Mining and petroleum drilling	33.0%
Textile and apparel products	31.7%
Wood, paper and leather products	29.8%
Lodging, hospitals and nursing facilities	26.5%
Total	*41.0%*

Source: Altman and Kishore (1996).

Table 6.2. Recovery rates by original debt seniority.

Debt seniority	Recovery rate average	
	Investment grade	Sub investment grade
Senior secured	54.8%	56.4%
Senior unsecured	48.2%	48.7%
Senior subordinated	32.7%	39.9%
Subordinated	31.9%	31.7%
Discount and zero coupon	24.1%	24.4%
Total	41.0%	

Source: Altman and Kishore (1996).

6.1.3 Credit spreads

There is no precise definition of a credit spread and it may be defined in slightly different ways and with respect to different rates (swaps or treasury bonds, for example). However, in general a credit spread reflects the difference in the risky versus the risk-free yield on a security and therefore defines the compensation for credit risk. It is not surprising, given the above comments, that credit spreads are highly volatile, driven by uncertain default and recovery rates. However, as is well known, credit spreads are high compared with actual credit losses over a reasonably long horizon. Put another way, investing in a diversified portfolio of corporate bonds over many years is extremely likely to produce a greater than risk-free return. Hull et al. (2004) show this relationship via the difference between market credit spreads and required credit spreads (to compensate for actual default losses historically). We see that actual losses explain only a fraction of observed credit spreads, especially for highly rated institutions.

Table 6.3. Comparison between actual and required credit spreads. All figures in basis points.

	Credit spread	Required credit spread	Ratio
Aaa	40	2	5.0%
Aa	47	4	8.5%
A	77	8	10.4%
Baa	143	28	19.6%
Ba	304	144	47.4%
B	542	449	82.8%
Caa	1,278	1,014	79.3%

Adapted from Hull et al. (2004).

There has been much work on understanding the components of credit spreads and their relation to actual default rates and recoveries. See, for example, Collin-Dufresne,

Goldstein et al. (2005) and Downing et al. (2005). These studies find that the difference between credit spreads and actual default losses is due to:

- the relative illiquidity of corporate bonds requiring a liquidity risk premium;
- the limited upside on holding a bond portfolio, or negative skew in bond returns;
- the non-diversifiable risk of corporate bonds requiring a systemic risk premium.

We do not require here to understand in detail the relationship between credit spreads and historical default losses but it is important to appreciate the impact on quantifying and managing counterparty risk. If one does not seek to hedge the default component of counterparty risk then it is more relevant to consider the default and recovery rates estimated empirically via historical data. If, on the other hand, one intends to hedge against counterparty defaults then it is important to consider market credit spreads. From Table 6.3 we expect the hedging costs to be significantly higher, especially for good-quality counterparties (for example, approximately 10 times higher for single-A rated names). Hedging will not only be more costly in the long run but will also be limited to the depth of liquidity of the credit derivative market for the counterparty in question. However, as discussed in more detail in Chapter 9, the hedging of default is a key aspect for any institution with a significant exposure to counterparty risk.

6.2 CREDIT DERIVATIVES

Credit derivatives instruments are important to our discussion since they represent opportunities for trading, hedging and diversification of counterparty risk. In addition, credit derivatives as a product class give rise to a significant amount of counterparty risk. Indeed, the continued development of the credit derivative market is contingent on control of this counterparty risk.

6.2.1 Market growth and uses

The credit derivatives market has grown dramatically (see Figure 6.3), fuelled by the need to transfer credit risk efficiently and develop ever-more sophisticated products for investors. A credit derivative is an agreement designed to shift credit risk between parties and its value is derived from the credit performance of a corporation, sovereign entity or security. Credit derivatives can be traded on a single-name basis (referencing a single component such as a corporate) or a portfolio basis (referencing many components such as 125 corporate names).

The CDS product was first used by banks in the late 1990s to reduce capital requirements. The market has grown substantially and covers new asset classes such as asset-backed securities (ABSs), mortgage-backed securities (MBSs) and other collateralised debt obligations (CDOs). Credit derivatives have grown due to demand by financial institutions (mainly banks) for a means of hedging and diversifying credit risks independently of other risks (such as interest rate risk and foreign exchange risk). They also have grown in response to demands for low-cost means of taking on credit exposure. Finally, a key driver of credit derivatives growth has been structured products. Credit has gradually become a more liquid risk that can be traded, albeit with numerous inherent challenges in doing so.

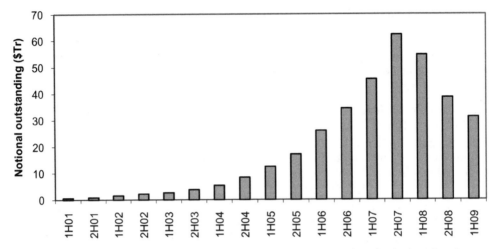

Figure 6.3. Total outstanding notional of credit derivatives transactions in the last decade. Source: ISDA (*http://isda.org/statistics/recent.htm*).

6.2.2   Credit default swaps (CDSs)

Many credit derivatives take the form of the credit default swap (CDS), which transfers the default risk of one or more corporations or sovereign entities from one party to another. In a single-name CDS, the protection buyer pays a periodic fee (the premium) to the protection seller for a certain notional amount of debt of a specified reference entity. If the reference entity specified undergoes a credit event (defined in Section 6.3.2) then the protection seller must compensate the protection buyer for the associated loss by means of a pre-specified settlement procedure (the protection buyer must also typically pay an accrued premium at this point as compensation due to the fact that premiums are paid in arrears). The premium is paid until either the maturity date or the credit event time, whichever comes first. The reference entity is not a party to the contract, and it is not necessary for the buyer or seller to obtain the reference entity's consent to enter into a CDS. The mechanics of a single-name CDS contract are shown in Figure 6.4 (index contracts are discussed later in Section 6.5.1).

CDSs are not securities and are classified and regulated as "security-based swaps"

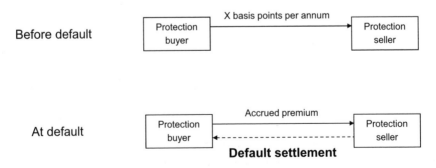

Figure 6.4. Illustration of a typical CDS contract on a single reference entity.

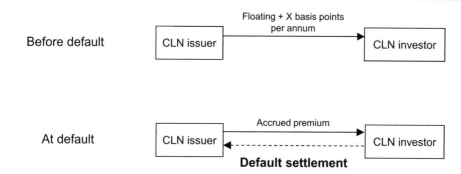

Figure 6.5. Illustration of a typical CLN contract on a single reference entity. Note that the investor would make an upfront payment of par and will receive par at maturity as long as there has not been a credit event. The default settlement of par minus recovery is effectively achieved via the loss of par from the termination of the floating rate note (floating payments and principal) and delivery of defaulted securities representing a recovery value.

under Federal securities law in the US. Although CDSs are illiquid compared with exchange-traded instruments such as stocks and futures, they are generally traded more than corporate bonds and are likely to become even more liquid as the market matures.

CDS premiums are much more dynamic and informative than credit ratings. For example, Bear Stearns' senior debt was not downgraded prior to its collapse in 2008 whereas its CDS premium increased dramatically.

6.2.3 Credit-linked notes

A credit-linked note (Figure 6.5) is simply a funded form of a CDS and consequently a CLN is a product that can be easily constructed as long as the relevant CDS can be traded. In a CLN the investor will make an upfront par payment and will then receive a running floating rate (for example, LIBOR) plus a spread in addition to receiving par back at maturity. If we compare a risk-free floating rate note, the CLN LIBOR payments can be seen as a pure interest rate component and the spread can be seen as the compensation for default risk. Hence, the spread should be similar to an equivalent CDS premium (this relationship will be discussed further in Section 6.2.5).

A typical CLN will be structured using an SPV (special purpose vehicle). This is in order to ring-fence the structure in the event of the issuer defaulting (although the investor does take risk to the SPV collateral). It therefore (in theory) removes the counterparty risk of the issuer from the point of view of the investor who takes credit risk to the reference entity only. See Section 3.2.2 for more discussions on SPVs, including recent problems arising from the Lehman Brothers' bankruptcy.

6.2.4 Asset swaps

Typically, bonds are fixed rate instruments, which pay a fixed coupon as compensation for the underlying interest rate and credit components. In a par–par asset swap contract (Figure 6.6), an investor will make a payment of par at inception (similar to purchasing a bond) and will then be paid a floating rate plus an "asset swap spread" linked to some

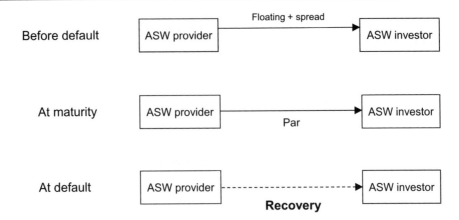

Figure 6.6. Illustration of a typical asset swap (ASW) contract. Note that the investor would make an upfront payment of par.

underlying credit. If there is a credit event on the underlying bond, then the asset swap investor will receive the recovery value of this bond (settlement methods discussed below). Asset swaps are interesting since, from an investor's point of view, they convert a fixed rate bond into a floating investment. The default risk of the bond is then unchanged but the interest rate risk has been extracted (thanks to floating rather than fixed payments).

6.2.5 Linkage between bonds, asset swaps and CDS premiums

It is informative to examine the relationship between CLN spreads, asset swap spreads and CDS premiums. One can view a CLN as simply a "funded CDS", as illustrated in Figure 6.7. If there is a credit event then the CLN issuer will effectively keep the initial

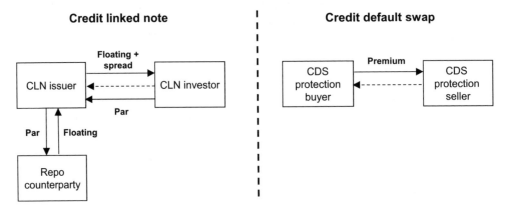

Figure 6.7. Schematic illustration of the relationship between a credit-linked note and a credit default swap. The dotted line represents the direction of the credit protection being provided. In the event of the credit event, each structure can be considered to be terminated with the par minus recovery value paid to the CLN issuer or CDS protection buyer.

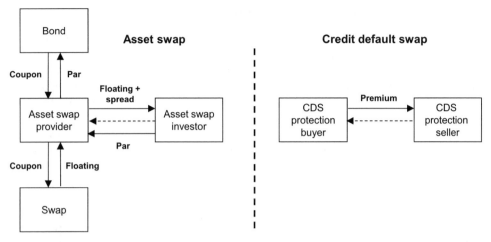

Figure 6.8. Schematic illustration of the relationship between an asset swap and credit default swap. The dotted line represents the direction of the credit protection being provided. In the event of the credit event, the structure would be terminated with the bond value (recovery) paid to the asset swap investor but with the potential additional cost of unwinding the (interest rate) swap.

investment of par, cease paying the floating coupons and deliver bonds to the CLN investor. This reproduces the payoff of par less recovery as seen in the CDS contract. This shows that the spread paid on the CLN and premium of the CDS should, theoretically, be equal as long as the repo can provide a floating payment equal to the LIBOR rate.

Comparing an asset swap and credit default swap is more complex, as shown in Figure 6.8. The ASW provider is paid par by the ASW investor and can use this to buy a fixed rate bond. The fixed coupons are swapped into floating payments via an interest rate swap. If there is a credit event then the structure terminates with a recovery value (of the defaulted bond) being paid to the ASW investor. Hence, the investor has essentially provided default protection and the ASW spread should be close to the CDS premium. The same argument would apply to the spread (above the swap rate) of a fixed rate bond. The added complication here is that, on the occurrence of a credit event, the interest rate swap must be terminated which will result in some MtM impact. In a dirty asset swap, this unwind risk may well be borne by the investor (often in a one-sided fashion so they will not take a gain when the swap MtM is positive but will be responsible for losses if it is negative). In a so-called clean asset swap, the issuer will take on the default contingent swap unwind risk.[1]

Whilst we have not given an exhaustive account of all of the cashflows concerned, to summarise, we can consider that the spread of a credit-linked note, asset swap, fixed rate bond and a CDS premium are all closely related and reflect the cost of transferring credit risk. Whilst this is approximately true, as we explore in more detail the CDS product we will find certain ways in which the above relationships should diverge.

---

[1] In the perfect asset swap the issuer takes on the default contingent swap unwind risk and additionally guarantees the recovery rate of the defaulted asset in the investor's base currency.

6.2.6 Contingent credit default swap (CCDS)

In a standard CDS, the protection buyer has protection on a certain notional amount, which works well for hedging typical credit exposures such as loans and bonds. For example, $10m of CDS protection would give protection against holding bonds with par value of $10m.[2] However, a key aspect of counterparty risk on a derivative is that the loss is determined by the credit exposure at the credit event time which is an unknown quantity.

A contingent credit default swap (CDS) is an instrument that is the same as a standard CDS but with one key difference in that the notional amount of protection is referenced to another transaction. This transaction can be potentially any product across any asset class. Hence, a CCDS can provide protection against the counterparty risk on a derivative since the protection amount can be directly linked to the exposure of that derivative (and this derivative must therefore be explicitly referenced within the CCDS term sheet). Therefore, whilst CDSs are generally products that have many applications, CCDSs are products that are tailor-made to hedge counterparty risk. Whilst this may seem ideal, there are many issues with CCDSs, which have inhibited their use as instruments for transferring counterparty risk. We will discuss this in more detail in Chapter 9.

6.2.7 Fixed and digital CDSs and recovery swaps

In a fixed recovery CDS, the recovery rate is pre-determined at the start of the contract. In a digital CDS, this fixed recovery rate will be zero leading to a unit payoff linked to the credit event. Fixed recovery CDS instruments have been sought by some investors in order to have no uncertainty on their loss if there is a credit event. They are not generally of use for hedging purposes since debt securities and derivatives have floating recoveries and are most efficiently hedged with instruments that behave in the same way.

A recovery swap is an agreement between two parties to swap a realised recovery rate (when and if the relevant credit event occurs) with a fixed recovery rate that is specified at the start of the contract. The reference price reflects the fixed recovery such that the recovery swap has zero value initially. Since the swap is issued at a price of zero, if the reference entity does not default in the term of the swap, then the swap expires with no cashflows having taken place. If the credit event does occur, the fixed recovery payer in the swap will compensate the other party if the actual recovery is less than the fixed recovery and vice versa.

In theory, a recovery swap is equivalent to buying protection on a fixed recovery CDS and selling protection on the standard CDS. In reality, there may be a difference in the settlement procedures. Fixed recovery CDSs are settled immediately, since there is no need to wait for recovery to be determined, whilst a recovery swap will wait until the ordinary CDS is settled before paying out.

As a name moves towards experiencing a credit event, the recovery rate naturally becomes better defined. Fixed recovery CDSs and recovery swaps have not been common but are potentially important since no other instrument allows one to imply the market expectation of recovery rate for a name other than those close to experiencing a credit event.

---

[2] This is only approximately true, for reasons discussed in Section 6.3.6.

6.3   CREDIT DEFAULT SWAPS

Having given a general overview of credit derivative and related products, we now go into more detail on the mechanics and risks of a CDS which represents a key product in the hedging of counterparty risk and credit risk in general. Moreover, CDSs themselves can also have significant counterparty risk due to wrong-way risk, as will be discussed in more detail in Chapter 9.

6.3.1   Reference entity and obligation

CDS documentation refers to a reference obligation and reference entity. The reference entity may be a corporate, a sovereign or any other form of legal entity which has incurred debt.[3] The reference obligation defines the seniority of the debt that can be delivered. Commonly, all obligations of the same or better seniority can be delivered (in the case of no reference obligation being specified then the seniority is senior unsecured).

It is critical to identify the correct underlying entity/obligation in the CDS contract since misidentification will result in inaccurate valuation of the trade and ineffective protection in the case of a credit event, leading to a hedge being completely inefficient. To help avoid such problems, RED[4] (reference entity database) codes legally verify CDS reference entity and reference obligations. Using unique alphanumeric RED codes helps reduce errors when confirming trades and ensures the correct representation of the underlying credit risk.

6.3.2   Credit events

Generally, the term default is used (as in default probability, for example) instead of the more relevant and generic term credit event. The payment in a CDS contract will be triggered if any one of the specified credit events occurs. These credit events will be defined in the CDS documentation and may vary, although certain standards have emerged. The three most important credit events are:

- *Bankruptcy*. This will be triggered by a variety of events associated with bankruptcy or insolvency proceedings, such as winding up, administration and receivership, under English and New York law or analogous events under other insolvency laws.
- *Failure to pay*. This event covers the reference entity failing to make a payment of principal or interest. A minimum threshold amount is normally nominated in the confirmation which must be exceeded before this event is triggered (default value $1m). Failure to make a collateral margin call after the relevant grace period probably falls into this category, as discussed in Chapter 3.
- *Restructuring*. This covers the reference entity arranging for some or all of its debts to be restructured causing a material adverse change in their credit-worthiness. There are four variations of restructuring which have developed historically due to the complexity of including restructuring as a credit event. This is discussed in more detail below.

---

[3] Occasionally, CDSs trade on names with little or no outstanding debt, often in the case of sovereign entities.
[4] RED is administered by Markit Partners, see *www.markit.com*

The final three credit events are of lesser importance but are included here for completeness:

- *Obligation acceleration.* Obligation acceleration concerns the situation, excluding a failure to pay, where the relevant obligation becomes due and payable before its normal expiration date. This normally would occur due to a default by the reference entity. The relevant sum being accelerated must be above a minimum threshold, which is defined in the contract.
- *Obligation default.* Obligation default covers the situation, other than a failure to pay, where the relevant obligation becomes capable of being declared due and payable for contractual reasons by the reference entity (before the time when such obligation would otherwise have been due). Again, the relevant sum must exceed a certain threshold.
- *Repudiation/Moratorium.* Repudiation/Moratorium deals with the situation where the reference entity or a governmental authority disaffirms, disclaims or otherwise challenges the validity of the relevant obligation.

6.3.3 Settlement of CDS

The fundamental aim of a CDS is to compensate the protection buyer for the loss of par value on a defaulted security such as a bond. However, debt securities will typically not be worth zero when there has been a credit event but will rather trade at some recovery value. Hence, the protection buyer needs to be paid par minus this recovery value. There are fundamentally two ways in which this payoff has been achieved in CDSs:

- *Physical settlement.* In this case, the protection buyer will deliver to the protection seller defaulted securities of the reference entity with a par value equal to the notional amount of the CDS contract. In return, the protection seller must make a payment of par in cash. For example, an investor buying a bond and holding CDS protection for the same notional may deliver the defaulted bond against receiving par. This mechanism is clearly attractive since no other parties need to be involved and there can be no dispute over payments. Indeed, this was the favoured settlement mechanism in the early years of the CDS market. However, there exist serious problems with physical settlement, described below, which have made it, more recently, less favourable.
- *Cash settlement.* Here, the protection seller will compensate the protection buyer in cash for the value of par minus recovery value. An obvious problem with this is that the recovery value must be determined through some market consensus of where the debt of the defaulted entity is trading (dealer poll or more recently an auction process described below). Due to the problems with physical settlement (discussed in Section 6.3.4), cash settlement is becoming the more popular way of settling CDS contracts.

In Table 6.4 we show recovery values settled following credit events for some CDS auctions in 2008. We see a wide range of recoveries from Fannie Mae and Freddie Mac that were close to 100% thanks largely to the guarantee from the US government, making this more a technical credit event, to Lehman Brothers and Icelandic banks that recovered very little.

Table 6.4. Recovery rates for CDS auctions for some credit events in 2008. The impact of a delivery squeeze (discussed in Section 6.3.5) can be seen in that Fannie Mae and Freddie Mac subordinated debt traded at higher levels than the senior debt.

Reference entity	Seniority	Recovery rate
Fannie Mae	Senior	91.5%
	Subordinated	99.9%
Freddie Mac	Senior	94.0%
	Subordinated	98.0%
Washington Mutual		57.0%
Lehman		8.6%
Kaupthing Bank	Senior	6.6%
	Subordinated	2.4%
Landsbanki	Senior	1.3%
	Subordinated	0.1%
Glitnir	Senior	3.0%
	Subordinated	0.1%
Average		*38.5%*

6.3.4 Cheapest-to-deliver option and restructuring

The classic case of the credit event of Conseco Corp. (see box) highlighted the problems with restructuring as a credit event.

Conseco Corp. credit event

In January 2001, Conseco Corp avoided an impending bankruptcy by negotiating an extension of $2.8bn of loans, which was technically a restructuring credit event (standard in documentation at the time). Some dealers who were long CDS protection triggered the contracts and delivered long-dated Conseco securities. A bond that had previously been trading at a price of around 60% of par could be delivered against par due to the possibility to trigger the CDS based on the restructuring credit event. Protection sellers were (not surprisingly) unimpressed that the protection buyers had found economic value in the CDS contracts unrelated to their initial intention to protect against credit losses (the cheap Conseco bonds were due to interest rate and not credit aspects).

In a CDS contract settled via physical delivery, since the credit event is not specific to a given security, there is no single bond that needs to be delivered. The protection buyer therefore has some choice over the security that can be delivered and will naturally choose the cheapest available in the market. For a hard credit event such as a bankruptcy, all bonds of a given seniority will be expected to trade at a similar price since they

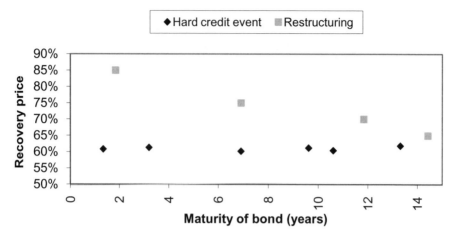

Figure 6.9. Illustration of cheapest-to-deliver optionality in a CDS contract. For a hard credit event, such as a bankruptcy, bonds of all maturities trade at similar prices (recovery value represented as a percentage). For a restructuring credit event, there may be dramatically different prices depending on the nature of the restructuring and the characteristics of the bonds outstanding.

represent an equivalent claim on the assets of the reference entity, irrespective of other bond features such as maturity or coupon. On the other hand, consider a restructuring credit event. In this case, the reference entity, whilst clearly having cashflow problems, is not in severe distress and may indeed recover to good financial health at some point in the future. Hence, bonds of different maturities may trade at different price levels. These levels will depend on future expectations of default probability and other aspects such as maturity and coupon.

The above difference is represented schematically in Figure 6.9. Suppose a 2-year maturity bond is being restructured and the impairment to face value (around 85%) likely represents a loss of 15% for the holder of that bond (one would expect short maturity debt to trade close to par unless there are significant credit problems for the issuer). On the other hand, longer maturity bonds need not trade at a similar level. Indeed, the market may have the view that the restructuring of the short-term debt is likely to be beneficial for the company in question and they are expected to be in good financial health when this debt matures.

What then determines the price of the longer maturity bonds in this example if they are not strongly driven by credit concerns? They could be trading far cheaper than their par value for a variety of reasons not linked to the issuer's credit spread. For example, long-dated bonds with some or all of the following characteristics will be trading cheaply with respect to their par values:

● low coupon;
● convertible (due to the low coupons associated with these instruments and being out of the money due to the equity value not having risen sufficiently);
● illiquid bonds.

How, then, can one deal with the inclusion or not of restructuring as a credit event? If it is included then it potentially gives rise to the classic Conseco case where protection buyers extract economic value from a CDS that is not related to credit aspects. On the other hand, if restructuring were not included then the holder of restructured debt would not be compensated for likely credit losses (the bond trading well below par due to the financial problems that have led the reference entity to attempt to restructure its debt). The solution to the problem has been to include restructuring in a limited way by restricting the maturity of debt that can be delivered. The market has then evolved to include four possible restructuring options:

- no restructuring;
- modified restructuring (US);
- modified modified restructuring (Europe);
- full restructuring.

The main point to take away is simply that in the event of a restructuring credit event only, under modified restructuring or modified modified restructuring limitations exist as to the maturity of the deliverable obligation. This maturity limitation is clearly to avoid the delivery of long-dated debt as in the Conseco case. The maturity limitations (restructuring maturity limitation date) are:

- *Modified restructuring (MR)*. The earlier of 30 months following the restructuring date and the latest final maturity date of any restructured bond or loan. However, under no circumstances shall the restructuring maturity limitation date be earlier than the scheduled termination date or later than 30 months following the scheduled termination date.
- *Modified modified restructuring (MMR)*. For a bond or loan, the later of 60 months following the restructuring date and scheduled termination date. For any other obligation, 30 months following the restructuring date.

Some further conditions apply to the MR and MMR restructuring clauses but the maturity limitation is the key consideration for the purposes of counterparty risk. We will need to consider the impact of a restructuring credit event when we discuss hedging counterparty risk in Chapter 9. As discussed in Section 6.3.7, the current market standards are no restructuring for the US and MMR for Europe.

6.3.5 Delivery squeeze

Around four-fifths of CDS protection buyers do so without being exposed to the underlying risk, i.e. holding a relevant debt security that would be deliverable if there is a credit event. For example, an arbitrageur or speculator may buy CDS protection but would not simultaneously hold the underlying debt. A delivery squeeze can be created if the amount of notional required to be delivered (total outstanding CDS protection on the reference entity) is large compared with the amount of outstanding debt. In the early years of the CDS market, a delivery squeeze would not have been an issue but due to the rapid growth in the amount of CDS protection traded on some names, the product has become a victim of its own success. In a delivery squeeze, the bond prices will increase to reflect a lack of supply and this in turn will suppress the value of the CDS (since the payoff is par less recovery). Delivery squeezes have been seen in several defaults such as Parmalat (2003) and Delphi (2005). For many counterparties the amount of CDS traded[5] is indeed larger than the available pool of bonds.

There have been calls to restrict the CDS market to protection buyers who hold the underlying debt security (as is the case in insurance contracts where the owner of insurance needs to own the insured risk at the claim time). Such an action would clearly avoid a delivery squeeze since no protection buyers would need to buy bonds when there is a credit event. However, this would presumably prevent CDS protection being held against credit exposure to hedge counterparty risk. Since future credit exposure is uncertain, it is not clear what would be a reasonable amount of CDS protection to hold. An institution may understandably want to buy more CDS protection than their current exposure to mitigate a potential increase in exposure in the future. If CDS protection could only be bought against existing claims then this hedge would not be possible. Furthermore, to ban or restrict trading in this way will make the CDS market inefficient and illiquid.

A delivery squeeze is an important consideration in the hedging of credit risk since it can create a significant discrepancy between the recovery value of the security itself and the recovery as defined by the CDS contract. In an ideal and liquid market, such differences would be small but technicalities like delivery squeezes can create significant basis risks. A solution to the delivery squeeze problem is to cash-settle CDS contracts via auctions for credit events (discussed further below) or other means. The process of holding auctions to determine a settlement price in respect of a credit derivative transaction (following the occurrence of a credit event) has been used since 2005 as the primary settlement method for credit events on widely traded reference entities. Whilst this solves the problem for the most liquid of traded CDS reference entities, it is probably not a viable solution for other less liquid names.

6.3.6   CDS risks

In addition to the delivery risk constituted by the cheapest-to-deliver option and delivery squeeze (covered in the Sections 6.3.4 and 6.3.5) and counterparty risk (covered in Chapter 8), CDS contracts are subject to several further risks that are worth mentioning:

- *Annuity risk*. Historically, CDS contracts have traded at market premiums, creating annuity risk between two opposite CDS contracts. Suppose one buys CDS protection paying 100 bps and then wishes to sell protection to lock in gains due to the CDS premium increasing to 150 bps. These gains are not completely hedged because there is a positive "carry" of 50 bps which is subject to interest rate risk and credit risk (if the credit event occurs then the remaining carry is lost). A second problem with unwinds is mismatched maturity dates that create marginal risks and imperfect hedges. Fixed premiums and standard maturity dates have been introduced to resolve these problems (see Section 6.3.7).
- *Economic loss but credit event not triggered*. Examples of this could be:
  - A debt-to-equity swap which may not trigger a credit event (or even if a credit event is triggered, protection buyers may not be able to find debt to deliver within the required 30-day period).

---

[5] Even after compression exercises.

- ○ A distressed exchange is also likely to create an economic loss but a credit event would only be triggered if there is a decrease in par value or coupon or a maturity extension in the context of the existing bond or loan (and all the holders are obliged to participate).
- ○ As discussed previously, a restructuring will probably result in an economic loss but would not trigger a credit event if the CDS contract specifies no restructuring.
- *Credit event triggered but no (or limited) economic loss*. This occurred in 2008 due to the conservatorship of Fannie Mae/Freddie Mac which triggered the bankruptcy clause without a bankruptcy filing. However, the bonds traded very close to par due to a delivery squeeze and the explicit guarantee by the US government. In this case, sellers of CDS protection faced costs due to settlement even though there was no economic loss.
- *Liquidity risk*. The liquidity of the CDS market in general can decline (as in 2007, for example, with dramatic effect). It is also important to consider that liquidity of a name declines as the spread widens – this is an important aspect for protection buyers hedging a name that becomes distressed.
- *Legal risk*. Credit event definitions must be well defined and understood as mistakes can give risk to significant risk.
- *Moral hazard*. The CDS market has been criticised for reducing the incentive for lenders to screen and monitor the credit quality of borrowers or counterparties. There is also the concern that protection buyers will push firms into bankruptcy in order to make economic gains (for example, see Soros, 2009). This is discussed again in Chapter 14.
- *Accrued interest*. In the event of default, a bond typically does not pay accrued interest whereas under standard CDS documentation, protection buyers must pay the accrued premium up to the credit event. This difference is small but will produce a loss for the hedger of a bond.
- *Funding*. CDS contracts require no funding so any funding cost in buying a bond and then hedging with CDS can be thought of as creating a cost on the hedge position.

Finally, we can identify an additional risk related to settled recovery which is specific to counterparty risk. Consider the hedge of a risky bond with a CDS where the reference entity suffers a credit event. Under physical delivery, one can transfer this bond to the protection seller in return for par and hence there exists a perfect hedge.[6] If the CDS is settled by an auction then it should be possible to sell the bond in the market for close to the auction price and still the hedge works well. But suppose one has a derivatives exposure to the reference entity which will not be recovered immediately (and may take a significant time). Then there is a potential mismatch between:

- *Settled recovery*. This is the recovery that is achieved following the credit event either from a CDS auction cash settlement mechanism or from simply trading the debt security in the market.
- *Actual recovery*. This is the actual recovery paid on the debt following a bankruptcy or similar process. This is the relevant recovery if one chooses not to sell the debt following a credit event and also applies to OTC derivatives.

---

[6] We note that there is some additional interest rate risk for fixed rate bonds due to the bond not trading at par as mentioned earlier. This is the same as the breakage of an interest rate swap in an asset swap.

Figure 6.10. Schematic illustration of recovery settlement after a credit event. The recovery rate relating to a CDS contract will be determined shortly after the relevant credit event whereas the actual recovery paid to creditors of the firm will be a significant time (potentially years) later.

In theory, settled and actual recoveries should be very similar but in reality, since bankruptcy processes take many years, they may differ materially. This is illustrated in Figure 6.10.

6.3.7 ISDA 2009, Big Bang Protocol, Small Bang Protocol and new trading conventions

In September 2006, ISDA first released a cash settlement protocol. A protocol involves a pre-planned auction of defaulted bonds to determine a price for cash settlement of CDSs. In 2009, there were a number of changes to CDS documentation and trading practices, aimed at reducing some of the risks described above and improving standardisation. These changes are summarised below.

The 2009 ISDA Supplement[7] has three main objectives:

- Establishment of credit derivatives determination committees. A determination committee (DC) will be comprised of dealers and will resolve credit event details (whether and when a credit event occurred, auction process, deliverable obligations and so on).
- The introduction of credit event and succession event backstop dates. Historically, in credit derivatives transactions, parties have the right to trigger the contract based upon events that occur between the effective date and the scheduled termination date, which can leave investors with basis risk due to trades with different effective dates. The 2009 Supplement creates a rolling effective date concept to create consistency across transactions.
- Incorporation of auction settlement provisions as the standard settlement method for credit derivatives transactions. The 2009 supplement hard-wires the CDS auction as a standard settlement method. The publication of the 2009 Supplement and the Big Bang Protocol is intended to standardise the auction settlement process across different credit derivatives transactions and credit events. The relevant DCs will decide whether to hold auctions in respect of each credit event and determine the necessary auction-specific terms. On 8 April 2009, ISDA incorporated the cash settlement auction into standard CDS documentation and over 2,000 dealers agreed to participate in incorporating this in existing CDS contracts via the Big Bang Protocol.

---

[7] For more details see *www.isda.org/credit*

Regarding the last point, since physical settlement potentially creates problems for hedging credit risk due to cheapest-to-deliver options and delivery squeezes, it is important to understand when auctions will not be held. In the following cases, auctions will not apply:

- restructuring credit events (a single auction may not apply but there may be multiple auctions according to the maturity bucket);
- illiquid reference entities;
- parties have not selected auction settlement in their confirmations;
- parties have not adhered to the Big Bang Protocol for older trades.

The 2009 ISDA Supplement applies to all future trades referencing the amended 2003 Definitions. Parties to existing trades that reference the previous definitions were able to amend these trades on a multilateral basis with all other adhering counterparties by adhering to the Big Bang Protocol. The Big Bang Protocol also covers future credit derivative transactions between 8th April 2008 and 31st January 2011 so that trading with previous documentation can still allow these changes to be incorporated.

At the same time as the above changes, the industry agreed a number of changes to US CDS contracts with European contracts later adopting similar changes (the so-called Small Bang Protocol). These changes are:

- *Fixed premium.* CDS contracts quoted with fixed premiums and upfront payments. This avoids annuity risk in the hedge and unwinding of CDS contracts. Although it is not compulsory, the standard is that CDSs on investment-grade reference entities will have a fixed premium of 100 basis points whilst high-yield reference entities will trade at 500 basis points. In Europe the fixed premiums used are expanded to 25, 100, 500, and 1,000 (with 300 and 750 also seen traded) basis points. Old trades would need to be renegotiated in order to adhere to these new fixed premiums.
- *Restructuring.* Trades on investment-grade credit (and fallen angels but not high yield) routinely included modified restructuring as a credit event but will now trade with no restructuring in the US. The European standard remains modified modified restructuring (MMR).
- *Scheduled termination dates.* These will be one of 20th March, 20th June, 20th September or 20th December.

The adoption of different restructuring standards in Europe and the US (MMR in Europe, no restructuring in the US) can be partially traced to the greater likelihood of debt restructuring of European names and restrictions over allowable capital reductions when hedging with CDSs in Europe.

6.4 ESTIMATING DEFAULT PROBABILITY

A critical component of assessing counterparty risk will be calculating the default probabilities (and their uncertainty) for all counterparties with which exposure or PFE exists. Here we review various methods of determining default probability, which may be relevant depending on the manner in which counterparty risk is to be managed

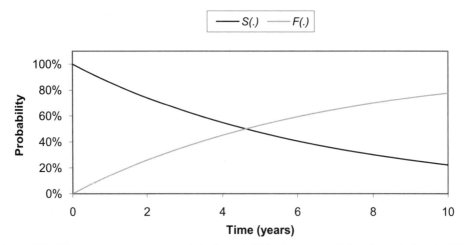

Figure 6.11. Illustration of cumulative default probability function, $F(u)$ and survival probability function $S(u)$.

(discussed in more detail in Chapter 12). Indeed, there is no "best" method to use for assessing default probability, there is only the most relevant choice depending on the ultimate risk management goal. Irrespective of the choice of approach, one must be cautious to understand the term structure (how default probability changes over time) due to the potentially time-inhomogeneous nature of credit exposure.

6.4.1 Defining default probability

In Appendix 6.A we define default probability in more mathematical detail. We will refer to the survival probability, $S(u)$, which gives the probability of *no default* prior to a certain time u (conditional upon no default at the current time). Alternatively, we may use the function $F(u) = 1 - S(u)$ to represent the cumulative probability of *default* prior to a certain time u (conditional upon no default at the current time). The survival and cumulative default probability functions are shown in Figure 6.11. Finally, we can consider a marginal default probability:

$$q(u_1, u_2) = S(u_1) - S(u_2) = F(u_2) - F(u_1) \qquad u_1 \leq u_2 \qquad (6.3)$$

which gives the probability of default between two future dates u_1 and u_2.

6.4.2 Historical estimation

Perhaps the most obvious assessment of default likelihood comes from examining historical data and using past default experience to predict future default likelihood. For example, in Table 6.5 we show default probabilities based on many years of data as published by Moody's (see Moody's Investors Service, 2007) and Standard & Poor's (see Standard & Poor's, 2008). Apart from the obvious conclusion that firms with good credit ratings default less often that those with worse ratings, we can also notice:

Table 6.5. Cumulative default probabilities, $F(u)$, by rating grade from both Moody's and Standard & Poor's rating agencies.

	Year	1	2	3	4	5	6	7	8	9	10
Triple-A	Moody's	0.00%	0.00%	0.00%	0.03%	0.10%	0.17%	0.25%	0.34%	0.42%	0.52%
	S&P	0.00%	0.00%	0.09%	0.19%	0.29%	0.43%	0.50%	0.62%	0.66%	0.70%
Double-A	Moody's	0.01%	0.02%	0.04%	0.11%	0.18%	0.26%	0.34%	0.42%	0.46%	0.52%
	S&P	0.01%	0.05%	0.10%	0.20%	0.32%	0.43%	0.56%	0.68%	0.78%	0.89%
Single-A	Moody's	0.02%	0.10%	0.22%	0.34%	0.47%	0.61%	0.76%	0.93%	1.11%	1.29%
	S&P	0.06%	0.17%	0.31%	0.47%	0.68%	0.91%	1.19%	1.41%	1.64%	1.90%
Triple-B	Moody's	0.18%	0.51%	0.93%	1.43%	1.94%	2.45%	2.96%	3.45%	4.02%	4.64%
	S&P	0.24%	0.71%	1.23%	1.92%	2.61%	3.28%	3.82%	4.38%	4.89%	5.42%
Double-B	Moody's	1.21%	3.22%	5.57%	7.96%	10.22%	12.24%	14.01%	15.71%	17.39%	19.12%
	S&P	1.07%	3.14%	5.61%	7.97%	10.10%	12.12%	13.73%	15.15%	16.47%	17.49%
Single-B	Moody's	5.24%	11.30%	17.04%	22.05%	26.79%	30.98%	34.77%	37.98%	40.92%	43.34%
	S&P	4.99%	10.92%	15.90%	19.76%	22.55%	24.72%	26.54%	28.00%	29.20%	30.42%
Triple-C	Moody's	19.48%	30.49%	39.72%	46.90%	52.62%	56.81%	59.94%	63.27%	66.28%	69.18%
	S&P	26.29%	34.73%	39.96%	43.19%	46.22%	47.49%	48.61%	49.23%	50.95%	51.83%

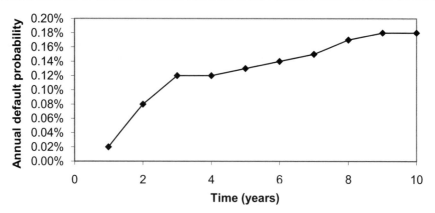

Figure 6.12. Annual historical default probabilities for Moody's A-rated firms computed using the data in Table 6.5. For example, the point at 3 years represents the default probability in the interval 2 years to 3 years which is $0.22\% - 0.10\% = 0.12\%$.

- Good-quality credits (investment-grade and above) tend to have default probability that increases strongly over time. For example, the 10-year Moody's triple-A (Aaa) default probability is more than five times the equivalent 5-year probability.
- Poor-quality ratings (sub investment-grade) tend to have default probabilities that increase much less strongly over time. For example, the 10-year single-B S&P default probability is only one-third higher than the 5-year probability.

> **Spreadsheet 6.1.** Analysis of historical default probabilities

From Table 6.5 we can compute quantities such as marginal default probability to illustrate the evolution of credit quality over time. For example, to calculate the (annual) default probability between 3 and 4 years we simply evaluate $q(3, 4) = F(4) - F(3)$. We show the annual default probabilities calculated in this way in Figures 6.12 and 6.13.

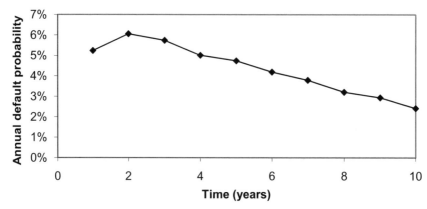

Figure 6.13. Annual historical default probability for Moody's B-rated firms computed using the data in Table 6.5. For example, the point at 6 years represents the default probability in the interval 5 years to 6 years which is $30.98\% - 26.79\% = 4.19\%$.

The graphs (Figures 6.12 and 6.13) can be explained by the mean reversion of credit ratings, indicating that historically good-quality firms tend to deteriorate and vice versa. Hence (conditioning on no prior default), a double-A firm is much more likely to be downgraded than upgraded whilst the reverse is true for an institution with a double-B rating. Such trends can be more easily seen when looking at transition matrices as shown in Table 6.6. Such matrices give the probability of moving from a given rating denoted by the left-hand column to any possible rating given across the top row. An institution can maintain the same rating, be upgraded or downgraded, default or have their rating withdrawn (WR). The last category is normally ignored although withdrawn ratings normally occur for negative reasons and so consequently this introduces some positive bias.

A final key point to consider when understanding the term structure of default probability is that poor-credit-quality firms have default probabilities concentrated in the short term, not necessarily because their credit quality is expected to improve over time. This is instead due to the simple fact that default in a future period can only be achieved by surviving to the start of this period. This point will be important when considering pricing and hedging aspects in Chapters 7 and 9, respectively.

6.4.3 Equity-based approaches

Equity-based approaches aim to estimate default probability from stock market information. In the classic Merton (1974) framework, the value of a firm (asset value) is considered stochastic and default is modelled as the point where the firm is unable to pay its outstanding liabilities when they mature. The original Merton model assumes that a firm has issued only a zero-coupon bond and will not therefore default prior to the maturity of this debt as illustrated in Figure 6.14. Through option-pricing arguments, Merton then provides a link between corporate debt and equity via pricing formulae based on the value of the firm and its volatility (analogously to options being valued from spot prices and volatility). The problem of modelling default is transformed into that of assessing the future distribution of firm value and the barrier where default would occur. Such quantities can be estimated non-trivially from equity data and capital structure information. A key contribution of the Merton approach is that low-frequency binary events can be modelled via a continuous process and calibrated using high-frequency equity data.

Spreadsheet 6.2. Implementation of Merton model

KMV^{TM} (now Moody's KMV) developed the Merton-style approach (for example, see Kealhofer and Kurbat, 2002 and Kealhofer, 2003) with the aim of predicting default via the assessment of 1-year default probability defined as EDF^{TM} (expected default frequency). The KMV approach relaxed many of the stylised Merton assumptions. Their approach can be broadly summarised in three stages:

- estimation of the market value and volatility of a firm's assets;
- calculation of the distance to default, which is an index measure of default risk;
- scaling of the distance to default to the actual probability of default using a default database.

The distance to default (DD) measure is a standardised distance from which a firm is away from default. A key element of the approach is to recognise the model risk inherent

Table 6.6. Historical transition rates (1-year) for Moody's-rated institutions.

	Aaa	Aa	A	Baa	Ba	B	Caa	Ca-C	Default	WR
Aaa	87.69%	7.38%	0.85%	0.16%	0.02%	0.00%	0.00%	0.00%	0.00%	3.90%
Aa	1.08%	85.96%	6.46%	0.68%	0.17%	0.04%	0.00%	0.00%	0.06%	5.55%
A	0.08%	2.76%	85.78%	5.23%	0.69%	0.11%	0.02%	0.01%	0.07%	5.26%
Baa	0.04%	0.29%	4.57%	81.77%	5.06%	0.78%	0.15%	0.02%	0.29%	7.03%
Ba	0.01%	0.09%	0.51%	5.75%	74.71%	6.75%	0.55%	0.05%	1.31%	10.29%
B	0.00%	0.06%	0.18%	0.64%	6.24%	72.45%	4.78%	0.51%	4.09%	11.05%
Caa	0.00%	0.03%	0.04%	0.23%	0.91%	7.90%	64.36%	3.62%	12.47%	10.44%
Ca-C	0.00%	0.00%	0.11%	0.00%	0.45%	3.01%	7.25%	56.74%	19.68%	12.76%

Source: Moody's Investors Service (2007).

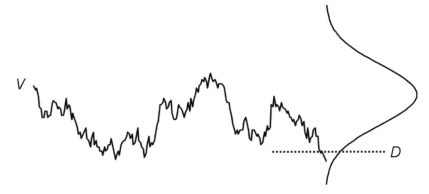

Figure 6.14. Illustration of the traditional Merton approach to modelling default based on the firm being below the face value of the debt (*D*) at maturity.

in this approach and rather to estimate the default probability empirically from many years of default history (and the calculated DD variables). For a firm with a DD of 4.0 (say), the question is how often have firms with the same DD defaulted historically? The answer is likely to be considerably higher than the theoretical result of 0.003%.[8] This mapping of DD to actual default probability could be thought of as an empirical correction for model error. Note that, although the KMV approach relies on historical data, the EDF measure will still be dynamic due to constantly changing equity data.

A more recent and related, although simpler, approach is CreditGrades[TM]. The aims of CreditGrades are rather similar to that of KMV except that the modelling framework (see Finger et al., 2002) is rather simpler and more transparent; in particular, there is no use of empirical data in order to map an eventual default probability. In CreditGrades, default probability is defined by a simple formula with just a few model parameters. For those against the use of complex models, CreditGrades is a candid (in the sense of model limitations) and open approach to a very difficult problem. However, the model risk inherent in such approaches should always be kept in mind.

Equity-based models for default probabilities have a place due to their ability to define default probability dynamically. This can be an advantage in a situation where historical default probabilities are considered too static a measure whilst probabilities defined directly from the credit market (discussed next) may be considered highly volatile and conservative due to the embedded risk premiums.

6.4.4 Market-implied default probabilities

In Appendix 6.B we show pricing formulas for CDSs and risky bonds and define mathematically the hazard rate of default at time u, h_u. The hazard rate defines the probability of default in a small[9] interval dt (conditional on no prior default before time u) as being $h_u \, dt$. The hazard rate is related to the cumulative default probability (or

---

[8] This arises since $\Phi^{-1}(-4.0) = 0.003\%$.
[9] Infinitely small interval to be exact.

equivalently the survival probability) via:

$$F(u) = 1 - S(u) = 1 - \exp(-hu). \tag{6.4}$$

(Here we have assumed a constant hazard rate, for a non-constant hazard rate the formula is given in Appendix 6.B.) In Appendix 6.B we show that an approximate relationship between the hazard rate and CDS premium is:

$$h \approx \frac{X_{\text{CDS}}}{(1 - \delta)}, \tag{6.5}$$

where X_{CDS} is the CDS premium (as a percentage) and δ is the assumed recovery rate (also a percentage). The above assumes that the CDS curve is flat (CDS premiums for all maturities are equal).[10] We can use equation (6.5) with the definition of survival probability to derive an approximate formula for the relationship between the cumulative default probability and the CDS premium at a certain maturity $T(X_T^{\text{CDS}})$:

$$F(T) = 1 - \exp\left[-\frac{X_T^{\text{CDS}}}{(1 - \delta)} T\right] \approx -\frac{X_T^{\text{CDS}}}{(1 - \delta)} T. \tag{6.6}$$

The above formula is a good approximation generally although to compute the implied default probabilities accurately we must solve numerically for the correct hazard rate, assuming a certain underlying functional form. The reader is referred to O'Kane (2008) for a more detailed discussion

---

Spreadsheet 6.3. Calculating market-implied default probabilities

---

Example. Suppose a reference credit has a CDS curve defined by the CDS quotes (100 bps, 150 bps, 200 bps, 250 bps, 300 bps) for CDS maturities (1Y, 2Y, 3Y, 4Y, 5Y) and an expected recovery rate of 40%. We obtain the hazard rates and cumulative default probabilities below.[11] We compare it with the approximate default probabilities given by equation (6.6) and show the annual default probabilities.

	Hazard rate	$F(T)$	$F(T)$ (approx.)	Annual default probability
1Y	1.658%	1.64%	1.65%	1.64%
2Y	3.352%	4.89%	4.88%	3.24%
3Y	5.155%	9.67%	9.52%	4.78%
4Y	7.089%	15.85%	15.35%	6.18%
5Y	9.220%	23.26%	22.12%	7.41%

We note that the annual default probabilities increase over time since the credit curve is increasing (upwards-sloping).

---

[10] It assumes also that CDS premiums are paid continuously, as discussed in Appendix 6.B.
[11] This assumes a piecewise constant representation of the hazard rate which means that the hazard rate is assumed constant between two adjacent CDS maturity dates.

6.5 PORTFOLIO CREDIT DERIVATIVES

In this final section, we give a brief overview of portfolio credit derivatives products such as index tranches and collateralised debt obligations (CDOs). A basic understanding of these structures is useful for the discussions on wrong-way counterparty risk in Chapter 8, monoline insurers and other aspects covered in Chapter 13. A more in-depth coverage of portfolio credit derivatives and their uses (and abuses) is given in Tavakoli (2008).

6.5.1 CDS index products

Up until 2004, the majority of credit default swaps were written on single names, but after the introduction of widely accepted credit indices in 2004, the major impetus to growth and liquidity of the credit derivative market has been credit default swaps on indices. A credit index can be usually thought of as an equally weighted combination of single-name CDSs and hence the fair premium on the index will be close to the average CDS premium within that index.[12] The two most common credit indices are:

- *DJ iTraxx Europe*. This contains 125 European corporate investment-grade reference entities, which are equally weighted.
- *DJ CDX NA IG*. This contains 125 North American (NA) corporate investment-grade reference entities that are equally weighted.

Other indices exist for different underlying reference entities and regions but they are less liquid. Indices can be traded in either CDS (unfunded) or CLN (funded) form. Buying CDS protection on $125m of the DJ CDX NA IG index is almost[13] equivalent to buying $1m of CDS protection on each of the underlying reference entities within the index.

An important feature of credit indices is that they "roll" every 6 months. A roll will involve:

- *Adjustment of maturity*. Typical traded maturities are 5 year, 7 year and 10 years. Fixed maturity dates[14] will be used such that the initial maturities are 5.25, 7.25 and 10.25 years. After 6 months the maturities will have become 4.75, 6.75 and 9.75 and these will be re-set to their original values.
- *Adjustment of portfolio*. Names will be removed from a credit index according to pre-defined criteria in relation to credit events, ratings downgrades and increase in individual CDS premiums beyond a certain threshold. The overall aim is to replace defaulted names and maintain a homogeneous credit quality. Names removed from the index will be replaced with other names meeting the required criteria.
- *Premium*. In the 6-month period before a roll, the index premium is fixed at a given level and trades on the index will involve an upfront payment from one party to the other to compensate for the difference between the fair premium and traded premium.

---

[12] This is not quite true for two reasons. First, there is a theoretical adjustment that must be made to the average CDS premium to account for the heterogeneity of the constituents. Second, the index will typically trade at a basis to the average CDS premiums (bid–offer costs will prevent arbitrage of this difference).

[13] Aside from the theoretical adjustment due to a premium mismatch and the fact that the index protection may involve an upfront payment.

[14] International Monetary Market (IMM) dates are used.

This greatly facilitates unwinded positions and monetarising MtM gains (or losses) and is similar to the switch to a fixed premium for US CDS contracts discussed in Section 6.3.7. At the roll, the index premium will be reset to something close to its fair theoretical level based on the individual CDS levels at that time.

We note that rolls only influence new trades and not existing ones (which still reference the old index and other terms).

6.5.2   Index tranches

Following on from the standardisation of credit indices was the development of index tranches. Whilst a credit index references all losses on the underlying names, a tranche will only reference a certain portion of those losses. So, for example, an $[X, Y\%]$ tranche will reference losses between $X\%$ and $Y\%$ on the underlying index. The "subordination" of the tranche is $X\%$ whilst $Y\%$ is referred to as the "detachment point". The size of the tranche is $(Y - X)\%$. The standard index tranches for the DJ iTraxx Europe and DJ CDX NA indices are illustrated in Figure 6.15.

The index tranche that takes the first loss, $[0–3\%]$, is referred to as the equity tranche, with the very high-up tranches referred to as senior or super senior and the intermediate tranches referred to as mezzanine. Although there is no standard terminology, we show one example naming convention in Table 6.7.

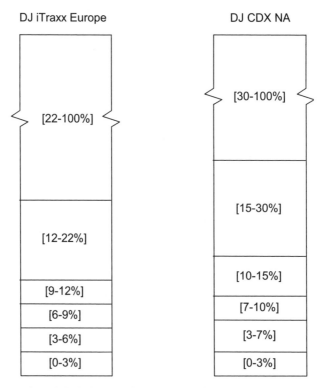

Figure 6.15. Illustration of the index tranches corresponding to the DJ iTraxx and DJ CDX North American credit indices. All tranches are shown to scale except the [22–100%] and [30–100%].

Table 6.7. Example naming convention for index tranches.

	DJ iTraxx Europe	DJ CDX NA
Index	[0–100%]	[0–100%]
Super senior	[22–100%]	[30–100%]
Junior super senior	[12–22%]	[15–30%]
Senior mezzanine	[9–12%]	[10–15%]
Mezzanine	[6–9%]	[7–10%]
Junior mezzanine	[3–6%]	[3–7%]
Equity	[0–3%]	[0–3%]

Like indices themselves, index tranches can be traded in both CDS and CLN form. The only additional point to mention is that the equity tranches ([0–3%]) have always traded with an upfront premium and fixed running spread of 500 bps to avoid the annuity risk that exists for such a relatively high-risk tranche. For iTraxx, more recently the [3–6%] and [6–9%] have changed to trade in the same way. The remaining tranches trade on a running basis. CDX tranches (which used to trade in a similar way to iTraxx) now trade at 500 basis points (bps) running for [0–3%], [3–7%] and [7–10%] and 100 basis points running for [10–15%], [15–30%] and [30–100%]. Example tranche quotes for iTraxx and CDX are shown in Table 6.8.

Table 6.8. Example tranche quotes for iTraxx and CDX investment-grade tranches at 5, 7 and 10-year maturities for 28th August 2009. The first three tranches in each case trade with a fixed 500-bps running coupon with the quote reflecting the upfront payment required. The final three iTraxx tranches trade with a variable coupon (shown in bps) only, whilst the final three CDX tranches trade at a fixed running coupon of 100 bps with the quote reflecting the upfront payment required. Upfront payments are negative when the fixed coupon is higher than the fair coupon.

DJ iTraxx Europe tranches

	5 Y	7 Y	10 Y
[0–3%]	38.00%	45.00%	50.75%
[3–6%]	2.000%	7.000%	12.750%
[6–9%]	−7.625%	−6.000%	−2.875%
[9–12%]	160	200	246
[12–22%]	66.5	92.0	101.5
[22–100%]	28.75	34.00	38.25

DJ CDX NA

	5 Y	7 Y	10 Y
[0–3%]	70.125%	76.250%	77.875%
[3–7%]	24.500%	32.375%	36.875%
[7–10%]	1.125%	6.000%	10.750%
[10–15%]	4.500%	9.438%	13.625%
[15–30%]	−1.280%	−1.150%	1.030%
[30–100%]	−2.300%	−3.400%	−4.800%

Irrespective of trading convention, the important aspect of an index tranche is that it covers only a certain range of the losses on the portfolio. Index tranches vary substantially in the risk they constitute: equity tranches carry a large amount of risk and pay attractive returns whilst tranches that are more senior have far less risk but pay only moderate returns. At the far end, super senior tranches might be considered to have no risk whatsoever (in terms of experiencing losses) but this is a point we will analyse in more depth in Chapter 8. Tranching creates a leverage effect since the more junior tranches carry more risk than the index whilst the most senior tranches[15] have less risk.

Example. An investor sells $10m of protection on the [3–7%] tranche of a 125-name index (for example, the DJ CDX NA) in CDS form. Since the contract is in CDS form, the investor will be paid a premium in basis points per annum on $10m notional.

Let us consider how many defaults are required to cause a loss. Since the investor is trading only 4% (7% − 3%) of the overall portfolio, the size of the full portfolio is $10m divided by 4% which is $250m. Hence, each name has a notional of $2m (250/125). Finally we also need to account for recovery. Assuming recovery of 40%, the actual loss on each name would be $1.2m (2 × 60%).

The size of the tranche is $10m (4% × 250) and the subordination is $7.5m (3% × 250). We can work out the number of defaults before the subordination has been wiped out:

$$7.5/1.2 = 6.25 \text{ defaults}$$

The investor will therefore suffer losses when 7 defaults have occurred but will only suffer 0.75 of the 7th default. The other 0.25 of this default passes to the equity tranche. After 7 defaults, the total loss is $7 \times 1.2 = \$8.4m$ and hence the loss to the investor is $0.9m.[16] The premium will now be paid on a notional of only $9.1m.

A similar analysis will determine that the tranche will be wiped out completely after 15 defaults. The table below shows the impact of defaults on the portfolio, assuming all recovery rates are 40%, and provides a summary of the losses.

Defaults	Portfolio loss	Tranche loss	Notional remaining	Defaults	Portfolio loss	Tranche loss	Notional remaining
0	0.0	0.0	10.0	8	9.6	2.1	7.9
1	1.2	0.0	10.0	9	10.8	3.3	6.7
2	2.4	0.0	10.0	10	12.0	4.5	5.5
3	3.6	0.0	10.0	11	13.2	5.7	4.3
4	4.8	0.0	10.0	12	14.4	6.9	3.1
5	6.0	0.0	10.0	13	15.6	8.1	1.9
6	7.2	0.0	10.0	14	16.8	9.3	0.7
7	8.4	0.9	9.1	15	18.0	10.0	0.0

---

[15] Due to its size usually only the super senior may have a leverage of less than 1 and all other tranches may be more highly leveraged than the index.

[16] With physical settlement they would be delivered $1.5m (2 × 0.75) of debt of the 7th reference entity to default and would recover the market value of this debt.

6.5.3 Super senior risk

As we shall see in Chapter 8, the more senior a tranche, the more counterparty risk it creates. Not surprisingly then, super senior tranches have created a big headache for the credit market in terms of their counterparty risk. Let us start by asking ourselves how many defaults would cause a loss for the super senior tranche of either DJ iTraxx and DJ CDX. Following from the previous example, we can represent the number of defaults a given tranche can withstand as:

$$\text{number of defaults} = n \frac{X}{(1 - \bar{\bar{\delta}})}, \tag{6.7}$$

where X represents the attachment point of the tranche in percent, n is the number of names in the index and $\bar{\bar{\delta}}$ is the (weighted[17]) average recovery rate for the defaults that occur.

Example. How many defaults can the super senior tranches of DJ iTraxx and DJ CDX withstand at assumed average recoveries of 40% and 20%?

From the previous formula we have for DJ iTraxx

$$125 \times 22\%/(1 - 40\%) = 45.8 \text{ defaults (40\% recovery)}$$

$$125 \times 22\%/(1 - 20\%) = 34.4 \text{ defaults (20\% recovery)}$$

and for DJ CDX

$$125 \times 30\%/(1 - 40\%) = 62.5 \text{ defaults (40\% recovery)}$$

$$125 \times 30\%/(1 - 20\%) = 46.9 \text{ defaults (20\% recovery)}$$

Super senior tranches clearly have very little default risk. Let us consider a super senior tranche of the longest maturity (10 years). From Table 6.5, the Moody's and S&P average cumulative default probabilities for the worst investment-grade rating of triple-B for this period are 4.64% and 5.42%, respectively. Then even assuming (conservatively) zero recovery, we still see the default rate over the 10-year period would have to be four to six times higher than the historical average to wipe out the subordination on the super senior tranches (for a 5-year trade, default rates of between eight and eleven times would be required). This default remoteness has led to terms such as "super triple-A" or "quadruple A" being used to describe the risk on super senior tranches since they constitute what we might call "end of the world" risk (this expression is not to be taken too literally but we will use it as a metaphor for super senior risk).

However, an institution needs to buy protection on end-of-the-world risk (we will describe in Sections 6.5.4 and 6.5.5 the motivation for doing this): What sort of counterparty do they need to trade with?

A final point to note on super senior tranches that detach at 100% losses is that they amortise with losses in the portfolio. When a name defaults then the notional of that name minus the recovery value is absorbed by the tranche as losses. The recovery value

---

[17] Since the default that actually hits the tranche may have only a fractional impact, as in the previous example.

is removed from the portfolio via an amortisation of the most senior tranche (i.e. the one detaching at 100%).

6.5.4 Collateralised debt obligations

There are many different types of collateralised debt obligations. They contain different asset classes and have different structural features. However, the approximate classification of risk defined in the last section (equity, mezzanine, senior) will always follow. For example, any CDO structure will have an associated super senior tranche that will be considered extremely unlikely ever to take credit losses.

CDOs can be broadly divided into two categories:

- *Synthetic CDOs.* Alternatively called collateralised synthetic obligations (CSOs), these are very similar to index tranches except that the underlying portfolio, attachment and detachment points, maturity and other specifics will be bespoke or tailor-made for a given transaction. Most commonly, a tranche will be traded in isolation from the rest of the capital structure. Banks have traditionally had large "correlation desks" that trade many different tranches of synthetic CDOs on various different portfolios.
- *Structured finance securities.* This very large class of securitisation structures covers cash CDOs, collateralised loan obligations (CLOs), mortgage-backed securities (MBSs) and CDOs of ABSs. The main difference between these structures and synthetic CDOs is that the structure and tranche losses occur by means of a much more complex mechanism. This means that tranches of these deals cannot be traded in isolation and all tranches must be sold more or less simultaneously[18] as a so-called "full capital structure" transaction.

From the point of view of counterparty risk, the key aspect is that all issuers of CDOs need to place (buy protection) on all tranches across the capital structure. In a full capital structure or structured finance-type structure this is clear from the need to place all of the risk. In a synthetic CDO it is less obvious but arises because a book cannot be risk-managed effectively unless it has a reasonable balance between equity, mezzanine and senior tranches. Therefore, issuers of CDOs are super senior protection buyers not necessarily because they think super senior tranches have value but rather because:

- They need to buy protection or place the super senior risk in order to have efficiently distributed the risk. Failure to do this may mean holding onto a very large super senior piece and potentially not being able to recognise P&L on a transaction.

OR

- Buying super senior protection is required as a hedge for other tranche positions. Without going into too much detail, we note that structured products traders may buy a product such as an option or tranche not because they think it is undervalued but

---

[18] Unless some can be "recycled" and put in the next structure, a practice that has become widely regarded as far from ideal from an investor's perspective.

rather because it allows them to hedge. In options terminology they may pay for the "gamma" (the convexity of the price with respect to market movements). In this case, a CDO correlation trader may buy protection on a super senior tranche not because he thinks it will have a payoff (losses hitting the tranche) but rather because it provides positive gamma.

See Chapter 13 of Tavakoli (2008) for a detailed description of the need for the creation of super senior tranches.

We are now back to our original question of from whom can you buy super senior protection? Let us in fact consider the range of investors across the full spectrum of seniority of index tranches and CDOs.

6.5.5   CDO investors

Given the dramatically different risk profiles across the tranche spectrum, as represented in Figure 6.15, there is not surprisingly a contrast to the different investors in tranche products. A CDO investor will take the risk on that given tranche and will therefore be a protection seller. Whilst tranches are highly specialised to the individual needs of investors, the investor spectrum can be broadly summarised as:

- *Equity tranches.* The most risky tranches which take the first losses on the portfolio and typically have no credit rating tend to fit the investment preferences of hedge funds since they typically have the appetite for the risk as long as the returns (typically easily in excess of 10% per annum) are suitable high. Institutions such as hedge funds will take equity risk in unfunded form to access the potentially high leverage offered. They will trade on a *collateralised* basis and also normally be required to post an *independent amount* against the protection they have sold to mitigate counterparty risk.
- *Mezzanine tranches (may include so-called senior tranches).* This represents the "sweet spot" in the capital structure since the mezzanine tranches can command a credit rating (often a strong one) given by the rating agencies whilst still paying a reasonable return. Most so-called "real money" investors will be interested in these tranches since they may give a reasonable risk/return profile (returns of 2% or 3% above the risk-free rate and an investment-grade rating). These products will often be structured on a funded basis, in which case they carry no counterparty risk for the issuer and little for the investor due to the SPV wrapper. If an investor sells protection on a mezzanine tranche in unfunded form via a CDS then they will be required to post *collateral* against potential market moves to reduce the counterparty risk for the issuer.
- *Super senior tranches.* Finally, we come to the most senior tranches in the structure. Whilst they generally have minimal default risk[19] as illustrated above, they correspondingly pay a relatively poor premium (historically in the region of 5 to 50 basis points per annum). Investors tend to be monoline insurance companies and (more recently) so-called CDPCs (credit derivative product companies). Super senior risk has also been sold to other investors via the so-called LSS or leveraged super senior

---

[19] Some so-called super senior tranches have indeed suffered losses but there are many that should be strongly expected to survive all but catastrophic market conditions.

structure. Monolines and CDPCs also tend to be highly leveraged with respect to the super senior risk they insure.[20] This means that they will trade in an unfunded manner, which potentially constitutes significant counterparty risk for the issuer. Interestingly, the way in which this counterparty risk is reduced is not via collateralisation but instead via the risk-takers (monolines and CDPCs) gaining triple-A ratings to provide confidence that they will never fail. However, there is a problem here: trading with a triple-A counterparty is certainly one way to minimise counterparty risk but it is key not to lose sight of the underlying risk that is being transferred. Buying super senior (super triple-A) protection from a triple-A counterparty is actually not particular safe. We explore this point in more detail in Chapter 8.

6.5.6   Rating of CDOs

The rating of CDOs and related products has been critical to their wide investor appeal. The key ratings agencies involved have been Moody's, Standard and Poor's and Fitch. Ratings approaches are generally highly quantitative and rely less on qualitative input. The statistical approaches used to assess ratings are highly subjective and depend on historical experience in some way being representative of future behaviour. A tranche may be given a triple-A rating due to its ability to withstand losses based on past experience. The same tranche may pay a substantial return due to the market prices of the underlying assets being favourable. Whilst it is not unreasonable to base credit ratings purely on historical data (ignoring current market parameters), this is clearly a slightly dangerous practice given the likely uncertainty in rating complex structured finance transactions. Hence, not surprisingly, the performance of high-rated tranches on many different types of transactions has been extremely poor – see Chapter 17 of Tavakoli (2008) for a frank description of the performance of rating agencies in assigned ratings to structured credit products.

More relevant to our perspective on counterparty risk, rating agencies have also provided the triple-A ratings that allow monolines and CDPCs to act as super senior protection sellers. This is a more complicated process because the rating should be based on not only the monoline or CDPC suffering losses that it cannot handle but also on the operating environment to which they must adhere. We will discuss this in more detail in Chapter 13.

6.5.7   Summary

In this chapter we have given an overview of credit risk and credit derivatives. Whilst most of the material is not integral to the understanding of counterparty risk, there are some key features to be understood. We have provided an understanding of the nature of credit spreads in relation to the traded products of credit default swaps, credit-linked notes, asset swaps and bonds. An assessment of default probability and recovery rates has been given, which is important in relation to our discussion of pricing in Chapters 7 and 8. A basic understanding of credit derivative structures will be useful since the counterparty risk of CDSs and tranches of credit portfolios will be considered in detail

---

[20] Being insurance companies, they have to take the risk via insurance contracts and not the sell of CDS protection that requires a derivatives instrument. However, the risk transfer process is equivalent.

in Chapter 8. Finally, in Chapter 13 we will look in detail at the counterparty risk of super senior protection sellers and an understanding of the mechanics of such tranches is therefore useful. Hence, much of the material in this chapter may be useful for reference at later stages in this book.

In Chapter 7 we combine the concepts of credit exposure and default probability to discuss the pricing of counterparty risk.

APPENDIX 6.A: DEFINING SURVIVAL AND DEFAULT PROBABILITIES

(i) Survival probability and default probability

The basic idea around pricing default-sensitive products is illustrated by considering a risky zero-coupon bond of unit notional and maturity T. We write the payoff at maturity as:

$$C(T, T) = \begin{cases} 1 & \text{no default} \\ \delta & \text{default} \end{cases}$$

where δ is an assumed recovery fraction paid immediately in the event of default. The price of a risky cashflow due at time T (assuming zero interest rates) is then:

$$C(t, T) = E[I(\tau > T) . 1 + I(\tau \leq T)\delta] = S(t, T) + [1 - S(t, T)]\delta$$

where $S(t, T) = E[I(\tau > T)]$ is the risk-neutral survival (no default) probability in the interval $[t, T[$ or, equivalently, $1 - S(t, T)$ is the risk-neutral default probability. This style of approach was developed by Jarrow and Turnbull (1992, 1995).

(ii) The hazard rate

In pricing a CDS or risky bond, the main issue is to define $S(t, u)$ for all relevant times in the future, $t \leq u \leq T$. If we consider default to be a Poisson process driven by a constant intensity of default then the survival probability is:

$$S(t, u) = \exp[-h(u - t)],$$

where h is the intensity of default, often described as the hazard rate. We can interpret h as a forward instantaneous default probability; the probability of default in an infinitely small period dt conditional on no prior default is $h\, dt$. Default is a sudden unanticipated event (although it may of course have been partly anticipated due to a high value of h).

APPENDIX 6.B: PRICING FORMULAS FOR CDSs AND RISKY BONDS

(i) Pricing a credit default swap (CDS)

In a CDS contract, the protection buyer will typically pay a fixed periodic premium, X_{CDS}, to the protection seller until the maturity date or the default (credit event) time.

The present value of these premiums at time t can be written as:

$$V_{\text{premium}}(t, T) = E\left[\sum_{i=1}^{m} I(\tau > t_i) B(t, t_i) \Delta_{i-1,i} X_{\text{CDS}}\right]$$

$$= \sum_{i=1}^{m} S(t, t_i) B(t, t_i) \Delta_{i-1,i} X_{\text{CDS}},$$

where m is the number of premium payments, $B(t, t_i)$ is the risk-free discount factor for time t_i as seen from time t and $\Delta_{i-1,i}$ represents the daycount fraction.

The protection seller in a CDS contract will undertake in the event of a default to compensate the buyer for the loss of notional less some recovery value, δ. The value of the default component obtained by integrating over all possible default times:

$$V_{\text{default}}(t, T) = -E[(1 - \delta) B(t, \tau) I(\tau < T)] = (1 - \delta) \int_{t}^{T} B(t, u)\, dS(t, u),$$

where we have assumed a constant recovery rate. Note that due to the required negative slope of $S(t, u)$, the above term will be negative and hence the sum of the previous two equations defines the value of a CDS from a protection provider's point of view. We note this by $V_{\text{CDS}}(t, T) = V_{\text{premium}}(t, T) + V_{\text{default}}(t, T)$.

(ii) Pricing a risky bond

Within a reduced-form framework, risky bonds can be priced in a similar way to CDSs:

$$V_{\text{bond}}(t, T) = \delta \int_{t}^{T} B(t, u)\, dS(t, u) + \sum_{i=1}^{m} S(t, t_i) B(t, t_i) \Delta_{i-1,i} X_{\text{bond}} + S(t, T) B(t, T).$$

The first term above is similar to the default payment on a CDS but assuming the bond will be worth a fraction δ in default. The second and third terms represents the coupon and principal payments on the bond, respectively. It is therefore possible to price bonds via the CDS market (or vice versa) and indeed to calibrate a credit curve via bonds of different maturities from the same issuer. However, the treatment of bonds and CDSs within the same modelling framework must be approached with caution. Components such as funding, the CDS delivery option, delivery squeezes and counterparty risk mean that CDSs and bonds of the same issuer will trade with a basis representing non-equal risk-neutral default probabilities. In the context of the formulas, the components creating such a basis, broadly speaking, represent different recovery values when pricing CDSs and bonds of the same issuer.

(iii) Link from hazard rate to credit spread

If we assume that CDS premiums are paid continuously[21] then the value of the premium payments can be written as:

$$V_{\text{premium}}(t, T) \approx X_{\text{CDS}} \int_t^T B(t, u) S(t, u) \, du.$$

Under the assumption of a constant hazard rate of default we can write $dS(t, u) = -hS(t, u) \, du$ and the default payment leg becomes:

$$V_{\text{default}}(t, T) = -(1 - \delta)h \int_t^T B(t, u) S(t, u) \, du.$$

The CDS spread will be such that the total value of these components is zero, hence from $V_{\text{premium}}(t, T) + V_{\text{default}}(t, T) = 0$ we have the simple relationship:

$$h \approx \frac{X_{\text{CDS}}}{(1 - \delta)}.$$

The above close relationship between the hazard rate and CDS premium (credit spread) is important in that the underlying variable in our model is directly linked to credit spreads observed in the market. Also, thanks to the definition of survival probability in terms of hazard rate (Appendix 6.A), we have the following approximation for the cumulative default probability up to a time u in terms of the CDS premium at that time X_u^{CDS}:

$$S(t, u) = 1 - F(t, u) = \exp\left[-\frac{X_u^{\text{CDS}}(u - t)}{(1 - \delta)} \right].$$

(iv) Simple formulas

Suppose we define the risk-free discount factors via a constant continuously compounded interest rate $B(t, u) = \exp[-r(u - t)]$. We then have closed-form expressions for quantities such as:

$$V_{\text{premium}}(t, T)/X_{\text{CDS}} \approx \int_t^T \exp[-(r + h)(u - t)] \, du = \frac{1 - \exp[-(r + h)(T - t)]}{r + h}.$$

The above expression allows a quick calculation for the value of a CDS, or equivalently a risky annuity (or DV01) for a particular credit.

(v) Incorporating term structure

For a non-constant intensity of default (h), the survival probability is given by:

$$S(t, u) = \exp\left[-\int_t^u h(x) \, dx \right].$$

To allow for a term structure of credit (for example, CDS premiums at different maturities) and indeed a term structure of interest rates, we must choose some functional

---

[21] CDS premiums are typically paid quarterly in arrears but an accrued premium is paid in the event of default to compensate the protection seller for the period for which a premium has been paid. Hence, the continuous premium assumption is usually a good approximation.

form for h. Such an approach is the credit equivalent of yield curve stripping although, due to the illiquidity of credit spreads, it is much less refined than was first suggested by Li (1998). The single-name CDS market is mainly based around 5-year instruments and other maturities will be rather illiquid. A standard approach is to choose a piecewise constant representation of the hazard rate to coincide with the maturity dates of the individual CDS quotes.

APPENDIX 6.C: PRICING OF INDEX TRANCHES

Here we give the basics of pricing index tranches and synthetic CDOs. Much more detail can be found in O'Kane (2008). The losses, $L(u)$, on a credit portfolio (or equivalently a credit index) at time u can be characterised by:

$$L(u) = \sum_{i=1}^{n} N_i (1 - \delta_i) I(\tau_i \leq u),$$

where N_i, δ_i and τ_i represent the notional amount, recovery rate and default time of name i, respectively. A tranche of a credit portfolio is characterised by losses occurring in a certain percentage range $[A, B]$. The loss on a tranche can be written as:

$$L(u; A, B) = \max[L(u) - A, 0] - \max[L(u) - B, 0].$$

A tranche with initial notional $M = B - A$ can be written in terms of premium and default legs in a similar way to a CDS as shown by Gregory and Laurent (2003):

$$V_{\text{premium}}^{\text{CDO}}(t, T) = E \left[\sum_{i=1}^{m} B(t, t_i) \Delta_{i-1,i} [M - L(t_{i-1}, A, B)]^+ X_{\text{CDO}} \right],$$

$$V_{\text{default}}^{\text{CDO}}(t, T) = E \left[\int_{t}^{T} B(t, u) \, dL(u, A, B) \right],$$

where the other terms above are as defined for a CDS in Appendix 6.A. The market standard model for pricing CDOs is the so-called "Gaussian copula model" attributed to Li (2000) but other more sophisticated models may also be considered.

7

Pricing Counterparty Credit Risk, I

> *"Do not worry about your difficulties in Mathematics. I can assure you mine are still greater."*
>
> Albert Einstein (1879–1955)

In Chapters 4 and 5 we discussed how to quantify credit exposure, whilst Chapter 6 concerned default probability. Now we proceed to combine these two components in order to address the pricing of counterparty credit risk. We will see that under certain commonly made assumptions it is relatively simple to combine default probabilities and exposures to arrive at an appropriate price for counterparty risk.

Accurate pricing of counterparty risk involves attaching a value to the risk of all outstanding positions with a given counterparty. This is important in the reporting of accurate earnings information and incentivising trading desks and businesses to trade appropriately. If counterparty risk pricing is combined with a systematic charging of new transactions, then it will generate funds that can be used to absorb potential losses in the event a counterparty defaults. Counterparty risk charges may also be associated with hedging costs in relation to credit risk aspects.

There have been many models proposed for pricing counterparty risk, which mostly cover the "classic" instrument types. For example, Sorenson and Bollier (1994), Jarrow and Turnbull (1992, 1995, 1997), Duffie and Huang (1996) and Brigo and Masetti (2005a) describe reduced-form models for counterparty risk and focus mainly on interest rate and foreign exchange products. Whilst there is a now a reasonably rich literature on pricing counterparty risk, it could be argued that many of the practical issues have been given only limited focus. In particular:

- Most models for pricing counterparty risk focus on specific instrument types and do not therefore account for netting effects.
- To a large extent, the literature ignores the treatment of collateral.
- Most theoretical papers on the pricing of counterparty risk do so from the point of view of risk-neutral valuation, as is standard for derivatives products. However, this point is debatable without a thorough analysis of hedging implications, which is why we dedicate Chapter 9 to hedging aspects.

Especially in the light of the credit crisis, there should be less focus on theoretical models for counterparty risk and more focus on the practical aspects. This will be our focus for this and Chapters 8 and 9.

7.1   PRICING COUNTERPARTY RISK

7.1.1   Motivation

Consider the following example:

> A trader wants to execute a swap transaction with a single-A counterparty whose outstanding debt is priced at a credit spread of around 300 basis points per annum. However, the size of the transaction is large ($1bn) and the maturity is long (10 years). The relevant credit officer is not comfortable with the transaction since he estimates that the exposure could easily reach $50m but the head trader is keen to proceed since profitability for the desk is excellent. Furthermore, the head of fixed income is also pushing to go ahead with this big trade since the counterparty is a good client trading across several different product areas. The trader has no credit background and cannot attempt to quantify the counterparty risk in the trade. There is a realisation by all concerned that the problem is more than simply deciding whether to trade or not. This trade should not be a simple yes/no decision.

In the above example, consider the following components that the trader concerned may have no knowledge or control over:

- The firm has potentially many other trades with the counterparty, which may be rather diverse and, thanks to netting, may lessen the risk of this new trade.
- The firm may have a collateral agreement (or could negotiate one given a large trade) with the counterparty that may further reduce the risk of this new trade.
- The default of the counterparty can be potentially hedged (at least to some degree) since it has debt trading in the market.

The following may be a better way to deal with the problem:

> Someone in the firm tells the trader what the cost of the counterparty risk should be, having considered the implications of exposure, default probability and accounting for all risk mitigation (netting, collateral, hedging). Only if the profit on the trade is *greater* than this cost should the trade go ahead. The trader's P&L will be reduced by this amount. Hence, the trader will be forced to factor in the cost of counterparty risk when pricing the original trade.

There are two key questions to answer:

- How to calculate theoretically the cost or price of the counterparty risk accounting for all risk mitigants such as netting and collateralisation.
- How to organise responsibilities and who within the firm should calculate the counterparty risk price.

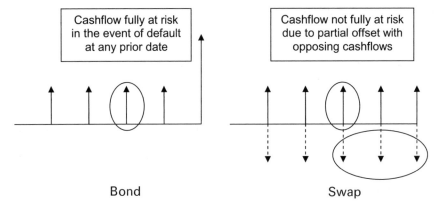

Figure 7.1. Illustration of the complexity when pricing the credit (counterparty) risk on a derivative instrument such as a swap, compared with an instrument such as a bond. In the bond the cashflow circled is fully at risk (less recovery) in the event of default of the issuer but in the swap the equivalent cashflow is not fully at risk due to the ability to partially offset it with current and future cashflows in the opposite direction (the three dotted cashflows shown circled).

In this chapter we will address the first point above and leave until Chapter 12 the discussion of the organisation aspects of pricing, hedging and managing counterparty risk.

7.1.2 Why pricing counterparty risk is not easy

Pricing the credit risk for an instrument with one-way payments, such as a bond, is relatively straightforward – one simply needs to account for default when discounting the cashflows and add any default payment (see Appendix 6.B for more technical details). However, many derivatives instruments have fixed, floating or contingent cashflows or payments that are made in both directions. It is this bilateral nature that characterises credit exposure and makes the quantification of counterparty risk dramatically more difficult. Whilst this will become clear in the more technical pricing calculations, a simple explanation is provided in Figure 7.1, which compares a bond with a similar swap transaction. In the bond case, a given cashflow is fully at risk (its value may be lost entirely) in the event of a default whereas in the swap case only part of the cashflow will be at risk due to partial cancellation with opposing cashflows. The risk on the swap is clearly smaller due to this effect.[1] However, the fraction of the swap cashflows that are indeed at risk is hard to determine as this depends on many factors such as forward rates and volatilities.

7.1.3 Credit value adjustment (unilateral)

Credit value adjustment[2] (CVA) is the key expression for defining counterparty risk. The full derivation is given in Appendix 7.A where we rigorously show that it is possible to

---

[1] It is also smaller due to the lack of a principal payment but this is a different point.
[2] Other names are sometimes used but this seems to be the most common name.

write the risky value of any number of transactions with a given counterparty as a combination of:

- The current risk-free value of the transactions(s). This is simply the sum of the individual transaction values whether those transactions are within a netting set or not.
- A term that is subtracted and accounts for the counterparty risk of the positions. We shall see that, unlike the term above, this term is not additive with respect to individual transactions. Hence, this term must be computed for each netting set and only these components are additive. This means that the risky value of a given transaction cannot be calculated individually, as it is defined with respect to other transactions within the *same* netting set.

The isolation of the above two terms is critical since it allows separation of responsibilities within a financial institution: one desk is responsible for risk-free valuation and one for the counterparty risk component. Derivatives and their associated counterparty risk may then be priced and risk-managed separately. In our above example the swap trader should be responsible for the first component (pricing the swap accurately as if it were risk-free) and may then rely on someone else in the institution to tell him what the counterparty risk charge or CVA should be.

7.1.4   Practical CVA formula (no wrong-way risk)

Wrong-way risk is dealt with in detail in Chapter 8. In this chapter we ignore any wrong-way risk, which amounts to assuming independence between default probability, exposure and recovery values. Under such assumptions the simplified CVA expression is presented in Appendix 7.B. This is given by:

$$\text{CVA} \approx (1 - \bar{\delta}) \sum_{j=1}^{m} B(t_j) \text{EE}(t_j) q(t_{j-1}, t_j). \qquad (7.1)$$

We can observe that CVA depends on the following components:

- *Loss given default*. The value of unity less the expected recovery fraction, $(1 - \bar{\delta})$, gives the loss given default. This is the percentage amount of the exposure expected to be lost if the counterparty defaults.
- *Discount factors*. The expression $B(t_j)$ gives the risk-free discount factor at time t_j. This is relevant since any future losses must be discounted back to the current time. It is sometimes hard to obtain risk-free discount factors that are not contaminated with some credit risk component and it should be emphasised that LIBOR rates have sometimes been above treasury bond yields. Indeed, in 2008, LIBOR rates, often regarded as the benchmark for risk-free borrowing, were several per cent higher than treasury rates.
- *Expected exposure (EE)*. The term $\text{EE}(t_j)$ is the expected exposure (EE) for the relevant dates in the future given by t_j for $j = 0, n \rightarrow m$. Calculating EE was the subject of Chapter 4.
- *Default probability*. The expression $q(t_{j-1}, t_j)$ gives the marginal default probability in

the interval between date t_{j+1} and t_j. Default probability estimation was covered in Section 6.4.

Hence, CVA simply depends on combining components from potentially different sources. For example, an exposure management team within a financial institution may compute EE, which is a market risk. The credit department and/or credit derivatives trading desk may provide loss given default and default probability information. Finally, the interest rate trading desk may provide the risk-free discount factors. Crucially, none of the areas needs to be aware of what the other is doing, as all the components are assumed independent.

A further important advantage of computing CVA via equation (7.1) is that default enters the expression via default *probability* only. This means that, whilst one may require a simulation framework in order to compute CVA, it is not necessary to simulate default events, only the exposures. This saves significantly on computation time by avoiding the need to simulate relatively rare default events.

Spreadsheet 7.1. Simple CVA calculation

In Table 7.1 we give an example of using the separate components described above to compute CVA according to equation (7.1). We use the implied default probabilities derived in Section 6.4.4 whilst the EE corresponds to that of a typical swap profile. In this case we have $m = 20$ (quarterly calculations) which will be reasonably accurate and may indeed be a limitation imposed by the systems in question only producing values at such an interval. The last column of Table 7.1 simply represents a multiplication of the four numbers and finally the sum of the CVA components gives the actual CVA. The EE is represented as a percentage of notional value and hence the CVA will be a percentage also. Therefore, for example, if the size of the trade were $10m then the CVA would be $20,899.

We emphasise that, under the assumption of no wrong-way risk, equation (7.1) provides a very efficient way to compute CVA from components that may already be calculated by a financial institution (exposures, default probabilities, discount factors and loss given default). Historically, for many institutions this route has been a very important way to price counterparty risk in a realistic and practical way.

7.1.5 CVA as a spread

Suppose that instead of computing the CVA as a stand-alone value, one wanted it to be expressed as a running spread (per annum charge). A simple calculation would involve dividing the CVA by the risky annuity for the maturity in question. For the previous calculation (Table 7.1), we would obtain[3] $0.209\%/4.32 = 0.048\%$ or 4.8 bps (basis points per annum).

In Appendix 7.C we derive an approximate formula for CVA that will be at least of intuitive interest and will also help in expressing CVA as a running spread. The formula assumes additionally that the EE is constant over time and equal to its average value

---

[3] The risky annuity approximation of 4.32 follows from Appendix 6.B. This is an approximation of the actual risky annuity of the swap that can be computed numerically via the sensitivity of the swap CVA to a small change in the swap rate.

Table 7.1. Example showing the components of CVA obtained from various systems and the overall calculation of CVA. The default probabilities are calculated assuming a CDS curve defined by the quotes (100 bps, 150 bps, 200 bps, 250 bps, 300 bps) for CDS maturities (1Y, 2Y, 3Y, 4Y, 5Y) and an expected recovery rate of 40%. The EE is defined by a typical swap profile as introduced in Chapter 4.

Time (years)	Loss given default	Discount factor	EE	Default probability	CVA component
0.00	60%	1.000			
0.25	60%	0.995	0.436%	0.41%	0.002%
0.50	60%	0.990	0.831%	0.41%	0.003%
0.75	60%	0.985	1.183%	0.41%	0.005%
1.00	60%	0.980	1.462%	0.41%	0.006%
1.25	60%	0.975	1.689%	0.82%	0.014%
1.50	60%	0.970	1.944%	0.81%	0.015%
1.75	60%	0.966	2.161%	0.81%	0.017%
2.00	60%	0.961	2.332%	0.80%	0.018%
2.25	60%	0.956	2.431%	1.21%	0.028%
2.50	60%	0.951	2.499%	1.19%	0.028%
2.75	60%	0.946	2.498%	1.18%	0.028%
3.00	60%	0.942	2.465%	1.16%	0.027%
3.25	60%	0.937	2.307%	1.56%	0.034%
3.50	60%	0.932	2.126%	1.53%	0.030%
3.75	60%	0.928	1.907%	1.51%	0.027%
4.00	60%	0.923	1.633%	1.48%	0.022%
4.25	60%	0.919	1.285%	1.87%	0.022%
4.50	60%	0.914	0.883%	1.83%	0.015%
4.75	60%	0.909	0.458%	1.79%	0.007%
5.00	60%	0.905	0.000%	1.75%	0.000%
				Total	0.209%

(EPE). This yields the following approximation based on this EPE:

$$\frac{\text{CVA}(t, T)}{\text{CDS}_{\text{premium}}(t, T)} = X^{\text{CDS}} \times \text{EPE}, \tag{7.2}$$

where $\text{CDS}_{\text{premium}}(t, T)$ is the unit premium value of a CDS (risky annuity) defined in Chapter 6 and X^{CDS} is the CDS premium corresponding to the maturity date T and hence can be thought of as a credit spread. The left-hand side of equation (7.2) therefore represents CVA as a running spread.

We can therefore quantify CVA from the right-hand side of equation (7.2). For the example shown in Table 7.1, calculating the average EE or EPE gives 1.63% and the 5-year CDS premium is 300 bps or 3%. Hence the CVA is obtained as $3\% \times 1.63\% = 0.049\%$ or 4.9 basis points per annum. The good accuracy can be explained by the fact that the exposure profile for the swap is rather symmetric so using the approximation that a single EPE can replace the exposure profile required for equation (7.2) overestimates the CVA in the short term and underestimates it in the longer term.

In the following cases, equation (7.2) will work well:

- EPE is reasonably constant over the whole profile.
- Default probability is reasonably constant over the whole profile.
- Either EE or default probability is symmetric over the whole profile such that there is a cancellation effect similar to that in the example above.

The third point is a little more subtle but the reader can use Spreadsheet 7.1 to gain further insight. In addition, this shows an example of a classic FX exposure and increasing default probability where the CVA is significantly underestimated by equation (7.2).

Returning to our example of the swap trader, we can illustrate why equation (7.2) might be very useful.

A trader needs to have a very quick idea of the CVA on the swap and has no time for complex calculations. The exposure management group work out that the EPE for a trade of this type is 5%. Since the credit spread of the counterparty is considered to be around 300 basis points per annum, the trader makes a very quick calculation of the CVA (as a running spread) as:

$$5\% \times 300 = 15\,\text{bps}.$$

The trader can now estimate approximately the P&L impact of this by pricing the same swap but paying 15 bps more on the pay leg (or receiving 15 bps less on the receive leg). Alternatively, the trader can add/subtract 15 bps to one leg of the trade as the credit charge or CVA.

The above calculations implicitly assume linearity in converting an upfront CVA to a running spread CVA. We should note that when adding a spread to a contract such as a swap, in theory the correct value should be calculated recursively (since the spread will be risky also) until the risky MtM of the contract is zero. Fortunately, such complexity is rarely required; for example, in the above example the CVA is almost linear with respect to the swap rate and therefore the simple approximation is very accurate as shown in Figure 7.2.[4] This will be a very small effect except for rather risky counterparties and large trades.

As counterparty risk became a common component of derivatives transactions from the late 1990s onwards, the above method of representing CVA would be rather common. For example, a bank might tell a corporate client that they would have to pay an extra X bps on a swap to cover the "credit charge" or CVA.

---

[4] Instead of using a risky annuity calculation, it is also possible to calculate the risky value for two different CVA spreads and then interpolate to find the correct CVA. For the same reason, this interpolated value will be very accurate.

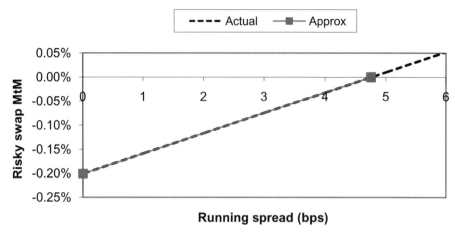

Figure 7.2. Illustration of approximation when converting a CVA to a running spread via a risky annuity calculation against the true behaviour of the risky MtM value. In this case, the approximation works almost perfectly due to the linear behaviour of the risky swap MtM: the approximation gives a CVA spread of 4.763 bps whilst the exact solution is 4.765 bps.

7.1.6   CVA semi-analytical methods

In the case of some specific product types, it is possible to derive analytical formulae for the CVA. Two commonly used examples are examined in Appendix 7.D. Whilst such formulas are of limited use since they do not account for netting or collateral, they are valuable for quick calculations and an intuitive understanding of CVA. With respect to the latter point, we would comment on the calculation of swap CVA as considered by Sorensen and Bollier (1994). These authors show that the counterparty risk on a swap can be expressed as a function of (reverse) swaptions with different exercise dates (Appendix 7.D). The intuition is that the counterparty might default at any time in the future and hence effectively cancel the non-recovered value of the swap, akin to exercising the reverse swaption.

The swap exposure and swaption analogy is illustrated in Figure 7.3. The expected exposure of the swap will be defined by the interaction between two factors: the swaption payoff and the underlying swap duration. These quantities respectively increase and decrease monotonically over time. The overall swaption value therefore peaks at an intermediate point.

> **Spreadsheet 7.2.** Semi-analytical calculation of the CVA for a swap

The Sorensen and Bollier formula gives us a very useful insight on CVA calculations, specifically that a CVA calculation will be at least as complex as pricing the underlying product itself. To price the swap CVA, one needs to know about swaption volatility (across time and strike), components far beyond those needed to price the swap itself. The value of the swap does not depend significantly on volatility and yet the CVA for the swap does.

7.1.7   How to calculate the EE for CVA

In Chapter 4 we discussed in detail how to quantify exposure, which covers the EE term in equation (7.1). Institutions will commonly take EE values from a risk management

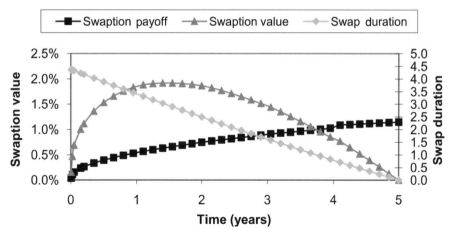

Figure 7.3. Illustration of swap CVA as defined by the sum of swaption payoffs. Note that the swaption payoff gives the expected exposure (EE) and the CVA is an integral involving the swaption payoff (EE) and default probabilities.

system, even though that system may have been set up for monitoring credit lines and not pricing counterparty risk. However, there is one caveat. For quantifying exposure for risk management, as discussed in Chapter 4, one should use the real probability measure whereas for pricing purposes the risk-neutral measure is commonly used. The risk-neutral measure, however, is justified by hedging arguments and hence its usage would imply that the CVA would be hedged. Unfortunately, the answer to the question as to whether CVA is hedged or not is usually not clear-cut since only certain aspects may be possible to hedge. The use of the risk-neutral versus real probability measure is an important point and hence will be discussed in more detail in Chapters 9 and 12.

7.2   PRICING NEW TRADES USING CVA

Being able to price the stand-alone CVA on a given transaction is useful for quick calculations but the need to account for risk mitigation such as netting and collateral is critical for any practical use of CVA.

7.2.1   CVA formula with collateral

Consider the influence of collateral on the standard CVA formula given in equation (7.1). The impact is to change only the EE (it does not change the default probability of the counterparty) and hence the same formula may be used with the EE based on assumptions of collateralisation, as covered in Chapters 4 and 5.

   To illustrate the impact of collateral, we have computed CVA corresponding to the EE profiles given previously (Chapter 5) where various different collateral assumptions were considered. The cases considered are ideal[5] collateralisation with a 10-day remargin period (EE shown in Section 5.4.4), the addition of a minimum transfer

---

[5] This means that, aside from the remargin frequency, collateral is posted (and returned) continuously, i.e. thresholds, independent amounts, minimum transfer amounts and rounding are ignored.

amount (Section 5.4.5) and the addition of a threshold (Section 5.4.6). These CVA calculations are compared with the case of no collateral and the results are shown in Table 7.2. The impact of collateral can reduce the CVA by over five times in the best case to just over half when there is a minimum transfer amount and threshold. The minimum transfer amount and threshold increase the CVA towards the no-collateral case, as would be expected.

Table 7.2. Illustration of CVA calculations for the EE profiles calculated with various collateral assumptions from Chapter 5. The CDS curve is assumed flat at 500 bps with a 40% recovery rate and constant interest rates of 5%.

Assumption	CVA (bps)
10-day remargin period	0.51
+ Minimum transfer amount of 0.5%	0.69
+ Threshold of 1.0%	1.57
No collateral	2.79

7.2.2 CVA formula with netting

To consider the impact of netting, the change in CVA, i.e. the CVA before and after a new trade has been executed, must be assessed. A new trade should be priced so that its profit *at least* offsets any increase in CVA. In other words, the risky value of the netted derivatives positions must not change. As shown in Appendix 7.E, we can derive the following formula:

$$V(i) = \text{CVA}(\text{NS}, i) - \text{CVA}(\text{NS}) = \Delta\text{CVA}_{\text{NS},i}, \qquad (7.3)$$

where $V(i)$ gives the risk-free value of the new trade i, $\text{CVA}(\text{NS})$ is the CVA on all existing trades within the same netting set and $\text{CVA}(\text{NS}, i)$ is the CVA included in the new trade in the netting set. Due to the properties of netting we must have $\Delta\text{CVA}_{\text{NS},i} \le \text{CVA}_i$, i.e. the impact trade i has on the netting set CVA must be no more than its individual CVA. Equation (7.3) defines that the profit (loss) made on the transaction must offset the increase (decrease) in the total CVA when adding the new trade.[6] If the increase in CVA is negative (due to favourable netting effects as described in Chapter 4), it may be possible to execute a trade at a loss due to the overall gain from CVA reduction.

To price a new trade with the impact of netting, one must calculate the change in CVA, termed the *incremental CVA* that the new trade will create. As with the case of collateral, this depends only on the EE and hence virtually the same formula as before

---

[6] We can note that if we charge for CVA by changing a parameter in the trade (such as a swap rate), in theory we must solve equation (7.3) in a non-linear fashion since the change in CVA will alter as we change the rate in the new transaction. However, as illustrated previously in Figure 7.2 this is generally a very small impact and can therefore be ignored.

will apply with just the incremental EE (ΔEE) replacing the EE:

$$\Delta\text{CVA} \approx (1 - \bar{\delta}) \sum_{j=1}^{m} B(t_j)\Delta\text{EE}(t_j)q(t_{j-1}, t_j), \qquad (7.4)$$

where $\Delta\text{EE}(t_j)$ represents the incremental change in EE at each point in time caused by the new trade whilst the other terms are as defined for equation (7.1). Incremental EE can be negative due to beneficial netting effects.

We emphasise the relationship defined above that, due to the properties of EE and netting (discussed in Chapter 3), the CVA in the presence of netting will never be higher than the CVA without netting (except in the bilateral CVA cases discussed later – see also Duffie and Huang, 1996). The practical result of this is that an institution with existing trades under a netting agreement will be likely to offer conditions that are more favourable to a counterparty with respect to a new trade. Cooper and Mello (1991) first quantified such an impact, showing specifically that a bank that already has a claim on a counterparty can offer a more competitive rate on a forward contract.

Whilst CVA calculations for single products are relatively simple and in some cases analytical formulae exist, the treatment of netting is more complex. Whilst some attempts have been made at handling netting analytically (for example, Brigo and Masetti, 2005b), CVA calculations incorporating netting require a general Monte Carlo simulation for exposures and resulting EE calculations. However, note that under equation (7.1) one does not have to simulate default events as mentioned before.

We illustrate the computation of CVA with netting by returning to the exposure examples shown in Section 4.4.3. Consider we are pricing the CVA on a new deal, a 5-year interest rate swap where we pay fixed and receive floating (IRS payer). We consider the impact of netting on the CVA of this new transaction as if there were already three different transactions with the counterparty. The CVA calculations are shown in Table 7.3.

Table 7.3. Incremental CVA calculations for a 5-year IRS payer with respect to three different existing transactions and compared with the stand-alone value. The CDS curve is assumed flat at 500 bps with a 40% recovery rate and constant interest rates of 5%. CVAs are given as percentages of deal notional and as a running spread (in basis points per annum) calculated by solving equation (7.3).

Existing trade	Incremental CVA	Incremental CVA (as a spread)
None (stand-alone calculation)	0.085%	2.36 bps
6-year IRS payer	0.084%	2.33 bps
6-year IRS receiver	−0.054%	−1.50 bps
Cross-currency swap	0.043%	1.19 bps

We can make the following observations:

- The incremental CVA is never higher than the stand-alone CVA (which assumes no netting benefit due to existing trades). This is not surprising since in Chapter 4 we saw that netting could not increase exposure.

- The incremental CVA is only slightly reduced for a very similar existing trade (6-year IRS payer). This follows from the high positive correlation between the two trades.
- The incremental CVA can be negative due to the strong negative correlation between the new trade and the 6-year IRS receiver. This implies that the risk-free value of the trade could be negative as implied by equation (7.3) but the overall impact of the trade is positive (if the change in CVA offsets the negative trade value). A trader may therefore expect a positive P&L in this situation due to reducing the overall risk to the counterparty in question and may therefore execute a trade with otherwise unfavourable terms. We discuss the mechanics of this in Chapter 12.
- In the case of netting against existing exposures that are not highly positively or negatively correlated to the new trade, as in the case of the cross-currency swap, then the CVA is still positive but significantly reduced compared with the stand-alone value.

7.2.3   Netting and trade size

The benefit of netting seen in the incremental CVA of a new trade depends also on the relative size of the new transaction. As the transaction size increases, the netting benefit is lost and the CVA will approach the stand-alone value. This is illustrated in Figure 7.4, which shows the incremental CVA of the 5-year IRS payer examined in Table 7.3 as a function of the relative size of this new transaction. In the base case (100%), the CVA is 1.19 bps, which approaches the stand-alone value of 2.36 bps as the transaction size increases. For a smaller transaction, the CVA decreases to a lower limit of 0.40 bps.

7.2.4   Marginal CVA

Whilst incremental CVA is important for pricing a new trade vis-à-vis existing trades, it might not always be the most useful measure. Consider the example at the top of the facing page.

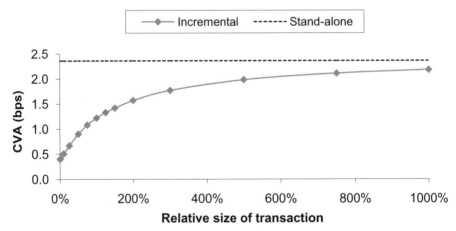

Figure 7.4. Incremental CVA (as a spread in basis points per annum) for a 5-year IRS payer with respect to an existing cross-currency swap as a function of the relative size of the new IRS transaction. The case of 100% corresponds to the value of 1.19 bps and the stand-alone value is 2.36 bps (Table 7.3).

Example. As part of a large transaction with a client, there are two trades being executed simultaneously, one with the interest rate desk and one with the foreign exchange desk. The total CVA number (measured on the full notional in basis points per annum and therefore to be compared with the average of individual CVAs) is 1.9 bps. The stand-alone CVA values are 2.4 and 2.6 bps, which have an average higher than the total CVA. However, the incremental CVAs of each trade in isolation are only 1.2 bps and 1.4 bps, which give an average of less than the total CVA. Hence, it is not clear how to allocate CVAs to the relevant trading desks.

Incremental risk measures are not additive and so, as shown in the above example, it is not possible to split the CVA numbers up into additive components. This makes it difficult to price trades transacted at the same time[7] (perhaps due to being part of the same deal) with a given counterparty.

By using a marginal CVA measure, it will be possible to break down a CVA for any number of netted trades into trade level contributions that sum to the total CVA. The mechanism for doing this follows directly from the marginal EE discussed in Chapter 4. Since CVA is just a linear combination of EE, then replacing the marginal EE in equation (7.4) will lead to a marginal CVA calculation.

As an example, we have computed marginal and incremental CVAs for a netting set of four trades, also used in the Chapter 4 analysis (Section 4.4.3) and the previous example (Table 7.3) with the results shown in Table 7.4. The sum of the marginal CVAs (3.79 bps) is also the total CVA[8] whereas the sum of the incremental CVAs is very different and essentially meaningless. The marginal CVA also shows that the 6-year payer and IRS receiver exactly cancel one another whereas the incremental results do not suggest this. Using the measure of marginal CVA, it is possible to drill down from the total CVA to look at the contribution from each individual trade. This is very useful in understanding the trades that contribute most to the CVA for a given counterparty.

Table 7.4. Incremental and marginal CVAs for a netting set of interest rate (IRS) and cross-currency swaps (CCS). The results are shown in basis points per annum (bps) on the total notional of all trades. Note that the total CVA is 3.79 bps.

	Stand-alone	*Incremental*	*Marginal*
5-year IRS payer	2.38	1.19	1.68
6-year IRS payer	3.44	1.21	2.32
6-year IRS receiver	2.35	−2.70	−2.32
Cross-currency swap	2.60	1.41	2.11
Total		*1.11*	*3.79*

---

[7] This could also cover a policy where CVA adjustments are only calculated periodically and several trades have occurred with a given counterparty within that period.
[8] To aid comparison, since the CVAs are expressed on a running basis, the total CVA is represented on a single-transaction notional with all transactions scaled to have the same notional.

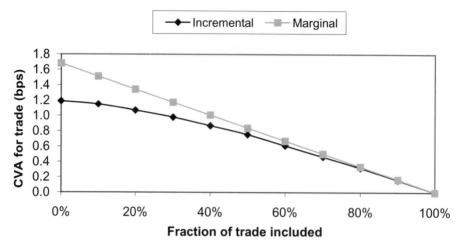

Figure 7.5. Comparison of marginal and incremental CVA numbers for the 5-year IRS payer from the example in Table 7.4.

In Figure 7.5 we show the comparison between marginal and incremental CVA calculations for the 5-year IRS payer. As the swap is removed gradually, the impact on the overall CVA becomes less significant leading to an eventual incremental CVA of 1.21 bps. The marginal CVA measures the impact on the total CVA of a small change in the size of the swap (the slope of the incremental CVA at 100%) leading to a higher value of 1.68 bps.

To summarise, incremental CVA (1.19 bps in the above example) is useful for looking at the impact of adding (or removing) a given trade to (from) the netting set of three existing trades. On the other hand, marginal CVA (1.68 bps) is more relevant for apportioning CVA contributions fairly across existing trades or assessing the CVA of more than one new trade. Both incremental and marginal CVA numbers will be less than or equal to[9] the stand-alone CVA (2.38 bps).

7.2.5 Exotic products

Calculating CVA on exotic derivatives can be highly challenging, which is not so surprising due to the previous intuition that calculating the CVA on a product is at least as complex (and often more complex) as pricing the product itself. Valuation of exotic products can be rather slow, requiring Monte Carlo or lattice-based modelling. Since each EE value needed in order to calculate CVA requires a rather large number of simulations (see Chapter 4), then this will probably be beyond realistic computational resources. Many pricing functions[10] used by traders may be inadequate to calculate EE.

Approximation to exotics products may be required in order to estimate their associated CVA values. Often simple approximations can be made; for example, a swaption

---

[9] Except in the case of bilateral CVAs discussed in Section 7.3.
[10] Exotic products in this context could imply any product that does not admit a very simple pricing formula (such as a swap or simple option).

might be treated as a forward swap (see Section 4.2.7) or a Bermudan product may be approximated by a European-style payoff. Knock-in and knock-out features may be assumed to have either triggered or not with 100% probability. Often, many of the approximations used will be chosen as a conservative representation of the future exposure.

Alternatively, methods such as described by Gordy and Juneja (2008) can be utilised to have a more efficient calculation of EE values. Such an approach makes use of the fact that, in exposure calculation, the *distribution* of instrument values is the key element to be estimated. Given this, the other uncertainties in quantifying CVA and associated hedging issues, using approximations for exotic products, should not be of great concern.

7.2.6 Path dependency

Path dependency in CVA calculations presents a problem since, in order to assess a future exposure at a certain date, one must have information about the entire path from now until that date. This aspect was discussed in Chapter 4 (for example, see the exposure profile of the swaption discussed in Section 4.2.7 showing that in a path-by-path simulation of exposures, such path dependency can be dealt with).

As shown in equation (7.1), the calculation of CVA will be approximated with reference to EE calculated at discrete points in time. Whilst this may be acceptable for certain kinds of path dependencies (for example, Bermudan swaptions), exotic derivatives prices are often based on a continuous sampling of quantities (for example, barrier options). Such cases will also require approximations such as those introduced by Lomibao and Zhu (2005) who use a mathematical technique know as a Brownian Bridge to calculate probabilities of path-dependent events that are intermediate to actual exposure simulation points. Again, we would argue that using such reasonable approximations for path-dependent products, whilst not perfectly accurate, should not be of great concern when put in the context of other uncertainties.

7.3 BILATERAL COUNTERPARTY RISK

7.3.1 Background

CVA has traditionally been a charge for counterparty risk that is incorporated in a transaction in favour of the stronger credit quality counterparty. Historically, banks trading with corporate counterparties have charged CVAs linked to the credit quality of the corporate and the exposure in question. A corporate would not have been able to credibly question such a charge since the probability that a bank would default was considered remote (and indeed the credit spreads of banks have traditionally been very tight and the credit ratings very strong). The suggestion that a large bank such as Lehman Brothers would default was until 2008 a laughable concept.

Now let us fast-forward to the credit crisis beginning in 2007. Gradually, the idea of "default-free" counterparties became laughable in itself and credit spreads of the "strong" financial institutions widened dramatically. Consider the following situation:

A corporate client has traded with a top-tier bank for a number of years. The credit ratings and credit spreads of each institution are as follows:

	Credit rating	Credit spread
Bank	Aa1/AA+	10–15 bps
Corporate	A3/A−	200–300 bps

The bank will always charge a CVA to the corporate on trades and will be transparent about the calculation; for example, explaining the quantities used to come up with the CVA and also giving benefit due to collateral and netting agreements that are in place. The corporate is quite used to the CVA charges (and one-way collateralisation that is also required by the bank) and has never been concerned that the bank could ever default. Now, during the credit crisis, the bank's own credit spread has widened to a level that is comparable with that of the corporate (the credit rating is unchanged but that offers little reassurance). The corporate believes that it should not be paying any significant CVA charge and indeed may even by able to make an argument for charging a CVA themselves. Of course, this means the bank would have to reduce their CVA charge significantly.

Question: How can the bank reduce the price of counterparty risk when the credit market is becoming more risky? What would be the economics behind such a reduction?

Question: How can two counterparties of similar credit quality ever agree to trade since they cannot both pay a CVA charge?

7.3.2 Bilateral CVA

A trend that has become increasingly relevant and popular, especially since the credit crisis started in 2007, has been to consider the bilateral nature of counterparty risk. This means that an institution would consider a CVA calculated under the assumption that they, as well as their counterparty, may default. In Appendix 7.F we derive the formula for bilateral CVA (BCVA) under these conditions. The definition of BCVA follows directly from that of unilateral CVA with the assumption that the institution concerned can also default. We obtain the following expression under the assumption of no simultaneous defaults[11] or wrong-way risk:

$$\text{BCVA} \approx +(1 - \bar{\delta}) \sum_{i=1}^{m} B(t_i)\text{EE}(t_i)S_I(t_{i-1})q(t_i, t_{i-1})$$

$$- (1 - \bar{\delta}_I) \sum_{i=1}^{m} B(t_i)\text{NEE}(t_i)S(t_{i-1})q_I(t_i, t_{i-1}), \qquad (7.5)$$

where the above terms are as defined previously – equation (7.1) – with $S(.)$ and $S_I(.)$ representing the survival probabilities of the institution and counterparty, respectively; $q_I(.)$ and $\bar{\delta}_I$ representing the default probability and recovery of the institution; and $\text{NEE}(.)$ representing the negative expected exposure (the EE from the point of view of

---

[11] This means one party will default first and the corresponding payments settled before the other party defaults.

the counterparty). Equation (7.5) is essentially a generalisation of equation (7.1) by assuming that the institution in question may default also. The first term in the BCVA formula is close to the usual CVA term but containing an additional multiplicative factor based on the institution's own survival probability. This is not surprising since an institution can argue that they should not consider losses due to their counterparty defaulting in scenarios where they themselves have defaulted first.

The second BCVA term is a mirror image of the first term and represents a negative contribution – this is often known as DVA (debt value adjustment). It corresponds to the fact that in cases where the institution defaults (before their counterparty), they will make a "gain" if the MtM is negative (a "negative exposure"). A gain in this context might seem unusual but it is, strictly speaking, correct since in default the institution will pay their counterparty only a fraction (recovery) of what they owe them. (Using the Sorensen and Bollier analogy, the institution is then also long a series of swaptions.)

There are some very important and attractive implications of the BCVA formula:

- The BCVA can be negative (if the second term is larger in magnitude than the first) unlike the CVA which is always positive. A negative BCVA implies that the risky value of a derivative (or netting set of derivatives) is *greater* than the risk-free value.
- If two counterparties agree on the approach and parameters for calculation of BCVA then they will agree on a price by the symmetry of equation (7.5). If one counterparty calculates BCVA from their point of view to be $+X$ then the other will calculate it to be $-X$. The latter counterparty will then pay the former an amount of $+X$ to compensate them for the counterparty risk.
- The impact of CVA caused by netting will not always be advantageous; in particular, if the second term in equation (7.5) dominates. This normally corresponds to a situation where the institution in question is more risky than their counterparty. Without netting, an institution can cherry-pick contracts, requiring those with a positive MtM to be settled and leaving those with a negative MtM as liabilities in the bankruptcy process. The lack of netting is clearly advantageous in this case.
- If all counterparties in the market agree on the approach and parameters for calculation of BCVA then the total amount of counterparty risk in the market (as represented by the sum of all BCVAs) will be zero. Again, this follows from the symmetry of equation (7.5).

7.3.3 Example

We now show an example of a BCVA calculation similar to that described by Gregory (2009). In order to understand the overall impact of bilateral pricing, three distinct CVA measures are considered as outlined below:

- *CVA:* this is the standard unilateral CVA formula given by equation (7.1).
- *Adjusted CVA:* this is the unilateral CVA but taking into account the default probability of the institution, i.e. this is the first term in equation (7.5). This will always be less than[12] the CVA above since it includes multiplication by survival probabilities that must be no greater than unity.

---

[12] Or equal to in the case the institution has a zero default probability.

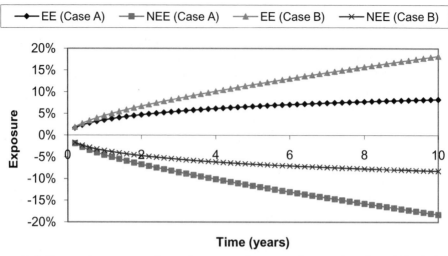

Figure 7.6. Expected exposure and negative expected exposure for case A and case B in the BCVA example.

- *BCVA:* the bilateral CVA given by equation (7.5). This will be less than the adjusted CVA and may be negative due to the second negative term in the formula.

Two cases are considered for which the exposure profiles (expected exposure and negative expected exposure) are shown in Figure 7.6:

- *Case A:* the institution has a default probability based on a flat CDS curve of 500 bps that is approximately double that of their counterparty whose CDS premium is at 250 bps. Furthermore the future MtM is skewed in the institution's favour, i.e. they are more likely to have a liability in the future (the NEE is larger than the EE).
- *Case B:* the opposite situation, i.e. both default probabilities and exposures reversed. This would therefore represent the counterparty's view of case A.

The results showing the three different CVA measures described above are shown in Table 7.5.

Table 7.5. Unilateral and bilateral CVA values for case A and case B under the assumption of independence of defaults and no wrong-way risk.

	Case A	Case B
CVA	1.235%	3.480%
Adjusted CVA	0.799%	2.766%
BCVA	−1.967%	1.967%

The adjusted CVA values are considerably smaller than the basic CVAs due to the reasonably high probability that the institution might default before its counterparty.

The relative reduction of adjusted CVA is greater in case A due to the higher default probability of the institution in this case.

Regarding bilateral CVA, case A represents a situation where the BCVA is negative due to the institution's higher default probability and the high chance that they will owe money on the contract (negative exposure). Case B is the opposite case and, since the counterparty is more risky than the institution, the BCVA is still positive although reduced by almost a half compared with the unilateral case. We see that since Case A and case B represent equal and opposite scenarios for each party, the sum of the bilateral adjustments is zero. This would correspond to parties agreeing on a CVA charge if they both use BCVA.

The above example assumes independence between the default probability of the institution and the counterparty. More details of similar calculations and the impact of correlation and joint default can be found in Gregory (2009).

7.3.4 BCVA formula from credit spread

In Section 7.1.5 we discussed a very simple CVA formula linked to the credit spread of the counterparty. A similar formula for BCVA is derived in Appendix 7.G and presented below:

$$\frac{\text{BCVA}(t,T)}{\text{CDS}_{\text{premium}}(t,T)} = \frac{\text{CVA}(t,T)}{\text{CDS}_{\text{premium}}(t,T)} - X_I^{\text{CDS}} \times \text{ENE}, \qquad (7.6)$$

where X_I^{CDS} represents the institution's own CDS spread and ENE represents the expected negative exposure (the exact opposite of EPE and defined mathematically in Appendix 7.E). As before, the $\text{CDS}_{\text{premium}}(t,T)$ term just means that the BCVA is represented as a running spread. This formula requires several approximations but, like equation (7.2), is reasonably accurate in the majority of cases. The intuition of equation (7.6) is basically that an institution may account for their own default by reducing the unilateral CVA charge according to their own credit spread multiplied by the ENE.

A trader needs to have a very quick idea of the BCVA on a swap. The EPE for a trade of this type is 5% whilst the ENE is 3%. Since the credit spread of the counterparty is considered to be around 300 basis points per annum and the credit spread of the trader's own institution is 200 basis points per annum, a very quick calculation of the BCVA is:

$$5\% \times 300 - 3\% \times 200 = 11 \text{ bps}.$$

Compared with the previous example, we can see that the BCVA is reduced from the (unilateral) CVA calculation of 15 bps. Hence, the trader may charge the counterparty 11 bps effectively for the overall counterparty risk.

Suppose the trader is looking instead at the reverse trade. In this case, the EPE and ENE will be reversed and the BCVA will be:

$$3\% \times 300 - 5\% \times 200 = -1 \text{ bps}.$$

Therefore, the trader will now need to pay the counterparty 1 bps to cover the overall counterparty risk that they take. Note that, although the trader's institution has a better credit quality, they still incur a CVA change due to the fact that the ENE in this case is significantly higher than the EPE (the institution is more likely to have a liability than their counterparty).

In the above cases, we assume the counterparty is using the same methodology and parameters and will hence come up with the opposite figures of -11 bps and $+1$ bps.

Referring to the above example, we make the following statements about BCVA compared with unilateral CVA:

- BCVA will always be smaller than CVA since the institution is pricing a "gain" from their future default.
- In general, BCVA is expected to be positive if the counterparty is more risky than the institution (their credit spread is greater) and negative otherwise.
- BCVA also depends on symmetry of future MtM (magnitude of EPE compared with ENE) although this is less likely to be as significant as the spread impact, as in many situations the EPE and ENE will be reasonably similar. Some products can have highly asymmetric future MtM, examples being cross-currency swaps and credit default swaps discussed later (Chapters 9 and 8, respectively).

7.3.5 BCVA or CVA?

With unilateral CVA, theoretically two counterparties will never agree to the terms of a new transaction since they will both seek to add a counterparty risk charge. Using bilateral CVA to price counterparty risk is compelling, largely since it has a symmetry that allows the counterparties to agree on a price.

However, the reader may rightly be concerned with the concept that an institution is attaching value to their own default and that a risky derivative can be worth more than the equivalent risk-free derivative. We would urge caution in relation to the use of BCVA in pricing counterparty risk for the simple reason that the second term in equation (7.5) is not easy to realise. This argument is discussed in more detail in Gregory (2009) who considers the ways in which a counterparty can in reality make a gain according to the BCVA term that relates to their own default:

- *File for bankruptcy.* An institution can obviously realise the BCVA component by going bankrupt but, since the component is directly related to their default, it only serves to increase the likely recovery value and not improve the credit quality of a firm in any other way. In fact, this becomes a circular argument; consider a firm with a bilateral counterparty benefit so substantial that it can prevent their bankruptcy. Yet bankruptcy may be the only way to realise[13] this gain!
- *Get very close to bankruptcy.* The institution may realise the BCVA component if a trade is unwound at some point probably due to their heavily declining credit quality. For example, as discussed further in Chapter 8, some monolines have gained from

---

[13] This might mean that shareholders would not consider BCVA to be relevant since it can only be realised in bankruptcy where they expected their investment to be worthless. Boldholders, however, may consider some benefit due to an enhanced recovery in default.

banks unwinding senior credit insurance. Such unwinds have represented large CVA-related losses for banks and associated CVA gains for monolines. However, we would suggest that an institution would need to be in severe financial distress and not expected to survive before being able to recognise gains in this way. Indeed, one way of interpreting the failure of monolines is through a naive use of bilateral counterparty risk pricing.

- *Return paid on collateral.* As discussed in Section 3.7.8, a giver of cash collateral is normally paid an overnight rate (such as EONIA in Europe). However, in certain situations, institutions have offered to pay in excess of this rate in order to encourage counterparts to post collateral in cash. If the receiver of collateral agreed to pay an overnight rate plus the spread of the institution giving the collateral then this would provide a means for that institution to monetarise the BCVA. Whilst paying the spread of the collateral giver might seem strange, this is aligned with the cost of buying CDS protection as a means to hedge an uncollateralised exposure.
- *Hedging.* We discuss this issue more in Chapter 9 but in summary, since a firm cannot sell CDS protection on themselves, it is hard to realise the BCVA component via hedging.
- *Funding arguments.* The argument that, whilst EPE represents a long-term receivable, ENE represents a long-term payable providing some funding benefit has also been used to justify bilateral CVA.

Take the scenario where two counterparties, each with significant default risk, find it difficult to trade with one another since they both wish to charge a positive (unilateral) CVA. Consider two solutions to the problem:

(1) Both counterparties price using bilateral CVA. This means they will agree on a price and the counterparty with the negative BCVA will effectively pay the other counterparty for what is essentially the overall net CVA. This counterparty will not be making any charge for counterparty risk, indeed they will actually be paying in order to trade.
(2) The counterparties realise that they are both taking significant risk to one another and *both* need to consider the implications of this and mitigate it as strongly as possible through netting, collateralisation, trading through a centralised clearing house or other risk mitigation techniques.

We would suggest that solution 1 is a quick fix to the problem whilst solution 2 is the correct but much more challenging solution to implement.

The question of bilateral CVA can be further generalised by asking if a firm's view that their own debt is too heavily discounted represents an economic profit for them. Credit value adjustments have allowed banks, for example, to book substantial gains by marking down the value of their own debt. If a firm takes the view that their debt is undervalued, as with BCVA, the question is how to realise this profit. The possible options could be:

- *Go bankrupt.*
- *Buy back debt cheaply with cash.* This is a valid argument except that in a crisis when a firm's credit spread is widening there is likely to be a shortage of cash.

- *Buy back debt by issuing new debt*. This does not work since market forces should price the new and old debt equivalently.
- *Buy back the debt synthetically*. This can be done using, for example, an asset swap (or total return swap but in this case the other party to the TRS will have significant counterparty risk). Whilst synthetic buybacks are relatively normal, they allow a firm to adjust its capital structure synthetically without the market prices of its securities adjusting naturally (since market participants do not need to be made aware of the synthetic buyback). Hence, it could be argued that synthetic buybacks are not beneficial for the efficiency and transparency of financial markets.

A firm buying its own debt can hedge the BCVA component since they will make money on BCVA when their spread widens but lose money on the debt position and vice versa. However, by buying their own debt in the market they should improve their own credit spread, leading to a loss due to BCVA increasing.

How to boost profits with accounting tricks

In the first quarter of 2008, a bank reported a loss of around $1bn, which was not as bad as analysts had expected. The bank had marked down the value of the debt on their books by $2.5bn dollars and therefore reduced their losses substantially.

(This is a true story although the name of the bank has not been included.)

An institution booking profits from their own declining credit quality, either due to the debt held on their books or with respect to derivatives via a bilateral counterparty risk adjustment is a subject that may be fiercely debated in the future. Consider the following quote[14] regarding the booking of gains by an institution based on their own default probability:

"It's not the kind of stuff you'd point to in earnings and say 'now that's sustainable income'. You would want to exclude it from earnings in evaluating how well a company performed."

In August 2009, this story became even more obscure as banks' own credit risk actually began to hamper their financial results. The above concept of including the default probability of an institution in the valuation of its liabilities had a significant impact on banks' profits in the first half of 2009, as credit default swap (CDS) premiums of referencing banks narrowed.[15]

7.3.6 BCVA and break clauses

In Chapter 3 we discussed break clauses or early termination options (ETOs) as a means to mitigate counterparty risk. Suppose an institution has a trade with a

---

[14] This is taken from the weblog published by Jack Ciesielski, dealing with accounting issues and news topics related to investment and finance, *www.accountingobserver.com*

[15] Banks' own credit risk hampers financial results, 5th August 2009, *www.risknews.net*

counterparty whose credit quality has declined significantly and hence the BCVA is extremely large and positive. The institution may want or need to unwind this transaction but, since their counterparty will have an equal and opposite BCVA, they would require this amount to be paid in order for the transaction to be terminated. In other words, the institution will be forced to unwind the transaction far away from market rates due to BCVA pricing. On the other hand, if there is an ETO or break clause then they can legally require an unwind at market rates. They would then gain since their positive BCVA would disappear along with the transaction. The situation is illustrated in Table 7.6. The cost of unwinding the transactions would normally be zero for both parties, reflecting a payment of X made by the institution to their counterparty. However, if there is an ETO, then the institution makes a gain of $+X$ since they can unwind the transaction without paying the BCVA and the counterparty makes a corresponding loss. A break clause or ETO should therefore be exercised at the first available opportunity by whichever party has the increasing BCVA.

Table 7.6. Illustration of unwind of transactions using BCVA calculations with or without an ETO. Assuming a transaction is marked-to-market with a BCVA adjustment, the cost to unwind the transaction will be zero. However, an ETO will allow an institution with a positive BCVA to gain (negative cost) via unwinding without any counterparty risk adjustments.

	BCVA	Unwind BCVA payment	Cost to unwind transaction (no ETO)	Cost to unwind transaction (with ETO)
Institution	$+X\%$	$+X\%$	—	$-X\%$
Counterparty	$-X\%$	$-X\%$	—	$+X\%$

7.3.7 BCVA and unwinding trades

A contrary example to that given above has been realised in the case of banks unwinding trades[16] with monolines (where X is of the order of billions of US dollars) in 2008/2009. As will be discussed in more detail in Chapters 9 and 13, such unwinds were forced upon banks by the realisation that these deals contained huge amounts of counterparty risk and the related point that monolines were in severe financial difficulty.[17]

Let us illustrate the impact of BCVA on unwinding a transaction with a simple example. We assume the expected exposure and negative expected exposure profiles shown in Figure 7.7. These are highly asymmetric reflecting, for example, the exposure of an instrument such as a cross-currency swap (discussed in more detail in Chapter 9) or a credit default swap (discussed in Chapter 8).

In Table 7.7 we show example BCVA calculations for differing CDS premiums of both an institution and their counterparty using the EE and NEE from Figure 7.7.

---

[16] Such transactions typically did not have any break clauses. Even if they did then they probably would not have helped in this situation unless they were activated very early on before monolines became severely financially distressed. This effect would be even stronger since it was accompanied by an increase in EE and decrease in NEE because the insurance purchased from monolines was extremely valuable.

[17] We can note that a break clause would have been of no use since the monolines were unable to settle the transactions at market rates.

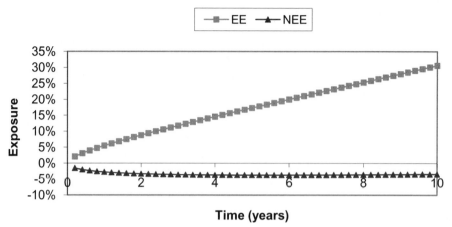

Figure 7.7. Illustration of expected exposure and negative expected exposure for the example described in the text.

Assume, for example, that case 1 corresponds to initiation of the trade. Although the counterparty is five times less risky than the institution, the BCVA is zero due to the highly skewed exposure profile. Suppose now that both parties become more risky but the counterparty's credit quality deteriorates more rapidly.[18] We see that the institution has a strongly positive BCVA and would need to compensate their counterparty by this amount to have any hope of unwinding the transaction. Furthermore, an institution in this situation would make a MtM loss due to increasing BCVA in this scenario unless hedged properly with respect to both its own and its counterparty's CDS premium (this is discussed in more detail in Chapter 9).

Table 7.7. Example BCVA calculations for the expected exposure and expected negative exposure calculations shown in Figure 7.7 as a function of the institution and counterparty CDS premiums (in bp pa).

	Case 1	Case 2	Case 3
Counterparty CDS premium	5	100	700
Institution CDS premium	25	100	200
BCVA	0.00%	1.11%	4.68%

7.3.8 Walkaway features

As described in Section 2.3.5, derivatives transactions have sometimes been traded with the (non-standard) feature that allows the transaction to be terminated in the event that the counterparty defaults. A walkaway feature means that an institution can gain from a negative MtM (liability) in the event that their counterparty defaults. On the other hand, assuming the walkaway feature is bilateral, the counterparty may also walk away from a positive MtM from the institution's perspective in the event that they default.

---

[18] This was the case with monolines and banks (in this case counterparty and institution, respectively) in the 2007–2008 period.

The BCVA formula under the assumption of a bilateral walkaway feature is derived in Appendix 7.H. In Table 7.8 we show the previous CVA calculations (Table 7.5) under the assumption of a bilateral walkaway agreement. Recall that case A corresponds to the institution being more risky than their counterparty and having a greater chance of a negative MtM whilst case B is the opposite scenario.

Table 7.8. Illustration of the impact of walkaway features on unilateral and bilateral CVAs computed using the parameters from Section 7.3.3.

	Case A		Case B	
	Base case	*Walkaway*	*Base case*	*Walkaway*
Unilateral (CVA)	1.235%	0.232%	3.480%	2.471%
Bilateral (BCVA)	−1.967%	−1.587%	1.967%	1.587%

Walkaway features reduce unilateral CVAs due to the gain that can be made. In case A the CVA is reduced substantially since the walkaway feature has significant value for the institution. In case B the value of the walkaway feature is similar since, whilst the chance of the institution having a liability is lower (ENE smaller than EPE in case B, see Figure 7.6), the default probability of the counterparty is higher. Indeed, a walkaway feature could cause even a unilateral CVA measure to become negative if the expected MtM in the future is sufficiently skewed in an institution's favour.

The impact of bilateral walkaway features on BCVA represents a balance between two components, the beneficial walkaway for the institution[19] less the negative benefit that their counterparty might walk away. We see that the overall magnitude of BCVA is reduced by walkaway features. In case A, BCVA is negative due to the significant chance that the institution may default but this high default probability means that there is also a net walkaway benefit in favour of the counterparty, hence the walkaway features reduce the BCVA benefit from −1.967% to −1.587%. In case B the positive BCVA is reduced in the institution's favour for similar reasons.

7.4 SUMMARY

This chapter has been concerned with the pricing of counterparty risk and we have described the way of doing this via an adjustment (CVA) to the risk-free value of a derivative or set of netted derivatives. The computation of CVA has been detailed from the commonly made simplification of no wrong-way risk, which assumes that the credit exposure, default of the counterparty and recovery rate are not related. We have shown the relevant formulas for computing CVA in their simplest possible forms (all the details can be found in the appendices to this chapter which can be considered by the reader to be optional). The concepts of incremental and marginal CVA have been introduced and illustrated in order to provide a means to price new or existing trades. We have discussed specifics of calculating CVA, including collateral and netting and covered some more complex aspects such as exotic products and path dependency. We have outlined

---

[19] This will therefore represent a negative term since CVA represents a cost.

bilateral CVA and discussed whether it is appropriate to use this to price counterparty risk. Finally, break clauses and walkaway agreements have been analysed.

In Chapter 8 we will continue to discuss pricing counterparty risk but will relax the assumption of independence between exposure and default probability. This will enable us to consider the case of wrong-way risk, which is particularly important for some specific cases and the general assessment of counterparty risk for credit derivative products.

APPENDIX 7.A: DERIVING THE EQUATION FOR CREDIT VALUE ADJUSTMENT (CVA)

We wish to find an expression for the risky value, $\tilde{V}(t, T)$, of a netted set of derivatives positions with a maximum maturity date T. Denote the risk-free value (current MtM) of the relevant positions as $V(t, T)$ and the default time of the counterparty as τ. Then $V(s, T)$ $(t < s \le T)$ will denote the future uncertain MtM accounting for discounting effects.

There are two cases to consider.

(1) Counterparty does not default before T

In this case, the risky position is equivalent to the risk-free position and we write the corresponding payoff as:

$$I(\tau > T)V(t, T),$$

where $I(\tau > T)$ is the indicator function denoting default (this takes the value 1 if default has not occurred before or at time T and zero otherwise).

(2) Counterparty does default before T

In this case, the payoff consists of two terms, the value of the position that would be paid *before* the default time (all cashflows before default will still be paid by the counterparty) plus the payoff at default.

(i) Cashflows paid up to the default time

$$I(\tau \le T)V(t, \tau).$$

(ii) Default payoff.

Here, if the MtM of the trade at the default time, $V(\tau, T)$, is positive then the institution will receive a recovery fraction (δ) of the risk-free value of the derivatives positions whilst if it is negative then they will still have to settle this amount. Hence, the default payoff at time τ is:

$$I(\tau \le T)(\delta V(\tau, T)^+ + V(\tau, T)^-),$$

where $x^- = \min(x, 0)$ and $y^+ = \max(y, 0)$.

Putting the above payoffs together, we have the following expression for the value of the risky position (we use the risk-neutral measure, as is common when pricing derivatives, although this point will be discussed in more detail later in Chapter 9):

$$\tilde{V}(t, T) = E^Q[I(\tau > T)V(t, T)$$
$$+ I(\tau \leq T)V(t, \tau)$$
$$+ I(\tau \leq T)(\delta V(\tau, T)^+ + V(\tau, T)^-)].$$

The above expression is general but not especially useful or even insightful. However, re-arranging and using the relationship $x^- = x - x^+$ we obtain:

$$\tilde{V}(t, T) = E^Q[I(\tau > T)V(t, T)$$
$$+ I(\tau \leq T)V(t, \tau)$$
$$+ I(\tau \leq T)(\delta V(\tau, T)^+ + V(\tau, T) - V(\tau, T)^+)]$$
$$= E^Q[I(\tau > T)(t, T)$$
$$+ I(\tau \leq T)V(t, \tau)$$
$$+ I(\tau \leq T)((\delta - 1)V(\tau, T)^+ + V(\tau, T))].$$

Now, realising that we can combine two terms since $V(t, \tau) + V(\tau, T) \equiv V(t, T)$ we have:

$$\tilde{V}(t, T) = E^Q[I(\tau > T)V(t, T)$$
$$+ I(\tau \leq T)V(t, T)$$
$$+ I(\tau \leq T)((\delta - 1)V(\tau, T)^+)].$$

Finally, since $I(\tau > T)V(t, T) + I(\tau \leq T)V(t, T) \equiv V(t, T)$, we have:

$$\tilde{V}(t, T) = V(t, T) - E^Q[(1 - \delta)I(\tau \leq T)V(\tau, T)^+].$$

The above equation is crucial since it defines the risky value of a netting set of derivatives positions with respect to the risk-free value. The relevant term is often known as CVA (credit value adjustment). It is an adjustment to the risk-free value of the positions within the netting set to account for counterparty risk:

$$\tilde{V}(t, T) = V(t, T) - \text{CVA}(t, T)$$
$$\text{CVA}(t, T) = E^Q[(1 - \delta)I(\tau \leq T)V(\tau, T)^+].$$

Note that we made the assumption that the future MtM value, $V(s, T)$, includes discounting for notational simplicity. If we drop this assumption, the above formula will include discounting:

$$\text{CVA}(t, T) = E^Q\left[(1 - \delta)I(\tau \leq T)V(\tau, T)^+ \frac{\beta(t)}{\beta(\tau)}\right],$$

where $\beta(s)$ is the value of the "money market account" at time s.

APPENDIX 7.B: APPROXIMATION TO THE CVA FORMULA IN THE CASE OF NO WRONG-WAY RISK

Here, we derive a commonly used approximation to the CVA formula that depends on the assumption of no wrong-way risk or, more specifically, no dependence between recovery rate, default and exposure.

We start from the expression for CVA derived in Appendix 7.A:

$$\text{CVA}(t, T) = E^Q[(1 - \delta)I(\tau \leq T)V(\tau, T)^+].$$

Assume there is no dependence between the recovery value and either the exposure or default event. We can then write:

$$\text{CVA}(t, T) = (1 - \bar{\delta})E^Q[I(\tau \leq T)V(\tau, T)^+],$$

where $\bar{\delta}$ is the mean or expected recovery value. Since the expectation in the above equation is over all times before the final maturity, we can integrate over all possible default times (similar to pricing a credit default swap in Chapter 6). We obtain:

$$\text{CVA}(t, T) = -(1 - \bar{\delta})E^Q\left[\int_t^T B(t, u)V^*(u, T)^+ \, dS(t, u)\right],$$

where $B(t, u)$ is the risk-free discount factor and $S(t, u)$ is the survival probability for the counterparty (probability of no default) as described in Chapter 6. We use $V^*(u, T)$ to denote:

$$V^*(u, T) = V(u, T) \, | \, \tau = u.$$

This is a critical point in the analysis as the above statement requires the exposure at a future date, $V(u, T)$, *knowing* that default of the counterparty has occurred at that date $(\tau = u)$.

For now, we will make the assumption for now that $V^*(u, T) = V(u, T)$ which is assuming no relationship between counterparty default and exposure (knowing the counterparty is in default does not change the expected value of the underlying positions). The case where $V^*(u, T)$ is different from $V(u, T)$, often described as wrong-way risk, will be dealt with in Chapter 8.

Assuming no wrong-way risk and that the discount factors and survival probabilities are deterministic, we have:

$$\text{CVA}(t, T) = -(1 - \bar{\delta})\left[\int_t^T B(t, u)\text{EE}(u, T) \, dS(t, u)\right].$$

We recognise the exposure term as being the EE calculated under the risk-neutral measure denoted by $\text{EE}(u, T) = E^Q[V(u, T)^+]$. Finally, we could compute the above equation via some integration scheme such as:

$$\text{CVA}(t, T) \approx (1 - \bar{\delta})\sum_{i=1}^m B(t, t_i)\text{EE}(t, t_i)[S(t, t_{i-1}) - S(t, t_i)],$$

where we have m periods given by $[t_0(= t), t_1, \ldots, t_m(= T)]$. As long as m is reasonably large (for example, 12 steps per year) then this will be a good approximation.

APPENDIX 7.C: APPROXIMATION LINKING CVA FORMULA TO CREDIT SPREAD

Here we show that, with further simplifying assumptions, one can obtain a simple expression for CVA linked to the credit spread of the counterparty. We start from the general formula for CVA given in Appendix 7.B and assuming no wrong-way risk:

$$\mathrm{CVA}(t, T) = -(1 - \bar{\delta})E^Q\left[\int_t^T B(t, u)\mathrm{EE}(u, T)\, dS(t, u)\right].$$

Suppose that we approximate the expected exposure term, $\mathrm{EE}(u, T)$, as a fixed known amount, we then obtain:

$$\mathrm{CVA}(t, T) = -(1 - \bar{\delta})E^Q\left[\int_t^T B(t, u)\, dS(t, u)\right]\mathrm{EPE}.$$

The fixed EPE (defined in Chapter 3) would most obviously be computed from the EE averaged over time, for example:

$$\mathrm{EPE} = \frac{\displaystyle\int_t^T \mathrm{EE}(u, T)\, du}{T - t} \approx \frac{1}{m}\sum_{j=1}^m \mathrm{EE}(t, t_j).$$

Clearly, the approximation will be a good one if the relationship between EPE, default probability (and indeed discount factors) is reasonably homogeneous through time. In the chapter we give an example where the approximation works very well and discuss cases where it will not be accurate (see also Spreadsheet 7.1).

Recalling from Chapter 6 that the simplified default leg of a credit default swap (CDS) is:

$$\mathrm{CDS}_{\mathrm{default}}(t, T) = (1 - \bar{\delta})E^Q\left[\int_t^T B(t, u)\, dS(t, u)\right].$$

We get:

$$\mathrm{CVA}(t, T) = \mathrm{CDS}_{\mathrm{default}}(t, T) \times \mathrm{EPE}.$$

Now we divide both sides of the equation by the unit premium leg of a CDS:

$$\frac{\mathrm{CVA}(t, T)}{\mathrm{CDS}_{\mathrm{premium}}(t, T)} = \frac{\mathrm{CDS}_{\mathrm{default}}(t, T)}{\mathrm{CDS}_{\mathrm{premium}}(t, T)} \times \mathrm{EPE} = X^{\mathrm{CDS}} \times \mathrm{EPE}.$$

The above results shows that the CVA as a spread (per annum) can be simply written as the market CDS premium X^{CDS} multiplied by the EPE.

APPENDIX 7.D: SPECIFIC APPROXIMATIONS TO THE CVA FORMULA FOR INDIVIDUAL INSTRUMENTS

Here, we give two well-known approximations to the CVA formula which give relatively simple analytical formulae. In both cases, we start from the CVA formula (under the assumption of no wrong-way risk) given at the start of Appendix 7.B.

(1) Long option position

In this case we have a simplification since the exposure of the long option position can never be negative:

$$\text{CVA}_{\text{option}}(t, T) = (1 - \bar{\delta})E^{Q}[I(\tau \leq T)]E^{Q}[V(\tau, T)]$$
$$= (1 - \bar{\delta})[1 - S(t, T)]V_{\text{option}}(t, T),$$

where $V_{\text{option}}(t, T)$ is the upfront premium for the option. This means that the value of the risky option can be calculated as:

$$V_{\text{option}}(t, T) - \text{CVA}_{\text{option}}(t, T) = V_{\text{option}}(t, T) - (1 - \bar{\delta})[1 - S(t, T)]V_{\text{option}}(t, T)$$
$$= V_{\text{option}}(t, T)S(t, T) + \bar{\delta}V_{\text{option}}(t, T)[1 - S(t, T)].$$

With zero recovery we have simply that the risky premium is the risk-free value multiplied by the survival probability over the life of the option.

(2) Swap

As noted by Sorensen and Bollier (1994), the CVA of a swap position can be written as:

$$\text{CVA}_{\text{swap}} \approx (1 - \bar{\delta}) \sum_{j=1}^{m} [S(t, t_{j-1}) - S(t, t_j)] V_{\text{swaption}}(t; t_j, T),$$

where $V_{\text{swaption}}(t; s, T)$ is the value today of the reverse swap with maturity date T and exercise date t_j. The intuition is that the counterparty has the "option" to default at any point in the future and therefore cancel the trade (execute the reverse position). The values of these swaptions are weighted by the relevant default probabilities and recovery is taken into account. Not only is this formula useful for analytical calculations, it is also quite intuitive for explaining CVA.

An interest rate swaption can be priced in a modified Black–Scholes framework via the formulas:

$$(F\Phi(d_1) - X\Phi(d_2))D(t^*, T) \qquad \text{(payer swaption)}$$
$$(-F\Phi(-d_1) + X\Phi(-d_2))D(t^*, T) \qquad \text{(payer swaption)}$$

$$d_1 = \frac{\log(F/X) + 0.5\sigma_s^2(t^* - t)}{\sigma\sqrt{t^* - t}} = d_2 + \sigma_s\sqrt{t^* - t},$$

where F is the forward rate of the swap, X is the strike rate (the fixed swap rate of the underlying swap), σ_s is the swap rate volatility, t^* is the maturity of the swaption (the time horizon of interest) and $T - t^*$ will be the maturity of the underlying swap. The exposure of the swap will be defined by the interaction between two factors: the swaption payoff, $F\Phi(d_1) - X\Phi(d_2)$, and the underlying swap duration, $D(t^*, T)$. These quantities respectively increase and decreas monotonically over time. The overall swaption value therefore peaks somewhere in-between, as illustrated in Figure 7.3 in the text and Spreadsheet 7.2.

APPENDIX 7.E: CALCULATION OF CVA INCREASE IN THE PRESENCE OF NETTING

We consider an initial set of netted trades with a counterparty denoted by NS (netting set) and assume that a new trade, denoted i, is to be executed. From the point of view of counterparty risk (i.e. ignoring other profit aspects), one must ensure that the risky value of all trades does not change when adding the new trade (otherwise there would be an increase in counterparty risk that is not being charged for). We represent this requirement as:

$$\tilde{V}(\text{NS}, i) = \tilde{V}(\text{NS}),$$

where $\tilde{V}(\text{NS})$ is the risky value of all existing trades (including netting and any other risk mitigants) whilst $\tilde{V}(\text{NS}, i)$ is the risky value including the new trade. We can write the above expression in terms of the risk-free values and CVA components:

$$V(\text{NS}, i) - \text{CVA}(\text{NS}, i) = V(\text{NS}) - \text{CVA}(\text{NS}),$$

where $V(\text{NS})$ is the risk-free value of all existing trades (including netting and any other risk mitigants) whilst $V(\text{NS}, i)$ is the risk-free value including the new trade. Since the risk-free values of the netted derivatives are linear with respect to each component we have:

$$V(\text{NS}) + V(i) - \text{CVA}(\text{NS}, i) = V(\text{NS}) - \text{CVA}(\text{NS}),$$

which simplifies to obtain:

$$V(i) = \text{CVA}(\text{NS}, i) - \text{CVA}(\text{NS}).$$

This shows that the risk-free value of a new trade must (at least) offset the change in CVA due to adding the counterparty risk of the trade. The change in CVA should then be subtracted from the P&L of the trade. In the event the CVA change is negative (due to favourable netting effects), then the P&L will increase.

APPENDIX 7.F: DERIVING THE EQUATION FOR BILATERAL CREDIT VALUE ADJUSTMENT (BCVA)

We wish to find an expression for the risky value, $\tilde{V}(t, T)$, of a netted set of derivatives positions with a maximum maturity date T as in Appendix 7.A but under the assumption that the institution concerned may also default in addition to their counterparty. Denoting the default time of the institution as τ_I, their recovery value as δ_I and following the notation and logic in Appendix 7.A, we now have the following cases (we denote the "first-to-default time" of the institution and counterparty as $\tau^1 = \min(\tau, \tau_I)$).

(1) Neither counterparty nor institution defaults before T

In this case, the risky position is equivalent to the risk-free position and we write the corresponding payoff as:

$$I(\tau^1 > T)V(t, T).$$

(2) Counterparty defaults first and also before time T

This is the default payoff as in Appendix 7.A:

$$I(\tau^1 \le T)I(\tau^1 = \tau)(\delta V(\tau^1, T)^+ + V(\tau^1, T)^-).$$

(3) Institution defaults first and also before time T

This is an additional term compared with the unilateral CVA case and corresponds to the institution itself defaulting. If they owe money to their counterparty (negative MtM) then they will pay only a recovery fraction of this whilst if the counterparty owes them money (positive MtM) then they will still receive this. Hence, the payoff is the opposite of case 2 above:

$$I(\tau^1 \le T)I(\tau^1 = \tau_I)(\delta_I V(\tau_1, T)^- + V(\tau_I, T)^+).$$

(4) If either the institution or counterparty does default then all cashflows prior to the first-to-default date will be paid

$$I(\tau^1 \le T)V(t, \tau^1).$$

Putting the above payoffs together, we have the following expression for the value of the risky position:

$$\tilde{V}(t, T) = E^Q[I(\tau^1 > T)V(t, T)$$
$$+ I(\tau^1 \le T)V(t, \tau^1)$$
$$+ I(\tau^1 \le T)I(\tau^1 = \tau)(\delta V(\tau^1, T)^+ + V(\tau^1, T)^-)$$
$$+ I(\tau^1 \le T)I(\tau^1 = \tau_I)(\delta_I V(\tau^1, T)^- + V(\tau^1, T)^+)].$$

Similarly to Appendix 7.A, we simplify the above expression as:

$$\tilde{V}(t, T) = E^Q[I(\tau^1 \le T)V(t, T)$$
$$+ I(\tau^1 \le T)V(t, \tau^1) + I(\tau^1 = \tau)V(\tau^1, T) + I(\tau^1 = \tau_I)V(\tau^1, T)$$
$$+ I(\tau^1 \le T)I(\tau^1 = \tau)(\delta V(\tau^1, T)^+ - V(\tau^1, T)^+)$$
$$+ I(\tau^1 \le T)I(\tau^1 = \tau_I)(\delta_I V(\tau^1, T)^- - V(\tau^1, T)^-)].$$

Finally obtaining:

$$\tilde{V}(t, T) = V(t, T) + E^Q[I(\tau^1 \le T)I(\tau^1 = \tau)(\delta V(\tau^1, T)^+ - V(\tau^1, T)^+)$$
$$+ I(\tau^1 \le T)I(\tau^1 = \tau_I)(\delta_I V(\tau^1, T)^- - V(\tau^1, T)^-)],$$
$$\tilde{V}(t, T) = V(t, T) - E^Q[I(\tau^1 \le T)I(\tau^1 = \tau)(1 - \delta)V(\tau^1, T)^+$$
$$+ I(\tau^1 \le T)I(\tau^1 = \tau_I)(1 - \delta_I)V(\tau^1, T)^-].$$

We can identify the BCVA (bilateral CVA) term as being:

$$\text{BCVA}(t, T) = E^Q[I(\tau^1 \leq T)I(\tau^1 = \tau)(1 - \delta)V(\tau^1, T)^+$$

$$+ I(\tau^1 \leq T)I(\tau^1 = \tau_I)(1 - \delta_I)V(\tau^1, T)^-].$$

Finally, under the similar assumptions of no wrong-way risk and of no simultaneous default between the default of the institution and its counterparty, we would have a formula analogous to that derived in Appendix 7.B for computing BCVA:

$$\text{CVA}(t, T) = -(1 - \bar{\delta})E^Q\left[\int_t^T B(t, u)V(u, T)^+ S_I(u)\, dS(t, u)\right]$$

$$+ (1 - \bar{\delta}_I)E^Q\left[\int_t^T B(t, u)V(u, T)^- S(u)\, dS_I(t, u)\right].$$

A simple approximation to compute this formula would then be:

$$\text{BCVA}(t, T) \approx (1 - \bar{\delta})\sum_{i=1}^m B(t, t_i)\text{EE}(t, t_i)S_I(t, t_{i-1})[S(t, t_{i-1}) - S(t, t_i)]$$

$$- (1 - \bar{\delta}_I)\sum_{i=1}^m B(t, t_i)\text{NEE}(t, t_i)S(t, t_{i-1})[S_I(t, t_{i-1}) - S_I(t, t_i)].$$

More details on these calculations and discussion on incorporating dependency between the default of the institution and the counterparty can be found in Gregory (2009).

In analysing BCVA, due to its symmetry, it will also be useful to introduce the ENE (expected negative exposure) which is the exact opposite of the EPE:

$$\text{ENE} = \frac{\int_t^T \text{NEE}(u)\, du}{T - t} \approx \frac{1}{m}\sum_{j=1}^m \text{NEE}(t, t_j).$$

APPENDIX 7.G: APPROXIMATION LINKING CVA FORMULA TO CREDIT SPREADS FOR BILATERAL CVA

In Appendix 7.C is shown a simple formula for CVA. We now calculate a similar formula for BCVA under the same assumption of no wrong-way risk. Additionally, we assume no joint default of institution and counterparty:

$$\text{CVA}(t, T) = -(1 - \bar{\delta})E^Q\left[\int_t^T B(t, u)V(u, T)^+ S_I(u)\, dS(t, u)\right]$$

$$+ (1 - \bar{\delta}_I)E^Q\left[\int_t^T B(t, u)V(u, T)^- S(u)\, dS_I(t, u)\right].$$

We first need to ignore the contribution from the terms $S_I(.)$ and $S(.)$. This will be reasonable if the institution and counterparty are of good credit quality (survival probabilities reasonably close to unity) and is also helped by a cancellation if the two terms are of similar magnitude.

Now we approximate both the positive and negative exposure component, $V(u, T)^+$ and $V(u, T)^-$, by EPE and ENE to obtain:

$$\text{BCVA}(t, T) = -(1 - \bar{\delta})E^Q\left[\int_t^T B(t, u)\, dS(t, u)\right]\text{EPE}$$

$$+ (1 - \bar{\delta}_I)E^Q\left[\int_t^T B(t, u)\, dS_I(t, u)\right]\text{ENE}.$$

Using again the expression for the premium and default legs of a credit default swap (CDS) but assuming that these are equal for the institution and counterparty (equal default probabilities):

$$\frac{\text{BCVA}(t, T)}{\text{CDS}_{\text{premium}}(t, T)} = X^{\text{CDS}} \times \text{EPE} - X_I^{\text{CDS}} \times \text{ENE}.$$

The above results shows that the CVA as a spread (per annum) can be approximately written as the institution's CDS premium X_I^{CDS} multiplied by the ENE subtracted from the counterparty's CDS premium X^{CDS} multiplied by the EPE. Alternatively, we can express the bilateral CVA as a spread via the unilateral CVA:

$$\frac{\text{BCVA}(t, T)}{\text{CDS}_{\text{premium}}(t, T)} = \frac{\text{CVA}(t, T)}{\text{CDS}_{\text{premium}}(t, T)} - X_I^{\text{CDS}} \times \text{ENE}.$$

APPENDIX 7.H: DERIVING THE EQUATION FOR BCVA UNDER THE ASSUMPTION OF A BILATERAL WALKAWAY CLAUSE

We now derive a formula analogous to the BCVA one (Appendix 7.F) under the assumption that each party may walk away from a liability (negative MtM) in the event the other party defaults (each party has a claim if their MtM is positive but does not pay anything when it is negative):

$$\tilde{V}(t, T) = E^Q[I(\tau^1 > T)V(t, T)$$

$$+ I(\tau^1 \leq T)V(t, \tau^1)$$

$$+ I(\tau^1 \leq T)I(\tau^1 = \tau)\delta V(\tau^1, T)^+$$

$$+ I(\tau^1 \leq T)I(\tau^1 = \tau_I)\delta_I V(\tau^1, T)^-].$$

We can again simplify the above expression as:

$$\tilde{V}(t, T) = E^Q[I(\tau^1 \leq T)V(t, T)$$

$$+ I(\tau^1 \leq T)V(t, \tau^1) + I(\tau^1 = \tau)V(\tau^1, T) + I(\tau^1 = \tau_I)V(\tau^1, T)$$

$$+ I(\tau^1 \leq T)I(\tau^1 = \tau)(\delta V(\tau^1, T)^+ - V(\tau^1, T))$$

$$+ I(\tau^1 \leq T)I(\tau^1 = \tau_I)(\delta_I V(\tau^1, T)^- - V(\tau^1, T))].$$

Finally obtaining:

$$\tilde{V}(t,T) = V(t,T) - E^Q[I(\tau^1 \le T)I(\tau^1 = \tau)(V(\tau^1,T)^+ - \delta V(\tau^1,T)^+)$$

$$+ I(\tau^1 \le T)I(\tau^1 = \tau_I)(V(\tau^1,T) - \delta_I V(\tau^1,T)^-)],$$

$$\tilde{V}(t,T) = V(t,T) - E^Q[I(\tau^1 \le T)I(\tau^1 = \tau)((1-\delta)V(\tau^1,T)^+ + V(\tau^1,T)^-)$$

$$+ I(\tau^1 \le T)I(\tau^1 = \tau_I)((1-\delta_I)V(\tau^1,T)^- + V(\tau^1,T)^+)].$$

We therefore see additional terms of $V(\tau^1,T)^-$, representing the institution's ability to walk away from a liability when their counterparty defaults and $V(\tau^1,T)^+$, representing the equivalent right for the counterparty when the institution defaults.

8

Pricing Counterparty Credit Risk, II – Wrong-way Risk

> *"I never had a slice of bread,*
> *Particularly large and wide,*
> *That did not fall upon the floor,*
> *And always on the buttered side."*
>
> Newspaper in Norwalk, Ohio, 1841.

8.1 INTRODUCTION

The last chapter was concerned with pricing counterparty risk under a key simplifying assumption of no wrong-way risk. Wrong-way risk is the phrase generally used to indicate an unfavourable dependence between exposure and counterparty credit quality – i.e. the exposure is high when the counterparty is more likely to default and vice versa. Whilst most derivatives transactions can be considered to have little or no wrong-way risk, its manifestation can be rather subtle and cause a substantial increase in counterparty risk. If wrong-way risk is possible then "right-way" risk must also exist in cases where the dependence between exposure and credit quality is a favourable one. Right-way situations will reduce counterparty risk.

In this chapter we will identify some causes of wrong-way risk and discuss the associated implications on exposure estimation and quantification of counterparty risk. We will consider the impact of wrong-way risk in forward contracts and options and show example approaches to quantifying the exposure in these cases. A significant amount of the chapter will be dedicated to the credit derivatives market since these products due to their very nature will always embed wrong-way risk. We will discuss credit default swaps (CDSs), tranches of credit portfolios and finally super senior risk. We will see that wrong-way risk in credit derivatives transactions can be devastating if ignored. The market is learning by experience about the counterparty risks inherent in credit derivatives products, which must be controlled in order for recovery and growth within this market to be possible.

8.2 WRONG-WAY RISK

Imagine tossing two coins and being asked to assess the probability of getting two heads – that is an easy question to answer.[1] Now suppose that you are told that the coins are linked in some way: the first coin to land can magically have some impact on which way up the other coin lands. Clearly, the question is now much more complex.

---

[1] It is of course 25% from one-half times one-half.

In the last chapter, we saw that the price of counterparty risk could be generally represented as default probability multiplied by expected exposure and loss given default (with some slight complications due to term structure). Multiplication of terms relies on a key assumption, which is that the different quantities are *independent*. If they are not independent then the analysis is far more complicated and the relatively simple formulas are no longer appropriate. Dependence between exposure and default means that it is not possible to multiply expected exposure and default probability. Dependence between loss given default (and equivalently recovery rate) and either exposure or default probability will also give rise to another form of wrong-way risk.

A simple analogy to wrong-way risk is dropping (the default) a piece of buttered bread. Many people believe that in such a case, the bread is most likely to land on the wrong, buttered side (exposure). This is due to "Murphy's law" that states that "anything that can go wrong, will go wrong". This particular aspect of Murphy's law has even been empirically tested[2] and, of course, the probability of bread landing butter side down is only 50%.[3] People have a tendency to overweight the times when the bread lands the wrong way against the times they were more fortunate. Since it is in human nature to believe in wrong-way risk, it is rather surprisingly that it has been significantly underestimated in the derivatives market! The market events of 2007 to 2009 illustrated clearly that wrong-way risk could be extremely serious, in particular in the area of credit derivative products. In this chapter, we will explain the origins of this wrong-way risk and consider solutions to ensure the stability of the credit derivatives market in the future.

Wrong-way risk is not always easy to identify, as we shall see. Let us start with an example.

Example. An institution is asked by a client (counterparty) to provide them with a cross-currency swap to exchange future cashflows from dollars into their own local currency. The deal is considered, the exposure quantified (as described in Chapter 4) and the counterparty risk priced (as in Chapter 7). The institution identifies that a missing key element in their analysis is that there might be a strong linkage between their counterparty's credit quality and the strength of their local currency. This is potentially dangerous since if the local currency is weak then the exposure on the trade is likely to be high (since they pay in the weaker currency and will have therefore made a MtM gain on the trade). A counterparty default at this time may leave a very significant loss.

Identifying wrong-way risk is not trivial since it requires a good knowledge of the counterparty and the potential linkage between their credit quality and the strength of their local currency. This linkage could be either way: first, a weakening of the currency could indicate a slow economy and hence a less profitable time for the counterparty. Alternatively, the default of a large counterparty may itself precipitate a weakening of its local currency. In some sense, the direction of the relationship does not matter – there is wrong-way risk and it must be understood properly.

---

[2] On the English BBC TV science programme *Q.E.D.* in 1993.
[3] Matthews (1995) has shown that a butter-down landing is indeed more likely but for reasons of gravitational torque and the height of tables rather than Murphy's law.

8.2.1 Empirical evidence of wrong-way risk effects

General empirical evidence supports the presence of wrong-way risk. For example, Duffee (1996b) shows a clustering of corporate defaults in the US during periods of falling interest rates. This would suggest that a receiver (payer) interest rate swap should have wrong-way (right-way) risk. On the other hand, a highly leveraged institution might be more likely to default in a high interest rate environment. Hence, the sign of the correlation between default rates and interest rates might even be uncertain.

Foreign exchange transactions are obvious candidates for wrong-way risk. An institution receiving a weakening currency that has significant overall exposure to that (or related currencies) will obviously present a challenge. This has led to the concept of currency devaluation on default, which is likely to be particularly extreme for sovereigns but also can be significant for corporate counterparties. Results from Levy and Levin (1999) look at residual currency values upon default of the sovereign and find average values ranging from 17% (triple-A) to 62% (triple-C). For not the first time, we observe that wrong-way risk is more significant for higher rated entities (since their default is more of a surprise).

Losses due to wrong-way risk have also been clearly illustrated. For example, many dealers suffered heavy losses because of wrong-way risk during the Asian crisis of 1997/1998. This was due to a strong link between the default of sovereigns and of corporates and a strong weakening of their local currencies. A decade later, the credit crisis starting in 2007 caused heavy wrong-way risk losses for banks buying insurance from so-called monolines, as discussed later (Section 8.7.2).

8.2.2 Right-way risk

If wrong-way risk exists then so too must right-way risk.[4] This would indicate a beneficial relationship between exposure and default probability that actually *reduces* counterparty risk.

Example. An institution is asked by a client to enter into an oil receiver swap. The client is an airline and such a contract allows them to hedge their exposure to rising oil prices (airlines will typically hedge in this way although sometimes only partially). Such a swap has exposure when the price of oil is low, but at this point the credit quality of the airline is potentially improving due to their reduced fuel costs. When the price of oil is high then the airline may be in a weaker financial situation but there will be no exposure for the institution. The institution then has right-way risk in this contract.

There is potentially a different linkage here, which is that a low price of oil might mean a severe recession in which case the airline may have financial troubles. This opposite effect was seen in the recent credit crisis. What was originally perceived as right-way risk in the sense of a small fall in the price of oil created wrong-way risk in relation to a more substantial price drop.

---

[4] The term "right-way exposure" might be more relevant since it might not actually be considered a risk but we refer to right-way risk to avoid confusion.

Wrong-way risk *should* be rather rare in an ideal world. Assuming users of derivatives are hedging and not speculating then they should generate right-way rather than wrong-way risk (for example, see the airline example above). Consider a counterparty that defaults due to a certain market event – any contract used as a partial hedge against such an event should be in the money for the counterparty and therefore have zero exposure for the transacting institution. Since right-way risk is beneficial, then to ignore it is conservative.

All transactions with corporate counterparties where a dealer receives a floating rate and pays a fixed rate should have right-way risk since during an economic downturn both treasury rates and default rates should increase. Right-way risk will potentially exist in any swap-type contract between two similar counterparties. If one party has wrong-way risk then the other will have right-way risk. This arises simply because if one party has a default probability with a positive relationship to the exposure on the trade then the other might have a similar negative relationship due to being on the other side of the trade.

There are two obvious cases where the above logic does not work, i.e. one party having wrong-way risk implies that the other party benefits from right-way risk:

- The business areas of each party are different. Just because one party has a credit quality linked to the exposure on the trade, it does not imply the other will have the opposite linkage. In the interbank market, wrong-way risk and right-way risk are likely to be always side-by-side. However, in the airline example above, the institution may have right-way risk in their trade with the airline but the airline will not obviously have wrong-way risk due to the credit quality of the institution they transact with declining when oil prices rise.
- If the trade payoff is highly asymmetric, so that only one party can have a significant exposure. This is the case in CDS contracts, which are discussed in Section 8.4.

It may be suggested that wrong-way risk will be offset by right-way risk. However, this logic ignores the fact that wrong-way and right-way trades may be with different counterparties. Nevertheless, it could then be argued that the offsetting works at a portfolio level. However, this also seems unlikely due to the often more extreme nature of wrong-way (compared with right-way risk) that we will highlight in this chapter.

In the real world, speculation and failed hedges mean the wrong-way risk seems to occur frequently. Institutions that have exposures to certain market events (such as hedge funds and monolines) will almost surely create wrong-way risk for those trading with them. We will mainly consider and discuss wrong-way risk from now on but, of course, hand in hand with every discussion is a similar (but opposite) one pertaining to right-way risk.

8.2.3   Examples of wrong-way risk trades

Let us give some examples of trades that obviously contain wrong-way risk across different asset classes:

- *Put option.* Buying a put option on a stock where the company in question has fortunes that are highly correlated to those of the counterparty. The put option will only be valuable if the stock goes down, in which case the counterparty is expected to be underperforming also. This does not of course mean that the counterparty will definitely default but just that they are more likely to. If the put option is very out of the money then this impact becomes more extreme because now the long option position will only have an exposure when the stock has dropped substantially, suggesting a more significant impact of the counterparty's credit quality. In the extreme case, it would be naive to buy an out-of-the-money put option from an institution on their own stock due to extreme wrong-way risk (the put option can only be worth something when the institution is in such trouble that their stock price has declined dramatically). Whereas put options represent potential wrong-way risk, the corresponding call options should be right-way products. These examples will be considered in more detail in Section 8.3.6.

- *FX forward or cross-currency products.* As illustrated in the example above, any FX contract must be considered in terms of a possible linkage between the relevant FX rate and the default probability of the counterparty. In particular, a potential weakening of the currency received by the counterparty vis-à-vis the paid currency should be a wrong-way risk concern. Another way to look at a cross-currency swap is that it represents a loan collateralised by the opposite currency in the swap. If this currency weakens dramatically, the value of the collateral is strongly diminished.

- *Interest rate products.* Although this is probably an area with limited wrong-way risk, it is important to consider a relationship between the relevant interest rates and the counterparty default probability. Such a relationship could be considered in either direction: high interest rates may trigger defaults whereas low interest rates may be indicative of a recession where defaults are more likely.

- *Commodity swaps.* In an oil swap, one party pays cashflows based on a fixed oil price and receives cashflows based on an average spot price of oil over a period. An oil payer swap will involve paying the floating price of oil against receiving a fixed rate. Hence, the exposure of the contract will be high when the price of oil has declined. Nevertheless, suppose the counterparty is an oil company: Will their credit quality be declining due to falling revenues from the low oil price? Brigo et al. (2008) consider the modelling of commodity derivatives CVA.

- *Credit default swaps.* When buying protection in a CDS contract, an exposure will be the result of the reference entity's credit spread widening. However, one would prefer that the counterparty's credit spread is not widening also! In the case of a strong relationship between the credit quality of the reference entity and counterparty then clearly there is extreme wrong-way risk. On the other hand, with such a strong relationship then selling CDS protection should be a right-way trade with little or no counterparty risk.

8.2.4 Wrong-way risk and CVA

The presence of wrong-way risk will (unsurprisingly) increase CVA. However, the magnitude of this increase will be hard to quantify, as we shall show in some examples. Wrong-way risk also prevents one from having the (relatively) simple formulas used for CVA in Chapter 7. There are, broadly speaking, two ways to go about computing CVA in the presence of wrong-way risk:

- Consider the exposure and default of the counterparty together and quantify the economic relationship between them. This method is the "correct" approach but the economic relationship may be extremely hard to define and there may be computation issues in calculating quantities such as CVA in this manner.
- Incorporate wrong-way risk via simple conservative assumptions or "rules of thumb". This is a much simpler and ad hoc approach that involves minimal effort in the way of systems re-engineering or additional computational requirements. This could be achieved, for example, by using the same approach as described in Chapter 7 but adjusting the exposure (or default probability) upwards to reflect the wrong-way risk. Such an approach is theoretically robust, as explained in Appendix 7.B, although the estimation of the "conditional EE" will surely not be straightforward.

8.3   MEASURING WRONG-WAY RISK

8.3.1   Correlation is not the same as dependence

Unfortunately, wrong-way risk may be subtle and not revealed via any historical data analysis. It may be a result of a *causality* – a cause-and-effect-type relationship between two events. Let us return to the first example in this chapter.

> **Example.** In the first example of this chapter, we considered a cross-currency swap with potential wrong-way risk due to a dependency between the credit quality of the counterparty and the strength of the pay currency in the swap (the counterparty's local currency).
>
> Suppose the institution involved makes a statistical study of the correlation between the credit quality of their counterparty measured by the market credit spread (or even from an equity-based approach such as CreditGrades^{TM}, as discussed in Chapter 6) and the FX rate underlying the swap. They find the correlation is close to zero.
>
> There seems to be little evidence of wrong-way risk in this transaction. Can it be ignored?

Correlation is only one measure of dependency. It measures only the linear relationship between variables. Suppose one believes that a small move in a market rate will have little or no impact on the credit quality of a counterparty but a much larger move will. This is a second-order relationship that will not be captured by correlation. There may be a causal relationship: for example, the counterparty defaulting will move market variables significantly even though the credit spread of that counterparty previously showed no relationship to the market variable during normal times.

8.3.2   Simple example

Sometimes very simple ad hoc solutions are used to quantify wrong-way risk. This can be either to assume that the MtM of the trade will have a higher volatility than is

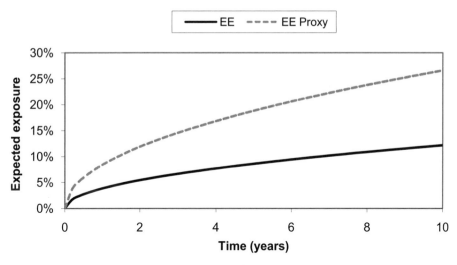

Figure 8.1. Simple example of quantification of wrong-way risk by using a conservative assumption when calculating the EE. The EE proxy is the PFE computed at the 84th percentile.

expected, or that it will be subject to a large drift or that one of the underlying variables may "jump" in the event the counterparty defaults. Expected exposure might simply be calculated using conservative assumptions, such as assuming a PFE[5] at some agreed confidence level. An example of an exposure profile defined in such as fashion is shown in Figure 8.1. Whilst this represents a simple way to incorporate wrong-way risk, it lacks any economic basis and may not give completely intuitive results as we will show later.

| **Spreadsheet 8.1.** Wrong-way risk calculations of expected exposure |

8.3.3   Forward trade example

Exposure should always be computed conditionally on the counterparty default. This has been mentioned many times and shown explicitly in the CVA formula in Chapter 7. In Appendix 4.A we derived a simple formula for the expected exposure (EE) of a forward trade under the assumption of a normal distribution driving the exposure. In Appendix 8.A we make a similar derivation but this time correctly conditioning on the default of the counterparty. In other words, the EE at time s is made under the assumption that the counterparty will have defaulted at some point prior to time s. The relationship between exposure and counterparty default is expressed using a single correlation parameter. This correlation parameter is rather abstract, with no obvious economic intuition, but it does facilitate a simple way of quantifying wrong-way risk. The formula in Appendix 8.A is a more general version of the previous calculation since, with the correlation set to zero, we retrieve the previous (no wrong-way risk) formula.

---

[5] We note that it is possible, especially if a low confidence level is used, for a PFE exposure to be less than an expected exposure.

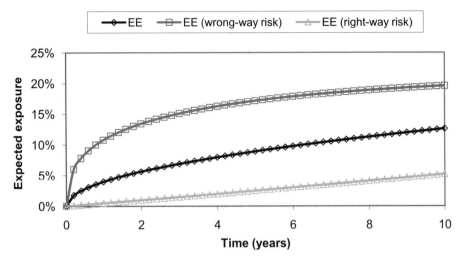

Figure 8.2. Illustration of wrong-way and right-way risk EE profiles using the base case scenario with correlations of 50% and −50%, respectively.

Let us now consider the impact of wrong-way risk on the forward contract similar to the analysis in Section 4.1.2 using the following base case parameters:

$\mu = 0\%$	Drift of the value of the forward contract.
$\sigma = 10\%$	Volatility of the value of the forward contract.
$h = 2\%$	Hazard rate of the default of the counterparty.
$\rho = \pm 50\%$	Correlation between the value of the forward contract and the default time of the counterparty.

In Figure 8.2 we show the impact of wrong-way (and right-way) risk on the EE. We can see that with 50% correlation wrong-way risk approximately doubles the EE whilst with −50% correlation the impact of right-way risk reduces it by at least half.

Consider now the impact of the counterparty default probability on the EE with wrong-way risk.

Figure 8.3 shows the EE using three different hazard rates[6] indicating that the exposure decreases with increasing riskiness of the counterparty. This result might at first seem counterintuitive but it makes sense when one considers that for a better credit quality counterparty, default is a less probable event and therefore represents a bigger surprise when it comes. We note the general conclusion:

> Wrong-way risk *increases* as the credit quality of the counterparty *increases*.

---

[6] See Section 6.4.4 for the definition of hazard rate.

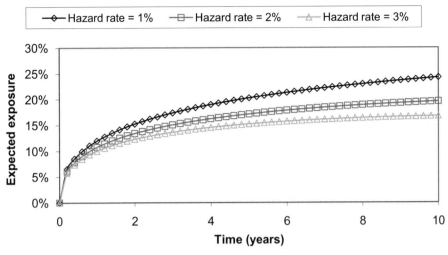

Figure 8.3. Illustration of EE under the assumption of wrong-way risk as a function of the hazard rate.

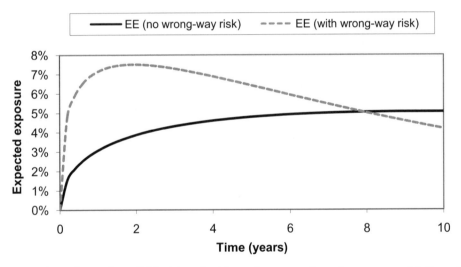

Figure 8.4. Illustration of EE with and without the assumption of wrong-way risk for a drift of $\mu = -2\%$ and hazard rate of $h = 6\%$.

The above conclusion has some interesting impacts across term structure. We now change the drift of the forward contract to be $\mu = 2\%$ and use a larger hazard rate of $h = 6\%$. The EE profile with and without wrong-way risk is shown in Figure 8.4. Negative drift will reduce the overall exposure, as we can see. However, there is another effect, which is that the wrong-way risk EE is actually smaller than the standard EE after 8 years. This is because counterparty default in later years is not such a surprise as in earlier years (with a hazard rate of 6% the 8-year default probability is 38% whilst the

2-year default probability is only 11.3%[7]). Hence, default in early years represents "bad news" whilst in later years default is almost expected! This creates a term structure effect on wrong-way exposure, which we note would not be easily captured via a simple approach, as described in Section 8.3.2.

8.3.4 Foreign exchange example

A simple approach proposed by Levy and Levin (1999) to model FX exposures with wrong-way risk is the following:

$$E[FX(s)\,|\,s = \tau] = E[FX(s)] \times RV. \tag{8.1}$$

The above simply states that the conditional expected FX rate, $E[FX(s)\,|\,s = \tau]$, at the counterparty default time is equal to its unconditional value $E[FX(s)]$ multiplied by a "residual value factor" (RV). This assumes that the currency devalues by an amount $(1 - RV)$ at the counterparty default time and the FX rate jumps accordingly.

Example. Consider a $100m forward contract where the counterparty receives in their local currency. Assume zero drift on the FX rate, which gives $E[FX(s)] = FX(t)$, meaning that the expected MtM on the contract is zero. Also, assume that the FX volatility is 10%.

Let us consider the expected exposure[8] of such a contract in 1 year. In the case of no wrong-way risk, this would be:

$$\$100m \times 10\%/\sqrt{2\pi} = \$3.99m.$$

Whilst there is no empirical evidence for a correlation between the credit quality of the counterparty, a conservative view is taken that if the counterparty were to default then the currency would be devalued to 80% of its previous value. This means that the expected MtM of the forward will be $[1 - FX(t)RV/FX(t)] = [1 - RV] = 20\%$.

The expected exposure based on this wrong-way risk assumption is:

$$\$100m \times [20\% \times \Phi(20\%/10\%) + 10\% \times \varphi(20\%/10\%)] = \$20.08m.$$

We see that in this example wrong-way risk increases expected exposure at default by a factor of 5.

8.3.5 Comparison of wrong-way risk approaches

Let us make a comparison of the wrong-way risk approaches shown above to understand how they differ. Specifically, we consider the simple approach (Section 8.3.2), the correlation-based approach (Section 8.3.3) and the devaluation example (Section 8.3.4). In Figure 8.5 we compare the expected exposure computed with the three methods (recall that in the simple approach the PFE is a proxy for the expected exposure with wrong-way risk). We can see that the simple approach might give similar

---

[7] Recall the simple relationship for the cumulative default probability at time s as being $1 - \exp(-hs)$.
[8] We use the previously derived formulae $\mu\Phi(\mu/\sigma) + \sigma\varphi(\mu/\sigma)$ and $\varphi(0) = 1/2\pi$.

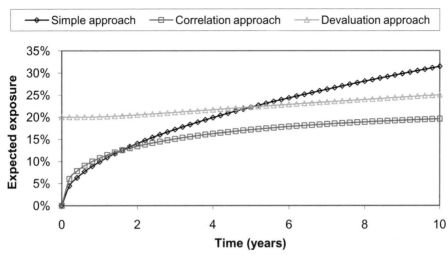

Figure 8.5. Comparison of three wrong-way risk approaches, as described in the text. All cases consider an FX forward position with $\mu = 0\%$ and $\sigma = 10\%$. The simple approach considers the PFE at the 84th percentile. In the correlation approach, we assume $h = 2\%$ and $\rho = 50\%$ (correlation between the value of the forward contract and the default time of the counterparty). In the devaluation approach we assume a residual value factor $RV = 80\%$.

behaviour but will likely underestimate short-term wrong-way risk compared with the other approaches where a default in the near future causes a significant jump in the exposure. The devaluation approach gives an expected exposure that is also constant over time due to the assumption that the currency will devalue when the counterparty defaults, irrespective of when this event occurs. The correlation model incorporates a time impact to wrong-way risk and a default in the near term represents bad news with a higher exposure whereas a later default does not produce such a dramatic impact (Figure 8.4). This feature of wrong-way risk is intuitive: the more unexpected the default, the greater the impact on exposure.

The three approaches also differ in estimation of the parameter required. In the simple approach, a certain percentile for the PFE must be chosen arbitrarily. The devaluation approach is intuitive since it is clear what the devaluation parameter represents although this might be more relevant for situations where there is a clear link between counterparty default and currency valuation, such as for a sovereign. Finally, the correlation approach represents a more traditional style of model and may be useful to apply in general to many trades, rather than a more specific trade-based approach. We note that estimation of the correlation parameter is not obvious and it may be best used as a means to explore the behaviour of a number of trades with a similar exposure in terms of wrong-way risk, rather than to attempt to quantify accurately the wrong-way risk of a given trade.

8.3.6   Risky option position

In Appendix 8.B we derive a simple formula for the value of a risky European stock option based on the classic Black and Scholes (1973) formula. The expression given allows computation of the risky option premium with the impact of wrong-way (and right-way) risk. We will use the following parameters in the examples below:

$A(t) = 100$	Current stock price.
$K = 105.1$	Strike price of option.
$r = 5\%$	Risk-free interest rate.
$\sigma = 25\%$	Stock volatility.
$T = 1$	Option maturity.
$h = 5\%$	Hazard rate of the default of the counterparty.
ρ	Correlation between the stock price and the default time of the counterparty.

The first five terms above are standard in the Black–Scholes formula. The magnitude of the counterparty risk impact will depend on the hazard rate, h, and the correlation parameter ρ. Increasing ρ in absolute terms will increase the wrong-way risk impact whilst changing the sign of ρ will generate right-way risk. The sign of ρ that gives rise to wrong-way or right-way risk will depend on the underlying contract considered.

Spreadsheet 8.2. Black–Scholes formula with counterparty risk

Since the strike of the option is "at-the-money forward"[9] then the standard (risk-free) value of both call and put options is 9.95. In Appendix 7.D we showed a simple expression for the CVA of an option. We will ignore recovery value (which is just a systematic effect), as a result of which the premium of a risky option (no wrong-way risk) can be obtained by simply multiplying the risk-free premium and the survival probability of the counterparty over the life of the option. This means that the risky value of the call or put in the current example is 9.46[10] – we will refer to this as the "risky Black–Scholes price".

We first show the impact of correlation on the premiums of European calls and puts in Figure 8.6. We can see that the call option value increases with correlation compared with the risky Black–Scholes value – this is a consequence of right-way risk. Due to the correlation between the stock price and the counterparty default time, a default becomes increasingly unlikely when the option payoff is positive. For the put option, there is wrong-way risk since a falling stock price leads to the option having a positive payoff but also increases the probability that the counterparty will default. This is intuitive behaviour: buying a put option from a counterparty whose credit quality is positively related to the underlying variable would be dangerous. On the other hand, the equivalent call option (which is in the money when the market is on the up) should be less of a concern. We can finally note that the impact of right-way risk is far less dramatic than that of wrong-way risk.

We can note that put–call parity, which normally gives a theoretical linkage between European call and put premiums, does not work in this case. Put–call parity involves comparing a long call and short put position (or vice versa). Since only the long position

---

[9] The strike of the options is determined by the forward value $F = A(t)e^{rT} = 100 \times e^{5\% \times 1} = 105.1$.
[10] The 1-year survival probability given the hazard rate of 5% is $S(1) = \exp(-5\% \times 1) = 0.951$.

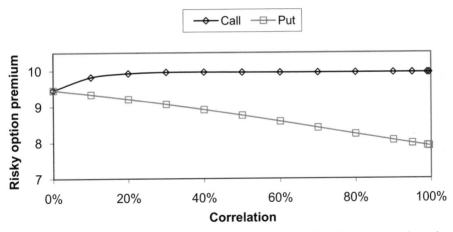

Figure 8.6. Premiums for risky European call and put options as a function of correlation using the base case parameters described in the text.

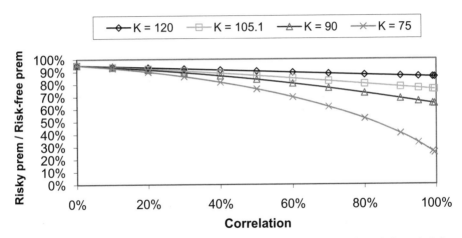

Figure 8.7. Risky option premium divided by the risk-free premium (Black–Scholes price) for put options of different strikes.

will have counterparty risk, it does not apply to risky options since a counterparty default will effectively break the underlying static hedge that leads to put–call parity.

We now investigate the relationship between counterparty risk on options and the strike of the option. In Figure 8.7 we show the ratio of the risky to risk-free put option as a function of strike. This ratio should always be no greater than 100% due to counterparty risk, and the lower the ratio the greater the wrong-way counterparty risk impact. We see that put options of lower strikes show a more significant behaviour. Indeed, for the most out-of-the-money put ($K = 75$) at high correlation the ratio shown approaches 0%, which means that the extent of the counterparty risk is to make the put option almost worthless. Again, this effect is intuitive: a very out-of-the-money put option will only have value when the underlying has dropped significantly, at which point the counterparty's credit quality should be expected to have deteriorated significantly.

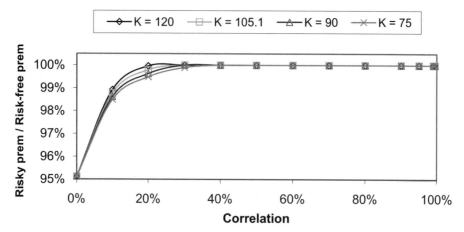

Figure 8.8. Risky option premium divided by the risk-free premium (Black–Scholes price) for put options of different strikes.

In Figure 8.8 we show the same graph for call options of differing strikes and see the opposite effect. An out-of-the-money call option will only have value when the underlying variable has risen sharply. If the counterparty is strongly correlated then they are very unlikely to default in such a scenario. As correlation increases, the risky call option premium tends towards the (risk-free) Black–Scholes value (ratio approaches 100%), and this convergence occurs more quickly for out-of-the-money options.

We have another general conclusion:

> Wrong-way risk *increases* for more out-of-the-money contracts.

This is a logical conclusion following the arguments above. Where there is wrong-way (or right-way) risk, its magnitude will increase for a contract that has more out-of-the-money characteristics. We will show later that this out-of-the-money analogy extends to products other than simple options.

8.3.7 Wrong-way risk and bilateral counterparty risk

Bilateral counterparty risk, as introduced in Chapter 7, is characterised by two components, representing the exposure that either party may have to the other. The two terms will then potentially represent wrong-way and right-way risk. Hence, one term will increase in magnitude whilst the other will decrease. Returning to the BCVA formula discussed in Chapter 7:

$$\text{BCVA} \approx +(1 - \bar{\delta}) \sum_{i=1}^{m} B(t_i) \text{EE}^*(t_i) S_I(t_{i-1}) q(t_i, t_{i-1})$$

$$- (1 - \bar{\delta}_I) \sum_{i=1}^{m} B(t_i) \text{NEE}^*(t_i) S(t_{i-1}) q_I(t_i, t_{i-1}), \qquad (8.2)$$

where $EE^*(.)$ and $NEE^*(.)$ indicate the expected exposure and negative expected exposure conditionally on the counterparty and institution default, respectively. Wrong-way risk will usually have the impact of increasing either EE or NEE and decreasing the other.[11] Therefore, one term on the right-hand side of equation (8.2) will increase whilst the other will decrease. The bilateral CVA (BCVA) will then become significantly positive for the party with wrong-way risk with an equal and opposite value for the other party, who has right-way risk. Indeed, wrong-way risk actually removes some of the complexity of bilateral counterparty risk and creates a situation closer to the unilateral treatment where only one party has risk to the other (although contrary to the unilateral case, the party with less risk will have a negative CVA). A classic example of this is in CDS trades (discussed in Section 8.4.5).

8.3.8 Wrong-way risk and collateral

Collateralisation is typically assessed in terms of its ability to mitigate exposure and hence the relationship between exposure and default probability might not be a concern when assessing the impact of collateralisation. However, if the impact of wrong-way risk could cause the exposure of certain transactions to move suddenly due to the counterparty defaulting then this aspect will be important. Consider the example of an FX transaction with wrong-way risk due to the dependency between the weakening of the paying currency and the counterparty default time. If currency weakening is gradual then the exposure can be well-collateralised prior to the default. However, if devaluation of a currency is linked very closely to a sovereign default, it may likely result in a jump in the FX rate that cannot be collateralised in a timely manner.

8.4 COUNTERPARTY RISK IN CDSs

Whilst many cases of wrong-way risk are rather subtle, there is nothing subtle about the wrong-way risk in CDSs and credit derivative products in general. It is a direct consequence of the nature of the products themselves and can clearly lead to serious counterparty risk issues. We start with a discussion of counterparty risk in the basic CDS product before extending our analysis to consider more complex credit derivatives structures.

8.4.1 CDS payoff under counterparty default

A protection buyer in a CDS contract has a payoff with respect to a reference entity's default but is at risk in case the counterparty in the contract suffers a similar fate. As mentioned earlier, the CDS product has a highly asymmetric payoff profile due to being essentially an insurance contract, as illustrated in Figure 8.9.

In addition to the asymmetry described above, there is also a correlation effect. Buying CDS protection represents a very definite form of wrong-way risk that is made

---

[11] Assuming there is no substantial difference between the impact of the counterparty or institution default on the exposure distribution.

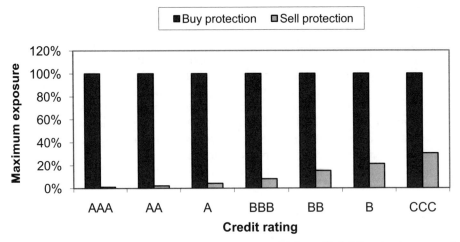

Figure 8.9. Illustration of the asymmetry of counterparty risk for a CDS. When buying protection, the maximum loss is 100% due to default, but when selling protection it is smaller since it is related only to a tightening of the reference entity CDS premium. We have used ratings as a proxy for credit quality changes and have assumed a 5-year maturity and CDS premiums of 25, 50, 100, 200, 400, 600 and 1,000 bps for AAA, AA, A, BBB, BB, B and CCC, respectively.

worse as the correlation between the credit quality of the reference entity and the counterparty increases. There are four possible cases of relevance when buying protection in a single-name CDS transaction, as illustrated in Figure 8.10:

- *Case 1 – reference entity defaults followed by counterparty.* Here, there is no loss since the reference entity defaults first.
- *Case 2 – counterparty defaults followed by reference entity.* Here, there is a significant loss since the counterparty defaults before the reference entity defaults and hence the default payment will not be made.
- *Case 3 – reference entity defaults first.* Here there will be no counterparty risk since the counterparty has not defaulted and the reference entity default will be settled as required.
- *Case 4 – counterparty defaults but reference entity does not.* This is the most complex case. The counterparty defaults and, although the reference entity does not default, any potential positive MtM of the contract will be lost, less some recovery value. If the counterparty default implies a significantly positive MtM on the CDS protection (since the correlated reference entity is expected to have a worsening credit quality), then this loss would be expected to be significant – this is the manifestation of wrong-way risk.

8.4.2   Quantifying CVA for a CDS

The CVA adjustment for CDS is best considered as a special case compared with the general formula presented in Chapter 7. This is because we have to consider the default time of both the counterparty and the reference entity, but, more specifically, the order

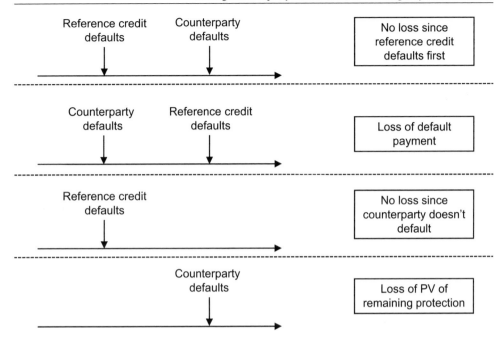

Figure 8.10. Illustration of counterparty risk scenarios for a CDS contract.

in which they occur. In Appendix 8.C we discuss the pricing for a CDS with counter-party risk. This requires valuing the two legs of a CDS contingent to the counterparty surviving (since once the counterparty has defaulted an institution would neither make premium payments nor receive default payments) and adding the usual term depending on the MtM of the CDS contract at the default time. The pricing of CDS counterparty risk is not trivial, as discussed in Appendix 8.C. However, an elegant solution is provided by Mashal and Naldi (2005), who show that there are upper and lower bounds for the value of protection that can be computed more easily. We will take this approach here and use a simple Monte Carlo simulation to value a CDS with counterparty risk. All details can be found in Appendix 8.C and the results are given in Section 8.4.3. Similar calculations have been shown by Turnbull (2005). We focus on computing fair premiums, and not MtM values as in previous papers.

We will ignore the impact of any collateral in the following analysis. This will be conservative since the use of collateral may be considered to reduce significantly CDS counterparty risk. However, due to the highly contagious and systemic nature of CDS risks, the impact of collateral may be hard to assess and indeed may be quite limited, especially in cases of high correlation. We note also that many protection sellers in the CDS market such as monolines and CDPCs (discussed later) have not traditionally entered into collateral arrangements anyway.

8.4.3 Buying CDS protection

We are interested in the risky value of buying CDS protection as a function of correlation between the reference entity and counterparty (the counterparty is selling

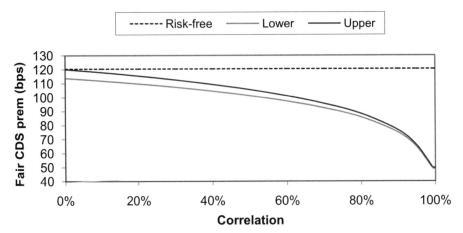

Figure 8.11. Upper and lower bounds for the fair CDS premium when buying protection subject to counterparty risk compared with the standard (risk-free) premium.

protection). We assume the following base case parameters:

$h = 2\%$	Hazard rate of reference entity.
$h_c = 4\%$	Hazard rate of counterparty.
$\delta = 40\%$	Recovery rate of reference entity.
$\delta_c = 40\%$	Recovery rate of counterparty.
$T = 5$	Maturity of CDS contract.

Using the simple formula discussed in Chapter 6, we can calculate the approximate CDS premiums for reference entity and counterparty from $X_{CDS} \approx h(1 - \delta)$ which gives 240 and 120 basis points per annum.[12] We start by considering the fair premium (i.e. reduced in order to account for counterparty risk) that one should pay in order to buy protection, which is shown in Figure 8.11. First, we see that the upper and lower bounds are quite close, making a more costly computation of the exact result unnecessary (for exposition purposes at least). We can also observe the very strong impact of correlation: one should be willing only to pay 100 bps at 60% correlation to buy protection compared with paying 120 bps with a "risk-free" counterparty. The CVA in this case is 20 bps (running) or one-sixth of the risk-free CDS premium. At extremely high correlations, the impact is even more severe and the CVA adjustment can be seen to be huge. At a maximum correlation of 100%, the CDS premium is just above 48 bps, which relates almost entirely to the recovery value.[13]

In Figure 8.12 we show the same example but with the hazard rates of the reference entity and counterparty exchanged. We can notice that the contract does not contain as much counterparty risk since the protection seller has a better credit quality than the reference entity. We also notice that the counterparty risk vanishes as the correlation goes to 100%. This is due to the fact that, with perfect correlation, the more risky

---

[12] The calculations used hazard rates to give precisely these CDS premiums.
[13] The premium based only on recovery value, i.e. there is no chance of receiving any default payment, is $120 \times 40\% = 48$ bps.

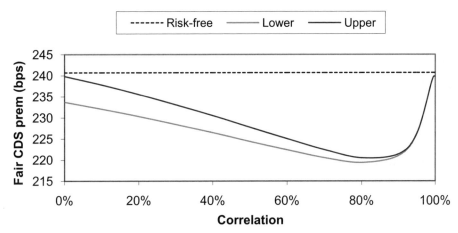

Figure 8.12. As previous figure but with the hazard rates of the reference entity and counterparty swapped.

reference entity will always default first. This feature might be considered slightly unnatural. An obvious way to correct for it would be to have some concept of joint default of the reference entity and counterparty or build in a settlement period to the analysis. These points are discussed, respectively, by Gregory (2009) and Turnbull (2005).

8.4.4   Selling CDS protection

We now consider the impact of selling CDS protection to a risky counterparty and use the same base case parameters as in Section 8.4.3. In Figures 8.13 and 8.14 we show the fair CDS premiums (increased to account for counterparty risk). The upper and lower bounds are not as useful in this case although they do show the limited nature of

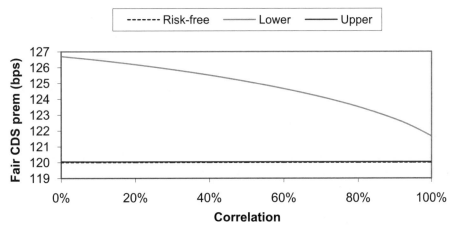

Figure 8.13. Upper and lower bounds for the fair CDS premium when selling protection subject to counterparty risk compared with the standard (risk-free) premium.

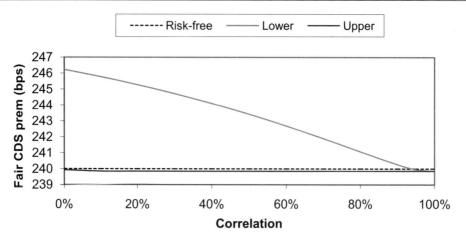

Figure 8.14. As previous figure but with the hazard rates of the reference entity and counterparty swapped.

counterparty risk for the protection seller. We will ignore the impact of negative correlations, which are highly unlikely in practice. For zero or low correlation values, the protection seller may possibly suffer losses due to the counterparty defaulting when the CDS has a positive MtM (requiring a somewhat unlikely tightening of the reference entity credit spread). However, for high correlation values, the MtM of the CDS is very likely to be negative at the counterparty default time and (since this amount must still be paid) there is virtually no counterparty risk.

8.4.5 Bilateral CDS counterparty risk

It is possible to do the above calculations under the assumptions that both counterparties may default, as described by Turnbull (2005). However, this has a limited impact on the calculations since all counterparty risk resides with the protection buyer in the contract. Hence, the BCVA component from the protection buyer's point of view will simply be reduced by a small amount due to the possibility that they may default first. Other than that, the conclusions are similar to those in Section 8.4.3.

8.5 COUNTERPARTY RISK IN STRUCTURED CREDIT

8.5.1 Overview

Whilst CDS counterparty risk represents a challenge to quantify due to the wrong-way risk and uncertainty of the correlation between the reference entity and protection seller (or buyer), structured credit has given rise to even more complex counterparty risk in the form of tranches. As discussed in Chapter 6, there exist many kinds of CDO structure, which are all broadly characterised by their exposure to a certain range of losses on a portfolio. The counterparty risk problem now becomes more complex since one needs to assess where the counterparty might default compared with all the reference names underlying the portfolio.

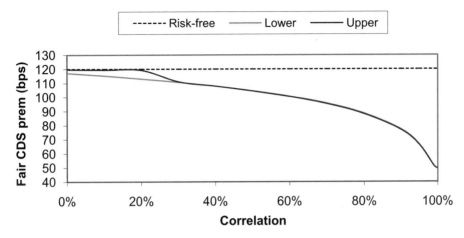

Figure 8.15. Upper and lower bounds for the fair CDS premium when buying protection on a CDS index subject to counterparty risk compared with the standard (risk-free) premium.

The goal is to understand the impact of counterparty risk for index tranches or CDO products traded in unfunded form. The pricing of these instruments and further references are given in Appendix 6.D. It is possible to extend the analysis of Section 8.4.2 (and Appendix 6.C) to calculate the upper and lower bounds on the value of a tranche product in the presence of counterparty risk. More details on this can be found in Turnbull (2005) and Pugachevsky (2005). Our calculations follow these authors, although we will calculate the fair premiums for risky tranche instruments, which are easier to follow than MtM calculations.

The following parameters will be used in the examples:

$n = 125$	Number of reference entities within the portfolio.
$\bar{h} = 2\%$	Average hazard rate of a name in the portfolio.[14]
$h_c = 4\%$	Hazard rate of counterparty.
$\delta = 40\%$	Recovery rate of reference entity.
$\delta_c = 40\%$	Recovery rate of counterparty.
$T = 5$	Maturity of CDS contract.

8.5.2 Credit indices

We first compute the fair CDS premium when buying protection on a CDS index. In Figure 8.15 we show the fair CDS premium upper and lower bounds compared with the risk-free value. We see almost exactly the same result as that previously for a single-name CDS with equivalent parameters in Figure 8.11. The only major difference is that the upper and lower bounds are tighter. This can be attributed to the fact that the value

---

[14] All of the following results have been computed with both homogeneous and heterogeneous hazard rates. There were no significant qualitative differences in the results and so for ease of replication of results we show the former results. We also note that the precise hazard rate was chosen so as to give a fair price for the index of 120 bps.

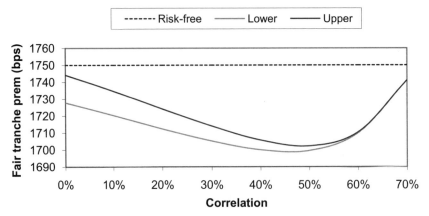

Figure 8.16. Upper and lower bounds for the fair premium when buying protection on the [0–3%] equity tranche (assuming the premium is paid on a running basis) as a function of correlation with the parameters given in the text.

of the protection at the counterparty default time is less uncertain for a portfolio than a single name due simply to the law of averages.[15] Hence we can conclude that a credit index behaves in a very similar way to a similar single-name CDS in terms of counterparty risk.

8.5.3 Index tranches

For tranches of a portfolio, it is important to understand how the impact of counterparty risk can change across the capital structure. We choose tranches according to the standard iTraxx Europe portfolio that are defined by the attachment and detachment points [0%, 3%, 6%, 9%, 12%, 22%, 100%]. Since we are only interested in understanding the qualitative impact of counterparty risk for different tranches, we choose the market standard Gaussian copula model (see Appendix 6.C) with a fixed correlation parameter of 50%.[16] Due to constraints on the correlation matrix, this means we consider the correlation between the counterparty default and the other names in the portfolio in the range [0, 70%].[17]

We first show the fair premium for buying [0–3%] protection[18] on the index with the parameters shown. We can see that the counterparty risk impact is actually quite small, even at high correlation values. At the 40% recovery rate assumed, the equity tranche covers the first 6.25 defaults[19] in the portfolio. Even though the counterparty is more risky, the chance that it defaults at some point before the equity tranche has completely

---

[15] In the single-name case there is a substantial variation in protection value essentially due to the binary nature of the payoff. In the index case the granularity from having a large number of names means that the payoff is more continuous and hence the variation is smaller.

[16] This does not produce prices close to the market but the standard approach of "base correlation" used to reproduce market prices does not have an obvious associated way in which to correctly price counterparty risk. We have checked that the qualitative conclusions of these results hold at different correlation levels.

[17] The upper limit for this correlation, due to constraints of positive semi-definiteness on the correlation matrix, is approximately $\sqrt{50\%} = 70.7\%$.

[18] For now, we assume the equity tranche trades on the basis of a running premium. Later on, we will consider the impact of paying upfront, as is more common in the market.

[19] $3\% \times 125/(1\text{–}40\%)$.

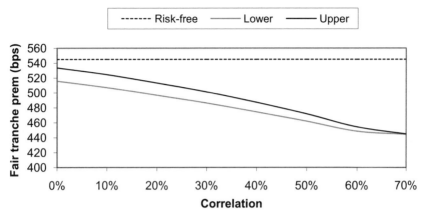

Figure 8.17. Upper and lower bounds for the fair premium when buying protection on the [6–9%] tranche as a function of correlation with the parameters given in the text.

defaulted is relatively small.[20] The impact of correlation (between counterparty default and the reference names in the portfolio) is quite subtle. As correlation increases, counterparty risk at first also increases (decreasing fair premium) due to the more risky counterparty being more likely to default earlier. However, for very high correlations, we see the effect reversing which is due to approaching the maximum correlation allowed, which makes the counterparty default times increasingly certain vis-à-vis the other defaults.[21]

We now look at a significantly more senior part of the capital structure with the [6–9%] tranche in Figure 8.17. We can see that the counterparty risk is much more significant, and increases substantially with the correlation between the counterparty and reference entities in the portfolio. At high correlation, the fair risky premium is decreased by around 100 bps compared with the risk-free premium. The impact of increasing correlation can again be understood by increasing the likelihood that the more risky counterparty will default sooner rather than later. Since the [6–9%] tranche is only hit after 12.5 defaults, there is more chance that the counterparty will have defaulted prior (or during) the tranche taking losses.

8.5.4 Super senior tranches

Finally, we consider the most senior tranche in the capital structure, the super senior [22–100%] in Figure 8.18. Assuming 40% recovery, there need to be 45.8 defaults[22] before this tranche takes any loss, and so the chance that the counterparty is still around to honour these payments is expected to be much smaller than for other tranches. Not surprisingly, the counterparty risk impact is now dramatic with the fair premium tending towards just a recovery value at high correlation (40% of the risk-free

---

[20] The counterparty must be one of the first seven defaults for there to be any counterparty risk since after this point the tranche is completely wiped out.

[21] This is a subtle point relating to the order of default times at high correlation. Due to the relative riskiness of the counterparty with respect to the other names and the correlation structure, the counterparty default is expected to be early but unlikely to be within the first seven defaults and hence the equity tranche has little counterparty risk.

[22] $22\% \times 125/(1-40\%)$.

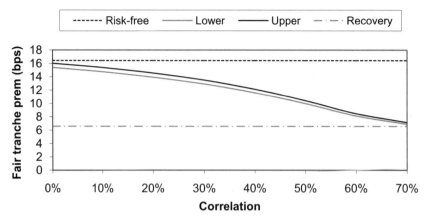

Figure 8.18. Upper and lower bounds for the fair premium when buying protection on the [22–100%] super senior tranche as a function of correlation with the parameters given in the text. The fair premium based on a recovery-only assumption is shown – this assumes the counterparty will never settle any losses before defaulting.

premium). In such a case there is virtually no chance to settle losses on the protection before the counterparty has defaulted.

8.5.5 Counterparty risk distribution across capital structure

We summarise the above results by showing the impact of counterparty risk across the entire capital structure in Figure 8.19. In order to compare all tranches on the same scale, we plot the ratio of fair risky premium (as an average of the upper and lower bounds) to the risk-free premium: this value will have a maximum at unity and decrease towards the recovery (of the counterparty) as counterparty risk becomes more significant. Whereas the equity tranche has less risk (traded on a running basis) than the index, all other more senior tranches have more risk – except the [3–6%] tranche at high correlations. Indeed, from a counterparty risk perspective, we can view tranching as segregating the counterparty risk: the more senior a tranche, the more risk it contains on a relative basis.

In the analysis of options and wrong-way risk (Section 8.3.6), we were able to conclude that wrong-way risk (where it exists) increases for more out-of-the-money contracts. We have now an analogous conclusion for tranches:

> Wrong-way risk *increases* for more senior tranches.

The above analysis concerned a situation where the counterparty is more risky than the average of the portfolio. We briefly summarise results for a less risky counterparty with a hazard rate of $h_c = 1.5\%$ in Figure 8.20. Whilst the overall impact is, as expected, not as significant, we still see that there is still considerable counterparty risk, especially for the most senior tranches.

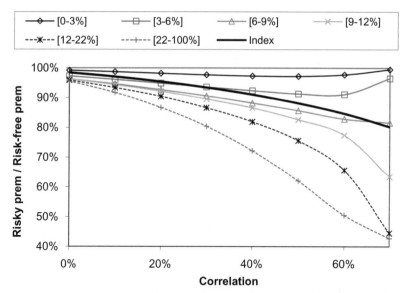

Figure 8.19. Impact of counterparty risk across the capital structure. Fair risky tranche premium divided by the risk-free premium for all tranches in the capital structure and compared with the index ([0–100%] tranche).

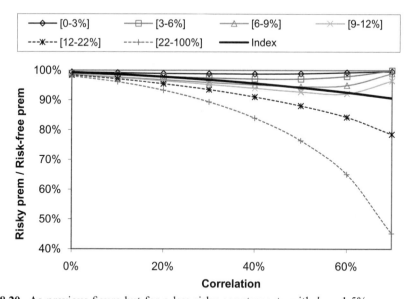

Figure 8.20. As previous figure but for a less risky counterparty with $h_c = 1.5\%$.

We can also note from the Figure 8.20 that the extreme counterparty risk of the [22–100%] tranche is not significantly decreased from trading with the counterparty that is two-and-a-half times less risky. It seems that seniority of tranche can dominate over even the credit quality of the counterparty.

8.5.6   Impact of upfront tranche payments

In the above examples it was assumed that all tranche premiums were made on a running basis to ease comparison across the capital structure. In reality, some tranches will trade on an upfront basis with a fixed 500 or 100 bps running premium. Historically, this has been the standard quotation method for the equity tranche, with a running premium of 500 bps but has more recently also been adopted for the [3–6%] and [6–9%] tranches (see Section 6.5.2). Some more senior tranches of DJ CDX NA now also trade with a fixed premium of 100 bps.

We will consider two contrasting examples of how fixed premiums and upfront payments can influence counterparty risk. First, we consider the counterparty risk of the equity tranche (previously shown in Figure 8.16 for an all-running premium with no upfront payment). We show the CVA[23] for the all-running and standard quotation method in Figure 8.21. Buying protection with an upfront payment can substantially increase counterparty risk, as shown. If the upfront payment made is uncollateralised then it can represent a substantial risk if the counterparty does not perform on payments linked to immediate defaults in the portfolio. A contrasting example is provided when looking at a super senior tranche. Consider the [22–100%] tranche (previously shown in Figure 8.18). In the example, this tranche has a fair running premium of 16.4 bps, and therefore with a fixed running premium of 100 bps there would be an upfront payment made to the protection buyer. This has the impact of reducing counterparty risk quite substantially, as shown in Figure 8.22.

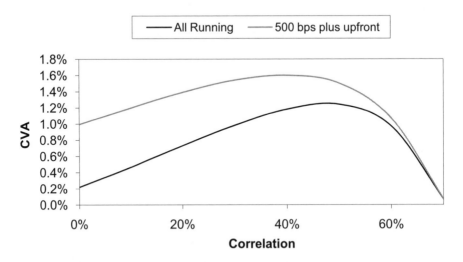

Figure 8.21. Impact of counterparty risk when tranches trade on an upfront basis. CVA for the [0–3%] equity tranche (long protection) when traded on an all-running basis and the more standard quotation of 500 bps running[24] plus an upfront premium.

---

[23] We compare CVAs rather than fair premiums since the premium is now fixed.

[24] In order to calculate the ratio of risky to risk-free premiums for the tranche with an upfront payment, we subtract from one the CVA of the tranche divided by the risk-free protection value.

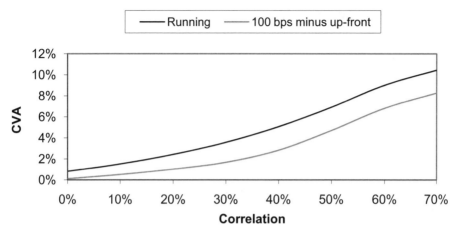

Figure 8.22. Impact of counterparty risk when tranches trade on an upfront basis. CVA for the [22–100%] super senior tranche (long protection) when traded on an all-running basis and the more standard quotation of 100 bps running minus an upfront premium.

8.6   COUNTERPARTY RISK AND GAP RISK

8.6.1   Motivation

As discussed in Chapter 4, a key aspect of collateralisation is that long-term exposure is mitigated at the expense of short-term market risk relating to the collateralised exposure and some margin call timescale. We now consider a class of structures where counterparty risk is potentially removed from the structure but at a cost of introducing market risk, or "gap risk" as it is often called. Such structures arise from leveraged transactions done in total return swap (TRS) or credit-linked note (CLN) form (TRSs and CLNs are described in Chapter 6).

8.6.2   TRS transactions

The general structure will involve the counterparty being paid the total return of an asset or portfolio of assets on a total notional, say N. There will be additionally an upfront collateral payment of say α (an independent amount), which means that the structure is leveraged by a factor of N/α. There may be additional collateral requirements depending on the type of structure:

- *Full recourse.* The client is potentially required to post additional collateral depending on the value of the transaction. Normally daily margining will occur independently of α (the independent amount). This is the standard form of collateralisation, as discussed in Chapter 3.
- *Non-recourse.* The client is not required to post additional collateral and the structure will unwind at a point where (hopefully for the arranger) the MtM of the transaction has not exceeded the value of α (the client is not obliged to make payments to cover losses above this amount). The client may be able to avoid an unwind by selling assets in the underlying portfolio rather than posting a cash amount.

- *Partial recourse.* In this type of structure, the counterparty may have the option to either post additional collateral or face an unwind of the structure. These structures are not so common, but often in a non-recourse structure the client may be given the option to post more collateral to avoid the structure being unwound. Hence, many non-recourse structures might be considered partial recourse in practice.

We note a subtle distinction between a full recourse trade, where the counterparty will only fail to post collateral if they default, and the other types where the counterparty has the choice not to post additional collateral. In the following analysis we will consider all cases to constitute counterparty risk, even though for non-recourse and partial recourse trades this represents the option for the counterparty to avoid posting more collateral.

TRS-type trades represent an extreme wrong-way risk, which is partially mitigated by the independent amount. They are often associated with assumptions that the counterparty will default or walk away at the worst possible time, i.e. when the exposure is highest.

8.6.3   Leveraged CLN

In a standard CLN (Section 6.2.3) a counterparty will commit par against receiving payments linked to some underlying credit risk, effectively selling protection on this risk. The protection buyer has no counterparty risk since the position is fully collateralised. In a leveraged CLN the counterparty will invest only an amount α but still receive payments linked to a larger notional amount of N. Again, this creates some implicit leverage and leads to a leveraged CLN behaving more like a CDS structure. Due to the leverage, there will be a pre-specified mechanism where the counterparty may have the choice to de-leverage by posting another block of collateral or otherwise have the structure unwound. Hence, there will be either a single or possibly a series of triggers for the structure either to de-leverage or unwind. The analysis is path-dependent since the decision to unwind or de-leverage at one trigger point impacts the risk at a subsequent trigger.

8.6.4   Converting counterparty risk to gap risk

The wide range of TRS, CLN and other structures are all characterised by an implicit leverage and unwind mechanism. The counterparty in such transactions will often be relatively risky and indeed hedge funds have commonly entered into this style of transaction due to the potentially high leverage offered. The counterparty risk in such structures is then often ignored for the following reasons:

- The counterparty may not be required to post more collateral (as in a non-recourse or partial recourse TRS structure). In this case, there is no way to estimate the probability of such a "walkaway". It is probably high since the typical counterparties involved in such transactions may want or need to exit the transactions after making significant losses and may not have sufficient funding to continue. Hence, the probability is, not unreasonably, often assumed to be 100%.
- The counterparty is obliged to post collateral, but the significant wrong-way risk (for example, a hedge fund likely to be in trouble due to large losses on this and similar

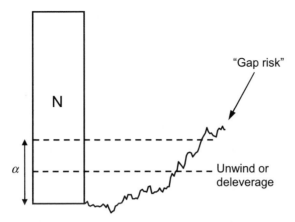

Figure 8.23. Illustration of the basic gap risk style trade. There is an overcollateralisation by an amount α and a pre-specified unwind trigger. The risk to the arranger of the structure is that the value of the structure from their point of view "gaps" above the value of α within some unwind or re-margining period. The counterparty default (or walkaway) probability in connection with this event is often assumed to be 100%.

positions) means that it may be assumed that the counterparty will default at the worst possible time, i.e. when they are required to post more collateral.[25]

The key aspect of the class of structure described above is that counterparty risk has been converted into gap risk, the form of which is illustrated in Figure 8.23. Regarding the choice of unwind point, it must be a balance between mitigating risk and making the structure attractive. A low unwind point will strongly mitigate the risk for an issuer but make the structure less attractive since it will be more likely to be terminated at some point. A high unwind point will make for a more attractive structure but with more significant gap risk.

> **Example.** Consider a $100m CLN indexed to a single-name reference entity, currently trading at 200 bps in the CDS market. The client posts only $10m of collateral but will be paid a return of up to LIBOR + 100 bps (paying a return below the traded level will enable the issuer to make a profit and cover gap risk costs) on the full $100m of risk (there is therefore an implicit leverage of 10 times) for a 3-year maturity. At maturity, the client will be repaid their original investment of $10m plus any additional collateral they have posted due to de-leveraging. The issuer of the structure has uncollateralised exposure when the MtM of the transaction goes above $10m and hence has counterparty risk due to the possibility that the client may default[26] and be not liable to cover more than $10m of the losses on the $100m notional. The issuer decides to set an unwind point when the CDS spread of the reference entity hits 500 bps. At this point the MtM of the transaction (assuming

---

[25] In the case of possible de-leverage then a worst case scenario might be considered to be an initial posting of additional collateral followed by subsequent default at a further trigger point.
[26] We note that in a case where the client is not required to post more collateral, it is not a default but a voluntary walkaway; however, from the issuer's point of view there is little difference.

a worst case duration of 2.6 years corresponding to the unwind happening immediately) would be:

$$(500 - 200)/10,000 \times 2.6 \times 100\text{m} = \$7.8\text{m}.$$

The unwind mechanism essentially converts counterparty risk into gap risk. The issuer has at least \$2.2m of MtM as a cushion against such gap risk. Assuming the counterparty will always default, the MtM of the transaction would have to increase by more than \$2.2m during the unwind period for the issuer to make a loss.

In the above example, the unwind is specified in terms of spread and not MtM value, which simplifies the definition and does not require any agreement on the valuation but does mean that the actual MtM on hitting the trigger is partially uncertain. There is initially \$2.2m or 2.2% of cushion against the gap risk and this cushion will increase over the life of the transaction due to the shortening maturity (unless the transaction references a rolling maturity). If the cushion is not deemed sufficient, then the unwind trigger of 500 bps must be lowered. The issuer is very likely to focus only on the definition of the trigger to control gap risk rather than the credit quality of the counterparty, especially in the non-recourse and partial recourse cases where the counterparty may choose to walk away. Effectively, they are assuming a 100% default probability of default of their counterparty and consider their risk to be purely market risk or gap risk.

8.7 SUPER SENIOR RISK

8.7.1 The leveraged super senior (LSS) trade

Super senior tranches are interesting due to their high subordination and therefore relatively minimal default risk. As discussed in Chapter 6, many market participants need to buy protection on super senior risk of various credit portfolios. However, there are two key obstacles to doing this:

- The returns offered by super senior tranches are typically not large enough to be attractive enough for most investors to sell protection (or insurance) on them.
- Buying super senior protection may lead to very significant counterparty risk, especially due to the possibility of wrong-way risk (as discussed in Section 8.5.4).

One way to attempt to get around the above problems is to buy super senior protection via a leveraged structure. The client will be able to get an enhanced return for taking the risk on a super senior, almost default risk free portfolio whilst the issuer converts the counterparty risk into gap risk as discussed in Section 8.6.4. The leverage in a LSS transaction reflects the fact that the investor's cash participation is less than the notional of the super senior tranche. For example, a \$100m investment may be leveraged 10 times into a super senior tranche with a notional of \$1bn. The investor has sold protection on \$1bn of protection but posted only \$100m initial collateral (the magnitude of these figures are representative of actual trades). Generally, for a leverage of x times, the investor will initially commit $1/x$ units of collateral, as illustrated in Figure 8.24.

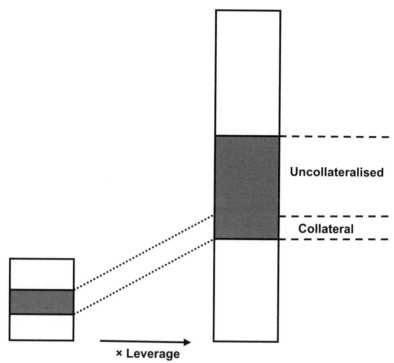

Figure 8.24. Illustration of the LSS concept. A tranche is effectively multiplied by a leverage factor and the resulting tranche is collateralised as shown.

LSS transactions were very popular during the 2005–2007 period in the credit derivatives market. Whether they will be popular again remains to be seen but they still represent an interesting case study of wrong-way counterparty risk.

As in the case of a leveraged CLN (Section 8.6.3), there needs to be a mechanism to mitigate the risk that the LSS issuer retains via the uncollateralised component. This is achieved using a "trigger event" where the investor might have the option to de-leverage by posting more collateral but will otherwise face the structure being unwound by the issuer at prevailing market rates.

In defining a trigger an issuer is trying to ensure that the percentage value of the tranche will always be below $1/\alpha$ with the likely incorporation of some cushion that will be appropriate given the risk in unwinding the trade. The trigger definition represents a balance between a simple definition that may ease documentation, understanding of the product and the related ratings process, and a more complex definition that leaves less unwind risk for the issuer. To understand the latter point, it is useful to have the possible trigger events in mind, and so we briefly describe the typical mechanisms that have been used in the market:

- *Loss-only trigger*. In this case, the trigger is defined by a certain loss on the portfolio (which may increase over time to reflect time decay). However, the issuer is potentially heavily exposed from movements in the underlying spreads and implied correlation levels.

- *Spread triggers.* Here, the trigger is defined by an average[27] portfolio spread as a function of portfolio loss and time to maturity. Although there is less uncertainty, the issuer still has risk over the (market-implied) correlation at the trigger time.
- *Market value trigger.* Finally, some structures reference the market value (MtM) of the tranche directly. This guarantees the cushion available when the trigger is hit although some gap risk still exists for the issuer.

The risk for an issuer of a LSS is that the MtM of the underlying tranche will gap through the value of $1/\alpha$ before the structure can be unwound or more collateral taken. In the case of loss-only and spread triggers, it may even exceed such a level before the trigger is breached. This would, of course, represent a bad assessment of the trigger definition.

A LSS might seem like a clever way to convert extreme uncontrollable counterparty risk into less extreme and controllable gap risk. However, a problem with LSS structures is that the underlying default risk of super senior tranches is so small. The single-name leveraged CLN example in Section 8.6.3 unwinds when the spread of the reference entity has widened from 200 to 500 bps, a potentially unexpected but hardly earth-shattering event. On the other hand, super senior tranches will only ever take losses in an "end of the world" scenario and a LSS typically could be unwound "half-way to the end of the world". Explained in such a way, it might seem that the ability to unwind the transaction is of extremely limited practical use.

Gregory (2008a) argues that a LSS is a fatally flawed structure and derives the valuation formulas for protection purchased in a LSS, which is argued to be substantially less valuable than "risk-free" protection (see Appendix 8.D). Essentially, the gap risk created in an LSS structure is potentially just as severe as the counterparty risk it replaced. The problem arises since, rather than having protection on an $[A, B]$ (say) less some gap risk, the LSS value can be shown to be equivalent to a much smaller tranche $[A, (B - A)/x]$ (where x is the leverage ratio as defined above) plus a complex "trigger option" due to the issuer's ability to unwind the transaction early. An illustration of this pricing result is shown in Figure 8.25. The difference between the incorrect value based on flawed gap risk assumptions and the actual LSS value is substantial.

In 2007 a sudden wave of volatility in the credit market meant that the triggers of LSS trades were severely tested. Super senior tranches suffered from both credit spread widening and increases in market-traded correlations. Fire sales from forced unwinding of troubled conduits and SIVs (structured investment vehicles) pushed credit spreads further out and exasperated losses on super senior tranches. By August 2007 many LSS structures were in significant danger of hitting unwind triggers[28] and the market was forced still wider (especially in terms of correlations) due to these fears. It was practically impossible to buy the protection on super senior tranches that would be needed in order to unwind LSS transactions. Hence, the gap risk was clearly severe and the chance of unwinding an LSS transaction without suffering massive losses was practically zero, despite the original optimism from issuers and rating agencies about the safety of the structures.

---

[27] The heterogeneity of credit spreads does not cause a problem here because the implicit assumption of equal spreads in defining average spread trigger levels will always overvalue a senior tranche.

[28] Amazingly, such triggers were considered just months previously to be almost impossible to hit and triple-A ratings were given to LSS structures on this basis.

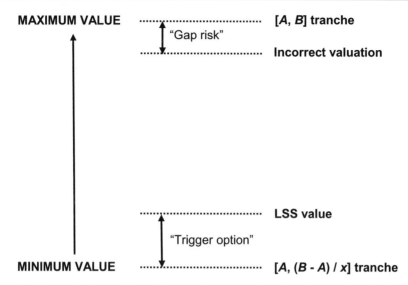

Figure 8.25. Schematic illustration of leveraged super senior valuation, as described by Gregory (2008a).

The LSS story is an important and cautionary one. Buying protection on super senior tranches represents extreme wrong-way counterparty risk. A LSS converts this counterparty risk into gap risk but this risk is also extreme in its nature. The LSS is an illustration of ineffective conversion of counterparty risk to another risk. There are no simple and cheap ways to remove counterparty risk. We will also see that monoline insurers and CDPCs, discussed in Sections 8.7.2 and 8.7.3, repeat the mistakes inherent in the LSS structure.

8.7.2 Monolines

Monoline insurers are financial guarantee companies that are triple-A rated and provide insurance for investment-grade transactions in structured finance. They are typically not required to post collateral on decline in value of contracts. A monoline will have some amount of equity capital and will then invest in a much larger notional of contracts with the ratio between the latter and the former defining an effective leverage of the company. They will typically achieve a triple-A rating based on a capital adequacy model agreed with the relevant rating agencies. This model tests if the required capital exceeds the current equity capital. Most importantly, monolines do not typically post collateral; this point both allows and probably also requires them to achieve a triple-A rating.

The last comment is a strange point. By not posting collateral, monolines can avoid MtM losses, which might otherwise push them into bankruptcy. However, does this enhance their credit quality from the point of view of an institution trading with them? If monolines did post collateral then an institution could always retain the option to waive a collateral call if they believed it would enhance the financial stability of the monoline (protection seller) in the long run. However, by doing this they would be taking a firm bet that the monoline's position would (re)gain value in the future. However, for the monoline to gain in the future, the institution (protection buyer) must lose money. The triple-A rating gained from not posting collateral just does not add up.

Since monolines do not post collateral, they will adhere to the strict operating guidelines summarised below which in theory justify the triple-A rating. The basic aim is to require that once the monoline no longer justifies triple-A credit quality, as measured dynamically via the capital model, it may be required to post collateral to mitigate the increased counterparty risk:

- *Normal state*. The monoline will typically be rated triple-A partly because of a (ratings-based) capital model which is run daily for the exposures it faces. As long as the required capital does not exceed the actual available equity capital (unexpected loss) then the company can operate within its normal operating guidelines.
- *Restricted state*. This typically is invoked if a capital breach has occurred and will result in restrictions on investments and funding. After a certain period, their triple-A rating may be withdrawn at the discretion of the rating agency and this in turn may trigger contractual clauses requiring the posting of collateral. In theory, a monoline can return to a normal state and regain their triple-A rating by raising new capital or restructuring/unwinding existing trades.
- *Run-off*. This corresponds to a hibernation state where the monoline will be essentially static, trades will gradually mature and any default losses will be settled as and when they occur (assuming there is equity capital to cover them). There is no recovery from this state and, whilst it is not the same as a bankruptcy, in practice the result is similar.

We note the posting of collateral means the crystallisation of losses for the monoline. Without the need to post collateral, a monoline can always hope that any MtM losses will be regained at some point in the future. However, in the common scenario that ratings worsening of a portfolio are preceded by MtM losses then a monoline will be forced to realise significant losses. This may lead to being forced into run-off due to being unable to post collateral or unwind/restructure trades to reduce the capital accordingly. The monoline would then enter a "death spiral" from which it is unable to regain its triple-A rating and hence would eventually be forced into run-off.

Many of the problems in 2008 and 2009 suffered by monolines were caused by high leverage coupled to the unprecedented increase in value of super senior protection leading to the death spiral effects discussed above. The credit spreads of monolines widened from 5–10 bps to several hundred basis points. Banks that had bought super senior insurance from monolines had to realise substantial losses due to the increased counterparty risk (see the bilateral CVA unwind example in Section 7.3.7). Many transactions were unwound with banks taking substantial losses due effectively to their positive CVA component. Monolines have therefore gained in such cases and realised a negative CVA component from unwinding contracts away from market prices. However, this has only been achieved due to the severe deterioration in credit quality of monolines and the fact that they were essentially no longer financially viable.

8.7.3 Credit derivative product companies (CDPCs)

Credit derivative product companies (CDPCs) are similar in concept to monolines but take on risk in the form of derivatives contracts rather than insurance policies. A CDPC is effectively a special purpose entity set up to invest in credit derivatives products on a leveraged basis, typically selling protection on corporate, sovereign and asset-backed securities in single-name or portfolio form as CDS contracts. CDPC sponsors include asset managers, hedge funds, insurers and banks. CDPCs, like monolines, will potentially benefit most from assets offering the most substantial risk premiums and therefore may find senior tranches the most attractive investments. Like monolines, CDPCs have the three operating modes described above.

Some CDPCs, like monolines, suffered problems in 2008 and 2009. Other CDPCs have fared better due to coming to the market relatively late and therefore not being highly exposed to the beginnings of the credit crisis in August 2007 (when significant losses would have been incurred by anyone selling super senior protection). A question that remains is to examine the structure of a monoline or CDPC to ask whether such an institution can have a viable business model as a seller of credit protection.

8.7.4 The value of protection purchased from monolines and CDPCs

Let us re-state two of the previous general conclusions made earlier in this chapter:

- Wrong-way credit exposure increases as the credit quality of the counterparty increases (Section 8.3.3).
- Wrong-way risk increases for more senior tranches (Section 8.5.5).

These conclusions would tend to suggest that the structure of a monoline or CDPC would represent a worst case scenario for wrong-way risk. We therefore return to the previous example (introduced in Section 8.5.1) and calculate the impact of the counterparty risk of trading with a monoline or CDPC. We use the same parameters as in the previous case but now assume the counterparty has a much better credit quality characterised by lower hazard rate assumptions. Due to the high leverage used by monolines and CDPCs, we assume a recovery rate of $\delta_c = 0$ (actual failures of monolines have supported this zero-recovery assumption). The fair premium for the protection purchased is shown in Figure 8.26.

Whilst the improving credit quality of the monoline or CDPC certainly reduces counterparty risk, with high correlation it is still significant even in the case of $h_c = 0.25\%$ (where the default probability of the counterparty is eight times less than the average default probability in the portfolio). An obvious conclusion is therefore that the monoline or CDPC is not a viable seller of super senior protection (insurance) unless significant risk mitigants such as collateral agreements are in place.[29] This argument is also made in more detail in Gregory (2008b) who argues that protection purchased from a monoline or CDPC is worth practically nothing unless the transaction can be unwound at some point in the future, long before losses occur. The impact of correlation would mean that the monoline/CDPC would be faced with unwinding all their positions at once and would be very far away from being able to meet all the MtM losses.

Super senior protection providers who do not post collateral must ensure their own default is *not* highly correlated to that of the entities in the portfolios upon which they

---

[29] By this we mean standard collateral arrangements and not the posting of collateral in the event of a credit-rating downgrade or other defined event.

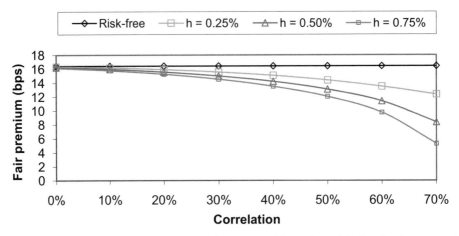

Figure 8.26. Fair premium (as the average of the upper and lower bounds) when buying protection on the [22–100%] super senior tranche from a monoline or CDPC with different hazard rate parameters as a function of correlation.

sell protection. This could be achieved by having an exposure to this type of instrument that is only a small part of a diversified set of risks, consistent with the aim of any insurance business. Alternatively, by both buying and selling protection and maintaining a reasonably flat position, the same low overall correlation may be achieved. Having specialised triple-A companies as providers of super senior credit protection may represent an advance in terms of efficient credit risk transfer. However, given the systemic nature of senior credit risk, it is critical that these companies have solid foundations. We re-address these points in Chapter 13 when discussing triple-A entities.

8.8 SUMMARY

In this chapter we have discussed wrong-way counterparty risk, which is a phenomenon caused by the dependence between exposure and default probability. Wrong-way risk is a subtle, but potentially devastating effect that can increase counterparty risk substantially. We have examined some classic examples of this risk arising in different trades and then discussed the calculation of CVA under wrong-way assumptions. A large part of this analysis has been dedicated to credit derivatives products, where CDS and tranches of credit portfolios have been shown to have substantial wrong-way risk. We have also described the possibility in extreme cases to mitigate wrong-way risk by converting counterparty risk into gap risk via overcollateralisation. Leveraged super senior tranches have been described as an example where the conversion of counterparty risk to gap risk is fundamentally flawed. Finally, following on from the LSS ideas, we have discussed the issues arising from monolines and CDPCs acting as super senior protection sellers in the credit derivatives market, probably the worst possible case of wrong-way risk. Indeed, the counterparty risk in transactions with monolines and CDPCs is so great as to potentially dwarf any value in the transaction itself. We have argued that monolines and CDPCs have a flawed business model but suggested some ways in which they may overcome this by limiting the counterparty risk they present.

APPENDIX 8.A: COMPUTING THE EE OF A TYPICAL FORWARD EXPOSURE WITH CORRELATION TO A TIME OF DEFAULT

(i) EE for a forward contract under the assumption of a normally distributed MtM value

In Appendices 4.A and 4.B we derived a simple formula for the expected exposure (EE) for an underlying MtM value (V_t) of the form:

$$dV_t = \mu \, dt + \sigma \, dW_t,$$

where μ represents a drift and σ is a volatility of the exposure with dW_t representing a standard Brownian motion. The expected exposure is given by:

$$EE = \mu(s-t)\Phi\left(\frac{\mu}{\sigma}\sqrt{s-t}\right) + \sigma\sqrt{s-t}\,\varphi\left(\frac{\mu}{\sigma}\sqrt{s-t}\right).$$

(ii) EE expression conditional on default

Now we derive a similar formula with conditioning on some actual default time. Under the above assumptions, the value of a contract at some time s in the future is given by:

$$V(s) = \mu(s-t) + \sigma\sqrt{s-t}\,Y,$$

where Y is a Gaussian random variable. Let us denote the time of default of the counterparty by τ and the survival probability of the counterparty up to time s as $S(0,s)$, which, as in Chapter 6, is defined via a constant hazard rate h or intensity of default:

$$S(0,s) = \exp(-hs).$$

Like the exposure, default is driven by a Gaussian variable, Z:

$$\tau = S^{-1}(\Phi(Z)).$$

Finally we link the Gaussian variables Y and Z via a correlation parameter ρ:

$$Y = \rho Z + \sqrt{1-\rho^2}\,\varepsilon,$$

with ε being a further independent Gaussian variable. We now need to calculate the expected exposure conditional upon default having occurred. This is:

$$EE(s\,|\,\tau = s) = E[\max(0, V(s))\,|\,Z = \Phi^{-1}(S(0,\tau))] = \int_{-\mu(t)/\sigma(t)}^{\infty} [\mu'(s) + \sigma'(s)]\varphi(x)\,dx.$$

Denoting by:

$$s = \Phi^{-1}(S(0,\tau)) \qquad \mu'(t) = \mu(t) + \rho\sigma(t)s'(t) \qquad \sigma'(t) = \sqrt{1-\rho^2}\,\sigma(t).$$

We can write:

$$EE(s\,|\,\tau = s) = \mu'(t)\Phi\left(\frac{\mu'(t)}{\sigma'(t)}\right) + \sigma'(t)\varphi\left(\frac{\mu'(t)}{\sigma'(t)}\right).$$

APPENDIX 8.B: FORMULA FOR A RISKY OPTION

The classic Black–Scholes formula for a European option can be extended to price a risky option (i.e. one that is extinguished when the counterparty defaults). As in Appendix 8.A, we link the default time to a standard Gaussian random variable, Z:[30]

$$\tau = S^{-1}(1 - \Phi(Z)).$$

Now, with the standard Black–Scholes assumption for the evolution of the underlying asset (for example, a stock paying no dividends):

$$A(T) = A(t) \exp\lfloor(r - \sigma^2/2)T + \sigma\sqrt{T}X\rfloor,$$

where $A(s)$ represents the asset price at time s, r is the risk-free interest rate, σ is the volatility, T is the option maturity and X is a standard Gaussian variable. The random term in the above expression is related to the default time via a correlation parameter ρ:

$$X = \rho Z + \sqrt{1 - \rho^2}\varepsilon,$$

with ε being a further independent Gaussian variable. Let us consider the impact of positive correlation on this relationship. If the variable Z is very negative then τ will be small (default relatively soon) and the return on the asset is likely also to be negative. Hence, the asset is expected to be low when the counterparty defaults.

In this framework, it is possible to price risky options using expressions similar to Black–Scholes formulas. The pricing formulas for call (C) and put (P) options are given by:

$$C = e^{-rT}(F \cdot A_1 - K \cdot A_2) \qquad P = e^{-rT}(-F \cdot A_{-1} + K \cdot A_{-2})$$

with the following definitions:

$$F = S\exp(rT),$$

$$d_2 = [\ln(F/K) - \sigma^2/2)T)]/\sigma\sqrt{T},$$

$$A_{\pm 1} = \int_{-\infty}^{\infty} \Phi\left(\pm\frac{\sqrt{\rho}u + \sigma\sqrt{T} + d_2}{\sqrt{1-\rho}}\right)\Phi\left(\frac{\sqrt{\rho}u + \rho\sigma\sqrt{T} - \Phi^{-1}(1-S(T))}{\sqrt{1-\rho}}\right)\varphi(u)\,du,$$

$$A_{\pm 2} = \int_{-\infty}^{\infty} \Phi\left(\pm\frac{\sqrt{\rho}u + d_2}{\sqrt{1-\rho}}\right)\Phi\left(\frac{\sqrt{\rho}u - \Phi^{-1}(1-S(T))}{\sqrt{1-\rho}}\right)\varphi(u)\,du.$$

In the case of zero default probability, $S(T) = 1$ and $\rho = 0$ we obtain $A_{\pm 1} = \sigma\sqrt{T} \pm d_2$ and $A_{\pm 2} = \pm d_2$ which correspond to the d_1 and d_2 terms in the standard Black–Scholes formula.

APPENDIX 8.C: FORMULA FOR PRICING A CDS CONTRACT WITH COUNTERPARTY RISK

In Appendix 6.B we gave a formula for pricing a CDS in terms of the value of the premium leg (present value of all premium payments made) and the default leg (present

---

[30] The $(1 - \Phi(Z))$ term rather than the previous $\Phi(Z)$ term simply allows the sign of the correlation to be intuitive.

value of all possible future default payments). These terms are denoted $V_{\text{premium}}(t, T)$ and $V_{\text{default}}(t, T)$, respectively. The present value of a CDS with no counterparty risk is then given by the sum of these two terms. The following analysis will extend these formulas to include counterparty risk and the reader should refer to Appendix 6.B for definitions.

Consider a CDS with counterparty risk. Denote by $S^1(t, T)$ the survival probability of the counterparty *and* reference entity. The counterparty default time is denoted by τ_C (note the difference in notion since τ has previously been used to define counterparty default). The premium payments will now not only be contingent on the reference entity *not* defaulting but also the counterparty *not* defaulting:

$$\tilde{V}_{\text{premium}}(t, T) = \sum_{i=1}^{m} S^1(t, t_i) B(t, t_i) \Delta_{i-1,i} X_{\text{CDS}}.$$

The default payments will be made when the reference entity has defaulted but only if the counterparty has not previously defaulted. The "contingent" default payment leg with $\tau^1 = \min(\tau_C, \tau)$ becomes:

$$\tilde{V}_{\text{default}}(t, T) = -E^Q[(1 - \delta) B(t, \tau) I(\tau^1 < T) I(\tau_C > \tau)].$$

Finally, we must add on the payment made at the counterparty default time. Denote by $V_{\text{CDS}}(\tau, T) = V_{\text{premium}}(\tau, T) + V_{\text{default}}(\tau, T)$ the (risk-free) MtM or replacement cost of the CDS at some future default date τ accounting for discounting. If this value is positive then the protection buyer will receive only a fraction $\delta V_{\text{CDS}}(\tau, T)$ of the amount whilst if it is negative then the MtM must be paid to the defaulted counterparty. Hence the payoff in default is $\delta V_{\text{CDS}}(\tau, T)^+ + V_{\text{CDS}}(\tau, T)^-$. Finally, we can write the total value of the CDS with counterparty risk as being:

$$\tilde{V}_{\text{CDS}}(t, T) = \tilde{V}_{\text{premium}}(t, T) + \tilde{V}_{\text{default}}(t, T) + E^Q[(\delta_c V_{\text{CDS}}(\tau, T)^+ + V_{\text{CDS}}(\tau, T)^-)],$$

where δ_c is the counterparty recovery (as opposed to the reference entity recovery). As in Appendix 6.B, this is from the protection provider's point of view, the protection buyer's position is given simply by reversing the signs on the terms $V_{\text{CDS}}(\tau, T)$, $\tilde{V}_{\text{premium}}(t, T)$ and $\tilde{V}_{\text{default}}(t, T)$.

We can define the random default time of the reference entity by $\tau = S^{-1}(\Phi(Z))$ (as in Appendix 8.A) and then the correlated default time of the counterparty can be given by $\tau_C = S_C^{-1}(\Phi(Y))$ where $Y = \rho Z + \sqrt{1 - \rho^2} Z$ with ε being an additional independent standard Gaussian random variable and ρ identified as a correlation parameter. The correlation between the reference entity and counterparty default times can also be represented via a bivariate Gaussian distribution. This would mean that the joint survival probability would be given by:

$$S^1(t, T) = \Phi_{2d}[\Phi^{-1}(S(t, T)), \Phi^{-1}(S_C(t, T); \rho)],$$

where $S_C(t, T)$ is the survival probability of the counterparty, $\Phi^{-1}(.)$ is the inverse of a cumulative Gaussian distribution function and $\Phi_{2d}(.)$ represents a cumulative bivariate Gaussian distribution function with correlation parameter ρ. The contingent premium and default terms, $\tilde{V}_{\text{premium}}(t, T)$ and $\tilde{V}_{\text{default}}(t, T)$, can be computed analytically.

Computation of the last term in the above formula is complicated since it involves the risk-free value of the CDS at some future date τ_C which is unknown. This gives rise to a classic American Monte Carlo problem in that one would have to do a Monte Carlo inside a Monte Carlo in order to evaluate the expression. However, Mashal and Naldi (2005) point out that upper and lower bounds for this quantity can be calculated. These are given by:

$$E^Q[\delta V_{\text{CDS}}(\tau, T)^+] + E^Q[V_{\text{CDS}}(\tau, T)] \leq E^Q[(\delta V_{\text{CDS}}(\tau, T)^+ + V_{\text{CDS}}(\tau, T)^-)]$$

$$\leq E^Q[(\delta C_{\text{CDS}}(\tau, T)^+ + C_{\text{CDS}}(\tau, T)^-)],$$

where $C_{\text{CDS}}(\tau_C, T)$ represents the value of the cashflows in the CDS contract at time τ_C in a given scenario, discounted back to today. The upper and lower bounds defined by the above equation can be computed by Monte Carlo simulation directly, as also discussed by Turnbull (2005). This is the approach used for the results given in the chapter to calculate the fair CDS premium in the presence of counterparty risk. We note a final complexity, which is that, since the term $V_{\text{CDS}}(\tau_C, T)$ depends on the premium itself, we need to solve recursively for this premium outside the Monte Carlo simulation. In practice, due to relative linearity in the region of the solution, convergence is almost immediate. Indeed, it is possible to accurately calculate the fair CDS premium by solving at two points and linearly interpolating or extrapolating to find the result.

APPENDIX 8.D: PRICING OF A LEVERAGED SUPER SENIOR TRANCHE

This appendix summarises a model-independent valuation of a leveraged super senior (LSS) tranche. We denote the leverage of the structure as x and so the initial investment (or collateral) will be $(B - A)/x = \alpha$. We denote by $\tilde{V}_{A,B,\alpha}(t)$ the time t value of LSS protection for a leverage defined by α. Issuers of LSS-type products may conveniently argue that the protection they buy in leveraged form is equivalent to the full value of protection on an $[A, B]$ tranche less some gap risk arising from possible losses from having to unwind the structure. This can be represented as:

$$\tilde{V}_{A,B,\alpha}(t) \equiv V_{A,B}(t) - E^Q[I(\tau < T)B(t, \tau)(V_{A,B}(\tau) - \alpha)_+],$$

where τ denotes the LSS trigger time, $I(\tau < T)$ is an indicator function defining whether the LSS trigger has been hit before the maturity date T, and $B(t, s)$ is the risk-free discount factor. The term $(V_{A,B}(\tau) - \alpha)^+ = \max(V_{A,B}(\tau) - \alpha, 0)$ corresponds to the payoff of the short gap option since the issuer will lose if they cannot unwind the trade without the value of the underlying tranche, $V_{A,B}(\tau)$, exceeding the collateral, α. The convenience of the above approach arises from arguing that the second term in the above equation is small as long as gap risk is controlled via a suitable choice of unwind trigger and leverage. However, it can be shown (Gregory, 2008a) that the correct valuation of an LSS structure gives the following result:

$$\tilde{V}_{A,B,\alpha}(t) = V_{A+\alpha,B}(t) + E^Q[I(\tau < T)B(t, \tau)\min(V_{A,B}(\tau), \alpha)].$$

The above result shows that the true LSS value is represented mainly by an $[A, A + \alpha]$ tranche. This tranche will have substantially less value than the larger $[A, B]$ tranche due to the large leverage that is typical in such structures. The second term in the equation above represents a complex "trigger option", arising from the optionality the issuer has to unwind the transaction at the trigger event. The ability to extract sufficient value from this option in order to justify the typical gap risk pricing approach is extremely unlikely.

9

Hedging Counterparty Risk

9.1 INTRODUCTION

This chapter deals with the hedging of counterparty risk, which has become a key activity over recent years. Whilst there are many ways to control counterparty risk, without the ability to hedge an institution may find themselves severely limited in the type and amount of transactions they take and the counterparties they trade with. Furthermore, an institution's total credit value adjustment (CVA) may exhibit severe volatility and therefore potentially lead to large losses. In Chapters 7 and 8 we have discussed CVA, which defines the difference between risk-free and counterparty risky derivative(s). Since CVA is presented as a price for counterparty risk, it is natural to ask what the associated "hedge" is. However, as we shall see, hedging counterparty risk poses many challenges due to the many different market variables involved and the potential linkage between them. Ultimately, the hedging will be far from perfect, the most pragmatic solution being to identify the key components of CVA that can and should be hedged, as well as those that cannot.

From an example in Chapter 7, if the EPE for a trade is 5% and the credit spread of the counterparty is 300 basis points per annum, an approximate CVA is:

$$5\% \times 300 = 15 \text{ bps}.$$

Let us suppose that the trade has a 5-year maturity and using an approximate duration of 4.0 years, a CVA of 0.6% is put in a reserve to absorb future losses on the trade. The reserve is only around one-eighth of the EPE.

In reality, if the counterparty does not default the actual loss on this trade will be zero whilst if the counterparty does default then it could well be substantially more than the 0.6% of reserve. Hence, the reserve will be either too big or too small.

There are two possible solutions to the above problem:

(1) The 0.6% is a static "reserve" against counterparty risk and will almost certainly not represent the actual losses experienced on this trade. However, since there are

many other trades with many different counterparties, the diversification impact means that 0.6% is the appropriate charge in a portfolio context.[1]

(2) The 0.6% represents the cost of hedging and will be used to hedge the counterparty risk of this trade whether or not the counterparty defaults.

We deal with the second case above in this chapter and discuss the portfolio concepts of the first case in Chapter 10. However, the reader should bear in mind that best practice management of counterparty risk probably represents a pragmatic combination of the two above general solutions. Whilst this represents a combination between hedging costs and capital costs, it does represent the real situation, as will be discussed further in Chapter 12.

9.2   HEDGING AND PRICING

The famous Black–Scholes (1973) approach to option pricing created a link between the price of an option and a dynamic hedging strategy. The option price is proved to be its expected return under the so-called risk-neutral measure. This is justified theoretically since the option can be replicated via a self-financing strategy. Anyone disagreeing on the price of the option can be proved wrong[2] via being arbitraged! This idea has been critical to the development of exotics options and structured products. To price any complex payoff, one specifies a model, calibrates it to the market (the hedging instruments) and then calculates the risk-neutral price. The underlying justification that there is a practical strategy for replicating the calculated model price is often not considered in enough depth.

Since CVA just involves pricing an exotics option type profile then surely it can be treated as an exotic derivative and priced and hedged accordingly? Whilst this point is not incorrect *per se*, some important considerations should be kept in mind with respect to hedging counterparty risk:

- *Variables.* The CVA for even a simple product will represent several underlying variables (for example, interest rates, FX rates and credit spreads), all of which may be important. Hence, hedging CVA involves several underlying risk factors.
- *Cross-dependency.* The dependency or relationship between different variables (for example, interest rates and credit spreads) may be important and should ideally be hedged. CVA therefore represents a complex credit hybrid payoff.
- *Term structure.* Hedges may be sensitive to term structure meaning that to hedge one underlying variable effectively may involve positions in hedging instruments with different maturity dates.
- *Inability to hedge some variables.* There may be some variables that have an impact on CVA but simply cannot be hedged, either because there is no instrument in the market with the required sensitivity or because, pragmatically, the hedging costs are prohibitive. Credit parameters, in particular, are rather hard to hedge.

---

[1] In this case we can comment that a risk premium has been implicitly added due to using a risk-neutral default probability via the credit spread. Since such a portfolio will have a degree of non-diversifiable risk then a risk premium is appropriate although there are potentially better ways to quantify such a component.

[2] Assuming of course the model's assumptions, in particular that of volatility, hold true.

None of the above points is specific to CVA and all arise in various exotic products. Having said that, from an exotics product perspective CVA represents a *highly complex multi-asset exotic option*. In addition, there is a further point when hedging CVA that should be considered:

- *Lack of arbitrage*. When pricing exotic products, arbitrage is a key determinant. If an institution overprices or underprices an exotic product then another institution can trade directly with them and dynamically hedge the risk to lock in the profit arising from the mispricing. However, if institution *A* misprices the counterparty risk to another institution *B* then an arbitrageur is less likely to be able to profit since they need to trade with institution *A* a contract referencing the credit quality of institution *B*. Whilst products like CCDSs (discussed later) make this potentially possible, their usage is still at a very low level.

All of the above five points (especially the last) potentially mean that pricing CVA is not a totally risk-neutral problem since hedging will be driven strongly by practicalities and not idealised risk management.

9.3 HEDGING A RISKY DERIVATIVE POSITION

A key aspect of CVA, as discussed in Chapter 8, was the ability to use it to separate the risk-free and risky value of a derivative (or set of netted derivatives). This approach extends to hedging as illustrated in Figure 9.1, which shows the impact of a market move on the risky and risk-free value of a derivative (or netting set of derivatives). A market move causes the position to increase in value by an amount ΔMtM that creates an associated loss on the hedge of $-\Delta$MtM. However, due to an increase in CVA, the risky value of the position actually decreases by an amount ΔMtM*. Since the large increase in CVA is hedged than the overall hedging gain ensures that the overall risky MtM decrease is neutralised. Without hedging the CVA, there would be a net loss on the risky position due to the CVA increasing (and a net gain if the CVA decreased). A corresponding numerical example of this is shown in Table 9.1.

Table 9.1. Numerical illustration of hedging of risky MTM via CVA and risk-free MtM. The numbers shown correspond approximately to the schematic depiction in Figure 9.1.

	Before	After	Hedge (after)
MtM	+10	+11	−1
CVA	+2	+4	+2
MtM*	+8	+7	
Gain/Loss		−1	+1

The above approach also implies that different trading desks can be responsible for hedging the MtM and CVA components, as discussed in more detail in Chapter 12.

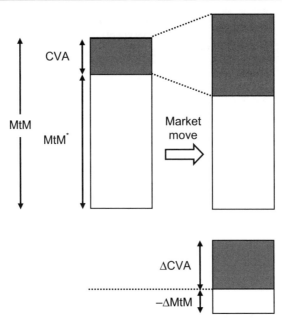

Figure 9.1. Illustration of the hedging of a risky derivatives position (MtM*) via hedging the risk-free (MtM) and the CVA component. The market move causes an increase in MtM which creates a loss on the corresponding hedging instrument. The CVA, however, increases and therefore the associated hedge produces a gain. Overall, the risky value (MtM*) decreases, which is hedged via an overall gain on the CVA versus a loss on the risk-free hedge.

9.4 TRADITIONAL HEDGING OF BONDS, LOANS AND REPOS

Traditional debt securities such as bonds and loans can be hedged using CDSs. Holding a bond with a $100m face value and buying the same notional of CDS protection referencing the bond issuer is a quite effective hedge for the credit risk of the bond. A potential default of the issuer is hedged against since the CDS payoff will compensate for the bond face value less recovery if there is a credit event. This is illustrated in Table 9.2. Furthermore, the position is hedged against credit migration and credit spread risk since a fall in the bond price triggered by a deterioration of the issuer's credit quality will be compensated by a MtM gain on the CDS position.

Table 9.2. Illustration of hedging the default risk in a bond with a CDS showing the payoff at default or maturity of the bond.

	Default	*No default*
Bond	Recovery	Par
CDS	Par – recovery	—
Total	*Par*	*Par*

Despite the relatively simple nature of the above example (after all this is more or less what the CDS product was designed for), there are a number of reasons why the above hedge will not be perfect. We start with the two obvious trading issues from the perspective of an investor holding a bond and buying CDS protection:

- *Bonds trading away from par.* CDS protection will settle based on a fixed notional value whereas bonds can trade above or below par for interest rate (or equity in the case of convertible bonds) reasons.[3] If the CDS hedge notional is equal to the par value of the bond then the hedge will make a loss[4] (gain) if the bond is trading above (below) par prior to default. This conditional interest rate (and equity) risk is analogous to the interest rate swap in an asset swap contract (discussed in Section 6.2.4).

This above point suggests that a static hedge with CDS protection is not appropriate and the hedge position should be adjusted as the bond price moves away from its par value. This point is particularly important since essentially the bond exposure can be considered not constant due to interest rate effects (and equity effects in the case of convertibles). This is therefore the most obvious case of a contract with a random exposure, although the uncertainly in the exposure is of course small compared with many derivatives instruments.

Now, suppose the bond credit risk will be dynamically hedged. There is now another point to consider which is *annuity risk*, as introduced in Section 6.3.6. CDS contracts have historically traded with a running spread and no upfront payments. This means that there is a mismatch between the duration of the bond and CDS contract due to the difference in credit spread (effectively a bond will be trading off-market).

The above point can be explained in another way. The delta and default hedges of the bond are not expected to coincide meaning that buying an amount of CDS protection in order to hedge a small change in the issuer's CDS premium will not hedge the default risk of the bond. We illustrate this in Figure 9.2, which shows an example of the CDS delta against the bond price as a function of the bond issuer's CDS premium. We can see that, due to the duration mismatch, a bond trading above par will have a CDS hedge notional that will be smaller than the bond price. This means that there will be so-called "jump to default" risk; if the issuer defaults before the hedge can be adjusted there will be a loss due to the notional of the CDS protection being too small to hedge the default risk. A bond trading below par will have the opposite effect. Only when the CDS premium and implied bond spread are equal[5] do the delta and default hedges coincide.

More recently, CDS contracts have started to trade with upfront payments and fixed premiums (see Section 6.3.7). This potentially helps solve this hedging dilemma since the duration of the CDS and bond may now more closely match. However, unless the fixed premium on the CDS coincides with the bond spread then again there will be an imperfect match. In the example in Figure 9.2 the fixed CDS premium is assumed to be 500 bps, which is higher than the bond spread, resulting in a systematic underhedge of the default risk by around 3–4%.

---

[3] The bond trading away from par for credit reasons is not relevant since the MtM impact of this will be mirrored by the MtM of the CDS protection.

[4] This assumes implicitly that the bond is marked-to-market and/or its interest rate risk is hedged.

[5] This occurs approximately at a level equal to the spread paid on the bond, which is 9% − 5% or 400 bps.

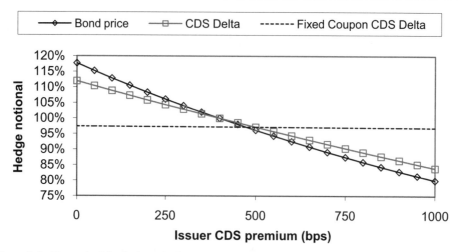

Figure 9.2. Example delta hedge of a fixed rate bond with a CDS, assuming both instruments have a maturity of 5 years. The bond coupon is assumed to be 9%, the risk-free interest rate 4% and the recovery rate of the bond in default 20%. Also shown is the fixed coupon CDS delta assuming a coupon of 500 bps.

We have shown that the hedging of a fixed rate bond with a CDS is not trivial because a CDS contract implicitly references a floating rate bond (one always trading at par). Such a hedge should be dynamic rather than static, and even then it is not possible to hedge both delta and jump-to-default risk with a single CDS instrument. A random exposure implies the need for a dynamic hedge and the more random the exposure the more hedging effort required.

There are other risks of CDSs, as described in Chapter 6, which could all cause problems for the hedging of counterparty risk, and a review of Section 6.3 is advised at this point. In summary, hedging the credit risk in a bond or similar security is not trivial, the bond exposure cannot be considered fixed at the par value and there are many pitfalls. The hedging of derivatives counterparty risk can also include all the above problems and more – due to the highly random nature of the exposure.

9.5   RISK-NEUTRAL OR REAL PARAMETERS?

In this section we consider whether parameters for computing CVA should be risk-neutral (derived from market data) or real (estimated from historical data). Risk-neutral parameters are typically used in pricing applications whilst real parameters generally form the basis of risk management models. Following our previous arguments that pricing counterparty risk should not be necessarily considered in a risk-neutral context, some comments on the differences between using risk-neutral and real parameters are relevant.

The types of parameters we must consider are:

- *Drift* – the trend of market variables.
- *Volatility* – the future uncertainty of market variables.
- *Correlation* – the co-movement between market variables.

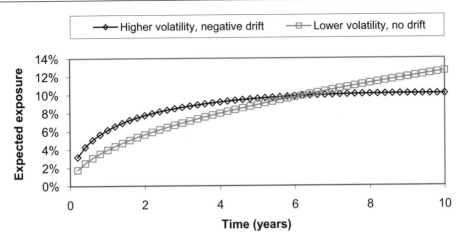

Figure 9.3. Illustration of the impact of a strong drift assumption on expected exposure. In the short term the higher volatility leads to more risk, but over a longer period drift is more important.

In addition to the above general parameters, effects like mean reversion should be considered. Mean reversion has an impact on future spot prices and future volatilities.

9.5.1 Futures prices and future spot prices

As discussed in Chapter 4, a difference between credit exposure and traditional market risk analysis is the time horizon concerned. In the relatively short market risk horizon (for example, 10 days in VAR approaches), the drift of an underlying asset is of secondary importance vis-à-vis its volatility. However, in the longer time horizons required for assessing credit exposure and counterparty risk, drift will be a key consideration alongside volatility. In other words, the *trend* of an underlying variable can be just as important as its *uncertainty*. This means one must consider the drift implications carefully and be cautious over the naive use of implicit risk-neutral drift parameters. This effect is illustrated[6] in Figure 9.3, showing that over a long time horizon the drift impact can dominate over the volatility. This is due to the drift being a linear effect whilst the volatility scales according to the square root of time.

Futures (or equivalently forward) prices have long been an important mechanism of price discovery in financial markets as they represent the intersection of expected supply and demand at some future point in time. A key aspect of financial markets is that spot prices and futures prices may be very far apart. For example:

- *Commodity prices.* Storage costs (or lack of storage), inventory and seasonal effects can move commodities futures apart from spot rates. Due to these aspects, together with the expectation that prices will rise or fall in future, backwardation and contango are common. For high inventories the futures price is higher than the spot price (contango). When inventories are low, commodity spot prices can be higher than futures prices (so-called backwardation).

---

[6] Here, we have used the simple approach given in Appendix 4.A for calculating EE based on drift and volatility. The two scenarios correspond to volatilities of 20% and 10% and drifts of −4% per year and zero.

- *Interest rates.* Yield curves may be upwards-sloping or downwards-sloping (and a variety of other shapes) due to the risk appetite for short, medium and long-term interest rate risk and the view that rates may increase or decrease.
- *Credit spreads.* Credit curves may be increasing or decreasing either due to demand for credit risk at certain maturities or the view that default probability will be increasing or decreasing over time.
- *Foreign exchange (FX) rates.* Forward FX rates are determined from an arbitrage relationship between the interest rate curves for the relevant currency pair. Expectation of future FX rates may have an influence on the current interest rate curves in the corresponding currencies.

All of the above examples of spot and futures price differences are driven by both *fundamental* and *technical* factors. Fundamental factors reflect the theoretical relationship between spot and futures prices due to interest rates, storage costs, dividend and convenience yields, and other aspects. In a perfect market, such a relationship will hold for arbitrage reasons. In practice, though, market imperfections mean that *technical* factors such as transaction costs, differential borrowing and lending rates, short selling and other aspects will influence the spot–futures relationship.

In a deep and liquid market, this supply and demand would be expected to balance out at a price that represents an unbiased (or slightly biased due to the presence of a risk premium or other fundamental factors) expectation of the future price of the actual asset and so be given by the simple fundamental relationship. There has been much empirical testing of the relationship between spot and futures prices across different markets. It is a generally held belief that the futures price is a biased forecast of the future spot price, contrary to the efficient market hypothesis, although the uncertainty of the future spot price will dominate this problem for shorter maturities.

The key point to take away is that markets are imperfect and so we cannot always expect current futures prices to be the best estimate of spot prices in the future. We should bear this in mind when assessing and pricing counterparty risk, especially for long time horizons.

9.5.2 Drift

Following on from the previous comments, let us consider the following example:

Example. Consider a transaction whose MtM value has a volatility of 10% and a drift of 5% over 1 year.

The expected exposure based on the usual formula is:

$$[5\% \times \Phi(5\%/10\%) + 10\% \times \varphi(5\%/10\%)] = 6.98\%.$$

On the other hand, consider the reverse transaction, the expected drift would by -5% and the expected exposure:

$$[-5\% \times \Phi(5\%/10\%) + 10\% \times \varphi(5\%/10\%)] = 1.98\%.$$

Is the first transaction actually three and a half times more risky than the second, opposite, trade?

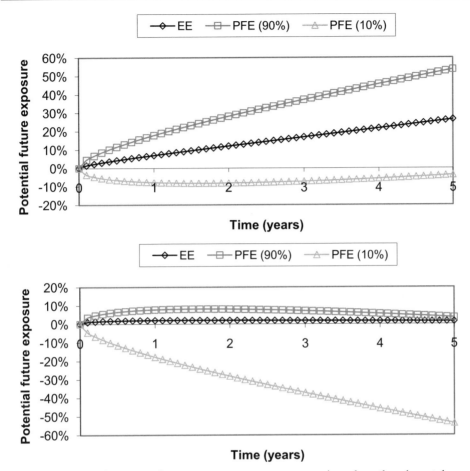

Figure 9.4. Expected exposure for a cross-currency swap transaction where the relevant domestic and foreign interest rates are 6% and 1%. The first case (top) corresponds to paying the domestic currency whilst the reverse swap (bottom) is also shown. Also shown is the PFE at the 10% and 90% points indicating the envelope of the future MtM distribution.

The above example could arise, for example, in a cross-currency swap. Suppose the 1-year interest rates of domestic and foreign currencies are 6% and 1%. The forward FX rate in 1 year, by arbitrage arguments, must be $(1 + 6\%)/(1 + 1\%) \approx 105\%$. Hence, the risk-neutral drift is approximately[7] 5%. Since the exchange of notional in the cross-currency swap is calculated using the spot FX rate, there is a large differential between the forward FX rate and the actual contractual rate. This means that the payer of the domestic currency will have a much greater expected exposure than the payer of the foreign currency. The above example is illustrated in more detail in Figure 9.4 for cross-currency swaps of 5-year maturity. The party paying the currency with higher interest rates expects to make larger interest payments (fixed or floating) over the life of the swap

---

[7] Depending on whether the swap legs correspond to fixed or floating payments and other effects such as daycount conventions.

and hence the expected exposure is high. In the reverse swap the chance of having positive MtM is small and hence the expected exposure is much smaller. This analysis is correct in the following situations only:

- The forward FX rate is the best unbiased estimator of future spot FX rates.
- The impact of FX moves on counterparty risk (CVA) is being perfectly hedged.

The former point is dubious since the relationship between today's forward rate FX and future spot rates tends to be rather weak. Forward FX does not even tend to predict direction, let only magnitude for FX moves in the future. This is why we advocate the use of real drifts in Section 4.3.2 for risk management purposes. In this chapter we need to consider whether for pricing CVA it is appropriate to use a risk-neutral drift, since the potential implications can be significant.

Another problem with defining the behaviour between real and market-implied drifts is mean reversion. Many market variables (for example, commodities and interest rates) tend to mean-revert over time which pulls long-term rates back to some average level. Risk-neutral mean reversions, whilst often hard to calibrate, tend to be smaller than mean reversions estimated from historical data.

9.5.3 Volatility

Options prices are sensitive to a number of variables, the only unobservable one being volatility. By equating market and model prices for options, we arrive at an implied (risk-neutral) volatility. For most markets, there is likely to be implied volatility information, potentially as a function of strike and the maturity of the option. For quantifying exposure, one might use an historical estimate of volatility. However, to calculate CVA, implied volatilities might be considered more relevant. Again there is the caveat related to the extent to which the volatility component of CVA can (and will) be hedged. We also note that (positive) mean reversion has the effect of reducing longer term volatilities and thus is an important parameter to estimate.

Whilst using risk-neutral drift parameters might be considered a subtle question, there might not be such an issue regarding volatility. Let us consider the estimate of volatility for risk management purposes (i.e. assuming no hedging). Using implied volatility might be expected to produce an upwards bias due to a risk premium, leading to higher risk numbers. However, it is often argued that implied volatility is a superior estimator of future volatility (for example, see Jorion, 2007, ch. 9) compared with historical estimation via time series approaches. The stability of the volatility risk premium and the fact that an overestimate of volatility will always lead to a more conservative risk number give greater credence to this idea.

We would therefore conclude that where a volatility market exists, implied volatility is the best measure to use for exposure estimation and CVA irrespective of hedging aspects. When no implied volatility is available then an historical estimate, potentially with some embedded risk premium for pricing CVA, should be used.

9.5.4 Correlation

Implied correlations are sometimes available in the market. For example, a quanto (or quantity-adjusted) option has a payoff in a different currency and thus gives information on the implied correlation between the relevant FX rate and the underlying asset. One key aspect of correlation is to determine wrong-way risk. For example, a quanto CDS (CDS where the premium and default legs are in different currencies) potentially gives information on the correlation between the relevant FX rate and the credit quality of the reference entity in the CDS.[8]

Whilst implied correlation can sometimes be calculated, for most quantities no market prices will be available. This also means that the sensitivity of CVA to correlation parameters cannot generally be hedged. We would suggest using implied correlations if possible since they are probably more forward-looking than historic data and are more likely to show any significant but subtle effects (variables that have not been correlated strongly in the past but for technical or fundamental reasons are expected to be strongly related in the future). Unlike volatility, however, it may not be obvious whether an increase or decrease in correlation will lead to a higher CVA. For example, the CVAs of two different trades may have opposite sensitivities to a correlation increase but both will increase with increasing volatility. A sensitivity analysis of correlation will also be required to understand in which direction it is appropriate to be conservative and/or add a risk premium.

9.6 COMPONENTS OF CVA

Having discussed some general points with respect to hedging CVA, we now focus on specific terms in the CVA formula. For the more technically minded, a derivation of these terms is given in Appendix 9.A although this is not required for the following discussion. The main components to be hedged are listed below:

- *Default probability.* This can be hedged with credit default swaps with the counterparty as the reference entity.
- *Recovery rate.* Most of the recovery risk will be hedged via the default probability above, but there can be a small amount of second-order risk and basis risk, which we will analyse.
- *Exposure.* All variables that have an impact on exposure will need to be hedged. For example:
    - for an interest rate swap, there will be the interest rate risk + interest rate volatility;
    - for an FX forward, there will be the FX risk and FX volatility;
    - for a cross-currency swap, there will be interest rate and interest rate volatility risk in each currency, as well as FX risk and FX volatility risk.
- *Cross-dependencies.* All terms where there is a correlation between the underlying variables will lead to a correlation risk. For example, in a cross-currency swap there are three correlations between currency 1, currency 2 and the FX rate. In the case of correlation between default probability and exposure, this corresponds to the hedging of wrong-way risk.

---

[8] Assuming we can also observe the premiums of the "vanilla" or single-currency CDS.

- *Term structure.* Finally, we note that all hedges should be done across the term structure. For example, hedging the CVA for a 5-year swap does not require only a single maturity swaption.

Clearly, even a single transaction such as a cross-currency swap will have many CVA terms to hedge, and a portfolio of netted derivatives may have a potentially huge number of terms arising from the different underlying trades with that counterparty. It is crucial to understand which terms are most important. In practice, cross-dependencies and term structure hedges may be ignored, unless they have a significant impact on the sensitivity of CVA and there are available instruments for hedging.

The next sections will examine all of the above CVA components in more detail and from a hedging perspective. The following assumptions will be used unless otherwise stated:

Trade	5-year payer interest rate swap.
Interest rates	Increasing term structure corresponding to 1 to 5-year interest rates of 4.0%, 4.25%, 4.5%, 4.75% and 5.0%, respectively.
Volatility	The interest rate volatility is assumed to be 25%.[9]
Credit quality	We assume the counterparty has an initial CDS premium of 500 bps.

For all quantitative examples, we will assume a complete liquidity of hedging instruments but also comment on the practicality of the strategies due to the availability of the hedging instruments in today's market.

9.7   RECOVERY RISK

Example. A trader has an uncollateralised exposure of $10m and has bought $10m of CDS protection on the counterparty for the same maturity.

If the name defaults, is there any risk? Does the trader have any sensitivity to the recovery rate?

In the above case, in theory there is no recovery risk as previously shown in Table 9.2. If the recovery rate is 20%, the derivative exposure produces a claim for $2m whilst the CDS contract pays $8m. For a higher recovery of 60%, the derivative exposure claim is $6m and the CDS payoff $4m. Whilst this is approximately true, there are some small technical factors we must examine which will give rise to risk. Whilst the default payoff might not be considered sensitive to recovery, this does not mean that the CVA is not sensitive to recovery. Second, one has to consider carefully if the recovery rate on the derivative and that referenced in the CDS contract are identical. This will require the reference entity in the CDS contract to match that of the derivatives counterparty and

---

[9] This is a lognormal volatility of the swap rate.

the seniority of the debt referenced by the CDS to be equivalent (*pari passu*) to the derivative.

9.7.1   Basis risk

Derivatives exposures normally rank *pari passu* with senior debt (referenced in CDS contracts) and would be therefore expected to have the same recovery rate. However, there are a number of complications that create recovery risk (see Chapter 6 for a more detailed description of the terms below):

- *Cheapest-to-deliver option.* If a CDS contract can be settled physically via the protection buyer delivering bonds then they have the option to find the cheapest bond that may be contractually delivered. A cheaper bond will lead to a lower recovery on the hedge than on the derivatives contract and result in a gain for the institution hedging counterparty risk.
- *Delivery squeeze.* Under physical settlement of a CDS, a delivery squeeze is caused by a lack of deliverable obligations in the market and causes bond prices to inflate due to strong demand. CDS protection buyers for the purposes of hedging counterparty risk will have to buy bonds in order to settle the CDS. This higher bond price will be likely to lead to a loss for the institution hedging counterparty risk.

As discussed earlier, the problems arising with physical settlement of CDSs have been resolved by adopting an auction method of cash settlement as the primary means of settling CDS contracts. Whilst this removes the problems related to the cheapest-to-deliver option and delivery squeeze, we must now consider any possible differences between the auction recovery rate and the actual recovery rate eventually received on the exposure. Assume that the institution issues a default notice with respect to their exposure at the same time as the CDS auction is being settled. There is one final problem:

- *CDS auction recovery versus actual recovery.* Whilst a CDS contract can (and must) be settled in a timely manner, an institution has to wait as an unsecured bondholder before being paid any recovery amount on the derivative(s) they had with that counterparty (see Figure 6.10). Bankruptcy proceedings involve long negotiations and legal proceedings that can last many years. The larger the counterparty, the more complex the bankruptcy period and consequently the longer an institution will have to wait to recover anything on their claim. Even if the recovery rate settled in the CDS contract is unbiased by technical factors such as delivery squeezes, it will be at best the market's expectation of the final recovery value of the counterparty. The more complex a bankruptcy, the more uncertain the final recovery may be.[10]

In general, in any hedging of credit risk there will be the above problem due to the almost immediate settling of the CDS contract but much slower recovery in relation to the claim from the defaulted entity.

---

[10] Of course, an exception to this is an extreme bankruptcy where the recovery may be so small that there can be little uncertainty regarding the final recovered amount.

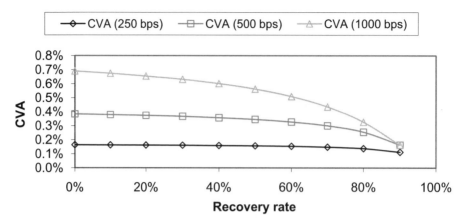

Figure 9.5. Illustration of the sensitivity of CVA to recovery rate assumptions for an interest rate swap and assuming the counterparty CDS premium is at levels of 250, 500 and 1,000 bps (flat CDS curve assumption).

9.7.2   CVA sensitivity to recovery

In most situations the sensitivity of CVA to recovery rate will be small assuming the CVA credit component is dynamically hedged with the CDS (as discussed later). A decrease in recovery not only causes an increase in CVA but also an equivalent increase in the value of the CDS protection used as a hedge. This is why the approximate CVA formula derived in Chapter 7 (equation 7.2) had no recovery rate parameter. In terms of pricing, the increase in CVA for a lower recovery is offset via a decrease in the implied default probability. This cancellation effect means that the impact is often quite small, as illustrated in Figure 9.5. Here, we show the sensitivity of CVA to a changing recovery rate under the assumptions that the recovery for the swap and the CDS contract are equal.

For the least risky case there is little sensitivity to recovery, but as the default probability of the counterparty increases so does the sensitivity. Recall that implied default probability is inversely related to 1 minus the assumed recovery rate (see Section 6.4.4). As the recovery rate increases so does the implied default probability. This implies the counterparty is more likely to default earlier where the exposure has not yet increased significantly. This effect is related to the discussion on jump-to-default risk later. For a risky name, a very high recovery decreases the CVA significantly just because the jump-to-default risk can be small.

Counterparties with low CDS premiums will have little recovery sensitivity. A counterparty close to default will also have little or no recovery sensitivity since the loss on the derivative and gain on the CDS contract are expected to net perfectly. A distressed counterparty not imminently likely to default represents the largest recovery risk, especially if the PFE may change substantially over time.

9.7.3   Recovery swaps

As discussed above, even if counterparty risk is well hedged with CDS contracts, there may be some residual recovery rate risk. Recovery swaps and fixed recovery CDSs

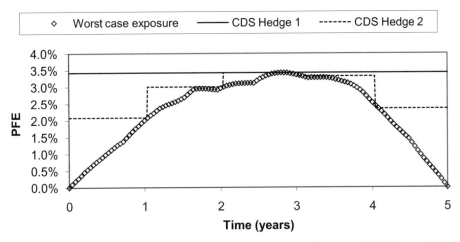

Figure 9.6. Example of static hedging of exposure with the PFE shown at the 90th quantile. CDS Hedge 1 corresponds to a single maturity instrument (5 years) whilst CDS Hedge 2 assumes a hedge involving 1, 2, 3, 4 and 5-year CDS protection.

(discussed in Section 6.2.7) potentially provide a means to hedge such risk but they do not trade with any frequency or liquidity for even the most common CDS reference entities.

9.8 STATIC HEDGING

9.8.1 Static CDS hedging of exposures

As discussed in Section 9.4, static hedging of a bond or similar security by buying CDS protection is a reasonable hedging strategy, albeit with many small potential risks (and technical risks such as delivery squeezes). Most fixed rate bonds are unlikely to trade more than 5–10% away from their par value[11] and hence a static hedge will, if implemented carefully, allow a major proportion of the credit risk to be eliminated.

The static hedging of derivatives exposures is much more complex due to the highly uncertain potential future exposure. As an example, we illustrate the hedging of the PFE of a swap contract in Figure 9.6. The hedge notional(s) are chosen to ensure that the worst case exposure (90th quantile) is hedged at all points in time. We consider a single CDS hedge and also a term structure hedge involving five CDS instruments of different maturities. The latter hedge allows a better replication of the PFE profile over time.

Since the static hedge is based on a worst case exposure, we would expect it to be costly since it will be an overhedge in 9 cases out of 10. Assuming a credit curve of (1Y = 100 bps, 2Y = 150 bps, 3Y = 200 bps, 4Y = 250 bps, 5Y = 300 bps), the total CVA, expressed as a running spread, for the exposure profile in Figure 9.6 is 1.5 bps. The initial cost of using only 5-year CDS protection is 10.3 bps.[12] The term structure hedge (CDS Hedge 2) provides a better match to the overall exposure profile and has an initial cost of 8.1 bps,[13] although it is highly debatable whether the liquidity of the single-name CDS

---

[11] Except for credit quality reasons, which will be hedged by the MtM value of the CDS protection.

[12] $300 \times 3.42\%$.

[13] $(100 \times -0.92\%) + (150 \times -0.42\%) + (200 \times 0.11\%) + (250 \times 0.97\%) + (300 \times 2.35\%)$.

market will allow such a hedge on even the most commonly traded names. We could of course choose a lower confidence level, which would make the hedge cheaper at the expense of increasing the probability that in default the exposure would be unhedged.

This style of static hedge, whilst extremely simple, is inefficient and costly. It can only be considered for extreme situations such as very profitable trading with a particular counterparty or the urgent need to reduce an exposure, either to within a confidence level or, equivalently, below a certain credit limit.

9.8.2   Contingent credit default swaps (CCDSs)

In a standard CDS the protection buyer has protection on a fixed contractual notional amount. Such a contract is reasonably well tailored toward credit exposures arising from instruments such as loans, bonds and repos. However, a key aspect of counterparty risk on a derivative is that the loss, as determined by the credit exposure at the credit event time, is an unknown quantity.

A contingent credit default swap (CCDS) is an instrument that is exactly the same as a standard CDS but with one key difference in that the notional amount of protection is referenced to the MtM value of a specific transaction. This transaction can be potentially any product across any asset class. Hence, a CCDS can provide perfect protection against the counterparty risk on a derivative since the protection amount can be directly linked to the exposure of that derivative. Whilst CDSs are generally products which have many applications, CCDSs are products that are tailor-made to hedge counterparty risk. As such, CCDSs potentially allow for the possibility of a complete disentangling of counterparty risk from all other financial risks.

Two obvious risks arise from a CCDS, as illustrated in Figure 9.7. A CCDS contract has to reference another transaction, and hence, in order to perfectly hedge the exposure, all the details of the transaction must be specified (maturity date, reference rates, underlyings, payment frequency, daycount conventions, etc.). If the exact transaction is not specified, for reasons of practicality or otherwise, then the exposure in question will not be precisely tracked by the MtM of the transaction referenced in the CCDS. For

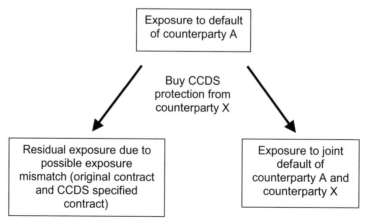

Figure 9.7. Illustration of the residual risks when using CCDS protection to hedge a derivatives exposure.

example, a non-standard transaction may be, for reasons of simplicity, hedged with a CCDS referencing a similar standard transaction. Such differences will give rise to residual exposure. A further consideration of CCDSs is that there is still risk due to the joint default of the original counterparty and the CCDS counterparty. Whilst this might seem a small issue, if the correlation between these counterparties is significant then the problem may be serious, as discussed in more detail in Chapter 10. For now we note that the "double default" aspect implies two important considerations when trading CCDSs (either or ideally both of the following conditions must be satisfied):

(1) The CCDS counterparty should be of an equivalent or better credit quality than the original counterparty.
(2) The default correlation between the CCDS counterparty and the original counterparty should be reasonably low.

The settlement of a CCDS will work in exactly the same way as that of a standard CDS except that the notional amount of protection will be determined by the current MtM value of the derivatives contract referenced by the CCDS. For example, if the derivative has an exposure of $10m at the counterparty default date then the CCDS protection buyer may exercise based on a notional amount of $10m. If a CCDS is physically settled then bonds with a face value of $10m must be purchased to deliver against the contract. If the recovery rate is 40% then the CCDS contract will have a payoff of $6m. The remaining $4m should be recovered from the counterparty. There has been discussion in the market of introducing swap-settled CCDSs where the actual derivative would be assigned to the CCDS counterparty, although legal obstacles of re-assignment may prohibit this. In any event, CCDSs will retain the problem of mismatch between CDS auction recovery versus actual final recovery (discussed in Section 9.7.1).

A CCDS represents a contract tailor-made to transfer counterparty risk from one institution to another. In buying a CCDS from X referencing a derivative traded with A, it is possible to transfer the counterparty risk of A to party X without permission from or the need to inform party A. However, except in limited cases, CCDSs have not proved particularly popular. The reasons for this are:

- *Complexity of documentation.* A CCDS must contain a "termsheet within a termsheet" since it must reference the transaction for which the counterparty risk is to be transferred.
- *No recognition of netting.* A CCDS references a single trade and not a netting set which would be more relevant. Since netting reduces exposure, a CCDS will likely be an overhedge with respect to a specific trade.
- *No recognition of collateral.* A CCDS does not account for the potential collateralisation of a credit exposure and therefore would represent a worst case hedge in such an instance.
- *Hedging of a CCDS.* A CCDS is not a magic solution to the very complex task of hedging counterparty risk. It is simply an instrument to pass this counterparty risk around from one institution to another. The hedging of a CCDS is, by construction, just as complex as hedging the counterparty risk of the underlying derivative itself.[14]

---

[14] Indeed, it may even be harder since the CCDS provider may not naturally have a good knowledge on the underlying transaction and/or the credit risk of the counterparty.

Whilst some of the above problems could be resolved, there will be increased complexity in doing this. For example, a CCDS could reference a whole netting set but this would give rise to extremely complex documentation of all trades within that netting set and agreements regarding their valuation. Even then, a CCDS would not reference subsequent trades within that netting set. Confidentiality may also be a problem since a CCDS counterparty would have information on all trades with the counterparty whose risk is being hedged.

A CCDS is probably best utilised as a means to transfer counterparty risk in extreme cases. For example, suppose an institution has a client who would like to execute a very large transaction that would lead to a very large uncollateralised exposure in excess of the amount with which the institution would be comfortable. Rather than refusing the business, the institution can use CCDS contracts to transfer the counterparty risk to other parties (whilst potentially keeping a tolerable amount themselves), without the client needing to be informed. Using CCDSs as a means to transfer and diversify particularly granular counterparty risk is potentially useful but their widespread use for hedging counterparty risk seems unlikely.

9.9 DYNAMIC CREDIT HEDGING

Whilst static hedging may be of some use in certain situations, hedging of the exotics risks represented by CVA must be done dynamically. In this section, we go through the relevant aspects and look at the overall implications of dynamic hedging of CVA.

9.9.1 Credit delta

Unlike a bullet structure, the credit spread hedging of the 5-year swap cannot be closely replicated with a 5-year CDS instrument. We first consider the sensitivity to the CDS spread, as shown in Figure 9.8. There is a significant impact across CDS tenor. An

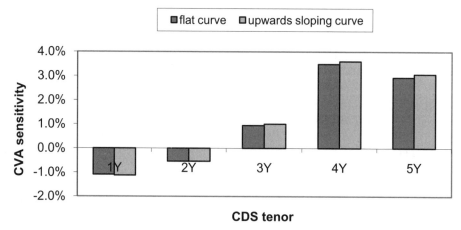

Figure 9.8. Sensitivity of the interest rate swap CVA to changes in CDS premiums of various maturities (represented in terms of CDS notional). The 5-year CDS premium is assumed to be 500 bps, with both a flat curve and upwards-sloping curve (300, 350, 400, 450, 500) considered.

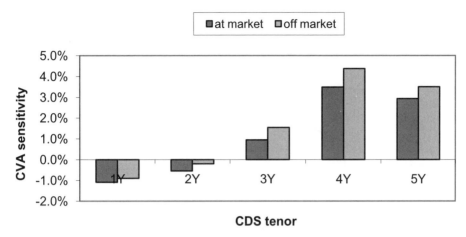

Figure 9.9. Sensitivity of the interest rate swap CVA to changes in CDS premiums of various maturities for an at-market swap and off-market swap (interest rates moved up by 50 bps). The CDS premiums are assumed to be flat at 500 bps.

increase in the 1-year CDS premium, for example, causes the 1-year default probability to increase and the 1-year to 2-year default probability to decrease. This means that the overall CVA will decrease since the EE is smaller in the first year compared with the second year – there is therefore a negative sensitivity at 1 year. An increase in the 3-year CDS will move default probability to the 2–3 year region from the 3–4 year region where the EE is higher and therefore creates a positive sensitivity. The impact of changes to the shape of the CDS curve (flat curve versus upwards-sloping curve) has little impact on CDS risk. This emphasises that the term structure impact arises almost entirely from the EE profile of the swap.

To emphasise the last point, we show in Figure 9.9 how the sensitivity of CVA changes as interest rates move up by 50 bps. In this example of a payer swap (receiving the floating rate), the swap becomes more in-the-money and there is a reasonable change in sensitivities. A move in interest rates means that the credit hedge will have to be adjusted significantly, even if CDS premiums have not moved.

The feature, illustrated above, that a move in interest rates requires a significant re-adjustment of the credit spread hedge is an important issue (and is clear mathematically from Appendix 9.A). Even without cross-dependencies, such constant re-hedging will be difficult and potentially costly.

9.9.2 Gamma

In Figure 9.10 is shown the sensitivity of CVA to the underlying CDS premium. We can notice that the profile is concave which will have an impact on delta-hedging and gamma.

Consider the delta-hedging of CVA assuming a starting CDS premium of 500 bps. We assume hedging with a 4-year CDS instrument since this represents the closest single-instrument hedge, as seen from Figure 9.9. The credit delta hedge at the current CDS premium of 500 bps is calculated to be 1.98%, meaning that one would need to buy

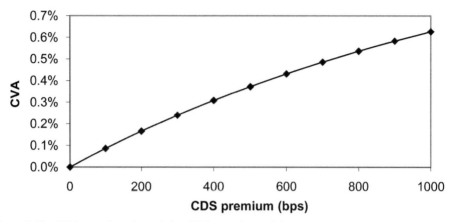

Figure 9.10. CVA as a function of the CDS premium of the counterparty.

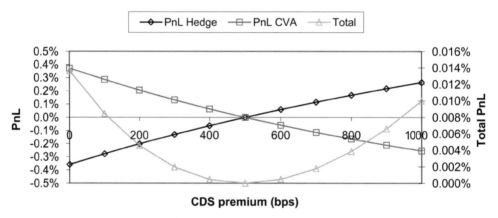

Figure 9.11. Illustration of hedging CVA by buying CDS protection. The initial CVA is 0.372%.

1.98% of the swap notional of CDS protection on the counterparty. The performance of this hedge against moves in the counterparty's CDS premium is shown in Figure 9.11. The concavity of the CVA profile is greater than the convexity of the CDS profile producing an overall small positive gamma. This means that the position is reasonable to manage since it requires buying CDS protection when credit spreads tighten and vice versa. Positive gamma means that unhedged moves in the CDS premium will create a gain on the hedge in the absence of transaction costs. Note that the effect depends on the maturity of the CDS contract used in the hedge since the overall gamma decreases with the increasing maturity of the CDS contract. For a CDS maturity of greater than 5 years, the overall gamma would be negative.

9.9.3   Jump-to-default risk

Whilst the hedging of the CVA for reasonable changes in credit spreads seems practical, we must also consider the potential impact of large increases in the spread of the

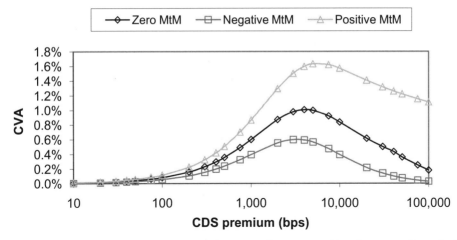

Figure 9.12. CVA as a function of CDS premium over a large range. Also shown are the equivalent swaps with negative and positive MtM values (created by moving interest rates up and down, respectively, by 50 bps).

counterparty due to severe credit deterioration and/or a sudden credit event (so-called jump-to-default risk).

Example. A trader has just executed a swap transaction with a risk-free value of zero and a CVA of 0.5%. The risky MtM of the swap is therefore −0.5%.

- Is it necessary to buy CDS protection to hedge the potential widening of the credit spread of the counterparty?
- Is it necessary to buy CDS protection to hedge the sudden default of the counterparty?

The above example illustrates the key point that the hedging of credit delta and default risk, whilst related, can require very different hedges. An instrument with no current exposure has *no* jump-to-default risk since an immediate default is of no concern. This is illustrated in Figure 9.12, which uses a very large scale to show the full range from current spreads to default.[15] The figure shows the CVA moving towards zero at default (or to the current MtM value for the positive MtM swap case). We can also see that highly distressed credits will have a CVA credit delta that changes sign at some point making hedging problematic.

In order to hedge both credit spread and jump-to-default risk one would require positions in at least two different CDS contracts. Whilst it is theoretically possible to hedge both credit spread sensitivity and the jump-to-default component, the liquidity in

---

[15] We note that this CDS will trade with an upfront premium when the name is severely distressed and so the numbers are for illustrative purposes only. Whilst a CDS premium of 100,000 bps might seem extreme, this is necessary to show the impact of almost immediate default. Indeed, this CDS premium implies that the expected default time is within the next month (the hazard rate at this CDS premium would be 1,000%/60% = 1,667%; the expected default time is the inverse of this, which is 3.12 weeks).

the single-name CDS market probably prohibits this. Assuming it is possible to buy CDS protection on the counterparty then the pragmatic approach will be to hedge the credit spread sensitivity unless the name becomes highly distressed, in which case the jump-to-default risk should be the key focus.[16] Figure 9.12 also shows that one can sell CDS protection against a potential gain if a counterparty defaults due to the CVA dropping to the current exposure (which may be zero). This corresponds to the highly distressed region in Figure 9.12 where there is a negative delta (slope).

9.9.4   Credit hedging with indices

Buying single-name CDS protection on some counterparties (or hedging their credit risk directly in other ways) is impractical. A CDS market may not exist, may be highly illiquid or an institution may simply not consider it worthwhile to trade CDS against certain counterparties. A possible solution is then to hedge credit delta via a credit index. Whilst this will hedge general credit quality changes, it will not allow any control over gamma and jump-to-default risk for a given counterparty.[17] Such an approach will hedge systemic credit quality changes but not idiosyncratic ones. A counterparty's CDS premium widening significantly for idiosyncratic reasons would be expected to give rise to an increase in CVA, which is unhedged. This effect was illustrated in Table 7.7.

Whilst hedging individual exposures is often impractical, a key advantage of using credit indices is the ability to hedge total CVA numbers across all counterparties. In a widening spread environment, a firm would have an increasing total CVA, which will create substantial losses for all cases where the default probability of the counterparties are not hedged.[18] For example, many firms suffered such problems when credit spreads widened dramatically in 2007. Macro-hedging of global credit spreads is possible by buying protection on the relevant credit indices. The use of credit indices will also simplify (perhaps incorrectly) the hedging of bilateral CVA. This is discussed in Section 9.11.4.

9.10   EXPOSURE

We now consider the hedging of the CVA component arising from the exposure that can be loosely divided into the impact of spot rates, volatility and correlation. The analysis will be made with CVA as a negative value with respect to the underlying transaction as it represents a cost.

9.10.1   Hedging spot rates

Interestingly, the hedging of underlying spot rates for CVA usually mirrors hedges corresponding to the risk-free instrument. In Figure 9.13 we show both the risk-free and CVA interest rate sensitivities for the interest rate swap in question.

We can understand the above graph as follows. The 5-year payer swap has a positive

---

[16] Although we can note that, due to the gamma effect, hedging credit spread risk will probably be an overhedge of jump-to-default risk.

[17] If the counterparty concerned is within the index used for hedging there may be some implicit hedging of these components.

[18] Unless the institution relies on bilateral CVAs to dampen this sensitivity, this may be considered merely a cosmetic solution to the problem (as argued in Chapter 7).

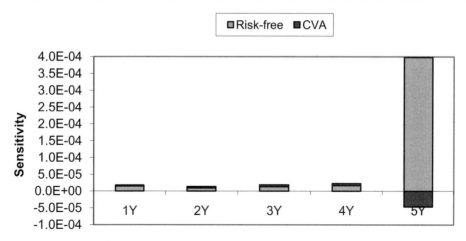

Figure 9.13. Sensitivity of the risk-free swap value and the CVA of the swap to a 1 bp move in the underlying interest rates assuming the counterparty CDS premium is 500 bps.

sensitivity to interest rates since, as rates increase, the value of the floating payments received will increase. Most of the sensitivity is concentrated on the 5-year point. When interest rates increase, the CVA will increase due to the increased exposure, but since CVA represents a cost this corresponds to a negative sensitivity. The CVA sensitivity on the previous tenors is slightly positive. A combination of the risk-free and CVA sensitivities gives the risky sensitivity, which involves reducing the 5-year hedge and increasing the (small) hedges on the shorter maturities.

A question that arises is whether to allow the swap trader to hedge the interest rate risk in the usual manner – as if the swap were risk-free and for another trader to have the responsibility to hedge the CVA component. Whilst this might seem the most obvious organisational split, it might seem perverse for one trader to execute one hedge position on 5-year rates and for the other essentially to "unwind" some of that position since they require to execute a trade with the opposite sensitivity. This topic will be discussed more in Chapter 12, but let us now present one justification for keeping the hedging separate. In Figure 9.14 we have recomputed the same sensitivities assuming the counterparty credit quality has deteriorated and the CDS premium has doubled to 1,000 bps. Whilst the risk-free hedges are unchanged, the CVA hedges have changed substantially. This is the reverse of the effect shown in Figure 9.9. Again, the need to re-adjust one risk factor (interest rates) due to a move in another (credit quality) is a difficult consequence of dynamic hedging of CVA.

In Figure 9.15 we show the sensitivities for the opposite receiver swap. Whilst the risk-free sensitivities are exactly equal and opposite due to the linearity of the product, the CVA components do not behave in this way. With an upwards-sloping interest rate term structure, the receiver swap will have a smaller sensitivity to interest rates since it has a lower expected exposure. The CVA sensitivities are of the opposite sign but approximately half those of the corresponding payer swap.

The above examples may well be interpreted as meaning that, whilst risk-free and CVA hedges could be combined, the complexity of hedging CVA means that it should be abstracted from the role of a typical trader.

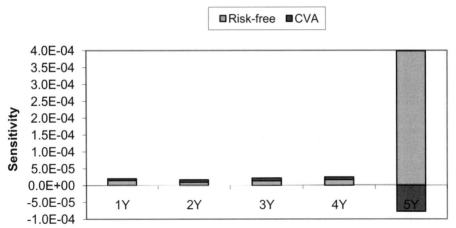

Figure 9.14. Sensitivity of the risk-free swap value and the CVA of the swap to a 1 bp move in the underlying interest rates assuming the counterparty CDS premium is 1,000 bps.

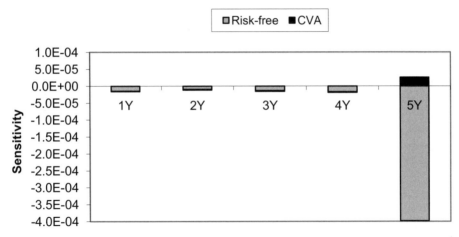

Figure 9.15. Sensitivity of the opposite risk-free receiver swap value and the CVA of the swap to a 1 bp move in the underlying interest rates assuming the counterparty CDS premium is 500 bps.

9.10.2   Spot rates and drift

Let us return to the discussion on using risk-neutral or real parameters and consider the hedging of the payer and receiver interest rate swaps according to the sensitivities shown in Figures 9.13 and 9.15, respectively. We therefore consider hedges based on all five annual maturities up to 5 years. By using the interest rate term structure given by the market, we are implicitly assuming that interest rates will increase over time. Let us assume that this is not the case, reflected by a flattening of the interest rate term structure. In Table 9.3 we show that the hedges perform well with the decrease in the CVA for the payer swap balanced by a loss on the hedge and vice versa for the receiver swap. The smaller hedge (Figure 9.15) required for the receiver swap is in line with the smaller change in CVA for the interest rate move.

Table 9.3. Illustration of hedging of CVA corresponding to a flattening of the interest rate term structure (1-year and 2-year rates move up by 5 bps, 4-year and 5-year rates down by 5 bps, 3-year rates unchanged).

	Payer swap	*Receiver swap*
Initial CVA	0.325%	0.166%
Final CVA	0.306%	0.177%
CVA P&L	0.019%	−0.011%
Hedge P&L	−0.020%	0.010%

If the interest rate component of the CVA is not being hedged then the use of risk-neutral parameters is dangerous. The implicit assumption that future spot interest rates will follow the current forward rates equates to making a bet that the interest rates will increase and hence the payer swap has a larger CVA than the receiver. If this is not the case, as seen by a gradual flattening of the interest rate curve, then the CVA will create a positive P&L on the payer swap and a negative P&L on the receiver swap. This illustrates the danger of a naive use of risk-neutral parameters without associated hedging.

9.10.3   Volatility

Managing volatility risk is, alongside CDS hedging, the most important aspect of hedging counterparty risk. Recall that, whilst the underlying derivative may have little or no sensitivity to volatility, the associated CVA will have substantial volatility risk. We show in Figure 9.16 the CVA for the payer and receiver interest rate swaps used in the

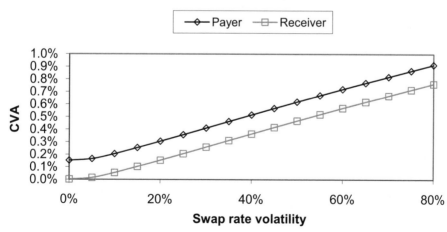

Figure 9.16. CVA as a function of swap rate volatility for the payer interest rate swap and equivalent receiver swap. This assumes a flat volatility term structure.

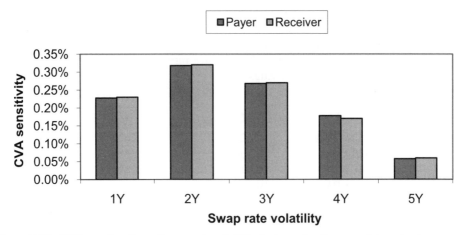

Figure 9.17. CVA as a function of swap rate volatility by tenor for the payer interest rate swap and equivalent receiver swap.

previous examples. The reader will find it helpful to recall that the CVA of an interest rate swap can be represented as a series of swaptions on the reverse swap (Section 7.1.6).

Both the payer and receiver swaps have a monotonically increasing relationship to volatility, as one would expect for an option-type payoff. For zero volatility, the payer swap has some CVA due to the swaptions being in the money for the upward-sloping interest rate term structure. At zero volatility the receiver swap has zero CVA since the swaptions are out of the money. This corresponds to zero probability of an exposure over the life of the swap (under the assumption of zero uncertainty of future value).

The sensitivity of CVA to interest rate volatility can be hedged via swaptions. However, we should also consider the term structure impact of volatility, which is illustrated in Figure 9.17. We can see quite a relatively complex pattern, which suggests that the volatility hedge should be term structure sensitive.

In order to understand the pattern in Figure 9.17, we must consider two effects:

- *Swaption value*. Short-term swaptions[19] will have little value due to the short maturity, whilst long-term swaptions will have little value due to the short duration of the underlying swap. The swaptions that have the most value are those at intermediate maturities.[20] Indeed, it is this effect that gives rise to the classic exposure profile of a swap product.
- *Moneyness of swaptions*. The swaptions that are at the money will have the largest volatility sensitivity whilst those in or out of the money will have smaller sensitivities.

The first factor above tends to dominate the second. In our example the payer swaptions will always be in the money by the same amount as the receiver swaptions are out of the money, hence the overall interest rate sensitivity is rather similar. The results in Figure 9.17 do not change substantially as the interest rate term structure changes.

---

[19] These swaptions follow the Sorensen and Bollier analogy (Appendix 7.D) and are not considered to be actual hedging instruments.

[20] A more detailed description of this is given in Appendix 7.D.

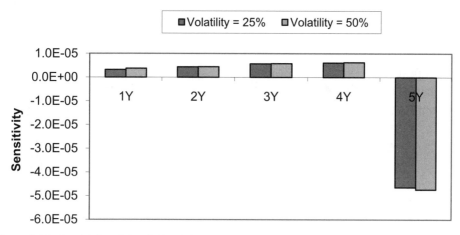

Figure 9.18. Sensitivity of the CVA of the swap to a 1 bp move in the underlying interest rates for swap rate volatilities of 25% and 50% assuming the counterparty CDS premium is 500 bps.

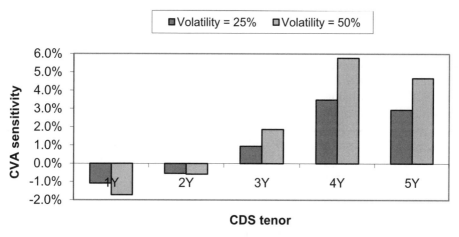

Figure 9.19. Sensitivity of the interest rate swap CVA to changes in CDS premiums of various maturities for swap rate volatilities of 25% and 50%. The CDS premiums are assumed to be flat at 500 bps.

Volatility sensitivity of CVA typically has a term structure similar to that of the EE profile – the more variable the EE profile, the more sensitive the volatility hedge to term structure.

Finally, we consider the impact of volatility on the other CVA hedges. Figure 9.18 shows the impact of volatility on the interest rate CVA hedge (Section 9.10.1) indicating only a minimal impact. However, CDS hedges change substantially, as illustrated in Figure 9.19. Whilst such effects should not produce gains and losses on CVA hedges (aside from cross-gamma issues discussed in Section 9.11.1), the effort of updating other hedges should be considered substantial.

Again, we see that changes in CVA variables can cause other hedges to be substantially re-adjusted.

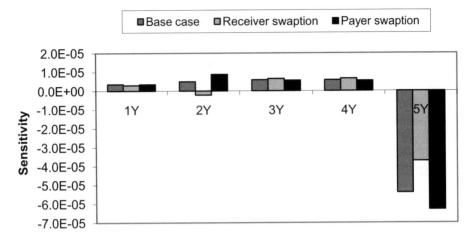

Figure 9.20. Sensitivity of the CVA of the (payer) swap to a 1 bp move in the underlying interest rates, as previously shown in Figure 9.13, but assuming that there is additionally a single volatility hedge corresponding to either a receiver or payer swaption of 2-year maturity.

9.10.4   Spot rate sensitivity under volatility hedging

We should finally comment that hedging volatility would also change the sensitivity to spot rates. In Figure 9.20 is shown the spot sensitivity of CVA, as previously shown in Figure 9.13, but assuming that the volatility will be hedged using a 2-year maturity swaption.[21] We can see that hedging volatility with the opposite receiver swaption will reduce the overall spot sensitivity whereas using a payer swaption to hedge volatility will increase the overall sensitivity and potentially increase hedging costs. From the Sorenson–Bollier analogy, it is not surprising that the more natural hedging instrument is the (opposite) receiver swaption.

9.11   CROSS-DEPENDENCY

9.11.1   Cross-gamma and wrong-way risk

Cross-gamma is the term used to describe a dependency between two underlying variables. If there is correlation between variables then the cross-gamma term(s) will be non-zero. In an ideal world, this implied correlation component would be hedged but it is unlikely that instruments with the relevant sensitivity will exist and the associated cross-gamma term will be unhedgeable. Nevertheless, it is important to consider and be aware of the potential problems causes by large dependencies and cross-gamma terms.

The most important manifestation of cross-gamma is that related to wrong-way risk. An unanticipated relationship between credit quality and exposure will cause hedging problems even if the credit and exposure terms are correctly hedged in isolation as we shall illustrate below.

---

[21] We assume a 2-year swaption to enter into a 3-year swap although the swap maturity has only a small impact on the results.

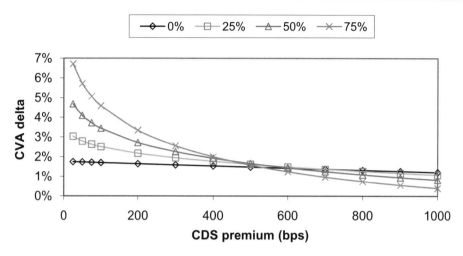

Figure 9.21. CDS hedge notional for the CVA of the interest rate swap for different wrong-way risk correlations (0% corresponds to no wrong-way risk).

9.11.2   Hedging wrong-way risk

We have used the simple approach described in Appendix 8.A to illustrate the wrong-way risk impact on hedging. We show the credit delta (as discussed in Section 9.9.1) in terms of the percentage of CDS notional required to hedge the CVA in Figure 9.21 as a function of different correlations (recall that a higher correlation implies a greater wrong-way risk).

We can see that the delta is very sensitive to wrong-way risk and, for good-quality counterparties, the failure to assess wrong-way risk can lead to a severe underestimate of the credit delta. If the CDS premium of the counterparty rises sharply, together with an increase in the exposure, the increase in CVA will be substantially underhedged.

9.11.3   Monolines

We now return to the monoline example from Section 8.7.4. Assume the monoline CDS premium is trading at 50 bps and the credit protection purchased has an identical spread. Suppose an institution buys protection on the monoline in order to hedge their CVA related to another transaction. Even though there is wrong-way risk, the hedge performs well as long as the correlation assumption made is correct. This is shown in Figure 9.22 where a correlation of 50% between the monoline credit quality and exposure of the underlying credit protection is assumed (this may have seemed a reasonable estimate when the monoline credit quality was good). There is even some positive gamma, suggesting that if the monoline credit quality deteriorates substantially then the hedged position will return a profit and the institution can unwind (sell back) the CDS protection at higher levels.

However, suppose the wrong-way risk was underestimated and the actual correlation parameter should have been 90%. In Figure 9.23 is shown the same position with this

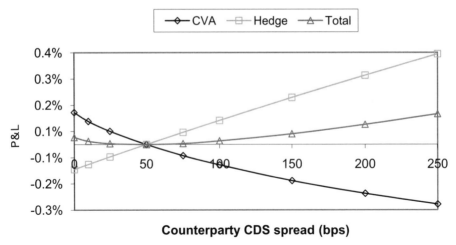

Figure 9.22. Illustration of hedging the CVA arising from CDS protection purchased from a high-quality counterparty on an uncollateralised basis such as a monoline. The CDS premium of the monoline (counterparty) is initially 50 bps and the delta hedge is calculated with a wrong-way risk assumption of 50% (correlation between monoline credit quality and underlying protection).

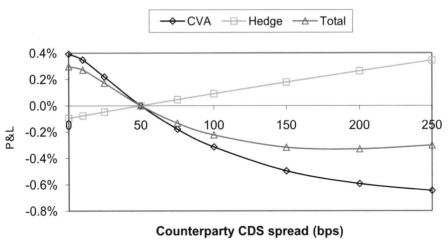

Figure 9.23. As for the previous example but assuming the hedge is calculated at 50% correlation whereas the actual correlation is 90%.

higher correlation parameter and the incorrect (50% correlation) hedge. We can see a major issue if the monoline CDS spread widens in that the CVA increase is only partially hedged. Worse still, it will be necessary to attempt to buy more CDS protection as the monoline spread widens. If the correlation used for hedging is too high then there will be losses when spreads tighten. It should be clear that the correlation between the credit quality of the monoline and value of contracts is critical and its uncertainty creates significant hedging challenges.

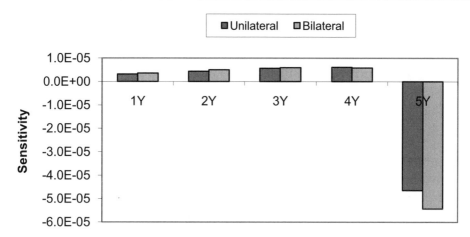

Figure 9.24. Sensitivity of the CVA to interest rates moves for unilateral and bilateral CVA for the payer interest rate swap shown previously in Figure 9.13.

9.11.4 Hedging bilateral counterparty risk

As discussed in Chapter 7, bilateral counterparty risk means that an institution manages CVA under the assumption that they, as well as their counterparty, may default. This aspect will always reduce the price of counterparty risk as defined by CVA since an institution will always "gain" when they default due to being not obliged ("able" would of course be a better word) to make contractual payments. In Chapter 7 we advised against the naive use of bilateral CVA for the simple reason that the gain that an institution would make when they default is very hard to monetise prior to their actual default (at least during normal times). Now we can look more deeply into the hedging of bilateral CVA, it may be useful to recall the intuitive approximate formula for bilateral CVA (Section 7.3.4):

$$\text{BCVA} = X^{\text{CDS}} \times \text{EPE} - X_I^{\text{CDS}} \times \text{ENE}, \tag{9.1}$$

where X^{CDS} is the counterparty's CDS premium, X_I^{CDS} the institution's own CDS premium, EPE the expected positive exposure and ENE the expected negative exposure (EPE from the counterparty's point of view). In all the examples we will assume that the institution is around half as risky as its counterparty with a CDS premium of 250 bps compared with 500 bps (both credit curves assumed to be flat).

We first show in Figure 9.24 the sensitivity to interest rates (shown earlier in Figure 9.13) for both unilateral (as discussed so far in this chapter) and bilateral CVA where the bilateral CVA hedge can be seen to have increased. This can be understood since an increase in 5-year interest rates will increase the EPE and correspondingly decrease the ENE. Due to their opposite signs, in equation (9.1) these effects both contribute a negative CVA sensitivity.[22]

We now consider how the sensitivity of CVA to swap rate volatility is impacted by the bilateral component. In the classic swaption analogy, an institution is short a series of

---

[22] Recall the CVA is a negative term in the context of the value of the derivative. Increasing EPE and decreasing ENE both have negative impacts and increase negative sensitivity compared with the bilateral case.

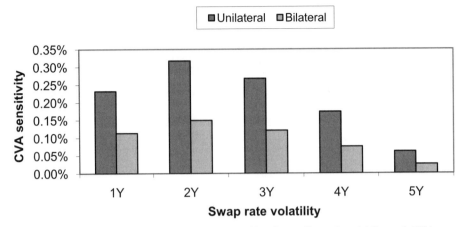

Figure 9.25. CVA as a function of swap rate volatility for unilateral and bilateral CVAs.

receiver swaptions (relating to their counterparty's default) but then long a series of the same swaptions (relating to their own default). These swaptions will not cancel perfectly due to the difference in credit quality and strike but one should expect some cancellation of the volatility risk. To put it differently, both terms in equation (9.1) will increase in absolute value with increasing volatility and so, overall, the second term will dampen the increase of the first. The balance of the sensitivity to volatility will be determined by:

- The relative riskiness of the institution and their counterparty – X^{CDS} and X_I^{CDS} in equation (9.1).
- EPE versus the ENE (this is related to the strike of the long and short swaptions).

Under the swaption analogy, one set of swaptions will be in the money whilst the other will be out of the money by the same proportion. Since both sets of swaptions will have comparable sensitivity to volatility, we expect the relative riskiness to be the key component. This is indeed the case, as seen in Figure 9.25 which shows the bilateral sensitivity reduced by around 50% in correspondence with the relative riskiness of the institution vis-à-vis their counterparty.

Finally, we look at the CDS sensitivities corresponding to bilateral CVA, which are shown in Figure 9.26. The sensitivity to the counterparty CDS premium is not changed substantially when using bilateral CVA (BCVA). The institution must still buy protection on their counterparty in almost the same amounts. The key impact is the sensitivity that the institution has to their own CDS premium, which is in the opposite direction. This, as discussed in Chapter 7, corresponds to an institution needing to sell CDS protection on themselves as a reference entity. This is a crucial component in the analysis and can be thought of as being required in order to partially fund the protection bought on the counterparty and therefore justify the lower bilateral CVA. If an institution is unable to monetise this component then using BCVA cannot be justified from a hedging point of view.

If the institution attempts to hedge their counterparty's CDS premium by buying index protection then the bilateral terms in Figure 9.26 can be combined (with some

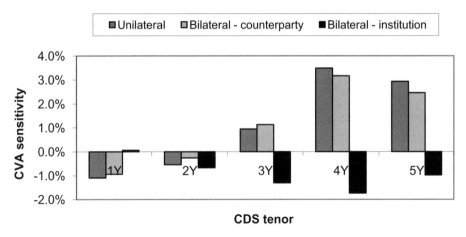

Figure 9.26. Sensitivity of the CVA to changes in CDS premiums for unilateral and bilateral cases. The case "Bilateral – counterparty" shows the impact of a move in the counterparty's CDS premium whilst "Bilateral – institution" refers to the CDS premium of the institution.

adjustment for the relevant betas[23]). This will dampen the overall CDS sensitivity by the long protection required to hedge the counterparty default being partially cancelled by the short CDS protection position to hedge the institution's own default. In terms of an index hedge, an institution needs to respectively buy and sell index protection to hedge the first and second terms in equation (9.1). The net position may turn out to be short protection, which can be seen as the institution monetising a negative bilateral CVA.

The idea of hedging with a credit index seems to fit naturally within the bilateral CVA concept and avoid the problem that an institution cannot sell CDS protection on themselves. However, such an approach might be considered to represent an illusion since it only works if neither the institution nor their counterparty becomes decorrelated with an index. The hedge is efficient for the systemic component of CDS premiums but does not hedge against idiosyncratic risks of either counterparty or institution. If the counterparty defaults then the resulting losses may be completely unhedged and yet there may have been zero (or even negative) BCVA initially.

An institution relying on bilateral CVA pricing, together with some systemic credit hedging via indices, will probably have few problems in normal markets where their counterparty's and their own credit quality is stable. However, in a turbulent period, when there are idiosyncratic credit quality concerns, the underestimation of counterparty risk by using the bilateral assumption and the inefficiency of credit hedges will become apparent.

9.11.5 Impact of collateralisation on hedging

We now show the impact of collateral on sensitivities and the hedging of counterparty risk. Since collateral reduces exposure then we should expect a reduction in the hedging requirements. All of the results below are based on the collateral simulations shown in

---

[23] In other words, adjusting for the correlation between the credit quality of the counterparty and institution and that of the underlying credit index.

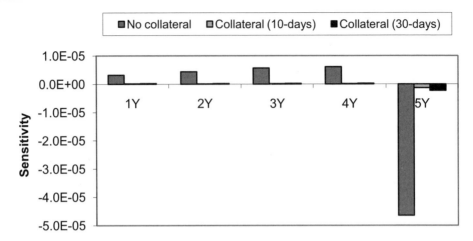

Figure 9.27. Sensitivity of the CVA to interest rate moves for collateralised and uncollateralised positions.

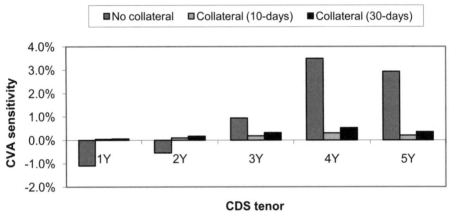

Figure 9.28. Sensitivity of the CVA to changes in CDS premiums for collateralised and uncollateralised positions.

Section 5.4 with the associated CVA calculations given in Section 7.2.1. A 10-day or 30-day remargin period is used (time before required collateral is posted) and there is assumed to be no threshold or independent amount. A 10-day period may be a reasonably conservative period with daily margining, as discussed in Chapter 4, whilst a 30-day period would correspond to a more stressed case.

The sensitivity with respect to interest rates (Figure 9.27) is almost zero, reflecting the fact that drift becomes unimportant with collateral due to the relevant time horizon being so short. For CDS (Figure 9.28) and volatility (Figure 9.29) sensitivities, there is a large reduction but still some sensitivity, reflecting the importance these factors have on the risk of a collateralised counterparty. As the period of risk is increased from 10 to 30 days, the sensitivity increases towards the non-collateral value. The results are, not surprisingly, highly sensitive to the assumptions regarding posting of collateral.

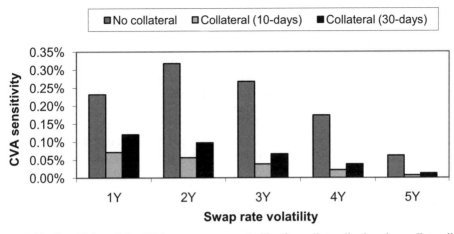

Figure 9.29. Sensitivity of the CVA to swap rate volatility for collateralised and uncollateralised positions.

The summary is that collateral can reduce hedging parameters substantially but that any residual sensitivity is very sensitive to the terms of the collateral agreement (thresholds, etc.) and the assumptions regarding receiving collateral (mainly the effective margin call frequency).

9.12 AGGREGATION OF SENSITIVITIES

The above sections have given a large amount of detail on the hedging of all possible CVA components. For a single trade, the extent of the required hedging is clearly complex, with many individual sensitivities. In reality, sensitivities can be aggregated according to:

- *General sensitivities.* All market parameters can be aggregated across counterparties. For example, sensitivities to spot and forward rates, volatilities and correlations. This may also include credit spread hedges via credit indices.
- *Counterparty-specific sensitivities.* This will include only single-name CDS (or CCDS) hedges referencing specific counterparties.

All general sensitivities can be assessed and hedged at the overall level. Sensitivities to spot and forward rates and correlations will tend to offset one another across counterparties. For example, if an institution has several trades with one counterparty and all the corresponding hedges with another counterparty of similar credit quality then there should be significant offsetting of sensitivities.[24] This can be seen for the opposite swaps shown earlier in Figures 9.14 and 9.15. If an institution's derivatives book is well hedged overall and its counterparties are of similar credit quality, then it can be expected that the hedging requirements of spot and forward rates and correlations will be reasonably limited.

---

[24] The offsetting requires that the counterparties have similar CDS premiums, and that exposure profiles are not highly skewed.

Whilst other market variables should require only limited hedging, under unilateral CVA, sensitivity to volatility is in the same direction for all trades (for example, see Figure 9.17). Hence, the overall volatility risk will be significant and should be hedged by trading options across the term structures for the different underlying asset classes. Foreign exchange volatility is likely to be a particularly important hedge due to the long-dated nature of many FX exposures, and interest rate volatility risk is likely to be significant due to the sheer notional amount of exposure. Failure to hedge volatility risk correctly could lead to sudden MtM losses caused by an increase in CVA values resulting from a spike in volatility in one or more asset classes. Volatility risk is reduced by using bilateral CVA (see Figure 9.25) due to a negative sensitivity linked to the institution's own default. This would mean that an institution would have to buy volatility when their credit quality is good but sell volatility when their credit quality worsens.[25] This might seem yet another strange quirk arising from the fundamentally flawed approach of bilateral counterparty risk.

Credit risk, like volatility, will be positive for all counterparties when using unilateral CVA. So, as with volatility, an institution will need to buy significant notional amounts of CDS protection to hedge an increasing CVA when credit spreads widen. Single-name CDS protection should, in theory at least, be traded against each counterparty individually to have control over gamma and jump-to-default risk. In practice, only the counterparties with significant risk and liquid CDS markets will be hedged in this way. Again, using bilateral CVA will reduce the net overall amount of CDS protection required. Indeed, an institution whose CDS premium is wide compared with the average of their counterparty's may be an overall seller of CDS protection in order to hedge a negative BCVA. Such an approach is perverse since a sudden improvement of the institution's credit quality (CDS premium tightens compared with the rest of the market) will create a large unhedged CVA loss. Trading single-name protection, an institution can be hedged against the idiosyncratic increase in the CDS premium of a counterparty. It does not, however, allow an institution to hedge a loss from a similar decrease in their own CDS premium without selling CDS protection on themselves. Alternatively, an institution can attempt to produce a similar position by buying their debt synthetically. As mentioned in Chapter 7, we would advise against using bilateral CVA without a full understanding of the associated hedging problems, which may be sometimes counterintuitive.

9.13 SUMMARY

This chapter has been concerned with a thorough analysis of the hedging aspects of counterparty risk. We have shown that a complete hedging of recovery rate, default probability and exposure components is complex due to the large number of variables, technical factors such as delivery squeezes, non-tradable variables, gamma, cross-dependency and jump-to default-risk. Sensitivities to spot rates, volatility, correlation, cross-dependency and default have all been described. We have also shown the impact of collateral on hedging and discussed the hedging implications of using bilateral counterparty risk. For an institution to effectively manage their counterparty risk requires a

---

[25] Very perversely, a highly distressed institution will need to be extremely short volatility to hedge the potential increase in BCVA – due to a decrease in the second term of equation (9.1) – if volatility declines.

prudent choice of which key variables to hedge. In Chapter 12 we will discuss more on managing counterparty risk and consider whether it is reasonable to choose not to hedge certain parameters and price them to their historical levels, taking a reserve against the associated hedging errors.

In the next chapters we tackle an alternative way to manage counterparty risk at the portfolio level via the consideration of unexpected losses and associated capital requirements.

APPENDIX 9.A: EXAMPLE OF CALCULATION OF CVA GREEKS

In Appendix 7.C we derived a simple formula for CVA in terms of the CDS premium and EPE under the assumption of no wrong-way risk. We now use this formula to illustrate the hedging of CVA. From Appendix 7.C:

$$\text{CVA}(t, T) \approx X^{\text{CDS}} \times \text{CDS}_{\text{premium}}(t, T) \times \text{EPE}.$$

Let us combine the current CDS and unit premium leg value of a CDS into a single-term CRD (which represents the value of a premium leg of the CDS on the counterparty) and drop time parameters for simplicity:

$$\text{CVA} = \text{CRD} \times \text{EPE}.$$

We can now write the change in the value of the CVA as:

$$\Delta\text{CVA} = \text{EPE}\left[\frac{\partial\text{CRD}}{\partial h}\Delta h + \frac{\partial\text{CRD}}{\partial\delta}\Delta\delta + \frac{\partial\text{CRD}}{\partial r}\Delta r\right] + \text{CRD}\left[\sum_{i=1}^{n}\frac{\partial\text{EPE}}{\partial x_i}\Delta x_i\right] + \cdots.$$

where the following partial derivatives refer to:

$$\frac{\partial\text{CRD}}{\partial h} = \text{sensitivity of the CRD to the hazard rate,}$$

$$\frac{\partial\text{CRD}}{\partial\delta} = \text{sensitivity of the CRD to the recovery rate,}$$

$$\frac{\partial\text{CRD}}{\partial S} = \text{sensitivity of the CRD to interest rates,}$$

$$\frac{\partial\text{EPE}}{\partial x_i} = \text{sensitivity of the EPE to the } i\text{th risk factor.}$$

The first two terms (hazard rate and recovery rate) can be hedged almost via a CDS contract with some small residual recovery risk. The interest rate risk in the CRD term is minimal and can be combined with any interest rate hedge in the EPE term. Finally, all of the risk factors of the EPE must be hedged.

Two important effects are ignored in the above analysis but must also be considered. The first is the cross-terms for every pair of sensitivities and the second is the time dependence of all hedge parameters. If the default probability and exposure are considered independent then these cross-terms can be ignored.

A very important point is that a change in EPE will change the CRD hedging terms and a change in CRD will change the magnitude of the EPE hedges. Several numerical examples in the chapter illustrate this.

Bilateral CVA will create sensitivities of opposite sign to the EPE components above and there will be therefore a net offsetting of the EPE and ENE-related components. In addition, using BCVA there will be additional CRD terms relating to an institution's own default.

10

Portfolio Models and Economic Capital

> *"The policy of being too cautious is the greatest risk of all."*
>
> Jawaharlal Nehru (1889–1964)

10.1 INTRODUCTION

So far, all considerations of counterparty risk have been made at the level of a single counterparty. This involves combining exposure, default probability, recovery and including all risk mitigation methods within a given netting set. The concept of a netting set can be quite complex, with many different trades covered and detailed aspects such as collateral agreements to consider. Nevertheless, a netting set applies only for a single counterparty (except in the case of multilateral netting discussed in Chapter 14). We have also discussed the pricing and hedging of counterparty risk mainly in relation to an individual counterparty.

The final component in quantifying and managing counterparty risk will be to introduce portfolio level aspects, which will require consideration of the risk posed by two or more counterparties. Even the smallest users of derivatives will typically trade with several counterparties, whilst many financial institutions will have hundreds or even thousands of counterparties to consider. Hence, understanding the interactions between these individual counterparty risks at a portfolio level is necessary.

Portfolio assessment of counterparty risk is critical since an institution must be prepared for the possibility that a relatively large number of their counterparties may default. Whilst this number is likely to be only a small percentage of the total, it will nevertheless represent an extreme situation. Having a good understanding of a "unexpected loss" due to counterparty risk is critical in order to make business decisions and assign capital. One of the critical issues for the Basel II internal ratings based (IRB) approach is calculation of the exposure at default (EAD). This chapter will provide the foundations for the calculation of EAD via a loan-equivalent measure. The precise details of Basel II implementation for counterparty risk will be dealt with in Chapter 11.

We will describe portfolio approaches to counterparty risk showing examples and including wrong-way risk aspects. We do not go into great detail on credit portfolio models which are covered in more depth by, for example, Gupton et al. (1997), Bluhm et al. (2003), Duffie and Singleton (2003) or, in relation to counterparty risk, by De Prisco and Rosen (2005). An implicit assumption will be that the marginal (individual) default probabilities of each counterparty are known – this aspect has been discussed in Chapter

6. The goal of this chapter is the consideration of multiple defaults knowing the probability of individual default events.

10.2 JOINT DEFAULT

10.2.1 Double-default approach

We start with the concept of "double default" as defined previously for CCDS contracts. Suppose an institution has an exposure to counterparty A and insures that exposure through counterparty X (as in the case of a CCDS discussed in Section 9.8.2). The institution now has a (reduced) risk due to both counterparties A and X defaulting. Let us consider four possible outcomes as illustrated in Figure 10.1. We need to consider the following relationships between entities A and X:

- *Mutually exclusive.* Mutually exclusive events cannot occur at the same time. For default events to be mutually exclusive, there would have to be negative correlation between them. This is unlikely to be the case for defaults, except in rare circumstances where two competitors may be considered unlikely to default together since the failure of one would give the other an increased market share.
- *Independent.* Independent events happen with no underlying linkage so that occurrence of one event makes it neither more nor less probable that the other event occurs. When throwing two coins, the outcomes are independent with respect to each other. Independent events can happen together, although this may be unlikely if their underlying probabilities are small.
- *Positive dependence.* Positive dependence means that if one event occurs then another is more likely to occur. This is the key area for portfolio defaults since one default may increase the probability of other defaults. Positive dependence means that the probability of two defaults is increased compared with the independent case.
- *Maximum dependence.* The maximum dependence between two default variables corresponds to the highest possible joint probability. Note that the circles cannot overlap perfectly (since the individual default probabilities differ). Hence, the

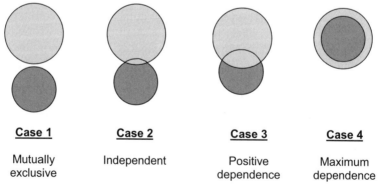

Case 1	Case 2	Case 3	Case 4
Mutually exclusive	Independent	Positive dependence	Maximum dependence

Figure 10.1. Illustration of the relationship between the defaults of two entities. The area of each circle represents the default probability (a larger circle is a more risky name). The overlap between the circles signifies joint default.

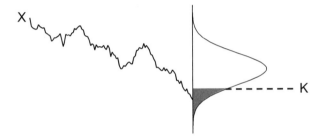

Figure 10.2. Illustration of the Merton approach to default modelling. If the underlying asset value falls below a certain default threshold (K) then default will occur.

maximum joint default probability is the minimum of the two individual default probabilities.

Example. Suppose an institution has exposure to a counterparty (A) with a default probability of 2% but then buys protection on that exposure (through a CCDS) with another counterparty (X) with a smaller default probability of 1%.

The institution now has risk to the "double default" (default of both counterparties A and X). What is this probability?

Answer. At this point we can do no more than attempt to put boundaries on the problem. Assuming that the default events of A and X cannot be mutually exclusive, the best case corresponds to independence when the joint default probability will be 0.02% (1% × 2%) – case 2 in Figure 10.1. The worst case of maximum correlation would correspond to a joint default probability of 1% (the minimum of the two default probabilities) – case 4 in Figure 10.1. The joint default probability will therefore be between 0.02% and 1% and the relative benefit of the CCDS could be anything from double (2% reduced to 1%) to 100 times (2% reduced to 0.02%).

10.2.2   Merton-style approach

The modelling of joint default events is conceptually difficult due to the binary[1] nature of default and the lack of data regarding default events, let alone joint default events. What is required is an intuitive way to generate dependence between defaults with some underlying economic structure. This has been classically achieved using a Merton-inspired approach. The Merton model was described in Chapter 6 for a single-default process and now is extended for multiple defaults.

In the Merton model we simply write default as being the point at which a process for the asset value falls below a certain "default threshold" as illustrated in Figure 10.2.

---

[1] Meaning simply that default can either occur or not, so there are just two (rather than a continuum of) states to consider. The nature of default, as in this two-state process, means that the application of classical statistical concepts such as correlation is not straightforward.

One can interpret X as being an asset value in the classic Merton sense (see Section 6.4.3) with the change in the asset value during a small time interval, the asset return, assumed to follow a standard normal distribution. Since the default probability of the firm is already known (by other methods as described in Chapter 6) then the precise distributional specification of the asset return (such as the drift and volatility) is unimportant. One must set the default barrier in order to retrieve the correct default probability which corresponds to $k = \Phi^{-1}(p)$, where $\Phi^{-1}(.)$ is the inverse of a cumulative normal distribution function and p is the default probability of the name over the time horizon of interest.

10.2.3 Impact of correlation

The above modelling framework[2] might first appear to be nothing more than a mapping exercise. However, the power of the approach is the elegance and intuition when introducing another default event. Now the joint default probability can be defined by a two-dimensional or bivariate Gaussian distribution function. Hence, in the double-default model of interest, the joint default probability of two names A and X, p_{AX}, is given by:

$$p_{AX} = \Phi_2(k_A, k_X; \rho_{AX}), \tag{10.1}$$

where Φ_2 is a bivariate cumulative distribution function, ρ_{AX} is the correlation between A and X (often referred to as the "asset correlation") and k_A and k_X are the default barriers as defined above. An illustration of this is given in Figure 10.3.

Spreadsheet 10.1. Calculation of joint default probabilities with a bivariate normal distribution function

---

We now have the means to calculate joint default probabilities as a function of correlation. This is shown in Figure 10.4 for the earlier example of names with default probabilities of 1% and 2%. We can see that with negative correlation, the joint default probability is extremely small, tending towards zero at maximum negative correlation (mutually exclusive). With zero correlation (independence), the joint default probability is 0.02% (1% × 2%) whilst at maximum correlation it increases to 1%.

We can see that the size of correlation is clearly crucial in determining the impact of counterparty risk for two or more names.

10.2.4 Impact on CCDS

In order to illustrate the last point fully, we now consider the effectiveness of a CCDS with respect to the example in Section 10.2.1. We look at the reduction in default risk corresponding to the unhedged default probability (original counterparty only) and the hedged case of joint default probability (both counterparties):

$$\text{CCDS effectiveness} = \frac{\text{default probability (no CCDS)}}{\text{joint default probability (with CCDS)}} = \frac{p_A}{p_{AX}} \geq 1 \tag{10.2}$$

---

[2] Although there is a clear link between this simple approach and the Merton model, we have ignored the full path of the asset value process and linked default to just a single variable. A more rigorous approach, however, does not differ significantly and is much more complex to implement (see Hull et al., 2004).

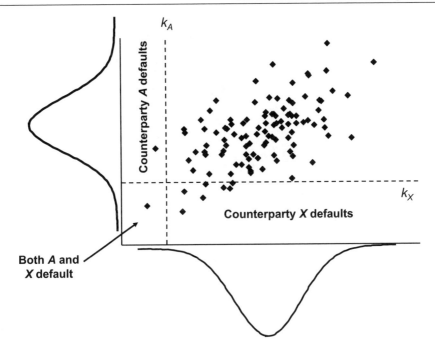

Figure 10.3. Illustration of the two-name correlation approach. The points shown are drawn from a bivariate Gaussian distribution with positive dependence. The asset returns, represented by the *x* and *y* coordinates, show positive dependence and the dots are clustered around the diagonal. There is then more chance that both asset returns are sufficiently negative to cause a joint default.

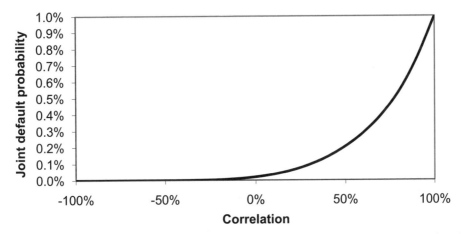

Figure 10.4. Joint default probability as a function of asset correlation for two counterparties with individual default probabilities of 2% and 1%.

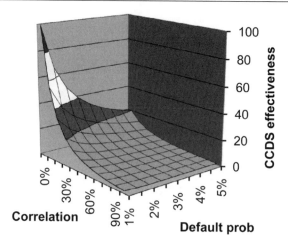

Figure 10.5. Illustration of CCDS effectiveness as a function of the default probability of the CCDS counterparty and the correlation between the CCDS and original counterparty. CCDS effectiveness is defined as the original counterparty default probability (2%) divided by the joint default probability.

The larger the above ratio, the more effective the CCDS. This is shown in Figure 10.5 for the example where the original counterparty default probability is 2%.

We can see that, not surprisingly, for a CCDS to be effective, the CCDS counterparty must have a low default probability (with respect to the original counterparty) and there should ideally be a low correlation between the CCDS counterparty and the original counterparty. If either of these points is not satisfied then the double-default probability will be potentially so large as to render the CCDS hedge largely ineffective. Indeed, at relatively high correlation and/or default probability in Figure 10.5, the ratio shown is close to unity, illustrating no CCDS benefit at all.

10.2.5   Distribution of losses

We now move on from the CCDS example but stay with a similar example, considering losses arising from the default events of two counterparties A and B[3] with a direct exposure of 100 to each counterparty and default probabilities of 10%. In Figure 10.6 we show the loss probabilities for the case of no correlation and a high correlation value of 75% obtained using equation (10.1). We can see that the impact of correlation is to increase the likelihood of extreme losses (in this case 200 due to both names defaulting). This is a key result relating to the correlation of defaults which will be addressed in more detail later.

10.2.6   Impact of random exposure

Now we consider the previous example but with random exposure, assuming that for each of A and B the MtM may be either $+200$ or -200, with 50% probability. This

---

[3] We use A and B to refer to two counterparties whose exposure is side by side rather than the previous notation of A for the original counterparty and X for the secondary CCDS counterparty.

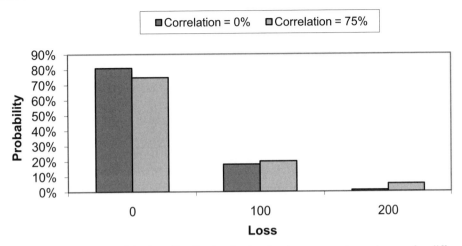

Figure 10.6. Illustration of the loss distribution in the simple two counterparty case for different correlation assumptions assuming individual default probabilities of 10%.

means that the exposure may be either +200 or zero and the expected exposure (EE) is +100, as in the previous fixed exposure example. We also assume that the MtM values are perfectly negatively correlated. This is not an extreme assumption since, as discussed in Chapter 4, it is common in the case of hedged positions. The perfect negative correlation means that if the MtM with respect to counterparty A is +200 then that with counterparty B will be -200 and vice versa. The direct implication of this is that a loss of +400 is not possible since, even in the event both counterparties default, there cannot be an exposure to both at the same time.

In Figure 10.7 is shown the loss probabilities for the simple random exposure example compared with the fixed exposure case. We use the same previous correlation parameter of 75%. Although, the expected exposure with respect to each counterparty is unchanged, the chance of a large loss (+200) is greater in the random exposure case. Random exposures increase the possibility of extreme losses.

10.2.7   Impact of correlated exposures

It is not only the correlation of defaults that is important in determining portfolio losses, but also the correlation of exposures. In the previous example, the MtM values to each counterparty were assumed to be perfectly negatively correlated. Now we compare this to the case when they are perfectly positively correlated (if one MtM is +200 then so is the other). In this case, a joint default will potentially create a large loss of +400. In Figure 10.8 we show that the impact of positive correlation between exposures increases the possibility of extreme losses still further.

10.3   CREDIT PORTFOLIO LOSSES

The concept of credit portfolio losses is fundamental to any quantification of credit risk. In order to properly account for counterparty risk at the portfolio level, there must be

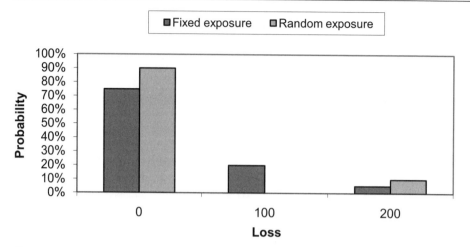

Figure 10.7. Illustration of the loss distribution in the simple two-counterparty case assuming individual default probabilities of 10%. The fixed exposure case corresponds to deterministic exposures of +100 for each counterparty whilst the random exposure case considers random exposures with an expected exposure of +100. A correlation of −100% between exposures and the previous asset correlation of 75% between the counterparty defaults is assumed.

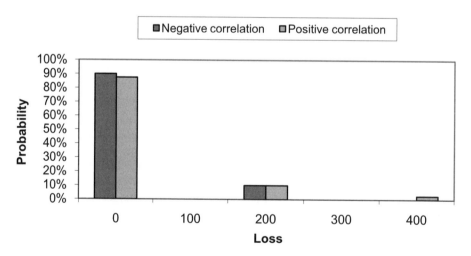

Figure 10.8. Illustration of loss distribution in the simple two-counterparty case assuming individual default probabilities of 10%. The negative correlation case corresponds to the MtM values with respect to each counterparty being opposite whilst in the positive correlation case, they are assumed equal. The previous asset correlation of 75% between the counterparty defaults is assumed.

some statistical estimate of the possibility of significant losses in the event that many counterparties were to default in a given period of time (such as 1 year).

The quantification of counterparty risk at the portfolio level requires knowledge of the following factors:

- counterparty default probabilities;
- correlations between counterparty default events;
- randomness of future counterparty exposures;
- correlation between future counterparty exposures.

Whilst the first two components above are standard inputs for most credit portfolio models, the last two are specific to counterparty risk and create significant complications when treating OTC derivatives within a typical credit portfolio framework. Whilst the randomness and correlations of exposures can be assessed accurately with a detailed knowledge of the relevant transactions with each counterparty, it may also be important to be able to treat these components in a simple fashion to avoid complex calculations.

10.3.1 Loss distributions and unexpected loss

Loss distributions are useful for understanding the nature of portfolio losses. Figure 10.9 illustrates the approach normally taken when considering portfolio losses. Using some measure of worst case loss (for example, VAR at a certain confidence level), it is possible to define an "unexpected loss". The unexpected loss represents the loss severity above that expected in a "normal" scenario and may be used either as a performance measure or to define economic capital requirements.

In the case of counterparty risk, we can relate unexpected loss back to the discussion on pricing in Chapter 7. CVA represents expected losses due to counterparty default (see

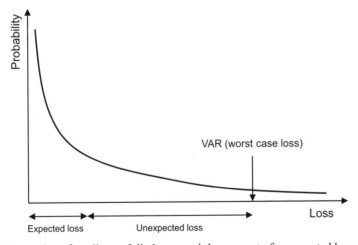

Figure 10.9. Illustration of credit portfolio losses and the concept of unexpected loss as defined by some worst case loss measure (such as VAR). The unexpected loss represents the uncertainty above the expected loss to a given confidence level.

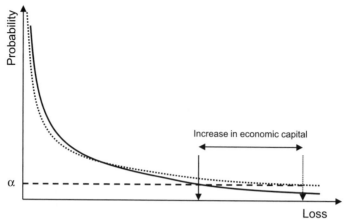

Figure 10.10. Illustration of the impact of correlation on credit portfolio losses. The dotted line represents a higher correlation of defaults and therefore corresponds to a higher worst case loss and a higher economic capital value. The dashed line shows the relevant tail probability (α).

Section 7.1.3). Suppose that an institution charges exactly the marginal (or incremental) CVA on all trades with all counterparties. This means that the total CVA will be exactly the expected losses due to counterparty risk at the portfolio level.[4] However, the institution will still be exposed to unexpected losses, which could cause significant problems if they are not anticipated and mitigated against. The unexpected loss may be significant and depend on many aspects such as the number of counterparties, their default probability and correlation. In addition, the characteristics of the exposure to each counterparty will be important (as illustrated in Figure 10.7). Hedging will tend to reduce the unexpected loss (in the case of perfect hedging then there is no uncertainty and the unexpected loss is zero).

Economic capital may be defined as either the unexpected loss or the unexpected loss plus the expected loss. Its purpose is to absorb losses in unexpected or bad scenarios. The probability attached to the severity of the scenario is a choice for the institution in question or their regulators. We will now seek to look at the impact of certain factors on the required economic capital to cover the counterparty risk of a given portfolio.

> **Spreadsheet 10.2.** Calculation of unexpected losses and "alpha" factor for a credit portfolio with random exposures").

10.3.2   Impact of correlation

The key driver of credit portfolio losses is correlation (or more generally dependence as discussed in Section 8.3.1). The impact of correlation on credit portfolio losses is shown in Figure 10.10. Correlation does not change the value of expected losses. However, positive correlation between default events makes large losses more likely and therefore increases the uncertainty of actual losses compared with expected losses. This will cause the unexpected loss, and consequently any associated capital number, to increase.

---

[4] Recall that the sum of marginal CVAs will give the total CVA for a netting set (Section 7.2.4) whilst the CVAs of netting sets are additive.

10.3.3 Default-only approaches

We can write the portfolio losses due to counterparty risk for some time horizon s as:

$$L(s) = \sum_{i=1}^{N} I(\tau_i \le s)(1 - \delta_i)V_i(s)^+, \tag{10.3}$$

where N represents the total number of counterparties, $I(\tau_i \le s)$ is an indicator function that defines which is unity if counterparty i has defaulted before the end of the time horizon of interest (s) and zero otherwise. Finally, δ_i is the assumed recovery rate with this counterparty and $V_i(s)^+ = \max(V_i(s), 0)$ is the positive part (exposure) of the netted MtM of all trades with counterparty i at time s.

In order to compute the distribution of losses according to equation (10.3), one must define a model for the behaviour of exposures and default events. In order to simplify the analysis, we will make the following assumptions:

- The recovery rates are fixed known percentages. This topic was discussed in Chapter 6.
- The default probabilities, which correspond to $p_i = E[I(\tau_i \le s)]$, are known. Again, the methods for doing this were described in Chapter 6.
- The exposure distributions are known for each counterparty, the calculation of these has been previously discussed in Chapter 4. The correct modelling of exposures will account for both the randomness of future exposures and the correlation between future exposures with respect to different counterparties.
- The exposures are independent of the default events.

The first three assumptions are common and will be assumed throughout the analysis of this chapter. The final point corresponds to the assumption of no wrong-way risk, which we will relax later.

Having made the assumptions above, the only remaining aspect is to define the basic default model. We will follow the two-name case introduced in Section 10.2.3 in which case the default events will be driven by a multivariate normal distribution. The addition of stochastic exposures to a credit portfolio model is possible, although the associated implementation is more complicated and/or time-consuming. We describe the basic modelling approach and implementation methods and provide further references in Appendix 11.A.

10.4 THE IMPACT OF STOCHASTIC EXPOSURE

Most credit portfolio models have focused on fixed exposures, which are characteristic of the classic debt instruments such as bonds and loans. Very little attention has been given to stochastic exposures although they have been described by Arvanitis and Gregory (2001), and several papers (for example, Pykhtin, 2003) have tackled the related problem of stochastic recovery rates.[5]

---

[5] The difference between random exposure and random recovery is simply that the recovery rate is bounded by zero and one, whereas the exposure is unbounded.

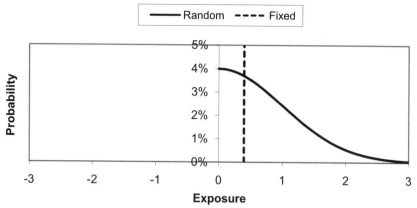

Figure 10.11. Illustration of random and fixed exposures used for the example.

10.4.1 Impact of random exposure on unexpected loss

We consider a heterogeneous portfolio with 200 counterparties and an average default probability of 1.5%. The asset correlations are assumed to be 20% for all counterparty pairs. We assume MtM values with each counterparty follow a standard normal distribution (mean of zero and standard deviation of one). This gives an expected positive exposure (EPE) of 0.399[6] as illustrated in Figure 10.11. Recovery values are assumed zero since they typically only manifest themselves as multiplicative factors. We calculate the distribution of losses in the following two cases:

- *Random exposure.* The MtM with each counterparty at the default point is assumed to follow a normal distribution with mean zero and standard deviation one. The values for different counterparties are independent.
- *Fixed exposure.* The MtM with each counterparty at the default point is assumed fixed and equal to 0.399.

All losses will be shown in percentages based on an overall portfolio size of the total EPE, which is $0.399 \times 200 = 79.8$.

The reason for the choice of fixed exposure is to give the same *expected* loss on the portfolio in each case (fixed and random). We assume all results are calculated with a time horizon of 1 year. This point is not important and any arbitrary choice could be used with the default probabilities adjusted accordingly. The 1-year time horizon is relevant in the last part of this section when we consider wrong-way risk and mark-to-market loss effects separately. In all results below we have used 500,000 Monte Carlo simulations for the calculations. This is relatively high in order to achieve a reasonably high resolution of the low-probability events.

Figure 10.12 shows the loss exceedance probabilities (probability that the loss will exceed a given level expressed as a percentage). We can clearly see that the impact of random exposure is to change the shape of the distribution of losses substantially and, in

---

[6] This is computed using the formula derived in Appendix 2.A. Since we are using a single time horizon, EPE is the same as expected exposure (EE). For reasons that will become clear, we will use EPE for all discussions.

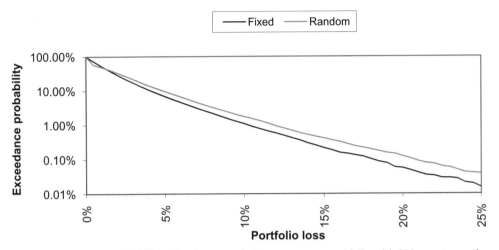

Figure 10.12. Loss probabilities for the example heterogeneous portfolio with 200 counterparties, an average default probability of 1.5% and a correlation of 20%. The random exposure case assumes normally distributed MtM values with zero mean and standard deviation of one. The fixed exposure case assumes deterministic exposures of 0.399 for each counterparty.

particular, to increase the possibility of larger losses. Indeed the 99% economic capital[7] of the random exposure cases is 11.9%, moderately larger than that in the fixed exposure case of 10.5%. For a 99.9% confidence level, these values are 21.0% and 19.0%.

The additional uncertainty introduced by random exposures creates a corresponding uncertainty in the portfolio loss. For fixed exposures, a given number of defaults results in a fixed loss. However, with random exposures, the loss for a given number of defaults is uncertain, depending on the exposures with respect to each defaulted counterparty. This additional uncertainty of exposure increases the unexpected loss.

10.4.2 The alpha factor

Practitioners have long used the concept of a "loan equivalent" in order to represent a random exposure in a simple way. Regulatory aspects are a key driver for this and will be discussed at length in Chapter 11. A loan equivalent represents the fixed exposure that would have to be used in order to mimic a random exposure. However, a loan equivalent must be defined with reference to a given characteristic of the loss distribution of the portfolio in question. It is important to emphasise that a loan equivalent will be an arbitrary correction or "fudge factor" and will be driven by the exposure of the counterparty in question but in the context of the underlying portfolio it represents the total counterparty risk and the measure chosen to represent that risk.

The basis of using loan equivalents is to separate the calculation of regulatory (or economic) capital into two stages as illustrated below:

$$\text{derivatives position(s)} \rightarrow \text{loan equivalent} \rightarrow \text{capital.}$$

---

[7] Economic capital is defined here as the 99% VAR number. As mentioned previously, it is sometimes defined as this value minus the expected loss, although given the latter quantity is quite small compared with the former this will not change the results substantially.

The above separation means that, from the point of view of capital calculations, derivatives positions can be treated in the same way as more simple positions such as loans. The main issue is then determination of the suitable loan equivalent amount.

The basis for calculating loan equivalents for random exposure derivatives portfolios is that, as shown by Wilde (2001), under the following conditions:

- infinitely large portfolio (number of counterparties) of small exposures (i.e. infinite diversification);
- no correlation of exposures;
- no wrong-way or right-way risk.

Then EPE is the true (accurate) loan-equivalent measure. Whilst this is only relevant as a theoretical result, it implies that EPE is the best starting point for a loan equivalent. One can then define a factor that will correct for the granularity of the portfolio in question. This factor has been named alpha (α). The loan equivalent used will be $\alpha \times$ EPE and can be calculated from the following expression:

$$\alpha = \frac{EC(\text{actual})}{EC(\text{EPE})}, \tag{10.4}$$

where EC(actual) is the actual economic capital (incorporating random exposures) and EC(EPE) is the economic capital using a fixed exposure for each counterparty equal to the EPE value.

The alpha factor defined as above will be greater than one[8] and reflect the extent to which the portfolio deviates from the stylised theoretical case. The advantage of defining a loan equivalent via $\alpha \times$ EPE is that the role of alpha is intuitive as it will correct for the granularity of the portfolio in question. Since alpha can be benchmarked against certain portfolio characteristics (as we shall do below), it may be reasonable to calculate a loan-equivalent value without time-consuming computation of equation (10.4). We will see that the following characteristics will be important in determining the magnitude of alpha:

- the granularity of the portfolio;
- the correlation between the exposures of different counterparties;
- the correlation between exposures and defaults (wrong-way risk).

Note that the same alpha parameter is typically applied to every counterparty within the portfolio. In theory, some more sophisticated analysis of the marginal risk with respect to each counterparty could be used to define separate alphas. For example, a counterparty with a larger exposure or high correlation may be expected to have a higher alpha since it contributes more to the granularity of the portfolio. However, in practice the application of a single-alpha factor is used for simplicity.

One might ask what could be the point of alpha given that its estimation requires knowledge of the correct economic capital anyway – by equation (10.4). The purpose of an alpha correction will be to allow calculations with fixed exposures to mimic the impact of random derivatives exposures. Suppose an institution runs a daily calculation

---

[8] Except in special cases such as right-way risk, which will be discussed in Section 10.5.3.

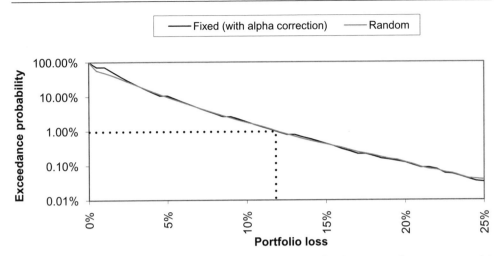

Figure 10.13. Loss probabilities for the example portfolio with fixed exposures (base case example) adjusted by the relevant alpha factor computed at a 99% confidence level. The dotted line shows the 99% economic capital, which is the same for each distribution.

of credit losses. In order to include derivatives positions in this calculation, they calculate some appropriate value of alpha using a simulation-based analysis of their total portfolio (or even some heuristic estimate). The daily calculations will then use $\alpha \times$ EPE as the fixed exposure for all derivatives counterparties. The value of alpha may be recalculated periodically, which is reasonable since the overall nature of the portfolio will evolve gradually and not change over a short timeframe. Alpha is also useful for defining regulatory capital (as discussed in Chapter 11). In this case, an institution may use a sophisticated approach to evaluating alpha for their own portfolio or they may revert to the regulator's (probably more conservative) estimate.

10.4.3 Example of alpha correction

We will now assess the impact of using the alpha measure in order to define loan equivalents. Using the values from Section 10.4.1, the base case alpha (assuming a 99% confidence level) is $11.9\%/10.5\% = 1.14$, as defined by equation (10.4). Hence, one can multiply all EPE values by this factor and re-do the calculations. In Figure 10.13 we show the same loss distribution as shown previously (Figure 10.12) but with the fixed exposures adjusted by the relevant alpha ratio. It is important to note that, whilst the fixed exposure now reproduces the true (random exposure) loss at the 99% confidence level (as shown), there is only a perfect match at this 1% probability point. This means the 99% economic capital values are the same with both calculations but any other measure is likely to differ. Other than the point used for the calculation of alpha, the distributions may differ substantially.[9] Furthermore, changes in both the portfolio and market variables will cause the true alpha measure to also change.

---

[9] Since they are plotted on a log-scale, the distributions shown in Figure 10.13 look rather similar, but there are material differences.

10.4.4 Sensitivity analysis on the alpha factor

In the following section, we present a sensitivity analysis on the value of alpha using the example portfolio introduced in Section 10.4.1. Similar results were originally presented by Canabarro et al. (2003). We show alpha as a function of various portfolio characteristics in Table 10.1.

Table 10.1. Illustration of change in alpha values computed for different portfolio characteristics. The base case is shown in **bold**.

Portfolio size	Alpha	Default probability	Alpha	Correlation	Alpha	Confidence level	Alpha
50	1.44	0.5%	1.28	0%	1.58	90%	1.25
100	1.24	1.0%	1.15	10%	1.28	95%	1.17
200	**1.14**	**1.5%**	**1.14**	**20%**	**1.14**	**99%**	**1.14**
400	1.07	2.0%	1.09	40%	1.04	99.9%	1.13
600	1.05	2.5%	1.08	60%	1.01	99.97%	1.10

We can see that the following aspects will all cause a decrease in the value of alpha:[10]

- larger portfolio;
- larger average default probabilities;
- larger correlations;
- higher confidence levels.

All of the above aspects can be understood by a single point. Suppose the economic capital is defined by a relatively large number of counterparty defaults. This could be due to a relatively large portfolio, higher average default probability, higher correlation or a higher confidence level. The law of averages now dictates that the total loss will be close to the sum of EPEs. Hence, the EPE will be a better approximation to the loan equivalent and the alpha value will be closer to unity.

10.5 SPECIAL CASES OF ALPHA

The sensitivity analysis shown in Table 10.1 illustrates that the value of alpha is dependent on a number of variables but generally varies from just above unity for a large portfolio to around 1.4 to 1.5 for a smaller portfolio. These results are consistent with previous studies (for example, Canabarro et al., 2003; Wilde, 2005) and seem to constitute a reasonable range. However, there are some important aspects that can lead to far higher alpha values, which we will consider next.

---

[10] We can also note that, as shown by Canabarro et al. (2003), the dispersion of exposures in a portfolio also causes the alpha value to increase. This is not surprising since it has a similar impact to decreasing the size of the portfolio.

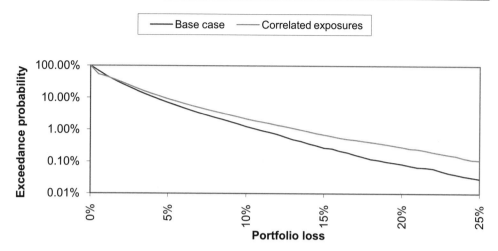

Figure 10.14. Loss probabilities for the example portfolio with fixed exposures (base case example) compared with random correlated exposures.

10.5.1 Correlation of exposures

So far, we have assumed a correlation of zero between exposures. We now impose a correlation structure, dividing the 200 counterparties into two groups. Within each group there is assumed a 60% correlation of all MtM values, whilst the correlation between values in opposite groups is −60%. This represents a case where exposures to counterparties have either strong positive correlation (due to similar instrument types such as payer interest rate swaps being traded), or strong negative correlation (due to hedging or offsetting effects such as for payer and receiver interest rate swaps). The loss distribution with correlated random exposures is shown in Figure 10.14. Due to the positive and negative correlations used, the average correlation is zero. Correlated exposures create a significantly "fatter tail" or higher probability of extreme losses due to the significant possibility of many exposures being simultaneously high. The value of alpha is increased to 1.24 due to the random correlation compared with 1.14 in the base case scenario.

10.5.2 Asymmetric exposure

A first key feature of a product such as a credit default swap is the asymmetry of the future MtM value. We therefore introduce asymmetric profiles[11] as illustrated in Figure 10.15. Case A is designed to mimic the impact of a long-protection CDS trade.[12] There is a large chance of negative MtM (no default) whilst a smaller chance of a large positive MtM (default). Case B represents the opposite case (for example, short CDS protection). We assume half of the counterparties have an exposure generated by Case A and half by Case B. The overall impact is to mimic a portfolio of CDS-like positions, which

---

[11] This is generated from a combination of two normal distribution functions with probability density function defined by $10\%\varphi(\pm40, 5) + 90\%\varphi(\pm3.5, 5)$. The expected exposure in each case is close to that used in the base case and so the fixed exposure is similar to the previous examples.

[12] The profile shown could represent either a single CDS trade or several highly correlated trades.

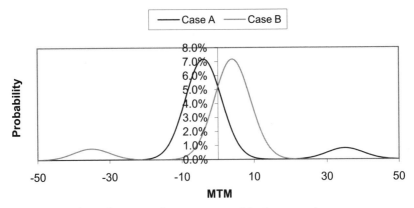

Figure 10.15. Illustration of asymmetric exposure used in the example.

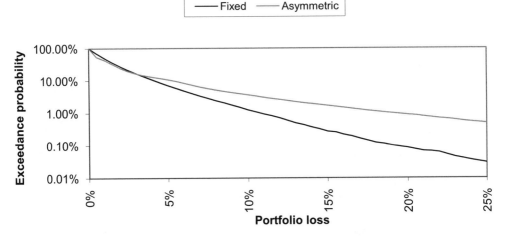

Figure 10.16. Loss probabilities for the example portfolio with fixed exposures (base case example) compared with asymmetric correlated exposures as, for example, in the case of a CDS contract.

is well balanced in terms of overall long and short positions (minimal market risk), but is not perfectly hedged with respect to individual reference entities (significant counterparty risk). The MtM values are also assumed to be correlated by 60% as in Section 10.5.1 (this means that long and short positions will have a negative correlation and the average correlation is zero).

The loss distributions for the asymmetric exposure case are shown in Figure 10.16. Since long positions are highly correlated, there is a chance of large losses due to high exposures with a relatively high number of the counterparties in default. This creates a skewed distribution and gives rise to a much higher alpha value of 1.77.

10.5.3 Wrong-way risk

The previous two examples illustrate the impact of portfolio losses caused by the asymmetry and correlation of exposures that is a strong characteristic of a portfolio of CDS instruments. However, as discussed in Chapter 8, a key feature of instruments such as CDS is the wrong-way risk that creates a correlation between exposure and default. Wrong-way risk has been previously studied by Wilde (2005) and Canabarro et al. (2003), who reported only modest increases in the value of alpha (for example, in Canabarro et al. the alpha increased from 1.09 to 1.21 when considering a market credit correlation of around 45%). In contrast to these previous studies that consider reasonably large diversified portfolios, it is highly relevant to look at the impact of wrong-way risk on a rather extreme and concentrated portfolio.

We use the simple wrong-way risk model described in Appendix 8.A to create a linkage between the exposure to each counterparty and the counterparty default time. This approach is a simple way to introduce correlation between the counterparty default and the realised exposure where the exposure has already been computed under the normal assumption of no wrong-way risk. Hence, whilst the approach is simple and the correlation parameterisation is rather abstract, the main advantage is efficiency since it is not necessary to jointly simulate exposure and default or re-simulate exposures given the counterparty default distribution. The approach is described in more detail in Appendix 10.B.

We retain the asymmetric exposures from the previous example and assume a correlation parameter of 60%, which means that early defaults (such as within the 1-year horizon in question) will make a large exposure from a long CDS-like position (Case B in Figure 10.15) more likely, whilst the exposure for short CDS protection is likely to be zero (Case A). In the simple case used, where the MtM with respect to each counterparty follows a standard normal variable, wrong-way risk approximately causes a shift in the exposure as illustrated in Figure 10.17.

The loss distribution including wrong-way risk is shown in Figure 10.18. We should note that, in contrast to the previous examples, wrong-way risk creates an expected loss that is higher than in the base case scenario (constant exposures). The impact of wrong-way risk is dramatic, with an alpha value of 4.48.

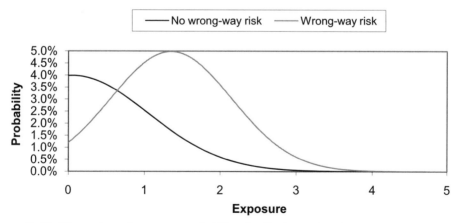

Figure 10.17. Illustration of exposure probability distribution using the simple wrong-way risk approach described in Appendix 10.B. We assume a default probability of 1.5%.

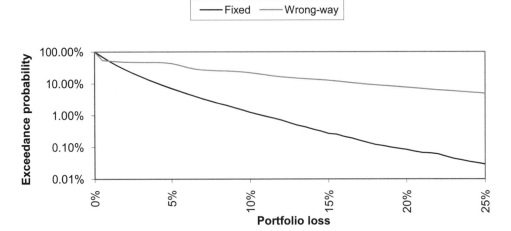

Figure 10.18. Loss probabilities for the example portfolio with fixed exposures (base case example) compared with the wrong-way risk example.

10.5.4   What is the correct value of alpha?

As we shall discuss more in Chapter 11, the regulatory value of alpha (for regulatory capital purposes) is set at 1.4. This value should represent a conservative estimate since it is used in cases where institutions are not computing alpha themselves. Previously published results and most of the standard results above (for example, see Table 10.1) add support to this as an upper estimate of alpha. Indeed, market participants have generally had the view that an alpha of 1.4 is rather conservative for most large portfolios. However, there are clearly cases such as small-portfolio or highly asymmetric exposures that could lead to a higher alpha. Furthermore, wrong-way risk can be seen (Section 10.5.3) to give a dramatically higher alpha value of over three times the conservative regulatory estimate of 1.4. Whilst a well-diversified portfolio may have an alpha within the regulatory level, a highly concentrated portfolio or those with significant wrong-way counterparty risks could be far more risky than such a multiplier might suggest. Whilst the true value of alpha is hard to determine, the depth and complexity of some counterparty risk has recently provided a lesson that it may in some cases be rather higher than has been generally believed.

Alpha is clearly a very useful measure for reasonably large multi-asset OTC derivatives portfolios and this is justified by estimated values not far above unity. However, the extreme cases of asymmetric exposure and wrong-way risk that may be characterised by specific instruments such as credit derivatives are more subtle. The use of alpha in such cases may give rise to a false sense of security as the true alpha may be significantly greater than one, be difficult to estimate and may change significantly over time. Even a large portfolio with a relatively small concentration of wrong-way risk exposures may have a significantly higher alpha. Dealing with instruments such as credit derivatives in a more sophisticated framework and not relying on loan-equivalent measures may be important.

10.6   CREDIT MIGRATION AND MARK-TO-MARKET

10.6.1   The importance of mark-to-market

All of the previous analysis has been made from a default-only perspective. This means that, for the time horizon of interest, any losses due to events other than defaults will not be accounted for. Changes in credit quality such as caused by credit migration events would be ignored. The inclusion of such losses is important since:

- The relevant time horizon (typically under 1 year) may be significantly shorter than the maturity of the instruments under consideration.
- Derivatives instruments are marked-to-market and so any change in credit quality over the period in question will lead to a gain or loss if the credit quality of a counterparty improves or deteriorates.

In particular, under a 1-year time horizon the default probability of high credit quality counterparties may be considered small, whereas the chance of a negative credit migration event may be far more significant. We will describe how to quantify such mark-to-market impacts and give an example to illustrate their importance.

10.6.2   Modelling credit migrations

Quantification of economic capital should include all potential losses at the time horizon of interest. The modelling approach described in Section 10.2.2 can be readily extended to incorporate credit migration events. Indeed, this leads to the well-known CreditMetrics^{TM} approach to credit portfolio modelling (Gupton et al., 1997). This framework assumes a default barrier as described above (Figure 10.2) and considers the mapping of credit migration probabilities onto the same normal variable. A downgrade can therefore be seen as a less extreme move not causing default. An illustration of the mapping is shown in Figure 10.19.

Calibration of the credit migration thresholds can be achieved using a transition matrix such as shown in Table 6.6. An example of this is shown in Table 10.2. For

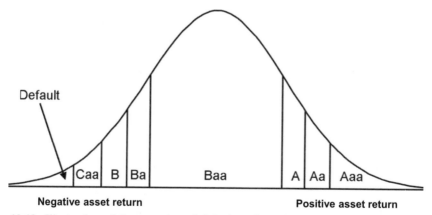

Figure 10.19. Illustration of the mapping of default and credit migrations thresholds for a Baa counterparty as used in the CreditMetrics^{TM} approach to credit portfolio modelling. This allows the simulation of credit-rating changes as well as default events. A positive asset return may lead to a credit-rating upgrade whilst a negative return may cause a downgrade or even default.

example, a random variable (asset return) of less than -2.735 will cause a default whereas one between -2.713 and -2.735 will cause a downgrade to the Ca-C category. We note that, in a portfolio, credit migrations will be correlated in the same manner as default events since they are driven by the same underlying variables.

Table 10.2. Illustration of credit migration thresholds calculated from Baa transition probabilities. For example, the default threshold is computed from $\Phi^{-1}(0.312\%) = 2.735$ and the Ca-C threshold then by $\Phi^{-1}(0.312\% + 0.022\%) = 2.713$ and so on. The transition probabilities are obtained from Table 6.6 and scaled for removal of the withdrawn rating category.

	Aaa	Aa	A	Baa	Ba	B	Caa	Ca-C	Default
Transition probability	0.043%	0.312%	4.916%	87.953%	5.443%	0.839%	0.161%	0.022%	0.312%
Threshold	$+\infty$		+3.333	+2.692	+1.619	−1.493	−2.216	−2.579	−2.713	−2.735

The above modelling of credit migration will simulate the impact of discrete changes in credit quality but not the impact of the stochastic nature of credit spreads. The latter impact can be modelled using an assumed process for risk premiums as, for example, described by Arvanitis et al. (1999).

10.6.3 Marking-to-market loans

The simulation of credit migration events through transition probabilities is reasonably straightforward as described above. However, it is also necessary to calculate the MtM impact of any change in credit quality. This requires knowledge of the future change in spread of the counterparty, which can be used together with the maturity of the instrument to then calculate the price impact. Consider the example credit spreads shown in Table 10.3 together with associated risky annuity (duration) values.

Table 10.3. Example credit spreads and risky annuity for various rating classes. The risky annuity values are calculated with the simple formula described in Appendix 6.B with an assumed recovery rate (δ) of 40% and risk-free interest rate (r) of 2%.

	Credit spread (bps)	4-year risky annuity
Aaa	50	3.78
Aa	100	3.72
A	150	3.66
Baa	250	3.54
Ba	400	3.38
B	800	2.99
Caa	1,200	2.66
Ca-C	2,000	2.14

Example. Suppose a 5-year Baa loan is downgraded in 1 year's time to Ba. What is the approximate MtM loss?

Answer. From Table 10.3, the change in spread is $400 - 250 = 150$ bps and the value of the remaining 4-year risky annuity is 3.38. The loss is therefore (dividing by 10,000 to convert bps to a percentage):

$$\text{loss} = (400 - 250) \times 3.38/10,000 = 5.07\%.$$

This is much smaller than the potential default loss of 60% (assuming 40% recovery) but from Table 10.2 it can be seen to be over 10 times more probable (5.443% versus 0.312%).

We can note that credit migration can have both a positive and negative impact since it may lead to gains (rating improvements) as well as losses resulting from downgrades. Correlation will become particularly important, since a counterparty defaulting will not only mean that other defaults are likely but will also imply related losses due to downgrades of non-defaulted counterparties. However, since the resulting credit migration losses are generally much smaller than potential default losses, this would imply that the impact on the "tail" or extreme losses of the distribution might be only moderate.

10.6.4   Marking-to-market derivatives

Whilst loans and other simple debt securities are quite easy to mark-to-market, derivatives are more complex to deal with since the loss on a derivatives position due to a change in credit spread will be driven by the change in CVA in the future. However, CVA calculation is significantly more complex and time-consuming than the simple loan formula given in the example above. A precise measurement of the portfolio impact of change in credit quality of derivatives counterparties would therefore require a double level of simulation (one simulation of credit migrations and default events and one to recalculate CVA values for counterparties whose credit quality had changed).

An alternative and much simpler way to incorporate credit quality changes on a portfolio of derivatives is to use the $\alpha \times$ EPE loan-equivalent approximation and apply a MtM based on the loan-equivalent exposures as described above. The relevant maturity to use is then the effective maturity (discussed in more detail in Chapter 11) of each counterparty at the horizon of interest. We note that the value of α might be benchmarked by using a default-only simulation and then used in a full credit migration simulation framework. This is clearly an approximation but should capture the key impact of credit migration behaviour.

10.6.5   Example

In order to look at the impact of credit migration, we take the following example. We use the transition probabilities in Table 6.6 (normalised for removal of the WR category). We assume an effective maturity of 4 years for all instruments and use the credit spreads and risky annuity values in Table 10.3 to define the MtM impact of ratings changes.

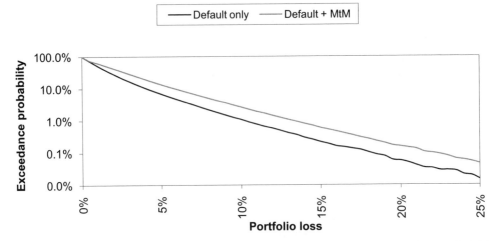

Figure 10.20. Loss probabilities for the portfolio with the impact of credit migrations and MtM losses as well as default losses, compared with the default-only case.

Finally, we assume the counterparties in the portfolio have ratings of Aa (10), A (20), Baa (40), Ba (100) and B (30) which gives an average default probability comparable with the base case scenario of 1.5%. All other parameters, such as correlation, are as in the base case scenario of Section 10.4.1.

The loss distributions for the default-only case and the default + MtM case (including the impact of defaults and MtM impacts from credit quality changes) are shown in Figure 10.20. The impact of MtM is reasonably large with the 99% economic capital increasing to 12.8% from 10.5% in the default-only case. The impact of credit migrations and MtM is clearly an important one and comparable in magnitude with many of the factors already considered.

The above example illustrates the importance of considering MtM losses arising from credit quality deterioration when assessing the unexpected losses due to counterparty risk at the portfolio level. The assessment of future MtM losses is difficult due to the required credit migration probabilities and associated spread assumptions. Furthermore, MtM impacts may be strongly driven by the nature of the portfolio in question (credit ratings and maturities, for example). Nevertheless, the importance of credit quality changes in assessing portfolio counterparty can be significant and should be quantified.

10.7   SUMMARY

In this chapter we have described the basics of modelling credit portfolio risk and therefore addressed the issue of defining the default of two or more counterparties. Initially, the two-name case has been described and the efficiency of a CCDS product in hedging counterparty risk has been assessed. Following this, the multiple-name case has been considered including the impact of random (derivatives) exposures on the distribution of losses. More extreme characteristics, such as correlation of exposures, asymmetric exposures and wrong-way risks, have been considered. Finally, the incorporation of credit migration and inclusion of mark-to-market losses has been considered.

In Chapter 11 we will discuss portfolio aspects in relation to the regulatory treatment of counterparty risk. Also in Chapter 11 we will describe in more detail how the concept of loan equivalents and the alpha factor has been incorporated into regulatory capital rules within Basel II.

APPENDIX 10.A: CREDIT PORTFOLIO MODEL

(i) Basic approach

We start from the definition of portfolio loss as given in equation (10.2) in the text:

$$L(s) = \sum_{i=1}^{N} I(\tau_i \leq s)(1 - \delta_i) V_i(s)^{+}.$$

Given the assumptions made, all that is required is to specify the dependence between the default events defined by $I(\tau_i \leq s)$. Using the multivariate Gaussian assumption then we can write $I(\tau_i \leq s) \equiv I(X_i < k_i)$ where k_i is the default barrier for the name, which is calculated from $k_i = \Phi^{-1}(p_i)$ with $p_i = E[I(\tau_i \leq s)]$. The X_i values follow a multivariate Gaussian distribution with some input correlation matrix.

(ii) Monte Carlo implementation

A Monte Carlo implementation of the above is rather straightforward (as can be seen in Spreadsheet 10.2) and consists of the following steps:

1. Simulation of a vector of N-correlated Gaussian variables denoted by $(X_1, \ldots, X_N)$. This can be done using methods such as the Box–Muller transform and Cholesky decomposition (see Press et al., 2007).
2. For each variable
   a. Check if $X_i < k_i$, in which case the name has defaulted
   b. If the name has defaulted then draw a possible value from the exposure distribution.
   c. If the above value is positive then multiply by $(1 - \delta_i)$ and update the total loss accordingly.
3. Proceed to the next simulation.

Monte Carlo simulation is completely general and easy to implement but is extremely slow. Monte Carlo acceleration techniques have been developed (for example, see Glasserman and Li, 2005). In addition, faster (but approximate) analytical approaches have been described for computing losses. We will review these approaches briefly next.

(iii) Conditional independence

Many different approaches have been developed for computing loss distributions in an analytical or semi-analytical way and avoiding the need for Monte Carlo simulation. All of these approaches rely on conditional independence. Writing the Gaussian variables in the following form:

$$X_i = \sum_{i=1}^{n} \beta_{ij} Z_i + \sqrt{1 - \sum_{i=1}^{n} \beta_{ij}^2} \varepsilon_j,$$

where Z_i and ε_j represent standard normal variables. This is an n-factor representation of the correlation structure depending on the quantities β_{ij}. Since default is defined by $X_i < \Phi^{-1}(p_i)$ we have:

$$p_i = \mathrm{Pr}\left(\sum_{i=1}^{n} \beta_{ij} Z_i + \sqrt{1 - \sum_{i=1}^{n} \beta_{ij}^2} \varepsilon_j < \Phi^{-1}(p_i)\right) = \Phi\left(\frac{\Phi^{-1}(p_i) - \sum_{i=1}^{n} \beta_{ij} Z_i}{\sqrt{1 - \sum_{i=1}^{n} \beta_{ij}^2}}\right).$$

The default probabilities are therefore independent conditionally on the realisation of the variables given by Z_i. In many cases, a one-factor homogeneous model is assumed, in which case we have the following representation:

$$p_i = \Phi\left(\frac{\Phi^{-1}(p_i) - \sqrt{\rho}Z}{\sqrt{1 - \rho}}\right),$$

where ρ can be interpreted as a correlation parameter since the correlation between any two variables will be $\sqrt{\rho}\sqrt{\rho} = \rho$.

Conditional independence is very useful since it allows conditional loss distributions to be calculated under the assumption of independence of default events. The unconditional loss distribution is obtained by integrating over the n-factors used above. Hence, using conditional independence, the challenge is computation of the conditional loss distributions and a low-dimensional integration.

The weakness of conditional independence is that it imposes restrictions on the correlation structure within the model and an arbitrary set of correlations cannot be chosen. Clearly the more factors that are used, the more flexible the correlation structure is but at the expense of additional computation cost. A balance between flexibility and computation requirements has been discussed by Gregory and Laurent (2004).

(iv) Implementation methods

Many methods have been developed using a conditional independence framework where the loss distribution can be calculated via conditional distributions in which defaults are independent, which we briefly review here. Most are implemented as single-factor models, although this is not a strict requirement:

- *Large pool approximation (LHP)*. The large homogeneous pool (LHP) approximation of Vasicek (1997) is based on the assumption of a very large (technically infinitely large) portfolio. The loss distribution of the portfolio is given as a simple formula. This approach is used for Basel II as discussed in the next chapter.
- *Homogeneous approximation*. Homogeneous approximations consider the names in the portfolio to be indistinguishable but do not assume a large portfolio. In this

simplified case, the conditional portfolio losses follow a simple binomial distribution (see, for example, O'Kane, 2007).

- *Conditional normal approximation.* This approach relies on the approximation that conditional distributions are Gaussian or normal as suggested by Shelton (2004). This method is most accurate in the tails of the distribution (more extreme, low-probability events).
- *Saddle point approximation.* The saddle point method (Martin et al., 2001; Gordy, 2002) is another method that is especially accurate in the tails of the distribution, making it ideal for computation of the small probabilities required for estimating worst case or unexpected losses.
- *Discrete methods.* Discrete methods for calculating credit portfolio losses have been described by Gregory and Laurent (2003), Andersen et al. (2003) and Hull and White (2004). They make no approximation to the loss distribution itself, but rely on some discrete bucketing of possible losses.

APPENDIX 10.B: SIMPLE TREATMENT OF WRONG-WAY RISK

Similarly to Appendix 8.A, we denote the time of default of the counterparty by τ and the survival probability of the counterparty up to time s as $S(0, s)$ which is defined via a constant hazard rate h or intensity of default:

$$S(0, s) = \exp(-hs).$$

Suppose default is driven by a Gaussian variable, Z:

$$\tau = S^{-1}(\Phi(Z)).$$

Now we generate another Gaussian variable Y via a correlation parameter ρ:

$$Y = \rho Z + \sqrt{1 - \rho^2}\varepsilon,$$

with ε being a further independent Gaussian variable. Finally we assume the MtM will be defined by:

$$G^{-1}(\Phi(Y)),$$

where $G(.)$ is the distribution function of the exposure in question. In the example in the text, the exposure is assumed to follow a standard normal distribution. Hence, the exposure would be simply defined by $\max(Y, 0)$ and the distribution function by:

$$\Pr(Y < y) = \Pr\left(\rho Z + \sqrt{1 - \rho^2}\varepsilon < y\right) = \Phi\left(\frac{y - \rho Z}{\sqrt{1 - \rho^2}}\right).$$

In the example given in the text, the default probability is assumed to be 1.5% (survival probability 98.5%) and hence the relevant value of Z for a default at the time horizon of 1 year is $Z = \Phi^{-1}(98.5\%) = 2.17$. We note this is approximate since defaults before 1 year are also to be considered and will lead to larger values of Z.

We note that any exposure distribution can be assumed for the above analysis and can be either continuous or discrete. In the latter case, exposures will be simply obtained by a quantile mapping procedure.

11

Counterparty Risk, Regulation and Basel II

> *"Hell, there are no rules here—we're trying to accomplish something."*
>
> Thomas A. Edison (1847–1931)

11.1 INTRODUCTION[1]

In most developed countries, banks are regulated by the government. A critical form of regulation is determining the minimum amount of capital that a given bank must hold. Capital acts as a buffer to absorb losses during turbulent periods and therefore partially defines the credit-worthiness of a bank. Ultimately, regulatory capital requirements partially determine the leverage that a bank can operate under. Since banks have historically sought to have strong credit ratings, regulatory capital requirements should be significant and easily cover losses in any plausibly bad financial scenario. On the other hand, banks have continually strived for ever-greater profits to be shared by employees (via bonuses) and shareholders (via dividend payments and capital gains). Banks will therefore naturally wish to hold the minimum amount of capital possible in order to maximise the amount of business they can do and risk they are able to take.

There is clearly a balance in defining the capital requirements for a bank; it must be high enough to contribute to a very low possibility of failure and yet not so severe as to unfairly penalise the bank (at least in comparison with competitors that operate under a different regulatory regime). The danger of overly optimistic capital requirements has been highlighted during the recent period, with several financial institutions failing or being bailed out after suffering losses (often in the form of writedowns). These losses have not just exceeded but dwarfed the capital set aside against them. Defining capital requirements is clearly a difficult task as financial markets have a habit of creating surprises that cannot be predicted by models and historical experience.

Aside from the problem of defining the approximate level of capital held by banks, there is the question of the precise definition of capital requirements for individual risk types and instruments. Note that, in contrast to economic capital considered in Chapter 10, regulatory capital does not need to follow from any model and may be defined by a simple look-up approach. Whilst such a simple approach will be transparent and easier to implement, it will not be able to capture any more than the key aspects of the risks arising from a complex web of positions often taken by a bank.

---

[1] I am grateful to Michael Pykhtin who collaborated on the writing of this chapter. Any remaining errors are the responsibility of the author.

As such, this may give rise to possible "arbitrages" of capital requirements arising from the ability to reduce capital without a corresponding reduction in the associated risk. (Indeed, the growth of the credit derivatives markets was largely driven by regulatory capital arbitrage.) A more sophisticated, possibly model-based, approach may more closely align capital and actual financial risk but will be less transparent and harder to implement.

11.2 THE BIRTH OF BASEL II

A further problem for regulatory capital "arbitrage" is conflicting capital requirements across jurisdictions. Most large banks operate in multiple countries. To minimise the effect that conflicting regulatory practices at different jurisdictions may have on international banks, the Basel Committee on Banking Supervision (BCBS) was established by the central bank governors of the Group of Ten (G10) countries in 1974. The Basel Committee does not possess any formal authority, and its conclusions do not have legal force. Instead, it formulates broad supervisory standards and issues recommendations that reflect its view on the current best practice. The supervisory authorities in the relevant countries follow the BCBS guidelines when they develop their national regulation rules.

In 1988 the BCBS introduced a capital measurement framework known as the Basel Capital Accord (nowadays often referred to as Basel I). This framework was adopted not only in the G10 countries, but also in other countries with internationally active banks. However, the Basel I Accord lacked risk sensitivities, and banks learned how to game the system: reduce the minimum capital requirements without actually reducing the risk taken. To reduce this practice, known as regulatory arbitrage, work on the more risk-sensitive *Revised Capital Adequacy Framework*, commonly known as *Basel II*, started in 1999. The Basel II Framework, now covering the G20 group of countries, which is now being implemented, is described in the Basel Committee's document entitled *International Convergence of Capital Measurement and Capital Standards* (BCBS, 2006). It consists of three "pillars":

- *Pillar 1, minimum capital requirements.* Banks compute regulatory capital charges according to a set of specified rules.
- *Pillar 2, supervisory review.* Supervisors evaluate the activities and risk profiles of banks to determine whether they should hold higher levels of capital than the minimum requirements in Pillar 1.
- *Pillar 3, market discipline.* Public disclosures that banks must make, which would provide greater insight into the adequacy of banks' capitalisation, are specified.

In this chapter, we will discuss only the minimum capital requirements according to Pillar 1 as they apply to counterparty risk in banks' trading books. For a comprehensive review of Basel II in general, the reader is referred to Ong (2006) and Engelmann and Rauhmeier (2006).

11.3 BASEL II FRAMEWORK FOR FIXED EXPOSURES

11.3.1 Overview

Two approaches are available under Basel II:

- *Standardised approach.* Banks assess the risk of their exposures using external ratings. All non-retail exposures are assigned to risk buckets. BCBS (2006) provides tables that specify a capital charge for each risk bucket. This approach is more granular than Basel I in that there are more risk buckets.
- *Internal ratings based (IRB) approach.* Banks rely on their own internal estimates of some (foundation IRB) or all (advanced IRB) risk components. These components are probability of default, loss given default (or recovery rate), exposure at default and effective maturity.

Whilst market risk capital requirements have since 1995 been fully model-based, Basel II has stopped short of allowing this for credit risk. Such a limitation can be put down to the increased complexity of modelling credit risk, together with the limited data and longer time horizons involved. The advanced IRB approach still uses a relatively simple formula to define economic capital, although the origins of this formula have a firm theoretical basis.

11.3.2 The advanced IRB approach

As discussed in Chapter 10, a thorough description of economic capital would require a model that, whilst relatively simple, represents some complexity to implement together with significant data requirements. The economic capital assigned to an individual asset would depend on the nature of that asset (exposure, default probability, loss given default) together with its correlation to the rest of the portfolio in question.

Under the advanced IRB approach, regulatory capital (RC) for a given instrument is first simplified by assuming that exposure at default (EAD) is independent of all other variables. Regulatory capital is then assumed linear in EAD and defined by the following formula:[2]

$$RC = EAD \times K(PD, LGD, M, \rho), \tag{11.1}$$

where PD is the obligor's probability of default (subject to a floor of 0.03%), LGD is expected loss given default in relation to the EAD (estimated conditionally on an economic downturn), M is the exposure's effective remaining maturity (defined in Appendix 11.A and subject to a floor of 1 year and a cap of 5 years) and, finally, ρ is a correlation parameter. The above formula is intuitive: the capital should depend on the size of the position concerned (EAD) and on the probability of default, loss given default, effective maturity and correlation within the portfolio concerned. However, it is the non-linearity and interaction between these final four terms that is complex and needs simplification in order to have a reasonable representation of the risk of an asset in a portfolio context.

The advanced IRB approach of Basel II follows the credit portfolio model described in Chapter 10. The theory rests on the large homogeneous pool (LHP) approximation

---

[2] Large exposures are therefore not penalised in such a formula.

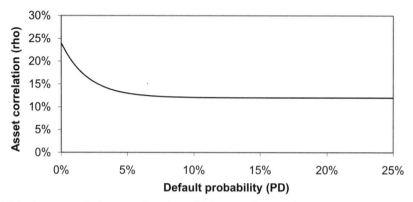

Figure 11.1. Asset correlation as a function of PD according to the Basel II capital rules.

described in Appendix 10.A. The term $K(\text{PD}, \text{LGD}, M)$ is a capital factor that is calculated according to:

$$K(\text{PD}, \text{LGD}, M) = \text{LGD} \times \Phi\left(\frac{\Phi^{-1}(\text{PD}) + \sqrt{\rho}\,\Phi^{-1}(0.999)}{\sqrt{1-\rho}}\right) \times \text{MA}(\text{PD}, M), \quad (11.2)$$

where functions $\Phi(.)$ and $\Phi^{-1}(.)$ are the standard normal cumulative distribution function and its inverse, respectively, ρ is the asset correlation parameter as introduced in Chapter 10 and MA is a maturity adjustment defined in Section 11.3.4. Equation (11.2) defines a conditional (on a confidence level) expected loss and is the result of the Merton-style model described in Section 10.2.2 under the LHP assumptions of Vasicek (1997) and granularity adjustment formula of Gordy (2004). The factor of 0.999 corresponds to the chosen confidence level of 99.9%.

11.3.3 Asset correlation

The asset correlation (ρ) in the above formula is assumed to depend on the default probability itself and is uniquely determined by the PD as shown in Figure 11.1 (the formula is given in Appendix 11.B). Whilst there is no obvious source of direct dependence of asset correlation on PD, it is generally believed for corporate exposures that asset correlation tends to decrease as the size of the obligor decreases. This can be explained by the fact that small obligors are more sensitive to local risk factors (which may be considered idiosyncratic) than large obligors. Since small obligors tend to have higher PD than small obligors, there may be indirect dependence on PD when size is not taken into account. It is possible that dependence of asset correlation on PD in the IRB formula reflects this indirect dependence. On the other hand, a decreasing dependence of asset correlation on PD makes the capital charge as the function of PD *flatter* than in the case of constant asset correlation. Because of this, it is quite possible that regulators' motivation for the declining dependence of asset correlation on PD is simply to make the capital charge a flatter function of PD. This would dampen the effect of procyclicality, which manifests itself in capital charges being low during good times and being high during bad times.[3]

---

[3] For a comprehensive discussion on procyclicality in regulatory capital and possible ways to reduce it see Gordy and Howells (2006).

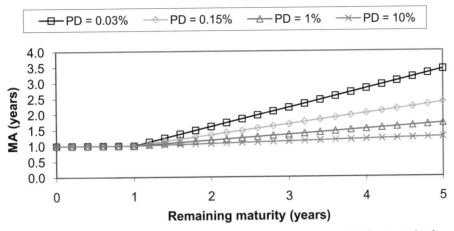

Figure 11.2. Maturity adjustment (MA) as a function of remaining maturity for several values of PD.

11.3.4 Maturity factor

The third factor in equation (11.2), the maturity adjustment, attempts to capture (crudely) credit migration risk (as discussed in Section 10.6). The Basel maturity adjustment is not derived from any model – it is a parametric function with its parameters chosen to match the output of a single-factor version of the KMV Portfolio Manager model (KMV Corporation, 1993) as closely as possible. The formula is given in Appendix 11.B. Figure 11.2 shows the dependence of the Basel maturity adjustment factor upon the remaining maturity for several values of PD. The idea behind the maturity factor is that longer maturity bonds, which are riskier, should attract a higher capital charge. However, for a higher PD, the maturity factor will fall because lower quality assets are exposed to less downgrade risk than higher quality assets (the mean reversion in credit ratings is discussed in Section 6.4.2). In other words, the scope for loss in value due to a downgrade is larger for a triple-A asset than for an asset with lower credit rating.

While the Basel parametric maturity adjustment is certainly a huge simplification over the real credit migration model, it does retain two major properties of credit migration risk that we would intuitively expect. First, for any given PD, the maturity adjustment factor increases with remaining maturity. We certainly would expect this behavior because, with longer remaining maturity, there is more time for the obligor to be downgraded. Second, the maturity adjustment factor is higher for obligors with lower PD. This behavior is also very intuitive because higher rated obligors have more "space" for downgrade than lower rated obligors, as illustrated by the mean reversion characteristics of credit migrations.

11.4 EXPOSURE AT DEFAULT AND BASEL II

A main emphasis of the Basel II framework is on instruments with relatively fixed exposures such as loans. Chapter 10 discussed the computation of economic capital and illustrated the additional complexity posed by derivatives due to effects such as random exposures, correlation of exposures and wrong-way risk. However, we have discussed that there also exist reasonable theoretical foundations for replacing derivatives exposures by their loan-equivalent values and an additional "alpha" multiplier.

The Basel II Framework very much follows the loan-equivalent style for derivatives with minimum capital requirements for counterparty risk in OTC derivatives and structured finance transactions (SFTs) calculated by applying Basel II rules for corporate, sovereign and bank exposures (BCBS, 2006). In applying these rules to counterparty risk in SFT and OTC derivatives, there are different methods of varying complexity for calculating EAD:

- the current exposure method (CEM);
- the standardised method (SM);
- the internal model method (IMM).

The first two approaches above are normally referred to as the non-IMM methods. These methods are designed to provide a simple and workable supervisory algorithm for those banks that are not able to model credit exposure internally. In addition, there are separate approaches to handle repo transactions. All of these approaches will be described in Sections 11.4.1 and 11.4.2 (CEM and SM, respectively) and Section 11.5 (IMM).

EAD is calculated at the netting set level. From the Basel perspective, a netting set is a group of transactions with a single counterparty that are subject to a legally enforceable bilateral netting agreement that satisfies certain legal and operational criteria described in Annex 4 of BCBS (2006). Netting other than on a bilateral basis is not recognised for the purpose of calculating regulatory capital. Each transaction that is not subject to a legally enforceable bilateral netting agreement is interpreted as its own netting set. The interpretation of a netting set according to Basel II is therefore consistent with our own usage and earlier definition in Chapter 3.

11.4.1 Current exposure method

Under the current exposure method approach (originating from Basel I), the EAD is computed according to:

$$EAD = CE + add\text{-}on, \tag{11.3}$$

where CE is the current exposure and add-on is the estimated amount of the potential future exposure over the remaining life of the contract. The add-on is calculated for each single transaction as the product of the transaction notional and the add-on factor, which is determined based on the remaining maturity and the type of underlying instrument (e.g., interest rates, foreign exchange, etc.) according to Table 11.1. For example, a 6-year interest rate swap with a current MtM of 1% would have an EAD of 2.5%.

Banks using the CEM are permitted to net fully the transactions covered by a legally enforceable bilateral netting agreement when they calculate the CE. In other words, CE for a netting set is calculated as the larger of *net* portfolio value and zero. The benefit of netting of future exposures via the add-on component is not obvious since the impact of

Table 11.1. Add-on factors of the current exposure method (CEM) by the remaining maturity and the type of underlying instrument.

Remaining maturity	Interest rates	FX and gold	Equities	Precious metals (except gold)	Other commodities
<1 year	0.0%	1.0%	6.0%	7.0%	10.0%
1–5 years	0.5%	5.0%	8.0%	7.0%	12.0%
>5 years	1.5%	7.5%	10.0%	8.0%	15.0%

netting can change significantly over time as the MtM values of individual transactions change. Consider two transactions that net perfectly today since they have equal and opposite MtM values. Only if they are mirror trades (perfect hedges) will the netting be perfect in the future. If the trades happened to net by chance then some or all of this netting benefit will be lost over time. The treatment of netting is described in Appendix 11.C. Essentially, only 60% of the current netting benefit is given as credit for netting of future exposures. This accounts for the fact that some netting benefit will not be structural (such as mirror trades or hedges) and will occur only transiently and by chance. This treatment is almost certainly conservative as it assumes that the current netting benefit will decay over time.

Finally, for a collateralised counterparty, unlike under Basel I, the current exposure for transactions within a netting set can be reduced by the current market value of the collateral, subject to a (sizeable) haircut. This is defined more thoroughly in Appendix 11.C. Essentially, the benefit of collateral on current exposure is recognised via the reduction of CE, but the ability to call for collateral against future exposure is not (no reduction of add-on).

11.4.2 Standardised method

The standardised method in Basel II was designed for those banks that do not qualify to model counterparty exposure internally but would like to adopt a more risk-sensitive approach than the CEM – for example, to account for netting. Under the SM, one computes the EAD for derivative transactions within a netting set as follows:

$$\text{EAD} = \beta \times \max\left[\text{MtM} - C, \sum_i |\text{RPE}_i - \text{RPC}_i| \times \text{CCF}_i\right], \tag{11.4}$$

where $\text{MtM} = \sum_i \text{MtM}_i$ and $C = \sum_j C_j$ represent, respectively, the current market value of trades in the netting set and current market value of all collateral positions assigned against the netting set. The terms $|\text{RPE}_i - \text{RPC}_i|$ represent a net risk position within a "hedging set" i which forms an exposure add-on then multiplied by a conversion factor CCF_i determined by the regulators according to the type of risk position. Finally, β is the supervisory scaling parameter, set at 1.4, which can be considered similar to the α-factor introduced in Chapter 10 and discussed later (Section 11.5.4).

A hedging set is defined as the portfolio risk positions of the same category (depending on the same risk factor) that arise from transactions within the same netting set. Each currency and issuer will define its own hedging set, within which netting effects are captured. However, netting between hedging sets is not accounted for. Instruments with interest rate and foreign exchange risk will generate risk positions in these hedging sets as well as their own (such as equities or commodities, for example). Within each hedging set, offsets are fully recognised; that is, only the net amount of all risk positions within a hedging set is relevant for the exposure amount or EAD. The long positions arising from transactions with linear risk profiles carry a positive sign, while short positions carry a negative sign. The positions with non-linear risk profiles are represented by their delta-equivalent notional values. The exposure amount for a counterparty is then the sum of the exposure amounts or EADs calculated across the netting sets with the counterparty. The use of delta-equivalent notional values for options creates a notable difference compared with the CEM. The CEM adopts a transaction-by-transaction approach instead of considering the netting set as a portfolio. The SM in contrast allows for the netting of positions and positions such as short options (that would not contribute under the CEM) will offset some of the exposure risk.

As with the CEM, collateral is only accounted for with respect to the current MtM component and future collateral is not specifically considered. The calibration of credit conversion factors (CCFs) is assumed for a 1-year horizon on at-the-money forwards and swaps because the impact of volatility on market risk drivers are more significant for at-the-money trades. Thus, this calibration of CCFs should result in a conservative estimate of PFE. Supervisory CCFs are shown in Table 11.2.

Table 11.2. Credit conversion factors (CCFs) for financial instrument hedging sets. These are given in paragraphs 86–88 of Annex 4 in BCBS (2006).

Instrument type	CCF
Foreign exchange	2.5%
Gold	5.0%
Equity	7.0%
Precious metals (except gold)	8.5%
Electric power	4.0%
Other commodities (except precious metals)	10.0%

11.4.3   Treatment of repo-style transactions

For repo-style transactions,[4] the EAD is calculated as the difference between the market value of the securities and the collateral received, and given by:

$$\text{EAD} = \max[0, \text{MtM}(1 + h_S) - C(1 - h_C)], \qquad (11.5)$$

where h_S is the haircut on the security and h_C is the haircut on the collateral. The haircuts must be applied to both the exposure and collateral received in order to account

---
[4] Only reverse repos attract credit risk capital.

for the risk arising from an appreciation in value of the underlying exposure and simultaneous decline in value of collateral received as a result of future market movements. The levels of haircuts are usually estimated according to market price volatility and foreign exchange volatility (in the case of securities denominated in foreign currency). Furthermore, haircuts take into account the type of security, its credit rating and the duration of its maturity. The standard supervisory haircuts are shown in Table 11.3. Netting of exposures can be done only within the same asset class. Across asset classes, the EAD represents the sum of the individual assets.

Table 11.3. Illustration of Basel II haircuts.

		Up to 1 year	*1–5 years*	*Above 5 years*
Sovereign debt	AAA/AA	0.5%	2%	4%
	A/BBB	1%	3%	6%
	BB		15%	
Corporates and financials	AAA/AA	1%	4%	8%
	A/BBB	2%	6%	12%
	BB		15%	
Other assets	Cash	0%		
	Equity	15–25%		
	Gold	15%		
	FX	8%		

Adapted from BCBS (2006).

Banks may be permitted to calculate haircuts themselves using internal models. In such cases the relevant confidence level should be 99% and the minimum time horizon 5 days. We can gain some intuition on the above haircuts by "backing out" a volatility parameter under the assumption that the numbers are computed using a simple normal distribution PFE formula (as given in Appendix 2.A, for example[5]). The results are shown in Table 11.4 under the assumptions of a 10-day time horizon and 99% confidence level.

From the reverse-engineering of volatility implied from haircuts, as shown in Table 11.4, we can see that the numbers generally make sense. We can also make the following observations:

1. The volatilities for equity, gold and FX all agree approximately with the historical observed volatilities in these asset classes.
2. The AAA/AA sovereign volatility might be considered to be mostly interest rate driven, whilst lower quality ratings and corporate debt have additional volatility due to potential credit spread changes.
3. High-quality debt instruments seem to be treated via a simple normal distribution formula (calculated volatilities agree across maturity).

---

[5] To back out the volatility, we simply need to divide by the confidence level multiplier (2.33), the scaled time horizon of 10 days ($\sqrt{10/250}$) and the assumed duration (for debt instruments only).

Table 11.4. Calculation of volatility implied from Basel II haircuts assuming a 99% confidence level, 10-day time horizon and durations of 0.75, 3 and 6 years for the three maturity buckets.

		Up to 1 year	1–5 years	Above 5 years
Sovereign debt	AAA/AA	1.43%	1.43%	1.43%
	A/BBB	2.86%	1.43%	1.43%
	BB		42.92%	
Corporates and financials	AAA/AA	2.86%	2.86%	2.86%
	A/BBB	5.72%	4.29%	4.29%
	BB		42.92%	
Other assets	Cash	0%		
	Equity	42.92%		
	Gold	32.19%		
	FX	17.17%		

4. Corporate debt is considered more volatile than sovereign debt (due perhaps to the additional credit spread volatility assumed).
5. Short-dated and BB debt clearly has some additional haircut, presumably to account for the possibility of severe credit quality change or default even during a short period.

To better account for netting, as an alternative method to the use of haircuts as above, banks may take a value-at-risk-based (VAR-based) approach to reflect the price volatility of the exposure and collateral received. Under the VAR-based approach, the EAD or exposure can be calculated for each netting set as:

$$EAD = \max(0, \text{MtM} - C + \text{VAR}), \tag{11.6}$$

where MtM and C again represent the current market value of trades in the netting set and the current market value of all collateral positions held against the netting set, respectively, and VAR represents a value-at-risk type assessment of the collateralised position over some time horizon. The advantage of the VAR model is to improve the rule-based aggregation under standard haircuts by taking into account correlation effects between security positions in the portfolio. The VAR-based approach is available to banks that have already received approval for the use of internal models under the Market Risk Framework – see BCBS (2006, Part 2, Section VI). Other banks can separately apply for supervisory recognition to use their internal VAR models for the haircut calculation on repo-style transactions.

The quantitative and qualitative criteria for recognition of internal market risk models on repo-style transactions and other similar transactions are, in principle, the same as under the Market Risk Framework. For repo-style transactions, the minimum holding period is 5 business days (rather than the 10 that is standard). The minimum holding period should be adjusted upwards for market instruments where such a holding period would be inappropriate given the liquidity of underlying security.

11.5 BASEL II INTERNAL MODEL METHOD

11.5.1 Introduction

ISDA concluded in 2001 that institutions with competence in market risk modelling were also suitably qualified to model exposures for derivatives using internal models. Banks with approval for market risk calculations would fall into this category. Under the IMM, banks are allowed to compute the distribution of exposure at future time points using their own models (with methods similar to those described in Chapter 4). Assuming that this distribution is available, the IMM prescribes a way of calculating EAD and effective maturity M from the expected exposure profile.

The internal model method (IMM) is the most risk-sensitive approach for EAD calculation available under the Basel II Framework. It is intended to provide incentives for banks to improve their measurement and management of counterparty credit risk by adopting practices that are more sophisticated. Under the IMM, both EAD and effective maturity M are computed from the output of a bank's internal models of future exposure. These models must be approved by the bank's supervisors for them to become eligible for the IMM.

Not only does the internal model method allow a realistic treatment of the important mitigants of netting and collateral, it permits full netting across asset classes and cross-product netting between OTC derivatives and SFT (i.e. repo style) transactions. In order to achieve cross-product netting, several legal and operational requirements must be met. In particular, there has to be a strong legal opinion that, in the event of default, the relevant courts and authorities (within all relevant jurisdictions) would recognise this form of netting. We note that netting is given only limited recognition under other approaches and cross-product netting has no recognition at all.

11.5.2 Effective maturity

Similar to the effective maturity measure (M) required in the standard Basel II formula – equation (11.1) – it is necessary to represent the effective maturity of a netting set of derivatives. This can be defined (for example, see Picoult, 2005) in terms of the expected exposure (EE) of each transaction in the netting set and the relevant discount factors as described in Appendix 11.A. Effective maturity can therefore be thought of as a duration or annuity-type measure. For exposures that show significant variation over time, effective maturity can be very different than for bullet structures that characteristically have a value slightly less than their maturity. However, the value of M is floored at 1 year and capped at 5 years.

We show some examples of calculations for M for different exposure profiles in Figure 11.3. Netting set 1 has a bullet exposure and its effective maturity is therefore slightly smaller than its maturity due to interest rates effects. Due to having a small EE in the first year,[6] netting set 2 has a high effective maturity of 6.51 years, which is capped at 5 years (according to the formula defined in Appendix 11.A). Finally, netting set 3 has an effective maturity of 3.21 years, which is relative small since the EE is concentrated within shorter maturities.

---

[6] This means that the denominator of the formula in Appendix 11.A becomes quite small resulting in the effective maturity being greater than the maximum maturity of the netting set (without the cap of 5 years).

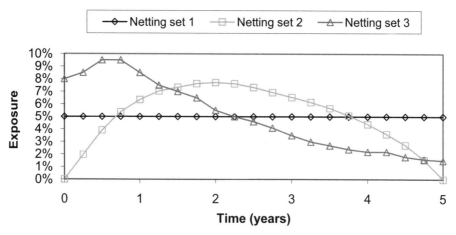

Figure 11.3. Illustration of effective maturity for different 5-year EE profiles. Interest rates are assumed to be 5% for all maturities. EE1, EE2 and EE3 have effective maturities of 4.81, 5.00 and 3.21 years, respectively.

As discussed above, the minimum value of the effective maturity is 1 year. Basel II does not recognise a more risk-sensitive treatment but allows a notional weighting scheme as described in Appendix 11.A. Transactions exempt from the 1-year floor must be classified as "non-relationship" transactions, i.e. there should be no relationship concerns that might hinder the termination or decision *not* to roll over the relevant transaction(s). OTC derivatives subject to this treatment must also be collateralised with daily margining and no room for undercollateralisation (such as thresholds).

11.5.3   Exposure at default

Under the IMM, EAD is calculated at the netting set level. Therefore, in contrast to non-internal methods, full cross-product netting is allowable. Given the potential benefits of netting, this is clearly highly advantageous. The definition of EAD under the IMM is based on an EE profile. Conceptually, the Basel II definition of EAD is consistent with the specification of loan-equivalent exposure that we have seen in Chapter 10:

$$EAD = \alpha \times EEPE, \qquad (11.7)$$

where EEPE is the effective expected positive exposure calculated for a given netting set from the effective EE profile and α is a multiplier. The effective EE measure is similar to EE, except that effective EE is constrained to be non-decreasing for maturities below 1 year. The motivation underlying the use of EEPE and its definition is given in Appendix 11.D. In essence, the non-decreasing constraint captures the roll-off impact of risk that would be otherwise missed for transactions that are close to maturity but likely to be replaced. An illustration of EEPE compared with EPE is shown in Figure 11.4. EEPE will typically be slightly greater than EPE as shown (unless EE is monotonically increasing, in which case they will be identical).

The intuition behind the α (alpha) multiplier is the same as discussed in Chapter 10, i.e. it corrects for the finite size and concentration of the portfolio in question. Since an

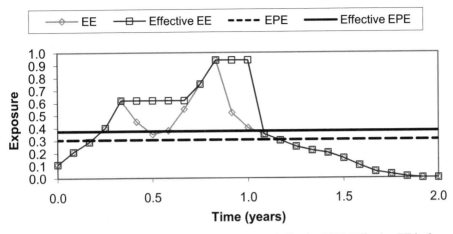

Figure 11.4. Illustration of the difference between EPE and effective EPE. Effective EE is the same as EE but is constrained to be non-decreasing in the first year. EPE is the average of the EE over time whilst effective EPE is the average of effective EE over time.

alpha of 1 is valid only for infinite diversification (see Section 10.4.2), alpha is interpreted as a multiplier above unity which depends on the nature of the portfolio in question.

11.5.4 Defining alpha

As we have seen in Chapter 10, EPE is the true loan-equivalent exposure for an infinitely fine-grained portfolio. The multiplier alpha, first suggested by Picoult (2002), is the correction that accounts for the finite number of counterparties, correlations between exposures and wrong-way risk.[7]

In other words, for the purposes of calculating capital, EPE should be multiplied by alpha in order to reproduce the same result as in the true random exposure case. The use of this loan-equivalent approach greatly reduces the complexity of Basel II since it permits a separate modelling of market and credit risk factors. To be clear, the IMM allows the EAD in equation (11.2) to be defined via a model-based computation of equation (11.7).

Under the IMM, α is fixed at a level of 1.4. While this number may be appropriate for banks with small derivative portfolios, it may be conservative when applied to large OTC derivatives dealers (assuming there is no severe wrong-way risk). Regulators agree that this level is high but argue that it is relevant to cover model and estimation errors. Alpha has been discussed in detail in Chapter 10 and we summarise some published estimates in Table 11.5.

Banks using the IMM have an option to compute their own estimate of α, subject to the supervisory approval. However, this estimate is subject to a floor of 1.2. In light of the results shown in Table 11.2, this floor seems to be conservative but could again be

---

[7] According to Picoult (2002), alpha "expresses the difference between calculating economic capital with full simulation and with a simulation assuming the exposure profile of each counterparty can be represented by a fixed exposure profile."

Table 11.5. Publicly available estimates of α. The study of Wilde (2005) includes wrong-way risk whilst the ISDA Survey involved four banks estimating based on their own portfolios and internal models.

Canabarro et al. (2003)	Wilde (2005)	ISDA Survey
1.09	1.21	1.07–1.10

argued to cover model risk and avoid overreliance on model-based approaches giving idealistic alphas close to unity.

We should emphasise that all of the above comments on the behaviour of alpha assume a reasonably large portfolio with no significant wrong-way risk. As discussed in Chapter 10, a portfolio containing a large credit derivatives exposure (for example) could have an alpha which is dramatically greater than the above estimates. All of the above results were made before the credit crisis that started in 2007 and do not benefit from the hindsight of the potential influence of large concentrated positions in instruments such as credit derivatives. As shown in Section 10.5, such aspects could lead to an alpha substantially above unity.

11.5.5 Effective EPE for collateralised counterparties

Under the IMM, there are two methods of calculating the effective EPE for netting sets covered by margin agreements. Banks that are capable of modelling collateralised credit exposure can use their internal models to calculate collateralised EE, subject to supervisory approval. Effective EPE is obtained from the collateralised EE profile according to the general rules described in Appendix 11.D. The modelling of collateralised exposures has been discussed in Chapter 5.

Banks that are capable of modelling credit exposure without collateral, but whose internal exposure models are not sophisticated enough to handle collateral agreements, can use a simplified method for calculating effective EPE for margined counterparties. Basel II does not give this method a name, but we will refer to it as the *shortcut* method. The shortcut method allows the effective EPE for a margined counterparty to be set as the lesser of the following two quantities:

- The contractual threshold amount, plus an add-on that reflects the potential increase in exposure over the margin period of risk. This add-on is defined as the expected exposure over some remargin period, which must be at least 5 business days for repo-style transactions and 10 business days for other netting sets.
- The effective EPE without a collateral agreement.

Note that the shortcut method does not make a distinction between unilateral and bilateral margin agreements – all margin agreements are treated as unilateral agreements in a bank's favour. Thus, a bank's risk of losing part of the posted collateral (discussed in Section 5.4.2) is ignored in the shortcut method. BCBS (2006) clearly states that the shortcut method is *conservative*, which is true because it makes the assumption that all

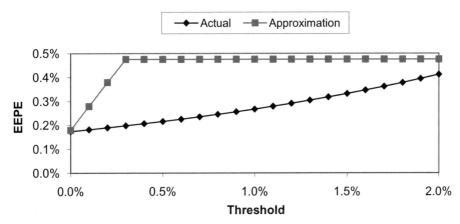

Figure 11.5. EEPE for a collateralised counterparty as defined by Basel II at 1 year for an interest rate swap calculated as a function of collateral threshold. The actual result computed using the simulations from Chapter 5 is shown in comparison with the approximation allowed under Basel II. The approximation corresponds to the uncollateralised EEPE (0.475%) for thresholds above 0.2%.

future exposures will be above the threshold or that there will be no benefit from collateral.

In Section 5.4.7 we have given an example of the calculation of EE as the sum of the threshold and an add-on defined by a simple EE formula. Returning to this example, we have computed the EEPE relevant for an economic capital horizon of 1 year as a function of the collateral threshold (Figure 11.5). We show the actual result compared with a shortcut method approximation of the threshold plus the EE.

We can make the following points:

  (i) For a threshold of zero, the shortcut method is quite accurate. This is because it is based on the EE approximation, which works well as shown in Section 5.4.4.
 (ii) For small thresholds, the shortcut method significantly overstates the true EEPE. For example, with a threshold of 0.3%, the shortcut EEPE is 2.3 times the true EEPE.
(iii) For large thresholds, the shortcut method converges to the true solution since this corresponds to taking the uncollateralised result.

11.6   BASEL II AND DOUBLE-DEFAULT

11.6.1   Background

Suppose the credit risk of an exposure is hedged with a product such as a credit default swap or otherwise guaranteed by a third party.[8] There should be potentially some capital relief due to this risk reduction since there is now only risk in the case both

---

[8] Only guarantees and credit derivatives meeting the minimum operational requirements in paragraphs 189 to 193 of *A Revised Framework* (BCBS, 2006) as well as additional requirements set out in this document are eligible.

parties (original counterparty and party providing the guarantee) default. Under Basel II there are two possible ways in which to account for hedged or guaranteed exposures:

- *Substitution.* The default probability of the "guarantor" (provider of protection or guarantee) may be substituted for the default probability of the original "obligor" (original counterparty). Assuming the guarantor has a better credit quality then this will cause some reduction in risk.
- *Double-default.* Since 2005, the "double-default effect" has been recognised via a formula to account for the fact that risk only arises from joint default. A key consideration in this formula is the correlation between the original counterparty and guarantor. The reader should bear in mind that the double-default treatment has likely been developed with mainly semi-fixed exposures such as loans and bonds in mind rather than the more complex case of derivatives products. However, we will discuss the combination of double-default and random exposure.

The double-default formula (BCBS, 2005) is based on the treatment of the two-default case as described in Section 10.2.1 and therefore respects the joint default probability in terms of a bivariate normal distribution function. This option is only available when using the IRB approach under Basel II.

11.6.2 Double-default formula

Appendix 11.E describes the double-default formula as used in Basel II for computing capital for hedged or guaranteed exposures. The main reduction in capital arises from the decrease in the default probability within the capital formula (there are less significant changes in effective maturity and loss given default). Hence, to keep the analysis simple, we shall focus solely on this term. Figure 11.6 contrasts the difference between an unhedged exposure, the substitution approach and the double-default approach. The substitution approach is preferable only if the conditional default probability of the guarantor is lower than that of the obligor. The double-default formula is always beneficial in recognition of the fact that the probability that both obligor and guarantor will default is usually significantly less that the probability of the obligor defaulting alone.

Clearly, the double-default formula will depend on the default probability of the guarantor as illustrated in Figure 11.7. When the guarantor default probability is low in relation to the obligor default probability then the capital reduction will be significant. For relatively high guarantor default probabilities the capital reduction will be small and may even be zero.

11.6.3 Double-default adjustment factor

The Basel Committee has also proposed a simple approach for double-default consisting of a parametric formula (adjustment factor) for the reduction in capital compared with the standard case. The capital requirement can be calculated by multiplying the capital for an unhedged exposure by this adjustment factor, which depends only on the probability of default of the guarantor. This approximation, described in Appendix 11.E, is compared with the actual double-default formula in Figure 11.8. For a guarantor

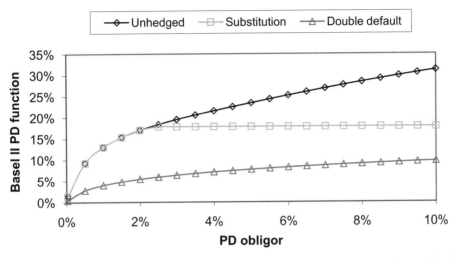

Figure 11.6. Default probability function in Basel II formula for unhedged and hedged exposures. In the latter case, both substitution assumptions and the double-default formula are shown. All details are given in Appendix 11.E. The obligor default probability is assumed to be 0.1%.

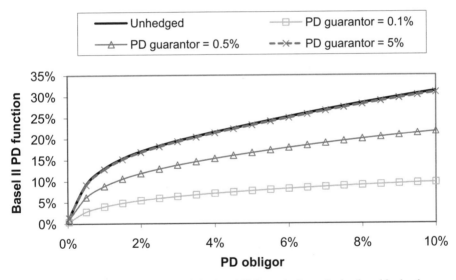

Figure 11.7. Default probability function in Basel II formula for unhedged and hedged exposures for different guarantor default probabilities. All details are given in Appendix 11.E. The obligor default probability is assumed to be 0.1%.

default probability of 0.1%, there is excellent agreement. For the higher default probability of 0.5% shown, the adjustment factor is systematically higher than the actual formula. Indeed, it is possible for the adjustment factor to give a capital requirement higher than that for an unhedged exposure. It is therefore only useful for the case of small guarantor default probabilities where the formula has clearly been benchmarked.

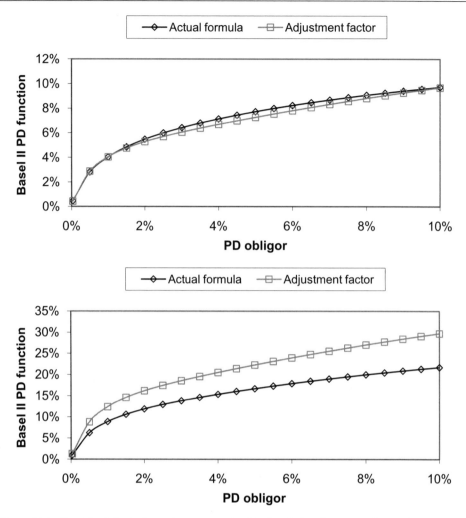

Figure 11.8. Double-default formula compared with Basel II adjustment factor for guarantor default probabilities of 0.1% (top) and 0.5% (bottom). All details are given in Appendix 11.E.

11.6.4 Accounting for double-default for derivatives

The above treatment implicitly assumed a perfect match of exposures in relation to double-default. Accounting for double-default for fixed exposures is relatively straight-forward. If there is an exposure of E and the institution has protection or a guarantee for the same notional of E (or higher) then the full double-default treatment can apply. However, for a random exposure that is being dynamically hedged, the hedged notional will likely be only the current exposure (which could even be zero) whereas the exposure for which the capital charge occurs may be greater even though the intention may be to hedge fully (i.e. buy more CDS protection if the exposure increases). This is illustrated in Figure 11.9. Whilst the position may be considered fully hedged by an institution, it is difficult to give regulatory relief for any more than existing positions.

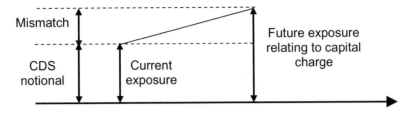

Figure 11.9. Illustration of the potential mismatch in relation to double-default. The current exposure is assumed perfectly hedged with CDS notional whereas the larger future exposure that forms the basis of the capital charge is not fully matched by the hedge notional.

The Basel Capital Accord does not seem to opine on the interaction between the double-default and EPE arising from derivatives exposures. This is probably simply because the double-default framework was put in place prior to the IMM approach. It would seem that there are two possible approaches to attempt to account for double-default for hedged or guaranteed derivatives positions:

- Apply the double-default treatment to the calculated EEPE for a given counterparty in the same way as a fixed exposure. The double-default benefit would apply to the minimum of the EEPE and hedge or guarantee amount (for example, CDS notional). Any excess of EEPE would be treated as direct exposure to the counterparty (the mismatch in Figure 11.9).
- Incorporate the protection or other guarantee (as a negative exposure) when calculating EEPE (similar to the impact of an independent amount under a collateral agreement). The value of alpha could also be computed under this assumption so, for example, hedged exposures would not influence the estimate of alpha. This could mean that a portfolio with well-hedged wrong-way risk exposures could give a low estimate of alpha due to recognition of the wrong-way risk reduction. The capital requirement for the protection or guarantee would need to be itself assessed with respect to the guarantor's counterparty risk.

The latter case above might seem a natural way forward since the impact of a hedge or guarantee is, for example, similar to the impact of an independent amount, which can already be considered when calculating EEPE. However, it does not consider the double-default impact directly.

11.7 SUMMARY

In this chapter we have described regulatory approaches to counterparty risk, in particular focusing on Basel II implementation details. We have considered the different approaches available to compute capital requirements for derivatives exposures, from the simple add-on rules to the more sophisticated internal model approach to estimating capital based on EPE multiplied by a factor known as alpha. We have discussed repo-style transactions and the treatment of collateral within the various approaches of the Basel II Framework. The treatment of double-default effects of hedged (or partially hedged) exposures has also been examined.

APPENDIX 11.A: EFFECTIVE REMAINING MATURITY

(a) Simple fixed exposures

Under Basel II, the effective remaining maturity in the case of simple instruments such as loans with fixed unidirectional cashflows is defined as the weighted average maturity of the relevant transactions given by a simple duration formula without interest rate effects:

$$\text{effective maturity } (M) = \frac{\sum_i \text{CF}_i t_t}{\sum_i \text{CF}_i},$$

where CF_i is the magnitude of the cashflow at time t_i (defining today as zero).

(b) Derivatives positions within a netting set

The cashflows of OTC derivatives are highly uncertain, and a more complex formula is required to calculate the effective maturity. The effective maturity is defined at the netting set level from the full EE profile that extends to the expiration of the longest contract in the netting set. If the original maturity of the longest dated contract contained in the set is greater than 1 year, the effective maturity is calculated according to:

$$M = 1 + \frac{\sum_{t_k > 1\,\text{yr}} \text{EE}(t_k)\Delta t_k B(0, t_k)}{\sum_{t_k \leq 1\,\text{yr}} \text{effective } \text{EE}(t_k)\Delta t_k B(0, t_k)},$$

where $B(0, t_k)$ is the risk-free discount factor from the simulation date t_k to today, Δt_k is the difference between time points, $\text{EE}(t_k)$ is the EE at time t_k and effective EE is basically a non-decreasing EE (defined in Appendix 11.D). Similar to the general treatment under corporate exposures, M has a cap of 5 years (a 1-year floor is implicitly present in the formula). Note that if the denominator in the above equation becomes rather small then the effective maturity can be large. This means that netting sets with rather small exposure up to 1 year (for example, due to the underlying market value being significantly negative) will have capital determined by a small exposure with a high maturity.

The above equation is conceptually consistent with the effective remaining maturity for more simple instruments. For more detail, see Picoult (2005).

(c) Impact of collateralised short-term instruments

For netting sets in which all contracts have an original maturity of less than 1 year, the effective maturity is set to 1 year. However, the 1-year floor does not apply to certain collateralised short-term exposures. The instruments included in this category are OTC derivatives and SFTs that have the original maturity of less than 1 year, are fully or nearly-fully collateralised and subject to daily re-margining. For such transactions, the effective maturity for a given netting set is calculated as the weighted average of the contractual remaining maturities, with notional amounts used as weights:

$$M = \frac{\sum_i A_i M_i}{\sum_i A_i},$$

where A_i is the notional and M_i is the contractual remaining maturity for contract i. This effective maturity is subject to a floor equal to the largest minimum holding period of the transactions in the netting set.

APPENDIX 11.B: THE ASSET CORRELATION AND MATURITY ADJUSTMENT FORMULAS IN THE ADVANCED IRB APPROACH OF BASEL II

(a) Asset correlation

In the Basel II advanced IRB approach the correlation parameter is linked to the default probability (PD) according to the following equation:

$$\rho = 0.12 \times \frac{1 - \exp(-50 \times PD)}{1 - \exp(-50)} + 0.24 \times \left(1 - \frac{1 - \exp(-50 \times PD)}{1 - \exp(-50)}\right).$$

Figure 11.1 shows the dependence of both asset correlation and the default-only capital charge on PD.

(b) Maturity factor

The factor $MA(PD, M)$ is the maturity adjustment that is calculated from PD and M according to:

$$MA(PD, M) = \frac{1 + (M - 2.5) \times b(PD)}{1 - 1.5 \times b(PD)},$$

where $b(PD)$ is a function of PD defined as:

$$b(PD) = [0.11852 - 0.05478 \times \ln(PD)]^2.$$

Note that maturity adjustment is capped at 5 and floored at 1.

APPENDIX 11.C: NETTING AND COLLATERAL TREATMENT UNDER THE CURRENT EXPOSURE METHOD (CEM) OF BASEL II

(a) Netting

The netting benefits of add-ons are handled in a simple but ad hoc fashion using a factor NGR, which is the ratio of the current net exposure to the current gross exposure for all transactions within the netting set. For n trades within a netting set, then NGR is given by:

$$\text{NGR} = \frac{\max\left(\sum_{i=1}^{n} \text{MtM}_i, 0\right)}{\sum_{i=1}^{n} \max(\text{MtM}_i, 0)},$$

where MtM_i is the MtM value of the ith trade in the netting set. NGR can be seen to define the current impact of netting in percentage terms (an NGR of zero implies perfect netting and an NGR of 100% implies no netting benefit).

Where legally enforceable netting agreements are in place, the total add-on is calculated according to the following formula:

$$\text{add-on} = (0.4 + 0.6 \cdot \text{NGR}) \cdot \sum_i \text{add-on}_i,$$

where add-on$_i$ is the add-on for transaction i. Only 60% benefit of current netting is therefore accounted for in any future exposure.

(b) Collateral

The impact of current collateral held against a netting set is incorporated into EAD as follows:

$$\text{EAD} = \max(0, \text{MtM} - C) + \text{add-on},$$

where MtM is the current mark-to-market of the portfolio, C is the volatility-adjusted collateral amount (i.e. the value of collateral minus a haircut) and "add-on" is the total add-on on the portfolio of transactions under the netting set.

APPENDIX 11.D: DEFINITION OF EFFECTIVE EPE

As we have discussed in Chapter 4, banks that model exposure internally compute exposure distributions at a set of future time points $t_1, t_2, \ldots, t_k, \ldots$ using Monte Carlo simulations. For each simulation time point t_k, the bank computes the expectation of exposure $\text{EE}(t_k)$ as the simple average of all Monte Carlo realisations of exposure for that time point.

To recap, EPE is defined as the average of the EE profile (in this case over a 1-year horizon). Practically, it is computed as the weighted average of $\text{EE}(t_k)$ as follows:

$$\text{EPE} = \sum_{t_k \leq 1\,\text{yr}} \text{EE}(t_k)\Delta t_k,$$

where weights are defined as time intervals between simulation dates $\Delta t_k = t_k - t_{k-1}$.

Generally, as the simulation time progresses, the number of remaining trades with the counterparty and the number of remaining cashflows in the portfolio decrease. Therefore, at some future time point, the "amortisation effect" starts dominating the "diffusion effect" so that the portfolio EE decreases as a function of time. In particular, the EE profile can start decreasing because of the expiration of short-term trades. However, these short-term trades are likely to be replaced by new ones, but the EPE does not consider this and may understate the risk.

To account for this "roll-over" risk, Basel replaces EPE with effective EPE obtained in two steps as follows. First, the effective EE profile up to the 1-year horizon is obtained by adding the non-decreasing constraint to the EE profile. In our notations, this non-decreasing constraint can be represented via a simple recursive relation given by:

$$\text{effective EE}(t_k) = \max\{\text{effective EE}(t_{k-1}), \text{EE}(t_k)\},$$

with the initial condition of effective EE(0) being equal to the current exposure. Figure 11.3 illustrates how the effective EE profile is obtained from the EE profile. In the second step, effective EPE is computed from the effective EE profile as the average over the 1-year horizon in the same way as EPE is computed from the EE profile:

$$\text{effective EPE} = \sum_{t_k \leq 1\,\text{yr}} \text{effective EE}(t_k)\Delta t_k.$$

The impact of roll-over adjustment is more significant for portfolios dominated by short-term OTC derivatives or repo-style trades.

APPENDIX 11.E: DOUBLE-DEFAULT TREATMENT OF HEDGED EXPOSURES IN BASEL II

(a) Double-default formula

From equation (11.1), the conditional default probability in the Basel II IRB capital formula is:

$$\Phi\left(\frac{\Phi^{-1}(\text{PD}_o) + \sqrt{\rho_o}\Phi^{-1}(0.999)}{\sqrt{1 - \rho_o}}\right),$$

where we denote specifically PD_o and ρ_o as the default probability and asset correlation parameter of the obligor (original counterparty). To compute capital for a hedged exposure in the advanced IRB framework (BCBS, 2005), it is necessary to calculate the conditional default probability that both the obligor and guarantor will default. It is also critically important to consider the correlation between obligor and guarantor as high correlations will make double-default more likely. By assuming an additional asset correlation parameter of ρ_g for the guarantor and an asset correlation between obligor and guarantor of ρ_{og}, the following conditional joint probability formula can be derived as a simple bivariate normal distribution function $\Phi_2(.)$:

$$\Phi_2\left(\frac{\Phi^{-1}(\text{PD}_o) + \sqrt{\rho_o}\Phi^{-1}(0.999)}{\sqrt{1 - \rho_o}}, \frac{\Phi^{-1}(\text{PD}_g) + \sqrt{\rho_g}\Phi^{-1}(0.999)}{\sqrt{1 - \rho_g}}; \frac{\rho_{og} - \sqrt{\rho_o\rho_g}}{\sqrt{(1 - \rho_o)(1 - \rho_g)}}\right).$$

The Basel Committee considers a value of $\rho_{og} = 50\%$ in order to account for a wrong-way risk due to a correlation between the default probability of obligor and guarantor. Nevertheless, an operational requirement for recognition of double-default is that there is no "excessive correlation" between the credit quality of obligor and guarantor and double-default is not recognised for an exposure to a financial institution. A value of $\rho_g = 70\%$ is used which essentially assumes (conservatively) that the systemic risk of the guarantor is high. This correlation parameter is substantially higher than that for the obligor, ρ_o, which will follow the standard calculation (Appendix 11.B) and will therefore be between 12% and 24%. A limiting case of the above formula (for example, as PD_g increases to unity) is:

$$\Phi\left(\frac{\Phi^{-1}(\min(PD_o, PD_g)) + \sqrt{\rho_o}\,\Phi^{-1}(0.999)}{\sqrt{1 - \rho_o}}\right).$$

This corresponds to the substitution approach.

The double-default capital formula also includes a loss given default function LGD_{og}, which corresponds to the worst case loss when pursuing recoveries from both an obligor and guarantor. Furthermore, the maturity adjustment component will also differ in the event of mismatch between the maturity of the original exposure and that of the protection or guarantee. Any charge for maturity mismatch would be based on the M calculated within the IMM approach (Accord Annex 4, paragraph 38).

(b) Adjustment factor

The Basel Committee proposed a simplified approach to the double-default formula where the capital is reduced by the following factor compared with the unhedged exposure case:

$$(0.15 \times 160 \times PD_g).$$

The unhedged exposure is calculated using the usual formula, but using LGD_g instead of LGD_o. The aforementioned parameters of $\rho_g = 70\%$ and $\rho_{og} = 50\%$ were assumed when deriving this formula. As shown in the text, the formula works well for small values of PD_g but can be seen to be more conservative than the unhedged case when $PD_g > 0.531\%$ (this corresponds to the above factor being greater than unity).

12

Managing Counterparty Risk in a Financial Institution

> "A banker is a fellow who lends you his umbrella when the sun is shining, but wants it back the minute it begins to rain."
>
> Mark Twain (1835–1910)

12.1 INTRODUCTION

In this chapter we deal with the management of counterparty risk within a financial institution. We make no particular assumptions about the type of institution in question although this practice has been generally pioneered by large banks and there will be a natural bias in this direction. Depending on the risk management sophistication of a particular institution and the overall amount of counterparty risk taken, the management approach will differ. Different institutions may have very different approaches towards aspects such as collateralisation, regulatory matters, pricing and hedging of counterparty risks. Here, we aim to discuss the high level issues around an overall strategy towards counterparty risk, the main aim being protection of revenues, balance sheets and general financial integrity in case of default of derivatives counterparties. Whilst we try to keep the discussion as general as possible, it will ultimately be biased towards large banks, who have been actively managing counterparty risk since around the 2000–2001 period. The focus will also be on OTC derivatives although other trades such as repos may also be managed centrally.

12.2 COUNTERPARTY RISK IN FINANCIAL INSTITUTIONS

12.2.1 Components

A basic strategy in managing counterparty risk should be based on the fact that it arises from the following components:

- credit exposure;
- default probability;
- expected loss given default (or equivalently recovery rate).

As discussed in previous chapters, the assessment of these components may be rather different and performed by separate divisions within an organisation (at least under assumptions of no wrong-way risk). However, as some point the components need to be combined. A counterparty with a large default probability and a small exposure may be considered preferable to a larger exposure and smaller underlying default probability. A counterparty with a high level of collateralisation and hence a lower loss given default may be considered preferable to a less risky counterparty with more limited arrangements.

For sophisticated derivatives users, the primary role of units responsible for counterparty risk has evolved from one of risk avoidance and trade approval to one of risk management, pricing and hedging. In reference to the exposure component of counterparty risk, there must be a detailed knowledge of the following aspects:

- *Credit lines.* The knowledge of credit lines is important since it relates to the potential approval of new transactions.
- *Netting agreements.* New transactions should ideally be priced incorporating netting with existing trades and therefore a full knowledge of all relevant master agreements is important.
- *Collateral agreements.* Transactions should be priced according to existing and possible future collateral held against potential losses. A detailed knowledge of all collateral agreements is therefore crucial.
- *Trade population.* Under the assumption that netting is possible, it is important to have a full knowledge of all relevant transactions across asset classes for a particular counterparty.

With respect to the second and third components of counterparty risk (default probability and loss given default), the following aspects should be considered:

- *Ratings.* Every counterparty should have a rating (internal and/or external) that allows it to be mapped to an agreed default probability.
- *Credit spreads.* For counterparties with traded debt or CDS markets, the relevant credit spreads are an important aspect for hedging counterparty risk.
- *Recovery rates.* An estimate of recovery rates depending on the characteristics of the counterparty and the seniority of any claim should be made.

Finally, when combining the three key components of counterparty risk to calculate a price, the following components should be considered carefully:

- *Expected losses.* Ultimately, the primary method of defining counterparty risk is via a price, which is akin to considering the expected losses on transactions (CVA).
- *Unexpected losses.* Whilst expected losses are useful, they are worth little (and can even be counterproductive) without some understanding of the variability of possibility losses or the unexpected loss. This may be linked to some concept of capital to support a derivatives business.
- *Risk mitigants.* Counterparty risk must be assessed taking into account all possible risk mitigants and both the cost and benefit of this hedging must be understood.

Regarding unexpected loss and hedging, it might be tempting to suggest that they do not both need be a consideration. If one can fully hedge counterparty risk then unexpected losses are irrelevant (since the cost of the hedge is known with certainty). On the other hand, if unexpected losses are fully under control (for example, by having capital held against them to a very high degree of confidence) then hedging is unnecessary. We will take the view that this argument is too idealistic: unexpected losses can never be fully under control and hedging is never perfect (some variables are unhedgeable and some hedges will have an uncertain cost). Our assertion will therefore be that the best practice of managing counterparty risk is to utilise hedging where practical and understand fully the residual unexpected losses. Hedging may reduce unexpected losses significantly but not eradicate them completely.

12.2.2   Counterparty risk group

From now on, we will refer to the counterparty risk group or CRG generically as the group(s) within a financial institution with the responsibility of managing counterparty risk.

Most large users of derivatives will have a group or groups dedicated to controlling counterparty risk for the different business lines. The existence of such groups may be critical and can add huge value to an institution's risk management. They can allow the firm to be competitive in certain transactions, but, just as importantly, to realise when to walk away from business or transact with another counterparty. A CRG may be able to facilitate increasing the level of business with a certain counterparty, whilst also reducing concentration risk by diversifying credit exposure. They may be able to focus attention in terms of risk mitigation on certain counterparties. In order to achieve all this, a CRG should have a close relationship with other groups such as collateral management, market risk, credit risk and credit derivatives trading. In a smaller institution, they may need to deal with such aspects directly.

12.2.3   Responsibilities

The CRG responsibilities could be reasonably widespread and might cover:

- *Pricing new deals/New trade approval.* There should be standard methods in place for pricing the credit aspect of new transactions (which have been *a priori* agreed with the relevant business areas, or trading desks). For new trades that are sensitive due to their large size, or the exotic nature or the counterparty involved, the CRG should at least opine on the fair price of counterparty risk.
- *Risk assessment.* Clearly, any institution needs to know in simple terms what parameters drive their counterparty risk: not only the level of credit spreads and default rates but also other aspects such as volatilities are important.
- *Hedging.* A CRG should offer an advantage in that many elements of counterparty risk can be hedged. After all other forms of risk mitigation have been exhausted, hedging is the only way in which to reduce risk. The ultimate aim should be that a transaction never needs to be refused outright, every potential trade with a given counterparty represents a price, competitive or not. The CRG should explore all ways in which to make a transaction or business opportunity achievable and economically viable.
- *(Economic) Capital management.* No matter how good risk mitigation and hedging are, counterparty risk will always give rise to unexpected losses. The likelihood of such losses needs to be understood, reserved against and should ultimately drive trading

and business decisions. This arises from the ability to define economic capital for counterparty risk (Chapter 10).

- *Regulatory aspects.* The regulatory aspects of capital requirements must be understood in terms of the chosen method and corresponding capital charge since this may influence decisions on new transactions.
- *Stress-testing.* Whilst a large counterparty risk book might be reasonably well balanced and the exposures diversified over many counterparties, there will be concentrations and potential systemic risks that may not be understood from typical credit portfolio models for calculating unexpected losses. Stress-testing provides a means to assess extreme impacts such as the default of one or more major counterparties and liquidity issues influencing the supply of collateral.

12.2.4   Organisational structure

CRGs may report to front office or control/risk management functions. They may function close to a credit derivatives trading desk or alongside a loan portfolio management group. The choice of organisation should compliment the degree to which the counterparty risk will be activity-managed. A CRG with the mandate to hedge counterparty risk and utilise trading opportunities should be front office based with a close link to credit trading desks. A CRG taking a more passive approach to counterparty risk management should be a control or risk management function linked to loan portfolio management.

In an ideal world, there will be only a single CRG since this maximises operational costs and the diversification offered. Whilst this might seem trivial, banks – being large and sometimes highly political organisations – may struggle to agree on the creation of such a group across all trading desks. However, many large institutions have indeed created a single CRG, which has sometimes meant less focus given to growing trading activities such as commodities and credit derivatives. In particular, in the latter case there was a lack of interest prior to 2007 to migrate counterparty risk for CDS, monolines and structured finance transactions to a CRG. In many large investment banks, such aspects were given low priority whereas, in hindsight, they should have been a key focus. Many CRG groups did not naturally assume responsibility for CDS counterparty risk (for example) as the credit derivatives market grew rapidly. This practice should be avoided as, knowingly or unknowingly, a CRG may avoid the most toxic counterparty risk. Business areas and trading desks may be "blinkered" or choose to ignore key problems such as wrong-way risk (for example, in search of short-term profits). The impartiality and cross-product focus of a CRG may make them best equipped to identify and avoid such issues (assuming they have the gravitas within an organisation to achieve this). By default, all counterparty risk in an organisation, especially that arising from new or exotic transactions, should reside with the CRG.

12.2.5   Mechanics of pricing

The role of a CRG is to take the problem of quantifying counterparty risk away from the individual businesses within an organisation. Hence, procedurally, the chain of events could be:

- A trading desk pays a "credit charge" or CVA to the CRG, which undertakes to underwrite any losses due to default of the counterparty of the trade at any time before maturity.

- The CRG uses the credit charge either as a reserve (buffer) against possible losses, as a means to absorb hedging costs or as a combination of the two.
- If the counterparty defaults then the CRG compensates the trading desk for the loss of the derivative. Any future credit charge (in the event the charge was not made fully upfront) due is then cancelled.
- If the counterparty does not default then no part of the credit charge is returned since it has been required either for hedging costs or to set off against other losses (possibly in the future).

A credit charge may be structured as an upfront or a running premium. From a trader's perspective, a running credit charge is often cleaner since it can be matched with payments on an underlying contract (for example, receiving a spread on a swap leg). A CRG would probably prefer a single upfront payment for simplicity and in order to avoid annuity risk (Section 6.3.6). In the case of a highly distressed counterparty, there is a strong argument for a running credit charge since the positive carry that this provides for the CRG should balance well the negative carry of buying CDS protection. However, since credit charges are normally relatively small and counterparty defaults are relatively unlikely events, the practical differences between running and upfront charges are not huge.

12.2.6 Default settlement

In the event of default, the CRG must compensate the original trading book for an amount corresponding to the exposure of the trade at default time less recovery value. As with CDS contracts (see Chapter 6), the settlement, although an internal matter, is not trivial. The most efficient methodology is probably if the CRG undertakes to cover the cost of the trading desk replacing the tranaction(s) concerned so they need have no concern over the bankruptcy process. The CRG should be aware of any liquidity risk they face due to this aspect. The CRG also needs to be actively involved in the lengthy process of pursuing any claim with the defaulted counterparty. Note that the CRG will be likely following claims arising from many derivatives transactions and there may be claims arising from other areas (for example, bond trading) also. This way, the CRG handles aspects such as delivery squeezes that they probably have the most expertise to deal with. Furthermore, the P&L of a trading desk will not be impacted by a lengthy bankruptcy process.

12.2.7 Technology aspects

For around two decades, large derivatives dealers have invested significant resource in order to build sophisticated systems for quantifying potential future exposure (PFE), the subject of Chapter 4. More recently, but for over a decade, some of these dealers have supplemented such systems with the ability to price (and hedge) counterparty risk according to typical CVA methods (Chapter 7). However, many financial institutions are only just beginning to implement CVA technology solutions. The systems for achieving this require:

(i) *Monte Carlo simulation engines.* PFE generation is normally supported by a generic Monte Carlo simulation. This must be able to run a large number of scenarios for each variable of interest and revaluate all underlying positions up to the netting set level normally in a few hours (via an overnight batch). Ideally, it will also be possible to simulate equivalent scenarios for new deals on a real-time basis to allow intra-day calculations of PFEs and CVAs to be made (Section 4.4.1).

(ii) *Pricing functionality.* After generating a large number of scenarios, it is necessary to revalue every single product in each scenario. Whilst most common products such as interest rate swaps, FX forwards and credit default swaps are almost trivial and extremely fast to value, the scale of the pricings required is huge. Consider simulating 50,000 trades at 100 time steps with a total of 10,000 scenarios. This requires 50 billion valuation calls via the relevant pricing functions that can easily take many hours of CPU time. Valuations can be speeded up significantly via applying both financial and computational optimisations. Examples include multi-dimensional interpolation of prices and the use of faster, but more approximate pricing functions. An institution should not feel shy of using simple pricing formulas: the key point is not to refine valuations far beyond the error margins of the underlying variables being simulated, especially in the case of long time horizons where there is significant uncertainty. This is particularly true of exotic trades, where work done to be able to use a related sophisticated and computationally intensive pricing model may be deemed irrelevant due to the margin of error surrounding the actual scenarios themselves.

(iii) *Databases.* Data collection and storage will be substantial and must be obtained from various front-office and back-office systems and external sources. The cooperation between various departments in order to retrieve such data is also crucial and has often proved a significant bottleneck for firms implementing a complex counterparty risk management system. Data requirements cover the following aspects:

- market data;
- trade details;
- legal entities;
- collateral agreements;
- other legal information;
- credit lines (limits);
- default probabilities and recovery rates;
- exposure simulations.

Rapid data retrieval is also extremely important. For example, the retrieval of exposure simulations, probably at the netting set level (as discussed in Section 4.4.1) is required for exposure calculations and the pricing of new trades.

(iv) *Exposure calculations.* Exposure metrics such as EE, PFE and EPE must be readily calculated from the simulation data stored from daily (overnight) computations. It must also be possible to re-aggregate on a real-time basis, including the impact of newly simulated trade(s) to look at the incremental impact on credit lines and pricing.

(v) *Trade pricing.* Systems must be capable of combining default probabilities with incremental expected exposures (Section 7.2.2) on a real-time basis to be able to price new trades. The ability to generate incremental exposures will enable the

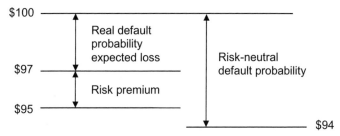

Figure 12.1. Illustration of the difference between real and risk-neutral default probability for the example bond described in the text.

appropriate incremental CVA to be calculated for new deals as required. It is highly desirable to be able to calculate incremental CVAs for new trades in real time, especially where the CVA may influence the profitability of the transaction in question.

(vi) *Reporting*. Reporting tools, showing credit limits breached and allowing drill-down of exposure profiles (via marginal exposures discussed in Section 4.5.1) as well as risk sensitivities for hedging are required.

We should note that systems for counterparty risk are typically built around the independence benefits of assuming no wrong-way risk. Indeed, historically many systems were put in place long before extreme wrong-way risks embedded in products such as credit derivatives were appreciated (or even present). The inclusion of wrong-way risk products, such as credit default swaps, in counterparty risk systems is therefore challenging and requires either crude simplifications or major systems engineering.

12.3 INSURANCE COMPANY OR TRADING DESK?

12.3.1 Background

Consider a bond with a notional value of $100 as illustrated in Figure 12.1. Assume an investor believes the probability of default of the bond is 3% and for simplicity that the associated recovery rate is zero: the expected loss is then also 3% or $3. However, this does not mean that the investor will be willing to pay $97 for the bond. In order for the investor to buy this bond then the market price must be below this amount in order to provide compensation for the credit (and other) risks. For example, suppose that the bond trades at a price of $95 since investors need to be paid a risk premium in order to buy the bond. In this case, the risk premium amounts to $2. However, consider now that an investor can buy insurance for the credit risk on the bond for $6. Now they may be willing to pay $94[1] for the bond since they can hedge the credit risk and require no risk premium on top of this. This implies a default probability of 6%. This probability is known as risk-neutral probability and should not be confused with the actual (real) default probability. Arbitrage will be likely to drive the price to $94.[2]

---

[1] Note that the price of $96 arising from real default probability + risk premium arguments and from hedging arguments need not be equal although market forces will tend to drive them together.

[2] This point is quite complex and depends on aspects such as the ability to short the bond. Since counterparty risk can generally not be easily arbitraged (last bullet point in Section 9.2), it is sufficient to think of the prices of $94 and $95 existing at the same time and depending on the view of the bond investor.

Counterparty risk should be analysed in a similar way to bonds as above. One could assess the real probability of default and other parameters and derive a CVA value on this basis. However, it would be important to consider the inclusion of a risk premium within the calculation. This risk premium should be made with respect to unexpected losses as discussed in Section 10.3.1. On the other hand, the CVA could be calculated by reference to hedging instruments (such as credit default swaps) in which case a risk premium would not be relevant. However, unlike the bond case where the hedging of credit risk is quite straightforward, hedging CVA is much more complex, as discussed in Chapter 9. Hence, an institution must understand both the real and risk-neutral approaches to counterparty risk and, more importantly, what their overall chosen approach will be. There must also be consistency within the approach chosen. For example, charging CVA according to real probabilities with the addition of risk premiums and then attempting to hedge the underlying risk may produce large losses associated with high hedging costs. On the other hand, charging risk-neutral CVAs when not actively hedging could lead to a CRG detrimentally becoming a profit centre at the expense of their internal clients.

Financial risk is – very broadly speaking – dealt with in two ways. It is either prudently controlled and managed as in traditional risk management or it is dynamically hedged. Value-at-risk (VAR) applied to market risk is an example of the former category whereas the trading of structured products is an illustration of the latter. In risk management applications, one seeks to quantify and understand all components of risk but generally not to actively trade them in any way. Risk management is applied under the real probability measure, i.e. using the actual subjective probabilities of market events.[3] Dynamic hedging, on the other hand, is based on the idea that risk can be neutralised by adopting the appropriate trading strategy. Dynamic hedging is based on the risk-neutral probability measure, i.e. market-implied probabilities which might not subjectively appear real but do reflect the actual cost of hedges through time.

One particularly interesting feature of the quantification of counterparty risk is that it represents an intersection between the two distinct financial worlds of risk management and dynamic hedging. Potentially significant default losses, together with aspects such as wrong-way risk, provide convincing evidence for the need to hedge counterparty risk. Yet, as discussed in Chapter 9, the hedging of counterparty risk is challenging and is unlikely to be achieved without significant residual risks.

12.3.2 Insurance approach

We will refer to traditional risk management applied to counterparty risk as the "insurance approach". In this case, the credit charges are insurance premiums, which will create a collective buffer against counterparty defaults. The credit charges should cover all expected future losses due to counterparty risk, which we refer to as the "actuarial CVA". We can note that this will correspond to charging the incremental (or marginal[4]) CVA on all individual transactions as they occur. However, additionally, there should be some charge relating to the unexpected loss as illustrated in Figure 12.2. Ideally, a new trade would be assessed in terms of its contribution to the actuarial CVA

---

[3] Aside from the discussion on using implied volatility in Section 9.5.3.
[4] As discussed in Section 7.2.4, the incremental CVA is appropriate for new trades whereas the marginal CVA would facilitate an analysis of existing trades.

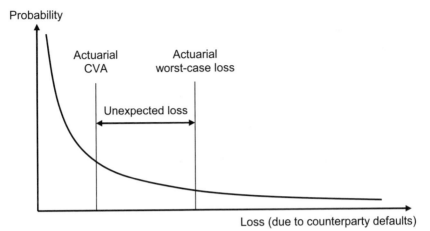

Figure 12.2. Schematic illustration of the quantification of counterparty risk using the "insurance approach". The figure shows the distribution of losses due to counterparty defaults over a time horizon covering the maturity of all trades. The "actuarial CVA" covers the expected loss, whilst the unexpected loss denotes the difference between this and a worst case loss at some confidence level.

and the unexpected loss. The former is naturally achieved by using an incremental (or marginal) CVA charge calculated for the counterparty in question.

However, the unexpected loss component is much harder to quantify since it depends on the risk to all counterparties, as discussed in Chapter 10. Rather than re-running lengthy capital calculations to assess the impact of a single trade on the portfolio risk, a quantification of unexpected loss can probably be best achieved via using a multiplier approach. This means that the total CVA charged to a trade would be the actuarial CVA scaled by a factor calibrated to the counterparty risk portfolio in question. The factor would represent one plus the ratio of unexpected loss to actuarial CVA for the portfolio in question and therefore measure the relative increase in expected CVA to account for the unexpected loss in a portfolio context. The ratio of unexpected loss to actuarial CVA could be estimated periodically based on the portfolio in question, similarly to the concept of alpha introduced in Chapter 10.

The magnitude of such a charge relating to unexpected loss is highly subjective. If it is too large then the counterparty risk charges will be excessive, with trading opportunities lost. However, if it is too small then the CRG will potentially experience significant losses when a larger-than-average number of defaults occurs within a given period. To assess the unexpected loss properly, the following components must be considered:

- *Time horizon.* The longer the time horizon, the smaller the unexpected loss charge will need to be since the law of averages will reduce the relative magnitude of unexpected losses (assuming of course that the actuarial CVA is a perfectly accurate measure of future losses).
- *Confidence level.* The higher the confidence level, the less likely that a CRG will experience losses over the period of interest. However, a high confidence level also gives rise to less aggressive pricing via the unexpected loss.

The more willing the management of a CRG team are to assess their performance on a long-term basis, the more aggressive pricing can be due to a reduction of unexpected loss, as described by the two above components.

We emphasise that actuarial CVA should be calculated out to the maximum maturity date to ensure that all possible future losses are covered. By contrast, and in line with economic capital approaches, unexpected losses may be considered over a shorter period such as 1 year. In this case, a final component, important when assessing unexpected loss, is credit migration and mark-to-market, as discussed in Section 10.6. The CRG may not just make losses because of defaults but also may lose due to increased CVAs as a result of default probability increases (credit migrations) and changes in other market variables. The unexpected loss should account for the potential for such losses. Again, a longer time horizon will tend to make such aspects less important as the residual maturity will be smaller.

12.3.3   Trading desk approach

An alternative way in which to manage counterparty risk is the "trading desk" approach. The booking of a CVA leads to linear and non-linear risk sensitivities to all underlying variables and credit (all discussed in detail in Chapter 9). The trading desk approach involves full hedging with respect to these sensitivities and hence to quantify with a high level of certainty the cost of counterparty risk as illustrated in Figure 12.3. Note that, in contrast to the insurance-style approach, there is no unexpected loss component to consider and therefore only default losses and not credit migration changes need be considered (since the CVA is calculated out to the maximum maturity). The risk-neutral CVA should define the hedging cost but a quantification of the residual hedging error is also required. The hedging error may reflect both uncertainty in hedging and a bias caused by aspects such as additional transaction costs.

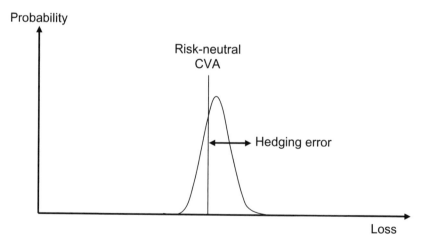

Figure 12.3. Schematic illustration of the quantification of counterparty risk using the "trading desk approach". The figure represents the "risk-neutral CVA" which should represent the cost of hedging in frictionless markets. There will be some additional hedging error as shown. This is likely to be positively biased due to transaction costs.

It would be expected that the risk-neutral CVA would be significantly larger than the actuarial CVA, since it is calculated from market-implied parameters which often involve substantial risk premiums.

12.3.4 Profit centre or not?

Ideally, a CRG should not be concerned with P&L generation since any profit will ultimately come only at the expense of the trading desks and/or businesses within a firm. For a trading desk approach, this is easy to monitor, as the P&L of the CRG should be relatively flat from month to month with some expected volatility due to hedging errors and (hopefully occasional) defaults. However, for an insurance-style approach, the assessment of whether P&L is being generated (or lost) can only be accurately made over a long time horizon of many years. Any CRG needs some reserve or buffer against potential (unhedged) default losses. A small reserve is likely to result in significant losses during periods when default rates are high. Such losses may need to be absorbed ultimately by the underlying clients of the CRG. On the other hand, a large reserve may mean overall losses are very unlikely but may also suggest that business lines are being overcharged for counterparty risk. It seems obvious, therefore, that a CRG should be using credit charges that are higher than expected losses, but the magnitude of the additional charge is a very subtle point: too small and it may destabilise the CRG, too large and it may adversely impact business.

12.3.5 Finding the balance

The insurance and trading desk approaches represent the extremes, with the most effective counterparty risk management representing a compromise in which key sensitivities are dynamically hedged whilst other risks are treated as insurance-style risks and reserved against. In the last decade, institutions active in managing counterparty risk have moved gradually to more of a trading desk approach, aided by the development of the credit derivatives market. However, hedging costs can be significant and an institution may want to consider the following equation:

$$\text{actuarial CVA} + \text{unexpected loss} = \text{risk-neutral CVA} + \text{hedging error}. \qquad (12.1)$$

It is interesting to calculate approximately the unexpected loss that satisfies the above relationship and translate this into possible time horizons and confidence levels. This then gives an idea of the relative size of hedging costs. For example, if the relevant unexpected loss is relatively large and implies a confidence level of 99.9% over a 1-year horizon then the institution may consider active hedging uneconomical.[5]

12.4 HOW TO CALCULATE CREDIT CHARGES

12.4.1 Real or risk-neutral?

In Chapter 7 we have described the formulas for CVA, which represent the price of counterparty risk. The CVA can be computed under either the real or risk-neutral

[5] This follows from the fact that switching to an actuarial approach would mean that there is only a 1-in-1,000 chance that they will suffer losses in excess of the hedging costs in the next year. This, however, crucially depends on the accuracy of the quantitative calculations and accountancy issues related to require MtM of CVA.

344 Counterparty Credit Risk

probability measure, in the former case using historical parameters and in the latter using market-implied parameters. In theory, the credit charge should be the CVA with an additional charge for risk and hedging costs:

- *Insurance approach.* In this case, the credit change should be the incremental CVA calculated with real parameters, which corresponds to the incremental expected losses due to the counterparty defaulting. In addition, some charge relating to the uncertainty of future losses in order to provide an additional reserve might be relevant ("risk premium"):

$$\text{credit charge} = \text{incremental CVA} + \text{risk premium.} \qquad (12.2)$$

Ideally, it should be possible to link the risk premium charged on an individual trade back to the unexpected loss as its magnitude can then be understood in terms of an overall time horizon and confidence level. As mentioned before, this might be achieved by scaling the marginal CVA by some multiplier for the appropriate portfolio in question.

- *Trading desk approach.* In this case, the credit charge should be the risk-neutral CVA, which corresponds to the expected losses due to counterparty defaults using market-implied parameters (i.e. including risk premium components). In addition, some charge for additional hedging costs may be relevant ("hedging error"):

$$\text{credit charge} = \text{incremental CVA} + \text{hedging error.} \qquad (12.3)$$

12.4.2 Default probabilities

As discussed before, the key aspect of real versus risk-neutral parameters relates to default probabilities, since market-implied default probabilities could be many multiples of long-run historical averages. In the insurance-style approach, default probabilities should in theory be real (rather than risk-neutral) and therefore estimated via counterparty rating (internal or otherwise) mapped to historical default experience. In the trading desk approach, risk-neutral default probabilities should be implied from the market using CDS or the price of traded debt.

12.4.3 Drift, volatility and correlations

As discussed previously (see Section 9.5.2), drifts should not be calculated from risk-neutral forwards unless the underlying variables are to be dynamically hedged. Like default probabilities, volatilities and correlations should be estimated historically unless they are to be hedged. An exception, as discussed in Section 9.5.3, is implied volatility which may be regarded as a superior estimator of future volatility and is likely to always lead to a conservative result.

In reality, many institutions use market implied default probabilities even when not actively managing default risk of all counterparties. Whilst this is arguably inconsistent, it can be justified by the fact that market-implied default probabilities would naturally add some risk premium component to the credit charge. The ability to link the risk premium back to unexpected losses at a portfolio level is therefore critical in understanding if the risk-neutral approach is covering unexpected losses to a reasonable time horizon and maturity.

12.4.4 Mark-to-market

The above comments imply that an institution should use a combination of real and risk-neutral parameters depending on the extent of dynamic hedging. Whilst technically there is nothing to prevent CVAs, and hence credit charges, from mixing real and risk-neutral probabilities, there is a significant and yet not mentioned point, which is the potential need to mark-to-market all credit charges (for example, under FAS 157[6].

The need for an institution to mark-to-market its counterparty risk alongside the value of the corresponding derivatives makes it difficult for a CRG to run an insurance-style book. It will be tempted to hedge at least at a high level; for example, buying CDS protection via indices and implied volatility in various asset classes to minimise MtM volatility linked to CVA and avoid large counterparty risk losses when markets become more volatile and credit spreads widen. Therefore, even a firm with a relatively passive approach to managing counterparty risk may be likely to base all calculations on market-implied parameters. A similar problem arises when putting reserves against trading books. A trading desk may want to try to hedge to minimise the volatility of the reserve, which goes against the nature of a reserve as an actuarial buffer against unexpected losses.

12.4.5 Bilateral credit charges

The question of whether or not to apply bilateral credit charges is a tricky one. On the one hand, especially in the interbank market, it will be impossible for trading terms to be agreed unless credit charges are made with bilateral CVA as a basis. On the other hand, this leaves the CRG with the problem of funding the negative component of the BCVA. Consider an institution executes a swap with a counterparty which has a similar credit quality (CDS premium) such that the overall BCVA is zero (for both parties). The CRG does not receive a fee from the desk executing the trade but still has to manage the risk that the counterparty defaults. Furthermore, an institution with a relatively wide credit spread will have negative BCVAs for new deals, implying that the CRG should be paying trading desks and businesses when they execute new trades. In such a situation, a CRG would have to be positioned close to a treasury unit to attempt to take advantage of funding opportunities. Furthermore, they would need to attempt to monetise the value of their institution's own default by synthetically trading their own credit quality, either directly via a synthetic buyback or indirectly via selling protection on highly correlated institutions. This may represent the only source of income for a CRG since the bilateral credit charges will be usually negative. As discussed in Section 7.3.5, we view such practices as cosmetic and likely to fuel future market instability.

12.5 HOW TO CHARGE FOR COUNTERPARTY RISK

The CRG will have the unenviable role of educating all of their clients (business areas and trading desks) as to the purpose and rationale behind credit charges. They will then

---

[6] An accounting standard issued in September 2006 by the Financial Accounting Standards Board (FASB).

be ultimately responsible for ensuring that credit charges can be calculated by all their "clients" on a timely basis. Whilst for large and/or complex transactions it may be reasonable to have some delay in assessing the relevant charge, in most cases there will need to be a significant amount of automation of the process.

12.5.1 Lookup tables

A lookup table will provide a rapid estimation of a credit charge or CVA based on grids, which may be produced for each product type separately. For example, an interest rate desk may have a grid giving credit charges as a function of maturity and credit quality (assessed by either counterparty rating or credit spread). Such calculations cannot, of course, account for trade specifics such as payment frequencies and currencies and, for this reason, the charges may be conservative in many cases (for example, an interest rate swap credit charge may assume a payer swap with an upwards-sloping curve). They do though make for a very simple, rapid and transparent approach to charging for counterparty risk.

12.5.2 Stand-alone pricing

Many institutions will have stand-alone CVA calculations for various different product types. For example, an interest rate swap CVA calculation may involve the analytical approach described in Appendix 7.D. Such calculations will still be conservative due to ignoring any risk mitigation but will at least capture trade-specific effects (such as a cross-currency swap paying the currency with lower interest rates having a smaller CVA than the reverse swap – see Section 4.3.2 for a detailed explanation). Such calculations may exist in spreadsheets and should be quite easy to use since they depend on just a single-deal definition.

12.5.3 Pricing incorporating risk mitigants

Stand-alone pricing can give a good measure of a credit charge without any benefit from netting or collateral agreements. In order to be able to price new trades with such aspects accounted for requires a significant amount of work in terms of systems development.

The most important aspect is that, in order to calculate an incremental CVA charge accounting for netting and collateral, it is necessary to have information on all other deals under the relevant netting agreement and terms of the collateral agreement (see Sections 7.2.1 and 7.2.2 for the technical details). Practically, this requires a simulation engine that generates all the relevant market variables and computes the values of the current transactions and the new transaction in many scenarios through time. From this data, the incremental CVA can be computed. Rather than doing all calculations on-the-fly, the simulation data for existing trades will probably be run in an overnight batch and then stored for aggregation with new trades during the next business day (see Section 4.4.1). Intra-day calculations are generally not required unless the market has moved significantly or there have been other trades with the counterparty on the same day. This latter case we deal with in Section 12.5.4.

12.5.4   Allocation of CVA

Incremental CVA provides a credit charge covering the increase in total CVA for a counterparty. It is an instantaneous measure, giving the current credit charge accounting for previous transactions and not, of course, accounting for any transactions in the future. This potentially can create some rather unusual effects depending on the ordering of transactions being executed.

Example. A trader executes a swap with a counterparty and is charged a certain amount X by the CRG for the counterparty risk. Later on, another trader executes the exact opposite swap with the same counterparty and therefore due to netting offsets removes all the counterparty risk. Should the second trader be paid X by the CRG since this would mean X has essentially passed from trader 1 to trader 2?

This example is unlikely to occur, but cases where trades remove a significant portion of existing counterparty risk, and therefore have a negative incremental CVA, are common.

The answer to the above problem is probably yes. The second trader must be given a strong incentive to do the offsetting swap. He may even transact the swap at a negative P&L knowing that this will be offset by the counterparty risk gain. Overall, the institution will benefit. The timing of trades is crucially important in determining incremental CVAs, as we shall show, and hence traders may be fortunate (or not) in the timing of a certain transaction with a specific counterparty.

Consider the four trades we described in Section 7.2.4. There are 24 possible combinations in which these trades could have been transacted over time.[7] In Table 12.1 we show the incremental CVAs under four possible trading sequences. In each sequence, the first transaction will have a CVA corresponding to its stand-alone value. Subsequent transactions will have an incremental CVA depending on the exposure profile at the relevant time. In the first sequence, the second transaction offers practically no netting benefit and so has an incremental CVA very close to the stand-alone value. However, the third transaction has a significant negative CVA due to cancelling all the risk of the previous (opposite) transaction. However, if this trade is transacted first (sequence 3) then it attracts a positive CVA charge which is potentially unfair since this offers significant risk reduction.

An incremental analysis might seem rather strange: new transactions can only be priced with information available at the time and it is (usually) not possible to predict what other offsetting transactions may be done in the future. However, this point might not be so clear, for example:

- several trades being executed almost simultaneously as part of a single deal;
- active trading with a given counterparty in a given period, potentially involving unwinds and/or restructured transactions.

---

[7] $4! = 4 \times 3 \times 2 \times 1 = 24$.

Table 12.1. Illustration of incremental CVA charges for four different trades with a given counterparty assuming that the order of the trades is altered. For example, in sequence 4 the ordering of trades is CCS, 5-year payer IRS, 6-year payer IRS, 6-year receiver IRS.

| | Stand-alone | Marginal | Incremental | | | |
			Sequence 1 (1-2-3-4)	Sequence 2 (1-3-2-4)	Sequence 3 (3-1-2-4)	Sequence 4 (4-1-2-3)
5-year payer IRS (1)	2.38	1.68	2.38	2.38	2.35	1.19
6-year payer IRS (2)	3.44	2.32	3.40	1.54	-1.51	2.70
6-year receiver IRS (3)	2.35	-2.32	-3.40	-1.54	1.54	-2.70
CCS (4)	2.60	2.11	1.41	1.41	1.41	2.60
Total	10.77	3.79	3.79	3.79	3.79	3.79

In such cases it may be counterproductive to have a credit-charging policy that may lead to particularly aggressive or conservative pricing for certain transactions. On the one hand, a trader may "get lucky" in competitive pricing on a trade that is not beneficial for an institution or, on the other hand, a trader might lose a deal that may have reduced the risk of future trades. For these reasons, an institution may consider pricing all the trades using marginal CVA as a more realistic representation of the true credit charge of each trade. Whilst most pricing decisions should only be made based on current conditions and not speculation on future business, taking a more high-level view can prove beneficial. Indeed, some institutions calculate approximate credit charges at the transaction time but then apportion actual CVA periodically such as on a monthly or a quarterly basis.[8] Doing this should dampen the large differences between incremental and stand-alone CVA values arising purely from the timing of transactions (as seen in Table 12.1), although there may still be some surprises due to the difference between the incremental CVA at the time of the transactions compared with the marginal CVA assigned at some later date.

12.6   SUMMARY

This chapter has considered the management of counterparty risk within a financial institution. We have outlined the important components to consider and the likely role and responsibilities of a CRG (counterparty risk group). Technology and data considerations have been discussed. The operation of a CRG between the extremes of an insurance company and a trading desk has been given careful consideration in light of the hedging aspects previously discussed in Chapter 9. Finally, we have discussed the mechanics of pricing new transactions and allocation of credit charges across transactions.

---

[8] Although this is often because systems do not allow real-time incremental CVA calculations.

13

Counterparty Risk of
Default-remote Entities

> *"The fact that a great many people believe something is no guarantee of its truth."*
>
> W. Somerset Maugham (1874–1965), *The Razor's Edge*, 1943

In this chapter we review the role of default-remote or triple-A type entities, a general concept that over the years has seen many forms. This area has proved to be the Achilles heal of financial markets with respect to counterparty risk. Triple-A ratings have been assigned to corporates or legal entities based on flawed logic in relation to aspects such as the underlying business model or legal structure. Furthermore, the behaviour of market participants in relation to the "too big to fail" institutions further accentuates the illusion that there is little or no underlying counterparty risk. As discussed already, the failure of institutions such as AIG, Fannie Mae, Freddie Mac and monoline insurers has forever shattered the "too big to fail" illusion. In this chapter we will review historically the role of the triple-A counterparty and assess the strengths and weaknesses of the default-remote entity with respect to counterparty risk. We look at the role of derivatives product companies, monoline insurers and credit derivatives product companies within the financial markets. The discussion will form the basis for some of the arguments in the next and final chapter examining the concept of central counterparties.

13.1 THE TRIPLE-A COUNTERPARTY

In the early days of the derivatives markets, there was a tendency to deal only with the most credit-worthy counterparties. Less credit-worthy counterparties were either excluded entirely or required to pay substantial premiums in order to trade. Financial institutions set up triple-A rated bankruptcy-remote subsidiaries – known as SPVs and discussed in Section 3.2.2 – to handle their derivatives dealing operations. Monoline insurers and derivatives product companies also entered the market. The concept of a triple-A counterparty is rather simple: if a counterparty is practically risk-free then any exposure an institution has with them should not present a major concern. There are two obvious issues with triple-A counterparties. The first and obvious one is that the triple-A rating may be misunderstood or incorrect and hence the concept that they are "practically risk-free" may be wrong. A more subtle problem, as discussed in detail in Chapter 8 in relation to wrong-way risk, is that the absolute credit quality of a counterparty should become less of a focus for very out-of-the-money products.

13.1.1 The need for institutions with long-term views

The concept of an institution with a long-term view is that they can look beyond short-term market volatility (and possible losses) and focus mainly on long-term returns. The concept of a "buy to hold investor" is a rather similar one; for example, an investor may be willing to take on a position with good expected long-term returns but with significant volatility and the possibility of short-term losses. Investors with such attitudes can stabilise markets since they may buy distressed and illiquid securities that have been under heavy price pressure. This will tend to balance out the herd mentalities that sometimes exist in volatile markets. The long-term risk view or buy-to-hold mentality is a particularly important one for the health of counterparty risk markets for the following reasons:

- *Central counterparties.* Like insurance companies and counterparty risk groups (CRGs), discussed in Chapter 12, central counterparties can ultimately perform over a long horizon. The relatively moderate profits made in normal years must not be dramatically wiped out during a bad year.
- *Credit derivatives products.* The CDS product represents an unusual challenge since its mark-to-market is driven by credit spread changes whilst its payoff is linked solely to one or more credit events. Buy-to-hold investors will ensure that these two elements are not driven too far apart. Suppose the CDS premium on a reference entity has widened dramatically due to institutions hedging counterparty risk. The CDS premium is driven to a level that is far too high in relation to the real default risk of the reference entity. This represents a problem for the entity itself and its counterparties, who may refuse trades and try to unwind positions due the inability to hedge their counterparty risk. An investor with a long-term or buy-to-hold view will sell the expensive CDS protection whereas other investors may not, due to their preoccupation with the short-term risks. The overall impact is a more liquid CDS market and more efficient counterparty risk hedging.
- *Super senior tranches.* As discussed at length in Chapter 6, super senior tranches represent a key element of the structured credit derivatives market and securitisation techniques. However, due to their underlying "end of the world" risk, they represent an extreme form of (wrong-way) counterparty risk. Only institutions with long-term views are viable risk takers of positions like this. An institution with a short-term view would simply maximise short-term returns by taking a leveraged exposure to super senior risk under the assumption that losses will never hit these tranches and the positions can be unwound at a profit at some point in the near future. Such a view will destabilise markets if and when unwinds of such leveraged positions occur.

We will now describe entities that have historically provided some mitigation of counterparty risk due to their own default-remoteness. Due to the nature of counterparty risk, such entities must be set up to be able to trade and make business decisions based on long-term views.

13.1.2 Derivatives product companies

The derivatives product company (or corporation) (DPC) was developed in order to mitigate OTC counterparty risk. The overall aim of a DPC is to provide a mechanism for institutions to trade through a triple-A rated entity in order to minimise any counterparty risk. DPCs are bankruptcy-remote entities that achieve a triple-A credit rating based on:

- *Minimising market risk.* In terms of market risk, DPCs can attempt to be close to market-neutral via trading offsetting contracts. Ideally, they would be on both sides of every trade as these "mirror trades" lead to an overall matched book.
- *Support from a parent.* The DPC is supported by a parent (for example, one of the first DPCs was Salomon Brothers' Swapco subsidiary). However, the DPC is bankruptcy-remote with respect to the parent to achieve a better rating. If the parent were to default then the DPC would either pass to another well-capitalised institution or be terminated with trades settled at mid-market.
- *Operational guidelines (limits, collateral terms, etc.).* Restrictions are also imposed on (external) counterparty credit quality and activities (position limits, collateral, etc). The management of counterparty risk is achieved by having daily MtM and collateral posting.

A DPC offers protection against default of the parent company of the DPC. However, should the parent become financially distressed or fail to meet its obligations, the soundness of the DPC may naturally be called into question.

The DPC idea has generally worked well since its creation in the early 1990s. DPCs have played a role similar to that of a counterparty risk group or CRG (discussed in Chapter 12) acting for all market participants. They have typically been involved in contracts such as interest rate swaps that have reasonably symmetric profiles and no wrong-way risk. By executing mirror trades and offsetting risk they can ensure that the risk they take is highly diversified (a mirror trade represents a correlation of -100% and so represents the maximum possible diversification). A DPC can be viewed as an insurance company that, whilst being specialised in a relatively small area, is highly diversified due to trading offsetting contracts, and different and imperfectly correlated asset classes.

13.1.3 Monolines

Monoline insurance companies utilise their triple-A ratings to provide *credit wraps*, which are *financial guarantees*. Monolines began providing credit wraps for US municipal finance but then entered the structured finance arena in a big way so as to achieve diversification and better returns. Monolines have capital requirements driven by the possible losses on the structures they "wrap". For example, a rating agency may consider both a base case and stress scenario and set the monoline capital requirements as a required percentage (100% or more) of the losses in these scenarios. The monoline capital requirements are also dynamically related to the portfolio of assets they wrap. However, the expected (and even stressed) losses for a monoline are likely to be low due to the good-quality assets they wrap (often triple-A themselves). This means that the amount of capital a monoline holds compared with the total amount of notional insured is small. The implicit leverage of a monoline is high (potentially a leverage of 100 is not unreasonable).

Due to the high leverage of a monoline, they have a problem with negative MtM changes on positions since losses will be magnified by the leverage factor. Monolines do not post collateral against positions (at least in normal times). One way to justify this is that since they take a long-term credit view, this avoids exposure to short-term market volatility and liquidity issues. Furthermore, since they carry triple-A ratings then surely it is unnecessary for them to post collateral since they are extremely unlikely ever to fail. By not posting collateral, a monoline can essentially try and "ride the wave" of short-term volatility and illiquidity that may imply large losses on positions. In the end this can be considered to be just "noise".

Nevertheless, there is another more worrying way to look at the need for monolines to not post collateral. They absolutely could not have entered the structured finance area in the same way if they had been required to post collateral since mark-to-market volatility would have severely limited their leverage capabilities. Consider the following example:

Example. A monoline provides financial guarantees or credit wraps on a total of $10bn notional of structured finance underlyings. Since these underlyings are of very good credit quality, the expected losses are 0.3% ($30m) and the losses in a stress scenario are 0.9% ($90m). The monoline has capital of $100m set against possible losses and achieves a triple-A rating.

Now suppose the monoline experiences MtM losses on its positions of 2%[1] or $200m. Does it still justify a triple-A rating?

The answer to the above problem is yes, ... and no. Yes, the monoline would still justify a triple-A rating based on the assessment of its capital against expected or stressed losses, which would not have changed since they are based on statistical estimates (this has been the standard practice of rating agencies). No, since if the monoline were forced to unwind its positions immediately then it would default with no better than a 50% recovery rate (likely worse due to the costs and impact of unwinding a large notional of positions). If the monoline were required to post collateral then it would be forced into bankruptcy.

In December 2007 the market was around 3 or 4 months into a credit crisis that was to prove longer and more painful than most market participants thought possible. Concerns started to rise over the triple-A ratings of monolines and that they had insufficient capital to justify their ratings. However, this placed the rating agencies in a subtle situation since the downgrading of monolines would potentially trigger a chain reaction. Investors would be required to mark down assets due to the loss of the triple-A ratings and monolines would potentially be forced to raise more capital due to being required to post collateral against positions with worried counterparties. Swift ratings action could have therefore triggered an immediate crisis with so much resting on the viability of the monolines triple-A ratings. On the other hand, by leaving the monoline rating alone, as long as the crisis did not worsen, then some MtM losses would eventually be recovered (due to spreads tightening again on assets that were of high credit quality) and the triple-A ratings would again look firm.

Of course, the rating agencies should never have been placed (or allowed themselves to be placed) in the difficult moral situation where removal of a triple-A rating, whilst the

---

[1] Assume the average duration of the positions is 8 years. A spread widening of 25 bps across the board would result in such as loss, i.e. it is not a particularly extreme event.

correct action, would cause default of the monoline and probable immediate systemic failure of all monolines. This situation should have been envisaged at the time of first awarding ratings and should have been a large clue that the whole concept of rating monolines was fundamentally flawed.

Rating agencies chose the wait-and-see approach to downgrading monolines at the start of the credit crisis, implicitly making a bet that the crisis would be a short one. For example, in December 2007, Standard & Poors reaffirmed the rating of XL Financial Assurance Ltd with a negative outlook. In late December, Fitch placed their triple-A rating under review, saying that $2bn of new capital needed to be raised (based on revised loss estimates that were still overly aggressive in retrospect). By mid-2008, XL Financial Assurance Ltd had been downgraded below investment grade by at least one rating agency. On 27th May 2009 an auction determined a final settlement value of 15 cents on the dollar for credit default swaps (CDSs) referencing Bermuda-based Syncora Guarantee (the monoline formerly known as XL Capital Assurance). This is one of several examples of failed monolines, such as Ambac and MBIA, and with the biggest insurer in the world (AIG) requiring an explicit guarantee from the US government in 2009 to prevent bankruptcy. The monolines' venture into structured finance was fundamentally flawed (as we explain in Section 13.2).

Many banks found themselves heavily exposed to monolines due to counterparty risk. For example, as of June 2008, UBS was estimated to have $6.4bn at risk to monoline insurers whilst the equivalent figures for Citigroup and Merrill Lynch were $4.8bn and $3bn, respectively (*Financial Times*, 2008). The monoline story has provided a note of caution for the concept of a large, specialised institution taking counterparty risk.

13.1.4   Credit derivatives products companies

A credit derivatives products company (CDPC) is essentially a vehicle inspired by the DPC and monoline concepts described above. It is structured like a DPC but, as its name suggests, specialises in dealing with credit derivatives products. A CDPC will typically offer to provide single-name and, more importantly, tranche protection on credit portfolios. CDPCs may have offsetting positions to some extent; for example, by buying and selling single-name protection. However, in general they break a key rule of a DPC, which is that they have significant market risk due to not having a balanced set of positions. CDPCs therefore have a problem created by the asymmetry of risk for CDS positions, compared, for example, with traditional swaps. They fill a role as a triple-A counterparty but do so largely on only one side of the market,[2] as sellers of credit protection.

CDPCs, like monolines, are highly leveraged and typically do not post collateral. They fared somewhat better during the credit crisis but only for timing reasons. Many CDPCs were not fully operational until after the beginning of the credit crisis in July 2007. They therefore missed at least the first "wave" of losses suffered by any party short credit protection (especially super senior[3]). The difference between a good and bad monoline or CDPC might simply be a matter of timing.

---

[2] Some CDPCs have taken both long and short positions but this has not been especially common.
[3] The widening in super senior spreads was on a relative basis much greater than credit spreads in general during late 2007.

13.2   THE VALUE OF MONOLINES AND CDPCs

In Chapter 8 we have given quantitative examples of the extreme wrong-way risk inherent in trading with entities such as monolines and CDPCs (described in the next sections generically as "credit insurers"). We showed that the presence of wrong-way risk could even make such protection practically worthless. We now give some qualitative background to this theory and explain in practice why the shaky foundations of credit insurers have caused such disruption in the credit markets. The reader may find it useful to (re)read Section 8.7.

13.2.1   Moral hazard

A key concern of credit insurers is moral hazard due to the seniority of the instruments in which they are concerned. Prior to 2007 there was little concern regarding monolines ever facing financial distress from the point of view of the monolines themselves, their counterparties and the rating agencies. Banks buying insurance on super senior tranches saw the resulting negative basis trade as an accounting trick and not insurance they would ever need. Criticism of the viability of a credit insurer (to be in a position to meet future claims) prior to the end of 2007 would be countered strongly with a defence like "this will never happen" or even "this might happen but far worse things will have happened first". Whilst this evidence is anecdotal, studies that are more rigorous exist. For example, Thompson (2009) shows that if an insurer has a belief that a claim is highly unlikely to occur, they will invest in more illiquid assets, which earn higher returns. The safer the underlying claim is perceived to be, the more severe the moral hazard problem and consequently the higher the counterparty risk. This result seems to link very directly to monolines looking to insure the illiquid triple-A tranches of structured finance transactions.

13.2.2   Rating agencies and triple-A entities

A key element of bankruptcy-remote entities such as DPCs, monolines and CDPCs is the triple-A rating since without this coveted measure of credit-worthiness they have practically no value. The crucial aspect of these triple-A ratings from the point of view of investors is that they are largely given after quantification of future losses based on historical data. Let us try to illustrate some potential pitfalls to understand where the ratings went wrong.

First, consider a simple credit insurer that sells protection on a single CDO tranche which itself has a triple-A rating. Rating agencies typically use an expected loss based measure to define such a triple-A rating.[4] Now, suppose the credit insurer has just a dollar of capital – a ridiculous notion. However, on an expected loss basis, the credit insurer is triple-A rated[5] since it can only make a loss when the CDO tranche takes a loss (a triple-A probability) and even then it has capital (albeit only one dollar!) to set aside against such a loss. This is illustrated in Figure 13.1. Assigning a triple-A rating to the credit insurer is meaningless since it just restates the fact that the underlying CDO

---

[4] Standard & Poors have always rated CDOs based on a first dollar of loss or equivalently default probability basis but the same argument will follow in this case.
[5] This follows from the simple mathematical idea that $E[(L - \alpha)^+] \leq E[L]$ as long as α is a positive quantity.

Triple-A Tranche   **Credit Insurer**

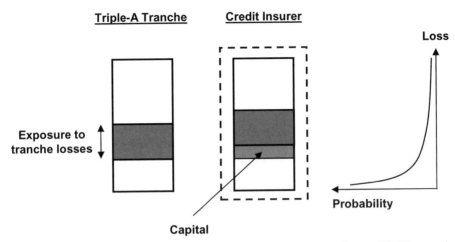

Figure 13.1. Illustration of the illusion by which a credit insurer (monoline or CDPC) may always appear to have a triple-A rating as long as they insure triple-A tranches. The credit insurer provides a guarantee on the triple-A tranche shown. As long as they have some additional capital (however small), the expected loss of the credit insurer can be no worse than the triple-A tranche.

tranche itself is triple-A which does not provide any additional information to a counterparty of the credit insurer.

Of course, rating agencies were not so naive as to apply such a flawed methodology to assign a triple-A rating (although they seemed to do little more than use metrics other than expected loss to quantify future losses of the vehicle in question; see, for example, Tzani and Chen, 2006 and Remeza, 2007). However, this example does illustrate a potential pitfall in that a monoline or CDPC-type vehicle might appear to have triple-A credit quality largely because they sell protection on (or wrap) triple-A underlyings. A counterparty buying protection from such a vehicle would need significantly more reassurance regarding their credit-worthiness since, if the tranche in question suffers losses, there should be a strong likelihood that the vehicle will still be around to honour their contract.

13.2.3 Credit insurer simple example

We can illustrate the problems with a credit insurer with a very simple model for the value of protection purchased on a non-collateralised basis. The model assumes a digital payoff for the protection purchased (this is relevant for a single-name CDS and hence is only an approximation for a tranche but the model is for illustration only). The model requires a correlation parameter that represents the relationship between the value of the digital contract and the inverse[6] credit quality of the counterparty. The formula is given in Appendix 13.A for reference. We assume the credit insurer has a default probability (during the life of the contact) of 0.1%. In Figure 13.2, we show, as a function of correlation, the CVA adjustment and risky value for a digital contract with a risk-free

---

[6] As the value of the contract increases, the credit quality of the credit insurer deteriorates.

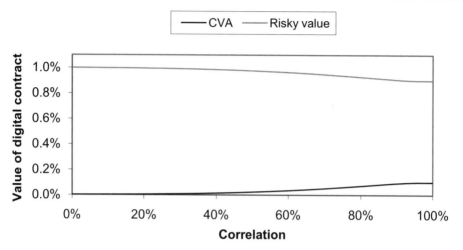

Figure 13.2. Simple credit insurer model showing the value of a digital contract purchased with no collateral posting as a function of correlation. The value of the risk-free digital contract is 1%.

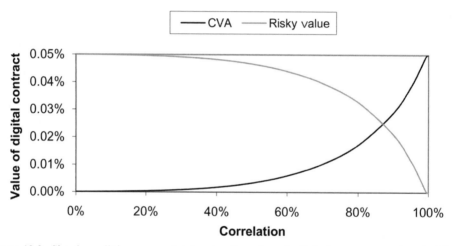

Figure 13.3. Simple credit insurer model showing the value of a digital contract purchased with no collateral posting as a function of correlation. The value of the risk-free digital contract is 0.05%.

value of 1%. We can see that the CVA adjustment is small for all correlations, although it is slightly larger when the correlation is high. In this case, counterparty risk does not appear to be a problem.

We show a similar example in Figure 13.3 but assuming that the risk-free value of the digital contract is just 0.05% (akin to a super senior tranche type probability). Now there is fundamentally different behaviour since, whilst at any "reasonable" level of correlation there is only a small counterparty risk adjustment (CVA), at a high correlation the contract value can be significantly less and eventually worthless.

Spreadsheet 13.1. Simple credit insurer example

This simple model has illustrated two important points we discussed in Chapter 8:

- Wrong-way risk increases with correlation (between credit insurer's default and the value of the underlying contract).
- Wrong-way risk is dramatically more severe for tranches that are more senior.

Consider one final example showing the monoline credit quality improved by a factor of 2 (default probability going from 0.1% to 0.05%). The risky value of the contract is shown in Figure 13.4. Whilst, the improvement in credit quality does have an impact (increasing the risky value for a given correlation level), this is secondary to that of correlation. For example, at high correlation values the doubling of credit quality has an impact similar to that of a decrease in correlation of only about 5%.

This final example emphasises a third point that was made before:

- Counterparty risk for a credit insurer depends less on the absolute credit quality of the credit insurer itself and more on correlation. The correlation concerned is that between the default probability of the credit insurer and the underlying exposure of the contract, which creates wrong-way risk.

The above point suggests that, when trading with a credit insurer, one should be less concerned about their *credit quality* and more concerned with *correlation* between this and the value of the underlying contract. This implies that a counterparty to a credit insurer, for example, should be highly concerned if the company is specialising in one area (credit derivatives, for example!).

Overall, monolines and CDPCs get very bad marks on all of the three aforementioned bullet points. First, they specialise in the rather senior (out-of-the-money) tranches. Second, their involvement in this market is so extreme that the correlation between the value of such assets and their own default probability is by construction extremely high. One could even argue that they are so highly exposed to an asset class that the

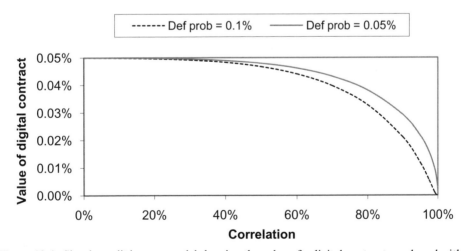

Figure 13.4. Simple credit insurer model showing the value of a digital contract purchased with no collateral posting as a function of correlation. Two different cases of the credit insurer default probability are shown.

correlation is close to unity. Third, they have focussed strongly on their triple-A ratings as a justification for having only minimal counterparty risk. Even if this triple-A rating is "correct" then there can be significant counterparty risk.

13.2.4   Suspension modes, downgrades and death spirals

The previous example illustrates that buying protection (especially super senior protection) from a counterparty not posting collateral can be extremely dangerous when there is a significant correlation between the value of the protection and credit quality of the counterparty (even if the current credit quality of the counterparty is triple-A). However, a further mitigating factor has been ignored in the analysis. Credit insurers can be put into a restricted state by a rating agency if their credit-worthiness is being compromised (for example, due to suffering losses). This restricted state can be explicitly defined (as is the case in many CDPCs) or more generally defined (as is more the case for monolines – see Section 8.7.2). The purpose of the restricted state is to strongly encourage the credit insurer to regain a sound credit quality. What is referred to as a restricted state can therefore be a very firm measure (such as downgrade or restriction on investing and funding activities) or a more general one (such as the suggestion that a certain amount of capital needs to be raised in order to keep a triple-A rating).

In order for a credit insurer to recover from a restricted state or "suspension mode", they will have to adjust their capital structure. This can be achieved by either raising additional capital or by unwinding or restructuring transactions. Either of these points might lead to a protection buyer avoiding counterparty risk losses (at least for the time being). The question is whether the protection buyer may believe that the mitigating features of the suspension mode act to reduce their counterparty risk to reasonable levels.

Whilst it is far from easy to make a quantitative assessment of the above points, we can note that raising additional capital for a credit insurer is likely to be difficult since it will be required at the worst possible time. This has been seen in the problems monolines had in attempting to recapitalise during the period from 2007 to 2009. If the credit insurer cannot return to normality by raising additional capital then they will have to attempt to restructure and unwind existing positions. In this event, they are faced with the following very simple condition

$$\text{decrease in capital} > \text{MtM loss.} \tag{13.1}$$

In other words, any crystallised[7] MtM losses must be smaller than the capital reduction achieved. This is very hard to assess since capital requirements are determined by credit ratings whilst any losses will be defined by market credit spreads. The most likely scenario of ratings lagging spread changes represents the worst case. Here, a credit insurer may realise significant mark-to-market losses and be forced into termination since it cannot find a way to restructure or unwind trades in order to reduce the capital requirement sufficiently. Indeed, if the above condition cannot be satisfied then it creates a "death spiral" due to the crystallised losses being greater than the associated capital relief.

---

[7] By this we mean "paper losses" that become real due to the requirement to post collateral.

Even if a credit insurer can avoid the dreaded death spiral and restructure its portfolio so as to return to a normal mode (for example, regaining its triple-A rating), it may only be a stay of execution. For example, suppose a credit insurer manages to restructure certain tranched investments to improve their ratings but without any associated losses. This will reduce their capital requirement at zero cost. Yet, all that has been achieved is a "ratings arbitrage" and this may be considered to be nothing other than a cosmetic change that will obscure the underlying problems for a brief period.

13.2.5 Termination mode and run-off

Assessing the rating of a credit insurer from a quantitative point of view is almost impossible. Such entities typically run capital models on a daily basis, the output of which could trigger some sort of suspension mode. Assessing the rating would then involve a simulation of the capital model used to monitor the integrity of the rating on a daily basis. Rating agencies have tended to avoid what would be a circular problem by assuming the credit insurer is in a run-off (see Section 8.7.2) or termination state when assigning the rating. This represents a worst case assumption since this is effectively the point at which the vehicle is being terminated (either immediately or gradually). From a quantitative point of view, it makes the problem much simpler because the credit insurer can do nothing more than settle losses on contracts as and when required. The rating agency will then simply consider the possible losses on the portfolio of the credit insurer in order to give a rating.

However, there are more problems. Consider a credit insurer is in run-off mode and will be static with default losses settled as and when they occur (from a total amount of equity capital equal to α). Suppose the rating agency originally assigned a triple-A rating on the worst case assumption that the credit insurer *would* be in a run-off mode. This then implies that the triple-A rating has not necessarily been violated. Consider now that there is only a single transaction with this credit insurer where an institution has bought protection on a tranche covering losses in the range $[A, B]$. This institution should work out quickly that they actually have protection on a smaller tranche $[A, A + \alpha]$, which follows from the simple fact that there is no chance of the credit insurer covering losses outside its current capital of α.[8] This point is illustrated in Figure 13.5.

A credit insurer could still be rated triple-A by virtue of the fact that the assessment of possible losses by the rating agency is still within the relevant thresholds. Such assessment will be of little consolation to an institution that purchased insurance on a $[A, B]$ tranche and subsequently has to recognise that they effectively have only $[A, A + \alpha]$ protection. The loss incurred at this point may be considerable since the leverage of the credit insurer (defined by $(B - A)/\alpha$) may be extremely high. As an example, in late 2007 it was revealed that ACA Financial Guarantee sold protection on $59bn against capital of $425m (Das, 2008) given a leverage of an enormous 138 times (ACA was being downgraded to triple-C at this point).

---

[8] Unless somehow the credit insurer can recapitalise which would seem unlikely given the likely underlying MtM losses that they would be facing.

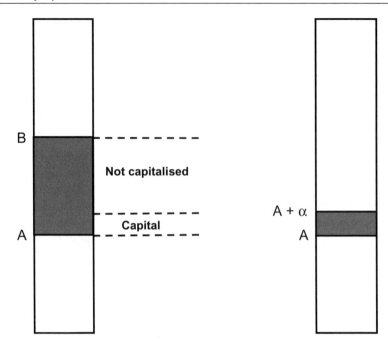

Figure 13.5. Illustration of the value of tranched protection purchased from a credit insurer in a run-off or termination state.

> **Example.** An institution buys super senior protection on a 5-year [22–100%] tranche from a credit insurer for a notional value of $100bn. The value of the protection is $725m. However, the institution then realises that the credit insurer is in severe financial difficulty and has an approximate leverage of 100 times. They now assess that they have only protection corresponding approximately to a smaller [22–22.8%] tranche, which has a value of $57m. They therefore realise a loss of $668m or 92% of the original value of the insurance.
>
> (The assumptions used to compute the above numbers are the same as those given in Section 8.5.3. The correlation skew observed in the tranche market is ignored in this example but will increase the estimated loss.)

The above example is representative of the writedowns made by many banks in relation to insurance purchased by monolines. The implication of the above is that a counterparty will want to buy protection from a credit insurer on a transaction that will take losses before all the other transactions made by that credit insurer – otherwise, there will be no capital left! This provides a qualitative understanding of the seniority point. Buying equity protection from a credit insurer who otherwise invests in super senior risk is fine (the "front of the queue" effect). The more senior the protection (compared with the others), the less chance of future losses being settled. We explore this point in more detail next.

13.2.6   The random leverage effect

In the previous example we considered only a single tranche and so an institution purchasing insurance from a credit insurer was exposed to a known and fixed leverage. In reality, a protection buyer will not have a claim on a specific amount of collateral and the effective leverage will be determined not only by the leverage of the credit insurer but also by the characteristics of the trades vis-à-vis trades with other protection buyers. The true value of α that a protection buyer "sees" will vary since claims would be settled according to the timing of losses. Indeed, there is likely to be significant heterogeneity over any unwound or restructured trades depending on the mark-to-market and marginal capital requirements in question.

In the previous analysis the leverage seen by a given counterparty now becomes α^*, a hidden random variable, and it is possible for the true value of the protection to be worthless. For example, if a credit insurer cannot recapitalise and will unwind trades with other counterparties in preference then the counterparty in question is not near enough to the "front of the queue" to receive settled losses. In this case the protection would be worthless. Let us briefly consider how a protection buyer might "enhance" the value of their protection by making it more likely that the credit insurer will unwind their transaction:

- Structure the tranche so it is likely to be downgraded (to create incentive for a later unwind).
- Create a tranche with a negative expected future value; for example, by paying a step-up coupon.[9]
- Ensure the tranche has smaller mark-to-market volatility (to reduce the chance of large losses); for example, having a shorter maturity compared with others. In the event of a parallel credit spread widening, a 5-year tranche would be likely to be unwound in preference to a 10-year tranche due to the smaller associated losses.
- Make the tranche sufficiently junior so that in a wind-down/run-off state it will be one of the first to take losses whilst there is still available capital for these to be settled.

Since the other institutions trading with the credit insurer may have been aware of these issues also, the buyer of protection only has real value if they can convincingly argue that they are at the front of the queue in their claim on the relatively small amount of capital.

This section has attempted to explain some intuitive reasons for the fact that protection purchased from a monoline or CDPC vehicle potentially has little or no value. A more mathematical treatment is given in Appendix 13.B that summarises the results in Gregory (2008b) with Figure 13.6 (see p. 367) providing a schematic illustration of the mathematical result. Such results have stood up to empirical tests. For example, in 2008 Merrill Lynch reported a net credit valuation loss of \$10.4bn[10] largely because of counterparty risk related losses with monoline insurance counterparties. Essentially, this stems from the realisation that insurance purchased had little or no value due to counterparty risk.

---

[9] Essentially, the institution is paying for protection in arrears and the credit insurer might unwind this tranche preferentially.
[10] Merrill Lynch form 10-K.

13.2.7 The future for credit insurers

In this section and previously in Chapter 8 we have presented strong qualitative and quantitative reasons against the business models of credit insurers such as monolines and CDPCs. Events of 2007 onwards, where some of these triple-A institutions have experienced severe financial distress (in some cases leading to default), provide further support that the underlying concept is fundamentally flawed. Yet, the credit derivatives market (and arguably financial markets in general) require investors to sell CDS protection and take the end-of-the-world risk than is present in, for example, super senior tranches. Such investors need to have and be able to make decisions on the basis of long-term views (Section 13.1.1). Having institutions of strong financial strength that can act as end-of-the-world risk takers through the credit cycle would create stability and reduce systemic risk episodes. Yet, as we have described in depth, the transfer of end-of-the-world risk is problematic because by its nature it generates extreme wrong-way counterparty risk.

However, there is still potentially some chance for a credit insurer to have a viable business model and strive to operate in a manner which a triple-A rating would be truly relevant. The key components would be:

- *Collateral posting*. As discussed, attaining a triple-A rating by being not obliged contractually to post collateral is a flawed concept. To justify strong credit-worthiness, a credit insurer would surely have to undertake some form of collater-alisation. This is probably the key point and one that simply cannot be ignored (following the arguments in Section 13.2.5) no matter what other safeguards and assurances are in place. At the time of writing, there are some CDPCs being set up that will indeed enter into standard collateral agreements.
- *Transparent operating structure*. Transparency is crucial to mitigating small problems cascading into more serious market disturbances and asymmetric information is a catalyst for such effects. Transparency over operating structure and key aspects like the leverage employed and positions taken will help to control such problems.
- *Diversification*. Correlation (between the value of the contract and credit quality of the credit insurer) is the key driver of wrong-way risk. To lower the correlation, the portfolio of the credit insurer must be well diversified. This favours the more general DPC concept over the highly specialised CDPC concept. Ultimately, diversification[11] is a key aspect of any insurance. A global insurance company with a small portfolio of structured credit is preferable to a monoline insurer with massive exposure to this area.
- *Hedging*. A possible compliment or alternative to diversification is hedging or trading offsetting positions (as in the mirror trades of the DPC). A CDPC buying and selling CDS protection is not so exposed to a sudden increase in the level of credit spreads.

Ultimately, a credit insurer following the above will represent a much safer counterparty for end-of-the-world (and other) trades. They should maintain a reasonable leverage, reserve gains against potential future losses when the credit cycle "turns" and apply prudent risk management. Ultimately, the ability the "ride the credit cycle" will be a key

---

[11] Monolines and CDPCs could be compared with, for example, an insurer who specialises in house insurance in only a single town. A policyholder would have much more faith if the company insures other areas and indeed other risks.

determinant in ensuring the long-term financial stability of a credit insurer and justifying that much-prized triple-A rating.

13.3 SUMMARY

In this chapter we have discussed the concept of the default-remote or triple-A entity in relation to counterparty risk. We have covered the DPC example where the mitigation of counterparty risk has been shown historically to work well. However, we have also highlighted some major problems that have arisen in relation to monoline insurers because of fundamentally flawed ideas that such an entity has little or no default risk. Ultimately, it should be clear that the existence of a true default-remote entity is extremely hard to justify and has many related pitfalls.

In Chapter 14 we move on to address a more general issue that has attracted significant interest since the beginning of the 2007 credit crisis. We will discuss central counterparties which are default-remote entities that aim to centralise, mutualise and, ultimately, reduce counterparty risk.

APPENDIX 13.A: SIMPLE MODEL FOR A CREDIT INSURER

Consider an institution has bought protection from a counterparty on a contract with a payoff defined by a binary event B (B is 0 if the event has not occurred and 1 otherwise). The counterparty will not post collateral against the position. Denote the current time by t and the maturity date of the contract as T. Assuming zero interest rates, the value of this contract is just the expected payoff $V(t) = E[B] = q$. Denoting the counterparty default time by τ and assuming zero recovery, the risky value is:

$$\tilde{V}(t) = E[I(\tau > T)B] = V(t) - E[I(\tau \leq T)B],$$

where $I(\tau \leq T) = p$ is the default probability of the credit insurer in the period of interest. Now assume a simple Gaussian relationship between the counterparty default and payoff. The last term in the above equation, which is identified as a CVA, can be written as:

$$E[I(\tau \leq T)B] = \Phi_{2d}(\Phi^{-1}(q), \Phi^{-1}(p); \rho),$$

where $\Phi_{2d}(.)$ is a cumulative Gaussian distribution function and ρ is a correlation parameter. This formula is illustrated in Spreadsheet 13.1.

APPENDIX 13.B: THE VALUATION OF CREDIT INSURER PURCHASED PROTECTION

This is a quantitative, model-independent analysis of the value of protection purchased from a monoline or CDPC adapted from Gregory (2008b), where more details can be found.

We focus solely on the value of the protection leg of a tranche since this is the key component in the analysis. We start with the stylised assumption that the credit insurer has a static leverage and furthermore allocates capital on a *pro rata* basis to each of its counterparties. This basically means that we assume a protection buyer on a tranche covering losses in the range $[A, B]$ has a claim on at least a certain amount of "available collateral" (as in the LSS case discussed in Appendix 8.D) which we denote by $\alpha(< B - A)$.

We denote the fully collateralised value of the underlying tranche at time t by $V_{A,B}(t)$. The counterparty risk occurs because of the fact that the protection buyer has only a sure claim on the available collateral α whereas the full value of protection is $(B - A)$. Given the possibility of a suspension mode (Section 13.2.4) then, before losses hit the tranche, there may be some mitigating action. The counterparty risk is characterised by $V_{A,B}(t) > \alpha$ where the mark-to-market of the tranche (potentially including losses) is greater than the available collateral. The protection buyer is therefore short an option with strike α referenced to $V_{A,B}(t)$ with payoff $(V_{A,B}(t) - \alpha)^+ = \max(V_{A,B}(t) - \alpha, 0)$.

From the point of view of the protection buyer, the following outcomes are relevant and lead to some payoff:

- The tranche suffers losses before any unwind or restructuring of the trade:
  i.   Losses occur without a change in the capital structure of the company.
  ii. Losses occur after the company de-leverages via receiving some additional capital or unwinding other trades.
- The tranche is unwound at a time τ (presumably, when the credit insurer is in a restricted or termination state).
  iii. The credit insurer can settle the mark-to-market in full since $V_{A,B}(\tau) \leq \alpha$.
  iv. The credit insurer cannot settle the mark-to-market in full since $V_{A,B}(\tau) > \alpha$.

The value of the protection leg of a CDO with maturity T at time t can be written (for example, Laurent and Gregory, 2005, see also Appendix 6.C):

$$V_{A,B}(t) = E^Q \left[\int_t^T B(t, u) \, dL(u, A, B) \right],$$

where $L(u, A, B)$ is the cumulative tranche loss and $B(t, u)$ represents the risk-free discount factor at time u. With the four scenarios above, we can generalise the above equation for the value of protection purchased from a CDPC or monoline with effective collateral of α as:

$$\tilde{V}_{A,B,\alpha}(t) = E \left[1_{\tau > s} \int_t^T B(t, u) \, dL(u, A, A + \alpha) \right] \qquad \text{wind-down value (i)}$$

$$+ E \left[1_{\tau > s} \int_t^T B(t, u) \, dL(u, A + \alpha, B) \right] \qquad \text{de-leverage value (ii)}$$

$$+ E \lfloor 1_{\tau < T} B(t, \tau) V_{A,B}(\tau) \rfloor \qquad \text{clean unwind value (iii)}$$

$$- E[1_{\tau < T} B(t, \tau)(V_{A,B}(\tau) - \alpha)^+] \qquad \text{counterparty risk (iv)}$$

The above equation shows that the bounds on the value of protection are $V_{A,A+\alpha}(t) \leq \tilde{V}_{A,B,\alpha}(t) \leq V_{A,B}(t)$. The minimum value for the protection corresponds to assuming that there is no chance of the credit insurer de-leveraging or unwinding the trade, whilst the upper bound would require the assumption of zero counterparty risk. These bounds will be wide since the credit insurer will be rather highly leveraged.

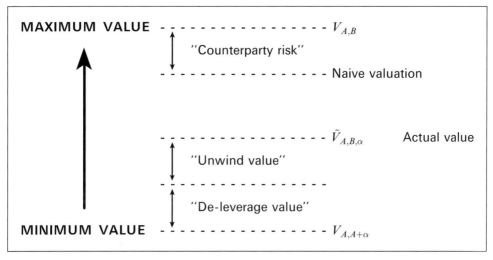

Figure 13.6. Illustration of valuation approaches for protection purchased from a CDPC or monoline insurer under simplified assumptions of executing a single trade. The naive valuation arises from simply assuming that there is a small amount of counterparty risk that can be assessed via the computation of a CVA. The actual value, which is calculated from a proper quantification of the relevant cashflows, is significantly less and very complex to assess.

Obviously, the protection buyer would like to argue that the value is close to the upper bound. However, returning to the value of protection and combining the third and fourth terms we obtain:

$$\tilde{V}_{A,B,\alpha} = E\left[1_{\tau>u}\int_t^T B(t,u)\,dL(u,A,A+\alpha)\right] + E\left[1_{\tau>u}\int_t^T B(t,u)\,dL(u,A+\alpha,A)\right]$$
$$+ E[1_{\tau<T}B(t,\tau)\min(V_{A,B}(\tau),\alpha)].$$

Rather than having a value of protection less some counterparty risk, the buyer of protection has a rather complex set of payoffs related to the precise structure and operating environment of the credit insurer. The first term gives a lower value for the tranche as being equal to a smaller $[A, A+\alpha]$ tranche. This is arguably the value for the tranche in a run-off mode as discussed in the text (see example in Section 13.2.5). The second term represents the value from a de-leveraging of the credit insurer (de-leverage value) perhaps due to the credit insurer unwinding transactions or recapitalising due to being placed in a suspension mode. The final term corresponds to value in case the transaction is itself unwound at some future point (unwind value). These last two terms clearly represent a challenge to value even in this rather simplified example. The situation is illustrated schematically in Figure 13.6. The real situation is even more complex due to the uncertainty regarding the value of α in the usual multiple counterparty case.

During the period 2007–2009, banks have had to make substantial writedowns (of the order of billions of US dollars) on protection that was priced at the level denoted by "Naive valuation" in Figure 13.6.

14

The Role of a Central Counterparty

In this chapter we consider the role of large central counterparties to provide a means for centralisation, mutualisation and reduction of counterparty risk. Following the credit crisis that started in 2007, there has been a significant interest in having centralised clearing entities for counterparty risk. In particular, the interest has been strong for credit derivatives products with their embedded wrong-way risks. We will discuss in detail the viability of reducing counterparty risk in the OTC derivatives market by using a central counterparty.

14.1 CENTRALISED CLEARING

The dramatic increase in counterparty risk due to the credit crisis and the realisation that no counterparty was immune to severe financial distress brought many calls for a solution to the global counterparty risk problem. Having a centralised clearing counterparty provides a potential solution to the problem of counterparty risk clogging up markets, especially those such as credit derivatives. Many operators of trading facilities, such as exchanges, are struggling to innovate in financial markets and cover new instruments without a partner clearing facility.

14.1.1 Background

Market risk can be eliminated by entering into an offsetting contract. However, unless this is done with the same counterparty as the original position(s), then additional counterparty risk will be generated. If the counterparties to offsetting contracts differ, and either counterparty fails, then the position is no longer neutral. Furthermore, the overall collateral needs with two counterparties are likely to be larger than those with just a single counterparty. This example represents a key limitation of bilateral netting.

The aim of a central counterparty (CCP) is to have an entity that stands between parties with respect to some or all contracts traded between them. Because it stands between market buyers and sellers, the CCP bears no net market risk, which remains with the original party to each trade. The CCP, on the other hand, does take the counterparty risk, which is centralised in the CCP structure. As a result, an institution no longer needs to worry about the credit quality of its counterparty, indeed the counterparty to a trade need not even be known. To all intents and purposes, the CCP is the counterparty to the trade.

Whilst the presence of one or more CCPs might seem like a "silver bullet" with respect to counterparty risk, it is not all good news. A CCP must have a fine-tuned structure with respect to collateralisation, settlement and risk management and ultimately must be extremely unlikely to fail. The bigger and better a CCP becomes, the more catastrophic its failure would be. Furthermore, the homogenisation of counterparty risk and removal of the need for institutions to assess their counterparty's credit quality may cause difficulties due to effects such as moral hazard.

In the next sections we will go through all the positive and negative aspects of trading through CCPs and then discuss the circumstances under which they can add value.

14.1.2 Systemic risk in the derivatives markets

One of the key concerns over the growing global derivatives market has always been systemic risk. Systemic risk does not have a firm definition but is essentially financial system instability exacerbated by distress of financial intermediaries. In the context of counterparty risk, systemic risk could arise from a number of situations:

- The failure of a large financial institution, leading to the knock-on failure of other institutions or the risk that one firm's default can leave another firm immediately insolvent.
- The failure of a key financial intermediary, meaning that a large number of counterparties simultaneously seek to replace contracts, resulting in severe liquidity issues and market gridlock. Asymmetric information may make this problem more severe as market participants struggle to comprehend the web of exposures in relation to the failed institution.
- A major economic shock or even natural catastrophe simultaneously affecting a large number of financial institutions.

Systemic risk is generally thought of as having an initial spark and a proceeding chain reaction, potentially leading to some sort of explosion of financial markets. Thus, in order to control systemic risk one can either minimise the chance of the initial spark, attempt to ensure that the chain reaction does not occur or simply plan that the explosion is controlled and the resulting damage limited.

Reducing the default risk of large, important market participants reduces the possibility of an initial spark caused by one of them failing. Capital regulation and prudential supervision can contribute to this but there is a balance between reduction of default risk and encouraging financial firms to grow and prosper. DPCs and monolines, discussed previously, are good examples of this balance. Placing very stringent capital and operational limitations on such an entity will make it extremely credit-worthy and yet simultaneously make it impossible to generate the returns required to function profitably as a corporation.

Given firms will inevitably fail, having efficient market mechanisms and structures for containing the failure of key firms and absorbing a large shock is key. Derivatives markets have netting, collateralisation and credit derivatives to help control such events. However, as argued in Chapter 3, such aspects may help to stabilise markets but also catalyse their growth to a level that would never have been otherwise possible. Hence, it can be argued that initiatives to stifle a chain reaction may achieve precisely the opposite and create the catalyst (such as many large exposures supported by a complex web of collateral) to cause the explosion. Whilst individuals working for financial institutions are compensated based on short-term rather than medium to long-term achievements, it seems hard to avoid such problems existing throughout the financial markets.

The ultimate solution to systemic risk may therefore be simply to have the means in place to manage periodic explosions in a controlled manner. A CCP can potentially achieve this by acting rather like an insurance company. If there is a failure of a key market participant then the CCP will guarantee all the contracts of that counterparty executed through them. This will mitigate concerns faced by institutions and prevent any extreme actions by those institutions that could worsen the crisis. Finally, the CCP will ensure that losses caused by the failure of one or more counterparties are shared amongst all members of the CCP (just as insurance losses are essentially shared by all policyholders[1]) rather than being concentrated within a smaller number of institutions that may themselves be heavily exposed to the failing counterparty. The potential subsequent failure of such institutions causes the domino effect that can cause a severe systemic risk failure.

14.1.3 Historical background to CCPs

One can trace the CCP idea all the way back to the 19th century where exchanges were used for futures trading. Originally, such exchanges were simply trading forums without any settlement or counterparty risk management functions. Transactions were still done on a bilateral basis and trading through the exchange simply provided a certification of one's counterparty via them being a member of the exchange. The development of "clearing rings" followed as a means of standardisation to ease aspects such as closing out positions and enhancing liquidity. After this, methods for mitigating counterparty risk, such as margining, were developed. Finally, by the late 19th century, there was some sort of loss mutualisation via financial contributions to form reserves to absorb member default losses. Many exchange-traded contracts are now, by default, subject to CCP clearing. The CCP function may either be operated by the exchange or provided to the exchange as a service by an independent company.

In the 20th century the concept of contract novation was added to exchanges. Novation means that the exchange essentially steps in-between parties to a transaction (see Figure 14.1) and therefore acts as an insurer of counterparty risk in both directions. In order for a clearing entity to act in this way, strong counterparty risk management techniques such as daily margining and loss mutualisation were required. Exchange-traded derivatives initially dominated OTC derivatives markets due to the benefits in terms of liquidity and counterparty risk management provided by exchanges. Exchanges are generally integrated, transparent and well regulated.

OTC derivatives growth has been substantial in the past three decades thanks to advances in quantitative finance, risk management and hedging. The notional size of the OTC derivatives markets has grown to significantly exceed that of exchange-traded

---

[1] We note that the precise mechanisms for loss sharing may differ since a CCP will share losses amongst current members whilst insurance losses may often be essentially covered by future policyholders.

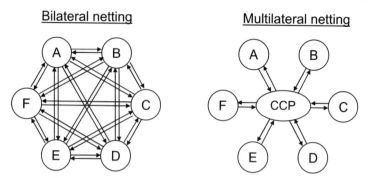

Figure 14.1. Illustration of the exchange and CCP concepts in reducing the complexity of bilateral trading.

derivatives. OTC and exchange-traded derivatives have generally two distinct mechanisms for clearing and settlement. Bilateral for OTC derivatives and CCP for exchange traded structures. Risk-management practices, such as collateralisation, are dealt with bilaterally by the counterparties to each OTC contract, whereas for exchange-traded derivatives the risk management functions are typically carried out by the associated clearing house.

Whilst counterparty risk in OTC derivatives markets has remained primarily a bilateral matter, the growth of the interest rate, foreign exchange, equity derivatives and commodities markets has not been dramatically held back (although firms have certainly needed to advance their methods for risk management). It is, arguably, the dramatic growth of the credit derivatives market in the past decade that has created instruments that (due to their inherent wrong-way risk) have triggered the massive interest in clearing houses. Whilst a clearing house may help, excessive overreliance on a CCP, especially for a single asset class, can potentially be even more catastrophic, as we shall argue in Section 14.2.3.

14.1.4 Bilateral netting versus centralised clearing

Let us compare the different netting schemes in relation to an example set of exposures between three counterparties as shown in Figure 14.2:

- *No netting.* Default of any institution will give rise to losses of 3 and 5 for the remaining institutions. For example, a default of A will cause a loss of 5 for B and 3 for C whilst A will still claim a total amount of 8 owed to them.
- *Bilateral netting.* Default of A will cause a reduced loss of only 2 for B whilst C will suffer no loss at all (since they owe A money).
- *Multilateral netting.* No institution is exposed to another since none has any outstanding exposure. Nor does the CCP have risk (in this stylised example) since all positions net.[2]

---

[2] In the example the matching exposures may be by chance or may arise due to perfectly matching (mirror) trades. In the former case, the CCP will have risk but the point is to illustrate that multilateral netting decreases exposure still further compared with bilateral netting.

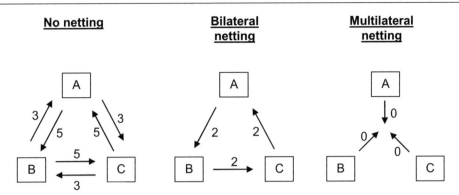

Figure 14.2. Comparison of netting schemes. An arrow indicates the direction of money owed (exposure) so that – under no netting, for example – entity *A* has an exposure of 3 to entity *B* whilst *B* has an exposure of 5 to *A*.

14.1.5 Novation

In centrally cleared derivatives markets, the original contract entered into by two parties is automatically replaced by two contracts, each of which arises between one of the original parties and the central counterparty. The legal process whereby the CCP is positioned between buyer and seller is known as novation. Novation is the replacement of one contract with one or more other contracts. The viability of novation depends on the legal enforceability of the new contracts and the certainty that the original parties are not legally obligated to each other once the novation is completed. Because of novation, the contract between the original parties ceases to exist and they therefore do not have counterparty risk to one another. Their only risk lies with the CCP itself.

From the point of view of trading through a CCP, one can consider three types of participant:

- General clearing member (GCM) – member of the CCP who is able to clear third-party trades as well as their own trades.
- Individual clearing member (ICM) – member of the CCP who clears only their own trades.
- Non-clearing member (NCM) – institution having no relationship with the CCP but can trade through a GCM.

All trades of a non-clearing member must be settled through a general clearing member. The process of novation is illustration in Figure 14.3.

A CCP is legally obligated to perform on the contracts to which it becomes a substituted counterparty via novation. However, as long as the CCP enters into two offsetting positions because of each novation, the CCP is "market-neutral" with no net market risk exposure. On the other hand, the counterparty risk taken by the CCP is substantial since if any counterparty defaults then they will have to honour all exposures other institutions had to that counterparty at the default time.

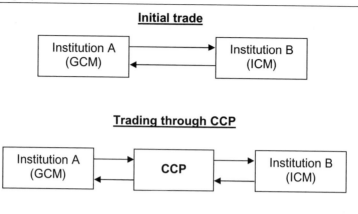

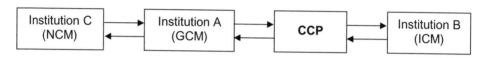

Figure 14.3. Illustration of novation.

14.1.6 The operation of a CCP

By becoming counterparties to derivatives contracts, CCPs guarantee the performance of those contracts for far longer than do financial institutions simply clearing payments or securities trades. In addition to standing in-between all transacting parties and hence guaranteeing all exposures, a CCP may perform other functions such as:

- trade matching;
- trade confirmation;
- netting;
- collateral management (margining).

Since a CCP will homogenise counterparty risk it must, for its own and other members' sakes, carefully vet all members. A CCP should only deal with credit-worthy counterparties who have the capacity to undertake all operational aspects required (such as daily margin posting). A CCP will utilise the counterparty risk mitigation techniques used by single institutions. Multilateral netting will be used to increase operational efficiency and reduce exposures as illustrated in Figure 14.2.

14.1.7 Impact of default of a CCP member

The viability of a CCP depends on its ability to withstand the default of one or more clearing members and it will therefore have several layers in order to absorb such losses. In the event of a default, the losses arising due to exposure to the defaulting member will typically be absorbed in sequence in the following way:

   (i) close-out of all positions for the member in question with netting of positive and
     negative positions where possible;
  (ii) collateral sale to cover any netted exposure from (i);
 (iii) relevant reserve fund (also known as a guarantee pool) of clearing house;
 (iv) contribution from other clearing members;
  (v) other guarantees, insurance or capital support.

In all but the most severe cases, (i) to (ii) above are expected to cover losses, and margin
requirements will be set on this basis. If this is not the case, the losses will essentially be
shared via all clearing members according to components (iii) and (iv). Since the reserve
fund is likely to be only moderate, then severe cases will rely on additional contributions
from clearing members or even other support (v).

14.1.8   Initial margin

Collateral requirements, referred to as initial and variation margin, are required by all
CCP members. The initial margin (similar in concept to independent amount discussed
in Chapter 3) is a buffer posted to cover the closing out of positions without loss to the
CCP in a worst case scenario. Initial margin requirements need to be set carefully
depending on the trade in question and any existing trades. Variation margin is collected
daily and should adjust for the previous close-of-business exposure of the positions. As a
counterparty to all trades, CCPs will be calculation agents, valuing all positions and
collecting or paying respective collateral amounts. Net margining will normally be used
by a CCP that allows long and short positions with different clients to be netted. Gross
margining is less common and leads to higher costs related to trading through a CCP. A
CCP may also make intra-day margin calls if large price movements threaten to exhaust
margin funds in a clearing member's account. Such practices are becoming increasingly
common and are supported by technology advances.
    The failure to meet a margin call will result in a clearing member being declared in
default and its positions being closed out. There will be a certain grace period before this
occurs but this will typically be short since the quicker the close-out can be done, the
smaller the risk for the CCP and its other members. However, in practice CCPs may take
longer than the grace period in order to decide whether a member should be declared in
default or not. Indeed, this may prove rather a subtle decision, as with the rating
agencies and monoline downgrades discussed in Section 13.1.3. Hence, as with our
previous modelling of collateralised exposure, the period of interest should be several
days or possibly more to account for this worst case scenario.
    Initial margin is the critical component in determining the efficiency and
credit-worthiness of a CCP. As an independent amount, it is a deposit intended to
cover a large intra-day price move against the institution in question with reference
to the replacement cost of the trade(s). Initial margin exists for the life of a trade and is
not returned until the trade is closed out. It is designed to cover all but the most extreme
daily price movements with protection against daily moves at an estimated level of
around 95–99% confidence being common. Since the posting of cash or high-quality
assets represents an opportunity cost for institutions, margin requirements must not be
too conservative as this may reduce trading volumes through the CCP. Some degree of
netting will be given with respect to initial margins (obviously offsetting positions should

have an overall much smaller initial margin requirement). When setting initial margin requirements, a CCP must attempt to be competitive by keeping margins reasonable low, otherwise participants will trade bilaterally or through another CCP. However, the initial margins charged also determine the credit-worthiness of the CCP, i.e. to what extent the default of a member can be absorbed without requiring losses to be passed on to other participants.

The following components are important in deciding on initial margin:

- *How volatile is the value of the transaction?* If the underlying market variable(s) are volatile and or the maturity of the trade is large then the overall intra-day volatility can be expected to be significant.
- *Asymmetry of exposure.* If the product has a significant asymmetric exposure profile (such as a cross-currency swap or more significantly a single-name CDS contract) then this must be understood and margins should be highly asymmetric.
- *Is there significant wrong-way risk?* Wrong-way risk will mean that the MtM of the position will be expected to jump in the event of default of a clearing member. The potential for jumps in MtM may cause an intra-day move of many multiples of the daily volatility.
- *What other trades should offset the margin of this trade.* A large naked position should attract a high initial margin whereas well-hedged and offsetting trades should reduce margin requirements.
- *How correlated is this counterparty to the other members of the CCP?* A CCP must be extremely well capitalised, since its failure could represent an extreme systemic risk scenario. Whilst a CCP can probably survive the default on a single member, the almost simultaneous default of several members is probably the critical event that could cause the CCP to fail. The determining factor for this is the default correlation amongst the CCP members.

Margin requirements have historically made use of normal distribution assumptions. However, not surprisingly, this can lead to an underestimate of required margin. For example, Figlewski (1984) has shown for equity markets that for a confidence level of 95% such an approach can work reasonably well whereas for a higher confidence level of 99% the empirical margin requirements are much higher than those predicted using normal assumptions. A more complex approach such as extreme value theory (EVT) potentially provides a more sophisticated way to attempt to capture the possibility of extreme price movements. A weakness of EVT is that it requires significant historical data whereas most clearing houses prefer to set margin based on a small and recent data sample. Whilst EVT may capture potential extreme moves, it may produce margin requirements that are too stringent.

Regarding margin requirements taking into account more than one open position, systems such as SPAN[3] have historically been used to calculate the next day's worst case directional move for all positions. In such cases, the losses on one trade may be offset by gains on another preventing a "double-charging" of initial margin. SPAN calculates margin by simulating risk factors separately within ranges covering 99% of historical

---

[3] Standard Portfolio Analysis of Risk, used by US futures clearing houses and the London Clearing House.

1-day movements. Using a matrix approach, losses are then aggregated to find the scenario that gives the worst case loss overall which determines the margin requirement.

The use of separate risk factors in SPAN is tractable for portfolios of futures and options but not for more complex instruments, as the number of risk factors required becomes unwieldy. One way to get around this would be to base margin requirement based on VAR-type approaches, which will aim to calculate the worst case loss for a set of trades of any dimensionality and accounting for all cross-dependencies.

14.1.9   Reserve funds and loss mutualisation

Ultimately, margin requirements will protect against losses in most scenarios but only up to a certain reasonable level of confidence. For more extreme cases, a CCP will have to deal with the possibility that a counterparty may fail and the available collateral will not be sufficient to offset the resulting losses arising from a close-out of all positions. Another important aspect of CCPs is loss mutualisation which means that losses above the level of collateral will be shared amongst clearing members in a pre-defined manner. Initially, this will come from a reserve fund that has been accumulated over time by initial and ongoing contributions from clearing members and/or built up from other sources such as CCP profits.

Losses above the existing reserve fund will be expected to be paid by the clearing members. There is also the possibility of some element of such losses being covered by third-party insurance. Loss mutualisation is a key point since it spreads losses from the failure of a single counterparty across all other clearing members. This has the potential to ameliorate any systemic problems arising in bilateral netting due to an institution being heavily exposed to a defaulted counterparty. Loss mutualisation (along with standard margining requirements) completes the process of homogenisation of counterparty risk across all clearing members. Whilst reducing systemic risk, this does potentially mean that poorer quality members or those with large exposures are gaining at the expense of others.

14.2   THE VIABILITY OF CENTRALISED CLEARING

CCP failures have been rare but have still occurred. Examples are Paris in 1973, Kuala Lumpur in 1983 and Hong Kong in 1987, as described in detail by Hills et al. (1999). Whilst lessons can be learnt from history, it is impossible to prevent CCP failures and the likely increasing reliance on centralised clearing makes the impact of a future failure even more severe.

Centralised clearing is therefore not without its dangers. As a result of the 1987 stock market crash, some options traders lost large amounts of money but losses were guaranteed by the firms clearing their trades. Since trades were reconciled only at the end of the day, traders were able to have highly leveraged positions and experienced losses far in excess of their capital. Many traders simply headed straight to the airport – the origin of the expression "airport play". Ultimately, support was needed to cover these losses and ensure the stability of the clearing system and banks had to fund the clearing houses that would otherwise have gone under. After the 1987 crash, electronic reporting of trades was introduced so that the system would not be exposed to these weaknesses again.

We will first summarise some obvious and clear advantages and disadvantages of CCPs and then move on to discuss some more subtle aspects that may contribute in either a positive or negative way in terms of the benefit of a CCP to the financial markets. Finally, we will assess the circumstances under which a CCP can be effective.

14.2.1   The advantage of centralised clearing

The advantages of trading through a CCP are:

- *Multilateral netting*. Contracts traded between different counterparties but traded through a CCP can be netted (Figure 14.2). This increases the flexibility to enter new transactions and terminate existing ones and reduces margin costs. Trading out of positions through a CCP is easy and, unlike bilateral markets, can be done with any other counterparty where the multilateral netting benefit is provided by the CCP.
- *Mutualisation*. Even when a default creates losses that exceed the financial resources within the CCP, these losses are distributed throughout the CCP members, reducing their impact on any one member. Thus, one counterparty's losses are dispersed partially throughout the market, making their impact less dramatic and reducing the possibility of systemic problems.
- *Independent valuation*. Derivatives traded through a CCP will be required to be priced on a daily basis due to daily margining and cashflow payments leading to a more transparent valuation of products.
- *Capital reduction*. The distinction between bilateral and CCP-cleared OTC transactions is recognised under Basel II which gives a 0% weighting of exposure to a CCP.
- *Legal and operational efficiency*. Whilst not the primary purpose of a CCP, their operation means that they need to offer services related to the trading of derivatives. The collateral, netting and settlement functions undertaken will increase operational efficiency and reduce costs. CCPs may also reduce legal risks in providing a centralisation of rules and mechanisms. A CCP working with regulators on the best procedures is more efficient than individual market participants taking this collective responsibility.
- *Liquidity*. A CCP will improve market liquidity through the ability of market participants to trade easily and benefit from multilateral netting. Market entry is enhanced through the ability to trade anonymously and the mitigation of counterparty risk. Firms with a lower credit quality that would be unable to enter a bilateral market will be able to enter the CCP-based market.

Overall, the role of a CCP is of course to reduce counterparty risk. CCPs may reduce the probability of failure of individual members through handling aspects of counterparty risk such as netting and collateralisation and enhancing liquidity. A CCP is also in a good position to manage the risks of a member that becomes financially distressed. Whilst it may require the tightening of risk mitigants such as margining it can also aid in the orderly unwinding of positions, without negative information leaking into the market and moving those positions against the distressed institution. The reduction in counterparty risk for an institution may be realised in many ways such as the ability to enter into trades that were not practical before, smaller required reserves, lower hedging costs, more favourable capital charges or reduced balance sheet usage.

14.2.2   The disadvantages of centralised clearing

At first thought, it might be easy to assume that having CCPs can only be advantageous and decrease counterparty risk but this is far from obvious. The obvious disadvantages of a CCP are:

- *Standardisation of products*. OTC market products tend to be customised, and relatively illiquid, which limits the ability to clear them through a CCP. A certain amount of standardisation – for example, of valuation approaches and documentation – is required before a product can be traded through a CCP.
- *CCP failure*. Although CCPs reduce counterparty risk for market participants, funnelling market activity through one institution leads to a concentration of risk. Since CCPs limit the risks to other market participants, their own potential failure becomes a critical component that would potentially lead to a severe systemic event.
- *Legal and operational risks*. The integrity of the legality of netting is absolutely critical for a CCP. Risk could arise if a netting agreement is not protected by national law in all relevant regions and jurisdictions. Additionally, like all market participants, CCPs are exposed to operational risk such as systems failures and fraud. A breakdown of any aspect of a CCP's infrastructure would be catastrophic since it would affect a relatively large number of parties within the market.

Having summarised the key advantages and disadvantages of CCPs, we will now discuss some more subtle points that can be both advantageous and yet also counterproductive for a CCP.

14.2.3   Risk homogeneity and asymmetric information

The homogenising of counterparty risk and use of mutualised loss sharing reduces asymmetric informational problems and allows anonymous trading and settlement. In a centrally cleared market using a CCP, all parties are essentially equal and the CCP acts as guarantor for all obligations. An institution has no need to assess the credit-worthiness of counterparties they trade with through the CCP and may therefore reduce resources spent on monitoring individual members. They just need only have confidence in the credit-worthiness of the CCP.

If a major derivatives player defaults, it may not be clear how big the associated counterparty risk losses will be, nor which institutions will bear the brunt of them. This uncertainty is mitigated through a CCP allocating losses across all of its members. A CCP is positioned to understand the positions of all market participants and therefore is privy to potentially sensitive trading information. Whilst this may be useful information during times of financial distress, since the CCP does not bear market risk, it has no incentive to use such information other than to stabilise the market. The neutrality and ability of a CCP to disperse losses mitigates information asymmetry that can propagate stress events in bilateral markets.

Risk homogeneity is not necessarily a good thing. An institution with better than average risk management (credit quality assessment, collateral management, hedging) will lose out by trading through a CCP. Indeed, a CCP takes away the incentive for an institution to monitor closely its key counterparties and take action if their credit quality deteriorates. In a bilateral market the pricing of CVA will naturally cause institutions with a worsening credit quality to have higher costs and therefore provide an incentive for them to improve this aspect. However, when trading through a CCP, as long as a member is posting the relevant collateral, the issue of their declining credit quality may be ignored (up to a point). This may allow poor-quality institutions to build up bigger positions than they would normally be able to do in bilateral markets. CCPs may be more popular with counterparties with below-average risk management abilities and firms with weaker credit quality who can only achieve a limited amount of bilateral trading. The products traded through the CCP may tend to be the more risky ones that an institution cannot manage easily in a bilateral market. Therefore, whilst a CCP can have tight control over all members, market forces may lead them to end up with the more risky counterparties in the market and the more risky products with wrong-way risk.

Asymmetric information can also cause problems since all risk transfer markets incur associated costs. Pirrong (2009) argues that asymmetric information costs will be higher in centrally cleared markets compared with bilateral ones, especially for exotic products traded by complex, opaque intermediaries. This is argued to be due to the specialisation of dealers with respect to valuing exotic derivatives together and the fact that dealers are more effective at and have more incentive for good monitoring and pricing of counterparty risk compared with a CCP. Market participants trading with a CCP may be incentivised to create larger positions than they would otherwise like to or even be able to occupy. Put another way, a CCP may therefore suffer from a form of "winner's curse". Such a phenomenon is well known in insurance markets where an insurance company will naturally end up with more risk due to policyholders automatically finding the cheapest premiums[4] given their circumstances.

14.2.4 Competition

The existence of a single CCP is clearly undesirable for monopolistic reasons. If more than one CCP exists then there will be a least a degree of competition. CCPs may reduce margins to be more competitive, which leads to an increased likelihood of members suffering losses and the CCP ultimately failing. An analogy can be made with respect to the structured credit market and rating agencies. Up to 2007 a plethora of ever-more complex products were given good-quality ratings. However, this could be seen to be driven by the fact that rating agencies were essentially paid for giving ratings together with competition between different agencies. In retrospect, it is clear that these ratings were overly optimistic to say the least, presumably due to a failure to assess properly the risks. The regulatory environment the rating agencies found themselves in meant that proper and accurate assessment of the likely risks could have put them out of business.[5]

---

[4] For example, an insurance company specialising in insuring drivers with motoring convictions may be able to charge higher premiums but market forces will ensure that they end up with more risky drivers on their books.
[5] Put very simply, if a particular rating agency refused to give (say) a triple-A rating then another agency may well do this and be paid the fee.

We could also argue that a CCP might take undue risk under the assumption that they are too big to be allowed to fail.

The failure of a CCP would necessarily lead to at least a temporary breakdown of the market as the whole structure through which positions are established, maintained and closed out would be disrupted. Such a failure should be expected to be far worse than the failure of any single institution. Of course, it might be assumed that lenders of last resort might come in to support the CCP but this might be a naive way to assess the probability of CCP failure as being small. Whilst the *probability* of CCP failure might be smaller than that of an individual institution (thanks to tight regulation and mutualisation of losses), it represents a far more extreme and systemic event.

Considering the two above conflicting points, it seems reasonable that the financial markets would be best served via a reasonable number[6] of CCPs that are large enough to offer good product coverage but not so large that their failure could trigger a global financial crisis. A key component for regulators is to ensure that, especially in buoyant markets, CCPs do not become more competitive and therefore increase the likelihood of failing during volatile markets and crashes.

14.2.5   Market coverage of a CCP

A CCP is ultimately a good idea if executed correctly but, like the monoline/CDPC example, could be highly counterproductive if not. Often a CCP may start with a single goal and therefore be focussed in terms of region and asset classes. Growth will naturally involve expanding the geographical base, markets and products covered. Let us consider the circumstances under which a CCP can be expected to operate efficiently. The following points require consideration:

- the type of asset classes covered by a given CCP;
- the number of asset classes covered by a given CCP;
- the number of CCPs in the market.

We start with the question of asset types to be covered by a CCP. Taking examples of some important product types with respect to counterparty risk, in Table 14.1 we give a ranking of those products against the five components introduced in Section 14.1.8 when discussing initial margin considerations.

For an interest rate swap, none of the components causes a particular concern. For a cross-currency swap with exchange of notional, MtM volatility is likely to be a key aspect and there may be some asymmetric exposure, as discussed in Chapter 4. For a CDS index, wrong-way risk may additionally become a problem since there may be a strong relationship between defaults in the index and that of the counterparty (as discussed in Chapter 8). Single-name CDS products may suffer additionally from the inability to offset positions (buy and sell protection on the same name). Finally, CDO tranches (especially super senior[7]) would be expected to have a serious correlation

---

[6] Whilst there are size and monopolistic concerns over a single CCP, in an ideal world this might represent the ideal solution. If it could be controlled at a high level such as through the G20, International Monetary Fund or World Bank then the integrity, operation and default-remoteness could be ensured. However, this is probably an idealistic view that would be unlikely to be politically achievable.

[7] We assume that the tranches would be rather senior in the capital structure (not equity tranches).

Table 14.1. Assessment of various products with respect to certain important characteristics from the point of view of trading through a CCP. A cross (×) indicates that the characteristic in question represents a negative aspect of trading that particular product through a CCP.

	Volatility	Asymmetric exposure	Wrong-way risk	Offset	Default correlation
Interest rate swap					
Cross-currency swap (with notional exchange)	×	×			
CDS (index)	×	×	×		
CDS (single-name)	×	×	×	×	
CDO tranches	×	×	×	×	×

impact since in a scenario where there are losses on these tranches it is likely that many CCP counterparties are in a distressed state.

The above analysis is to some degree subjective but one general point – probably beyond argument – is that the most important products to be traded through CCPs are arguably the most risky from the point of view of the stability of the CCP, and vice versa. There has been much recent interest to trade all CDS index products and single-name products[8] through CCPs, whereas over a long time period prior to this, a much larger notional of interest rate swaps has been comfortably managed within a bilateral market. The general point is that the products that market participants will most want and need to trade through a CCP will be the precise products that are most difficult to handle in this way.

A simple and intuitive quantitative treatment of the benefits of a CCP is given by Duffie and Zhu (2009). Their results are based on considering the netting benefit (based on EPE) for trading a single class of contracts through a CCP as opposed to bilateral clearing. They show, using a simple model,[9] the required number of dealers trading through the CCP for a single asset class to achieve netting reduction. We have plotted the results in Figure 14.4 as a function of correlation and number of asset classes. For example, for 4 uncorrelated asset classes, there must be at least 15 dealers to make clearing a single asset class through the CCP valid. Interestingly, the impact of correlation between asset classes makes a CCP more effective since bilateral netting is less effective in this case.

The above example assumes equal distribution of exposure across asset classes. Duffie and Zhu also consider a non-homogeneous case and derive an expression[10] for the fraction of dealer's exposure that must be concentrated in a particular asset to make a CCP for that asset class viable. This fraction is shown in Figure 14.5. For example, with 10 dealers, using a CCP for a given class of derivatives will be effective only if three-quarters of the dealers' bilaterally netted exposure resides in that class of products. This

---

[8] Whilst single-name CDS and CDO tranches would be even more relevant for a CCP, the complexity they represent has presumably been enough to prevent them being tackled before indices.

[9] Simplifying assumptions of symmetry and equal variance of exposure are used in this case.

[10] This assumes independence between asset classes.

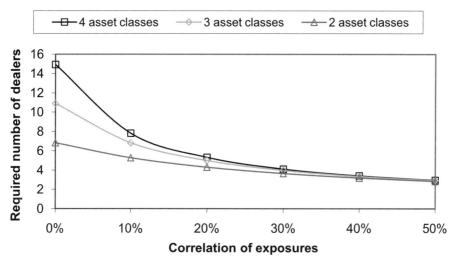

Figure 14.4. Required number of dealers for a single asset class CCP to improve netting efficiency calculated using the formula of Duffie and Zhu (2009).

Figure 14.5. Required fraction of exposure attributed to a single asset class ("critical exposure fraction") to make a CCP for that asset class effective. The results as a function of the number of dealers are calculated using the formula of Duffie and Zhu (2009).

is potentially an unrealistically large fraction to make centralised clearing beneficial in this case.

A further result of Duffie and Zhu shows that, not surprisingly, if a CCP is viable then it is inefficient to have more than one CCP in the market. Obviously, this purely theoretical result does not account for aspects such as monopolistic effects and the catastrophic failure of such a CCP. However, it is perhaps damning that, even without consideration of the more subjective disadvantages discussed above, there are clear cases where a CCP could simply be counterproductive by increasing the total exposure in the market compared with bilateral netting.

14.2.6 Central counterparties and credit derivatives

The housing crisis, credit crunch and financial and economic downturns during 2007–2009 led US policymakers to consider and fast-track a number of changes to improve the derivatives markets, in particular with respect to CDSs. In May 2009 the Obama Administration (through the US Treasury) proposed a new framework for greater market regulation and oversight of the OTC derivatives market.[11] This framework seems to mandate centralised clearing of all CDS transactions as well as prudent regulation of CDS market participants and increased transparency.

At the end of 2008, the SEC approved a series of temporary conditional exceptions allowing certain users of CDS contracts to trade through LCH.Clearnet as a CCP for certain index CDS contracts only. In March 2009, the SEC made similar arrangements for ICE US Trust LLC. These exceptions facilitate trading index CDSs through CCPs without the delays and hurdles that full regulation would create. In March 2009, ICE began clearing index CDSs and plans to handle also single-name trades.[12] The SEC believes that a CCP can reduce systemic risk, operational risks, market manipulation and fraud and contribute to overall market stability.[13] In addition, a bill was introduced to allow the Commodity Futures Trading Commission (CFTC) to suspend CDS trading in certain reference entities to prevent potential market manipulation.

The motivation for the actions outlined above arises from strong concerns regarding the regulation and practices within the CDS market. However, such concerns must not be overstated due to the unprecedented nature of the 2007–2009 credit crisis. The crisis was largely the result of systematic mispricing of mortgage-related debt and not directly due to the growth of the credit derivatives market. The systemic failure of counterparty risk in CDSs occurred only because of regulated financial guarantors (such as AIG) selling risky protection on assets such as MBS. AIG's excessive risk taking via CDSs was part of a broader problem related to seeking returns from mispriced mortgages and mortgage-backed securities.

Problems with CDS counterparty risk have stemmed from the underlying assets referenced but not flaws in the product itself or the underlying market. Warnings that dealer defaults could spread contagion through the CDS market have not materialised. Whereas issuance of securities such as MBS dramatically declined in 2008, CDSs have not suffered a similar fate, being traded actively through the crisis. The majority of CDS contracts on corporate names and indices have shown stability. The relatively large numbers of credit events experienced in the second half of 2008 were handled well.[14] Even the large number of payouts linked to Lehman Brother did not cause problems – indeed due to offsetting trades, only 7.2% of CDS notional value written on Lehman needed to pay out. CDS markets have been becoming more transparent since even before the crisis.[15]

---

[11] Press Release, US Department of Treasury, *Regulatory Reform OTC Derivatives*, May 13, 2009 (*http://ustreas.gov/press/releases/tg129.htm*).

[12] Leising, M. (2009) *ICE Starts Credit Default Swap Clearing to Increase Revenue*, Bloomberg, March 9th.

[13] See *http://sec.gov/rules/exorders/2008/34-59164.pdf*

[14] According to the Senior Supervisors Group in *Observations on Management of Recent Credit Default Swap Credit Events*, March 2009 (*http://www.newyorkfed.org/newsevents/news/markets/2009/SSG_030909.pdf*). CDS credit events were "managed in an orderly fashion, with no major operational disruptions or liquidity problems" demonstrating "the effectiveness of the existing auction-based settlement mechanism".

[15] For example, in 2006 the Depository Trust Clearing Corporation (DTCC) established a centralised repository for information relating to CDS trades. Almost all major global CDS dealers signed up to this initiative, and since the beginning of 2009 the DTCC has been publicly disclosing CDS trading activity on a weekly basis thereby increasing transparency within the market.

Mandatory clearing of all or almost all CDSs is a step too far since a CCP may not reduce counterparty risk and bilateral markets may be able to operate more efficiently on their own. Policymakers should certainly attempt to prevent concentration of CDS risks but dramatic reform of all CDS transactions will be a knee-jerk overreaction. Shadab (2009) argues that a significant portion of CDS transactions will not be improved by centralised clearing and furthermore that this will not reduce CDS counterparty risk and may increase it. CDSs allow banks to hedge their credit risk to clients without undermining their business relationship. The increase in transparency of a CCP would be counterproductive to such goals.

14.2.7   Under what circumstances will a CCP work?

CCPs provide an institutional structure for managing counterparty risk that has proven successful in exchange-traded derivatives. By mutualising counterparty risk, CCPs provide a broad base for absorbing losses and may therefore minimise systemic risk and create better liquidity. However, we have argued that it is not at all clear that a CCP will be effective in reducing risk in the market. Just like the monoline debacle, CCPs could do more harm than good if their introduction is not carefully assessed and monitored by policymakers and market participants. CCPs are not a quick fix or a silver bullet but may represent a step forward in managing risk in the global derivatives market.

A CCP should not cover only those products that have particular features that create a strong requirement for a centralised counterparty. For a CCP to be effective, it should cover several asset classes and not be specialised to a single asset class. Gemmill (1994) has illustrated the diversification offered to a clearing house from clearing several markets that are not highly correlated. This suggests that the idea of a CCP for clearing credit derivatives, which initially is further limited to index trades, is not viable. Due to the size of the interest rate market, combining credit derivatives and interest rate products within a single CCP would seem to represent a strong argument, especially due to the fact that high correlation between these asset classes seems unlikely. This conclusion is supported by the arguments based around Table 14.1, the historical success of DPCs (Section 13.1.2) and by Duffie and Zhu (2009).

On the one hand, the market is best supported by a single CCP, since this maximises netting, cross-product netting and collateral efficiencies. Furthermore, a CCP for a relatively small number of dealers will be less efficient than one covering a greater fraction of market participants. On the other hand, the ideal of a single CCP must be balanced against monopoly concerns and cross-border issues due to regulatory and operational differences. The best compromise would probably see a small number of global CCPs all of which cover a wide range of product types.

CCPs must not only focus on having margin requirements that cover losses in all but the most extreme cases. They must also ensure that there is adequate coverage of losses due to the default of a member following a margin-depleting price move. Margin should be at a level to cover all but the most extreme price movements, but not so high so as to damage market liquidity and/or discourage the use of the CCP. High margins have been shown empirically to have a detrimental impact on trading volumes (for example, see Hartzmark, 1986 and Hardouvelis and Kim, 1995). Brady (1988) discusses the crash of 1987 and its impact on some clearing houses arising in an extreme market event with associated liquidity problems. Bates and Craine (1999) showed that following the 1987 crash, the expected losses conditional on a margin call being breached increased by an order of magnitude.

Whilst keeping the likelihood of exceeding margin over a single day to a high confidence level (such as 99%) is viable, breaches will always be possible. The ability of a CCP to survive such extreme losses, potentially arising from the default of several members, is critical. One lesson from many years of application of value-at-risk methodologies (discussed in Chapter 1) is that "reasonable" losses (for example, at the 99% confidence level) can be quantified with some success, whereas more severe losses fall outside the abilities of quantitative approaches. Such an observation is an important lesson for a CCP since margin requirements may be set at VAR-type confidence levels whereas losses above such levels may still be extreme and hard to quantify.

The setting of collateral (margin) requirements and structure of other risk mitigation methods is a critical component of CCP design. Operational procedures should be carefully implemented and, in particular, collateral should be monitored extremely carefully. Stress testing should be used to assess the market risk resulting from the case of simultaneous default of a few members with large exposures. Finally, CCPs will need to develop more sophisticated portfolio models to capture possible losses arising from a potentially diverse and complex set of positions. CCPs clearing different markets must develop sophisticated modelling techniques to provide an aggregate assessment of the overall risk of open positions. The elements for this have already been described in Chapters 4 and 5 covering the quantification of credit exposure, including netting and collateral. Such an analysis must also include the assessment of the possibility of multiple defaults, which has been discussed in Chapter 10.

There is one problem with CCPs, which cannot readily be solved and may prove a significant weakness. Based on the survey for this book, low credit quality financial institutions were the strongest proponents of a CCP, almost unanimously saying that they believed it would reduce counterparty risk. The sceptics towards CCPs tended to be from strong credit quality institutions. Whilst this empirical evidence could easily be interpreted in other ways, it may be a suggestion that CCPs will be favoured only by counterparties of questionable credit quality and risk management capabilities. The asymmetric information problems faced by a CCP should be considered carefully.

14.3 CONCLUSIONS

In this chapter we have discussed the subtle problems of high credit quality central counterparties as a means to limit or reduce counterparty risk. We have argued that, whilst such entities have a crucial role to play, they can be counterproductive. The financial integrity of a central counterparty is critical, yet there are many ways in which this can be compromised, from poor collateral management to lack of diversification and asymmetric information problems. The lessons from problems experienced by the triple-A rated monolines during the 2007–2009 period must serve as a warning. Indeed, the success of exchanges and DPCs over the years suggests that it is the wrong-way risk inherent in credit derivatives that creates the biggest problem for credit insurers such as monolines and CDPCs and therefore also for CCPs.

A question as to whether CCPs really reduce counterparty risk should be carefully considered. In bilateral markets, dealers compete for business partially on the basis of their ability to manage counterparty risk. A CCP takes away the incentive to properly price and manage the counterparty risk created when entering a trade. Regulation may favour a certain CCP and this will create suboptimal outcomes and market instability. A CCP would, of course, have its own risk management capabilities and be subject to prudent supervision and capital requirements in order to make its failure highly unlikely. Yet these are exactly the same measures applied to banking institutions before the 2007 crisis! Ensuring that a CCP might not default one day is surely impossible in the light of the lessons from massive failures such as Lehman Brothers and AIG. Would a clearing house have prevented an institution like AIG selling significant protection on toxic assets or would it have been blinded by AIG's size and perceived concrete financial stability?

Bilateral OTC markets have been extremely successful and their growth has been greater than that of exchange-traded products over the last 15 years. Whilst it seems obvious that a bilaterally cleared market is more vulnerable to systemic risk, this is not an argument for the naive introduction of CCPs. As the derivatives markets become large and more global, the role of default-remote or triple-A counterparties will become increasingly important. Perhaps the greatest challenge will be for market participants to understand fully what a default-remote or triple-A counterparty really means and appreciate that a "too big to fail" corporate, bank, insurance company or CCP does not exist.

15
The Future of Counterparty Risk

At the time of writing, counterparty risk is one of the hottest topics within the financial markets with much interest around aspects such as collateral management, credit value adjustments (CVAs) and central counterparties. The credit derivatives market is in a state of flux with opinion divided somewhat between whether the underlying instruments represent important risk transfer and hedging tools or are simply dangerous weapons that will serve only to cause future disturbances within the financial markets. Many institutions are trying to recover from the crisis and improve profitability and capital ratios whilst at the same time beginning to consider what steps need to be taken to avoid being so heavily exposed to the next major financial disturbance. There is much research and discussion around the precise causes and catalysts of the credit crisis and debate and inquisition will probably continue for years.

Whilst the future of counterparty risk is likely to be changing significantly in the coming months and years, we will attempt to summarise briefly some of the key areas for development and improvement.

15.1 A COUNTERPARTY RISK REVOLUTION?

In the mid-1990s, market risk experienced a revolution due to the VAR concept together with regulatory rules around calculation of market risk capital using internal models. It is perhaps time for counterparty risk to experience a similar revolution. As we have argued several times, counterparty risk is significantly more complex to analyse than market risk for the following reasons:

- the inherently longer timeframes involved;
- the requirement to assess both exposure and default probability together with the potential presence of wrong-way risk;
- the difficulty in assessing the benefits of risk mitigants such as collateral and hedges;
- the complexity of calculations required in order to calculate prices (CVAs) and associated sensitivities (hedges) on a pre-deal basis.

Given the complex aspects involved in the assessment of counterparty risk, there are many different areas for researchers to focus on and, undoubtedly, banks and other financial institutions will increase their headcount of professionals working on counterparty risk and related functions, a trend that seems to have started already.

15.2   CONTROLLING CREDIT EXPOSURE

Gross credit exposure has increased exponentially over many years due to the frantic growth of the OTC derivatives market, the complex web of traded contracts required to connect the final risk-takers and due to practices such as offsetting rather than unwinding trades. Often credit exposure can be limited reasonably well structurally through compression exercises and transaction-specific terms such as resets. Early termination features could potentially become more common although it is unlikely that market participants will see the value of relating these to credit ratings and may seek to link contractually such a feature to a more continuous measure of credit quality such as a traded credit spread or stock price. Structurally limiting the potential future exposure of new transactions is a first line of defence in minimising counterparty risk.

Historically, credit lines have been a key tool to limit credit exposure and therefore control counterparty risk at the portfolio level. The more recent approach to systematically charge for counterparty risk (e.g. via CVA) might be viewed as making the more limited role of credit lines obsolete. However, given counterparty risk is generally priced at the netting set (single counterparty) and not portfolio (multiple counterparties) level, the role of credit lines in avoiding large exposures and concentration of counterparty risks is still valuable. Credit lines and CVA charging of incremental expected losses are complementary in controlling counterparty risk.

15.3   COLLATERAL MANAGEMENT

Collateral agreements are one of the strongest ways to reduce counterparty risk and can be applied to both parties in a transaction. Collateral management is no longer a back-office cost centre and can be an important asset optimisation tool if collateral is delivered and called in the most effective way. However, in a highly automated OTC derivatives market, collateral management is still an area relying on manual processes and data entry. Portfolio reconciliations are performed as part of the dispute resolution process but a large percentage of transactions typically need to be handled manually within spreadsheets and the inefficiencies of portfolio reconciliation can lead to lengthy disputes. Large institutions are investing heavily in resources to improve overall collateral management and, in particular, dispute prevention. Systems can streamline the collateral management function still further by, for example, allowing STP collateral calls to minimise operational workload and human error. Margin call frequencies are being reduced, with daily margin calls being the standard although this can often cause operational problems for smaller, less sophisticated institutions.

The modelling of collateralised exposures requires more study, in particular with respect to the remargin period that should be assumed in a worst case scenario and the assumptions with respect to closing out positions in the event of counterparty default. Systems should be able to account properly for the risks of non-cash collateral held against credit exposure. Efficient reporting tools and the ability to run stress tests is also important. Whilst they are often rather different, merging collateral management for banking and trading books within one system will also reduce risks and improve efficiencies.

15.4 THE TOO-BIG-TO-FAIL CONCEPT

The too-big-to-fail concept was at the heart of obscuring counterparty risks to the financial markets for many years. We would argue that any bank (or other institution) that is deemed too big to fail will create moral hazards. First, the bank itself may take unnecessary risks under the assumption that the taxpayer will effectively always be there to provide a last line of liquidity during turbulent times. Second, institutions trading with that bank as a counterparty may naturally take more risk than they would otherwise do. A solid bilateral derivatives market it not based around too-big-to-fail institutions but rather around institutions of varying credit-worthiness, where credit quality has an impact on trading terms (CVA, collateral requirements, etc.) with institutions incentivised to have a strong credit-worthiness by the more favourable terms available to them. Furthermore, in such a market the failure of any institution is likely or not a realistic possibility. Regulators should perhaps focus on ensuring that no institution is allowed to exist in a state where it is too big to fail or at least ensuring that the cost of an ongoing guarantee is treated as an insurance contract and paid for by the institution during profitable times.

There will be much debate for years to come over the negative aspects following the decision not to bail out Lehman Brothers, an iconic failure at a pivotal moment during the credit crisis. It could be argued that if the full extent of the Lehman positions were known (CDS transactions, for example) then the powers that be (US Government, Federal Reserve Bank of New York and banks themselves) may have taken a different course of action. Certainly, with the benefit of hindsight then it could be argued that those involved in failing to save Lehman should have acted differently. However, whilst Lehman Brothers was a victim, it is likely to prove to be a hugely important lesson in years to come, providing a constant reminder that institutions are not always too big to fail or even too big to be allowed to fail. The recent events have also highlighted the fact that complex documentation and legal terms relating to netting, collateral and entities such as SPVs are typically defined during good times but will be tested in crises and must be completely watertight under all market conditions.

15.5 CREDIT VALUE ADJUSTMENT (CVA)

There is huge interest around CVA as firms seek to build their systems' capabilities to actively price counterparty risk on a real-time basis and build CVA into all new transactions. Banks and other institutions are tending to form front-office based CVA groups that take overall responsibility for charging and management of counterparty risk. This is likely to continue to be a big effort with any major user of derivatives needing to have state-of-the-art assessment of their counterparty risk on a dynamic basis. This is a key challenge due to the large number of asset classes that need to be included in such a system and the presence of exotic derivatives and wrong-way risk transactions such as credit default swaps. Furthermore, such systems must have all relevant netting, collateral and other contractual details for every counterparty.

Bilateral CVA (BCVA) or DVA (debt value adjustment) is becoming rather standard for institutions with large amounts of OTC derivatives and counterparty risk. This is partly driven by the possibility to recognise one's "own credit" under fair value accountancy rules (SFAS 157 and IAS 39) via pricing liabilities at market value on one's balance sheet. However, the key driver for institutions using BCVA is simply that they cannot agree on transacted counterparty risk charges, otherwise most counterparties would refuse to trade at unilateral CVA prices. Many users of BCVA are uncomfortable with it as a general concept and agree that many features are counterintuitive; for example, the MtM benefits relating to an institution's deteriorating credit quality. Whilst some unpleasant features of DVA can be brushed under the carpet, the monetisation of the liability benefits of counterparty risk is a question that institutions will likely struggle with for some time to come.

15.6   HEDGING

Much of the derivatives market has been developed on the back on quantitative analytics, models and dynamic hedging. Given that counterparty risk is now a component of any OTC derivatives price, there will undoubtedly be much discussion about hedging CVA with fair value accountancy standards also pushing banks to hedge as thoroughly as possible their CVA books to minimise the underlying volatility. Whilst accurate hedging of highly complex structured products (exotics) is often one of the most challenging and quantitative aspects for a bank, hedging CVA may even take the problems to a new level. The challenge of risk-managing what is effectively an exotic multi-asset credit hybrid book is not to be underestimated. Furthermore, the assessment of how aspects such as collateral and bilateral charging influence sensitivities (hedges) is important to get right. Finally, good CVA risk management must involve a realisation and quantification of unhedgeable risks and a strategy to absorb idiosyncratic events and other unexpected losses.

15.7   CREDIT DERIVATIVES

The law has long prohibited people from taking out life insurance policies on people in whose lives they have no insurable interest since such a policy gives its buyer a motive for murder. Those against the use of credit derivatives may use such arguments to explain why the instrument should be outlawed or at least very heavily regulated. Leaving aside the more complex credit derivative products, it could be argued that the basic credit default swap (CDS) contract provides a very efficient mechanism for transfer of credit risk and that the CDS market is providing robustness to actual credit events and is becoming more transparent and standardised. The CDS instrument is ubiquitous within counterparty risk, giving market-implied default probabilities and being also a key hedging instrument. However, the potential presence of unpleasant wrong-way risks within CDS contracts creates additional complexity for those buying CDS protection.

15.8   CENTRAL COUNTERPARTIES

Central counterparties (CCPs) offer a quick and one-time solution to many counterparty risk problems, such as the wrong-way risks and informational asymmetries inherent in CDS contracts. On the one hand, a CCP could be argued to represent a key way to control systemic risk via loss mutualisation and overall homogenisation of counterparty risk. On the other hand, a CCP might be simply another flawed too-big-to-fail entity that leads market participants to increase their exposure under the incorrect assumption that their derivatives positions have zero counterparty risk. It is likely that market participants may also have strongly diverging views on the benefits of a CCP, some seeing it as the only realistic entry route into the derivatives market and others as introducing needless additional costs and complexity.

It may be possible that a careful introduction of CCPs, in terms of their overall number, operating structures, capital bases and so on, will benefit greatly the OTC derivatives market. However, regulators need to carefully consider both the benefits and drawbacks of CCPs and heed the lessons to be learned by experiences such as the failure of monolines. One way to look at a CCP is that via loss mutualisation they effectively force members to bail out a defaulting competitor (as, for example, occurred in the cases of Long Term Capital Management and Bear Sterns but not in the case of Lehman Brothers).

15.9   THE OVERALL CHALLENGE

Counterparty risk is present in many transactions for banks, other financial institutions and many corporates. It covers many different instruments across all asset classes and contains both market risk (credit exposure) and credit risk (default probability and credit migration) components. It must be measured over a long time horizon (often many years), accounting for the many possible risk mitigants. Pricing counterparty risk must be done at the counterparty (netting set) level and not for individual transactions in isolation, and wrong-way risks and other subtle aspects must be given careful consideration. It is possible to hedge large components of counterparty risk but this is a challenge and residual risks will be present. Counterparty risk at the portfolio level is complicated by the uncertainty of exposure as well as the problem of measuring default correlations. Good management of counterparty risk is certainly achievable but comes via careful control and quantification of many aspects simultaneously.

Counterparty credit risk is indeed the new challenge for financial markets and there is much work to do before the next inevitable financial crisis.

Glossary

Accrued interest   Interest that is due on a bond or other fixed income security since the last interest payment was made.

Additional termination event (ATE)   Pre-defined event (such as a ratings downgrade) that allows a transaction to be terminated at (mid-) market rates.

Annuity   A series of payments of fixed size and frequency.

Arbitrage   A transaction that generates a profit without any associated financial risk.

Asset swap   A swap contract used to convert one type of investment into another. Usually, a fixed investment such as a bond with guaranteed coupon payments is swapped into floating payments.

At the money   An option is at the money if the strike price of the option equals the current (spot) market price of the underlying security. At-the-money forward refers to the forward value of the underlying security and not the spot price.

Backwardation   The situation where spot prices exceed futures prices. Backwardation implies a downward-sloping (or inverted) forward curve and can imply an immediate shortage of the underlying asset (such as an oil shortage due to political reasons).

Bankruptcy   A legally declared inability of an individual or entity to pay its creditors. The bankruptcy may be voluntary and filed by the individual or organisation concerned or it may be involuntary and filed by the creditors. Creditors may file a bankruptcy petition in an effort to recoup a portion of what they are owed or initiate a restructuring.

Basis   The difference in price or yield between two underlying rates or indices.

Basis points per annum (bps or **bp pa)**   A basis point is one one-hundredth of a percentage point so, for example, 50 basis points is the same as a 0.5%. We will typically use basis points (bps) to indicate a running premium and so 50 bps refers to a annual premium of 50 basis points or 0.5%.

BCVA (*see also* **CVA**)   CVA taking into account one's own default as well as that of one's counterparty.

Bermudan option   An option where the buyer has the right to exercise at a set of discretely spaced times. It is intermediate between a European option (which allows exercise only at expiry) and an American option (which allows exercise at any time).

Bilateral netting (*see also* **netting and multilateral netting**)   A netting agreement between two parties.

Black–Scholes formula   A closed-form formula for valuing plain-vanilla options developed by Fischer Black and Myron Scholes in 1973 that led to the birth of pricing by replication for derivatives products.

Capital (*see* **regulatory capital and economic capital**)

Capital asset pricing model (CAPM)   A model that describes the relationship between risk and expected return in the pricing of risky securities. The CAPM postulates that investors need to be compensated for the risk-free rate of interest and the additional investment risk they take. The model states that an investor will require a return equal to the risk-free rate of interest plus a risk measure (beta) that depends on the correlation between the returns of the asset and those of the market.

Carry   Net gain or expense on a position due to interest, dividends and other payments, normally expressed in annual terms (such as basis points per annum).

Cashflow   An individual fixed or floating payment made on a specific date, such as a bond coupon.

Centralised counterparty   An entity that interposes itself as the buyer to every seller and as the seller to every buyer of a specified set of contracts.

Clean price   The price of a bond without accrued interest.

Clearing   To settle a trade by the seller delivering securities and the buyer delivering funds in the proper form. A trade that does not clear is said to fail.

Clearing house   A corporation, normally used in conjunction with an exchange, that facilitates the execution of trades by transferring funds, assigning deliveries and guaranteeing the performance of all obligations.

Collateral (or **margin**) **agreement**   A contractual agreement under which one party must supply collateral to a second counterparty when an exposure of that second counterparty to the first counterparty exceeds a specified level.

Collateralisation   The process of agreeing to and exchanging collateral or margin between two or more parties.

Collateralised debt obligation (CDO)   A broad type of instrument that repackages individual (usually debt) securities into a product that can be sold on the secondary market. The underlying securities may be, for example, auto loans, credit card debt, corporate debt or even other types of CDOs.

Conduit   An entity set up to assemble securities into a pool and issue other securities to investors that are ultimately guaranteed by the original pool of securities.

Contango   The situation where futures prices exceed spot prices (the opposite of backwardation). Contango implies an upward-sloping forward curve often due to the underlying cost of storage.

Contingent CDS (*see also* CDS)   A CDS contract that has a notional value linked to the value of another contract and therefore isolates counterparty credit risk arising from a reference derivative.

Convexity   A financial instrument is said to be convex if the price increases (decreases) faster (slower) than corresponding changes in the price of the underlying.

Correlation   Correlation measures linear dependence between variables. A correlation coefficient provides a measure of the degree to which random variables are linked in a linear fashion. A correlation coefficient will be positive when relative large or small values are associated together and vice versa. Financial instruments that move together in the same direction to the same extent have highly positive correlations. Instruments that move in the opposite direction to the same extent have highly negative correlations.

Credit default swap (CDS)   A specific swap transaction involving the transfer of a third party's credit risk from one party to another.

Credit event   Trigger event in a credit default swap, determined at the outset of the transaction. Markets standards include the existence of publicly available information confirming the occurrence, with respect to the reference credit, of bankruptcy, repudiation, restructuring, failure to pay, cross-default or cross-acceleration.

Credit exposure (*see* exposure)

Credit-linked note (CLN)   A funded credit derivative structure which is structured as a security with an embedded credit default swap allowing the issuer to transfer a specific credit risk to credit investors in note form. A CLN is therefore a synthetic bond.

Credit migration   A discrete change in the credit quality of an entity such that their credit-worthiness improves or worsens by a significant amount, often due to an up or downgrade in the underlying credit rating.

Credit rating   A published ranking, based on financial analysis that is supposed to measure the ability of a corporate, entity or individual to meet future obligations. The highest rating achievable is usually triple-A.

Credit spread   A yield measure reflecting the cost of credit risk in a security.

Credit Support Annex (CSA)   A legal document regulating collateral for derivatives transactions. A CSA defines the terms or rules under which collateral is posted or transferred between swap counterparties to mitigate exposure. Terms defined include thresholds, minimum transfer amounts, eligible securities and currencies, haircuts and rules for the settlement of disputes.

Credit support amount   The total net exposure that an institution has to their counterparty used in the context of a collateral agreement. Any independent amounts specified by a collateral agreement would be included in the CSA.

Credit value adjustment (CVA)   The difference between the risk-free and credit-risky values of a netting set where the risky value takes into account the possibility of the counterparty's default. CVA is the expected loss or value of counterparty credit risk. By convention, a positive CVA represents a cost.

Cross-currency swap (or **currency swap**)   A foreign exchange agreement between two parties to exchange principal and fixed rate interest payments in different currencies. Unlike interest rate swaps, cross-currency swaps involve the exchange of the principal amount at maturity.

Debt restructuring   A process that allows a company or a sovereign entity facing cashflow problems and in financial distress to renegotiate its debt payments (such as extending the maturity date) in order to improve or restore liquidity so that it can continue its operations and avoid often-impending bankruptcy.

Debt-to-equity swap   A restructuring where a company reduces their leverage by exchanging debt for equity with the original debt cancelled.

Debt value adjustment (DVA)   The opposite component to CVA which stems from a liability due to a negative exposure that would give rise to a gain if an institution were to default. There is some debate over the relevance of institutions "pricing in" their own default probability when assessing counterparty risk.

Default probability   Likelihood that an entity will default a some pre-defined interval in the future.

Dirty price (*see also* **clean price**)   A quoted bond price, including accrued interest.

Distressed exchange   An exchange of a security for another security or package of securities that amounts to a reduced financial obligation (such as a lower coupon or par amount).

Duration   The change in the value of a security resulting from a 1% change in interest rates and expressed in years. Unlike maturity, duration takes into account interest payments that occur throughout the course of holding an instrument. Duration therefore represents a weighted average of the cashflows from one or more securities.

Economic capital   The amount of actual risk capital that a firm requires to cover the risks that it takes, such as market risk, credit risk, operational risk and counterparty risk. It is the amount of capital that is needed to secure survival in a worst case scenario.

Effective EE   Same as EE but must be non-decreasing over a certain time period (typically 1 year).

Effective EPE   Average of effective EE over time (*see also* **EPE**).

Effective maturity   A duration-based measure for a portfolio of derivatives reflecting the average lifetime of the transactions scaled by the exposure over time.

Exchange (or **bourse**)   An organised market where standardised tradable securities, such as commodities, foreign exchange, futures and options contracts, are bought and sold by brokers and dealers who are members of the exchange.

Expected exposure (EE)   Average or expected value of the exposure at some point in time.

Expected positive exposure (EPE)   Average of the expected exposure (EE) over some pre-defined period (usually from the current time to the maximum maturity of the transactions in question).

Expected shortfall   An alternative to value-at-risk (VAR) which is more sensitive to the shape of the loss distribution in the "tail" or extreme, high-loss regions. The expected shortfall gives the expected loss on a portfolio in the worst case scenario, defined by a quantile. Expected shortfall is also called **tail VAR**.

Exposure (or **credit exposure**)   Positive value of one or more transactions with a counterparty. Should represent a net value where netting of transactions is possible.

Exposure at default (*see* exposure).

Fannie Mae (Federal National Mortgage Association)   The largest player in the secondary mortgage market.

Flight to quality   The flow of funds from riskier to safer investments in times of market uncertainty.

Freddie Mac (Federal Home Loan Mortgage Association)   The second largest player in the secondary mortgage market.

Futures   A standardised exchange-traded contract that requires delivery of a commodity, bond, currency or stock index, at a specified price, on a specified future date. Futures are typically cash-settled and so allow an investor to go long or short an underlying for speculation or hedging purposes without ever having to deliver or take delivery of the underlying.

Gamma   Gamma (or convexity) is the degree of curvature in the financial contract's price curve with respect to its underlying price. It is the rate of change of the delta with respect to changes in the underlying price.

Gaussian distribution (*see* **normal distribution**)

Haircut   A deduction in the market value of a security held as collateral reflecting the price uncertainty of the underlying security.

Hazard rate   An instantaneous default probability.

Hedge   An instrument traded in order to reduce the risk of adverse price movements in another instrument or portfolio of instruments. A hedging instrument therefore has price movements opposite to those of the underlying instruments. It may consist of cash instruments or derivatives.

Historical volatility   A measure of the actual volatility observed in the marketplace over a given time horizon in the past.

IMM dates   The four dates of each year which most credit default swaps and option contracts use as their scheduled termination date. The dates are the third Wednesday of March, June, September and December.

Implied volatility   Volatility required to reproduce a traded price (normally an option) in relation to a certain model (usually the Black–Scholes formula). Often thought of as the market's view of expected future volatility.

Independent amount   Usually an upfront cash amount that is posted from one party to another and is independent of any other collateral or margin terms. Also referred to as **initial margin**.

Initial margin (*see* **independent amount**)

Interest rate cap   A derivative in which the buyer effectively caps their exposure to rising interest rates by receiving payments at the end of each period if the interest rate exceeds an agreed strike price.

Interest rate floor   A derivative in which the buyer effectively floors their exposure to rising interest rates by receiving payments at the end of each period if the interest rate falls below an agreed strike price.

Interest rate swap   A contract requiring the exchange of interest payments on a specific notional amount. Usually fixed payments are swapped against floating payments in a particular currency.

In the money   The situation where an option has value if exercised immediately (although that may not be contractually possible). For a call (put) option, the current underlying price must be above (below) the strike price. In-the-money forward refers to the forward value of the underlying security and not the spot price.

Intrinsic value   Difference between the exercise price of an option at any time and its market price at the same time. It is therefore the value if the contract were to expire immediately as distinct from any potential value (time value for an option).

Investment grade   A bond considered "likely" to meet payment obligations. Corresponds to ratings as good as or better than Baa and BBB for Moody's and Standard & Poor's, respectively.

ISDA (International Swaps and Derivatives Association)   A trade organisation of participants in the market for OTC derivatives which publishes the *Code of Standard Wording, Assumptions and Provisions for Swaps.*

LIBOR (London Inter-Bank Offer Rate)   This is the rate of interest at which banks offer to lend money to one another in the so-called wholesale money markets in London.

Liquidity risk   The risk of not being able to trade within a reasonable tolerance in terms of the deviation from prevailing, expected or fair prices.

Loss given default (LGD)   The amount of loss on a credit instrument after the borrower has defaulted. It is typically stated as a percentage of the debt's par value.

Margining (*see* **collateralisation**)

Margin call frequency   The contractual period between which an institution may request collateral (or margin) from a counterparty. Can vary from a few days to continuous with daily margin calls being most common.

Margin threshold   The largest amount of an exposure that remains outstanding until one party has the right to call for collateral.

Mark-to-market (MtM)   The process of recording the price or value of a security, usually on a daily basis, to calculate profits and losses. MtM is used to refer to the current value of one or more derivatives instruments.

Market risk   The risk of losses due to daily fluctuations in the prices of securities such as equity, FX, interest rates and commodities.

Mean reversion   The statistical tendency of an underlying financial variable to gravitate back towards some long-term average.

Minimum transfer amount   The minimum amount that can be requested to be transferred as collateral (margin).

Monte Carlo simulation   A technique for working out an integral (often in many dimensions) by generating uniformly distributed pseudo-random numbers and evaluating the underlying function at all of these points.

Multilateral netting (*see also* netting and bilateral netting)   A netting agreement between three or more parties which is typically utilised by a central counterparty.

Netting set   A set of transactions with a single counterparty that are subject to a legally enforceable bilateral netting arrangement.

Netting   A legally enforceable arrangement covering two or more underlying contracts so that, in the event of the default or insolvency of one of the parties, positive (receivable) and negative (payable) MtM values of contracts can be netted against one another to arrive at a total liability or claim representing the value of all underlying contracts.

Normal (Gaussian) distribution   The most common of statistical distributions, which typically results from a large sample of uncorrelated random events.

Over-the-counter (OTC) contract   A privately negotiated derivatives contract that is transacted away from an exchange.

Options   A contract giving the right but not the obligation to sell or buy a commodity, financial instrument or index, at a specified price for a certain period.

Out of the money   The situation where an option has zero value if exercised immediately. For a call (put) option, the current underlying price must be below (above) the strike price. Out-of-the-money forward refers to the forward value of the underlying security and not the spot price.

Par or **principal value**   The amount of an obligation upon which interest is calculated.

Pari passu   Equal in all respects or enjoying the same rights without bias or preference. If a derivatives exposure is said to be *pari passu* with a senior unsecured bond then it means that the same percentage amount can expect to be recovered on both contracts.

Path dependency   A financial contract whose value depends on the path taken by the underlying market variable(s).

P&L (profit and loss)   A quantification of gains or losses on one or more financial contracts in a given period.

Put–call parity   An arbitrage relationship that must exist between the prices of European put and call options that both have the same underlying, strike price and maturity date.

Quantile   Point on a distribution of values such that a given proportion of the values are less than or equal to the point. For example, the 0.99 or 99% quantile represents a point where 99% of the values fall below (and correspondingly 1% fall above).

Rating   An evaluation of a corporate or municipal bond's relative safety, according to the issuer's ability to make required payments. Bonds are rated by various rating agencies such as Standard & Poor's and Moody's. Ratings range from triple-A (AAA or Aaa for Standard & Poor's and Moody's, respectively) to D, which represents a company in default.

Recovery rate   The percentage amount that a creditor receives in relation to claims on a defaulted counterparty.

Regulatory capital   The amount of Tier I and Tier II long-term funding that commercial banks are compelled to hold based upon the Basel Accord regulations for risk adjustment.

Remargin period   Used to denote the time from when collateral (margin) is called for until it is actually received accounting for some worst case delays. This will be equal to the margin call frequency with some additional conservative delay added.

Replacement cost   The amount it would cost to replace an asset or derivative contract at current market rates. Accounts for liquidity and transaction costs.

Risky annuity (*see also* **annuity**)   An annuity taking into account the probability of default of the annuity payer with respect to each cashflow. A risky annuity will be worth no more than the equivalent annuity.

SFT (structured finance transaction)   A non-standard lending arrangement customised to the needs of a specific client which is more complicated than traditional loans, bonds and equity. Complicated leveraged products such as CDOs fall under the definition of structured finance.

SIV (structured investment vehicle)   A fund with the strategy to borrow money by issuing short-term securities at low interest and then lend that money by buying long-term securities at higher interest, making a profit for investors from the difference. SIVs were a casualty of the credit crisis and ceased to exist by the end of 2008.

SPE (special purpose entity, *see* **SPV)**

SPV (special purpose vehicle)   A legal entity (usually a limited company of some type or a limited partnership) created to fulfil narrow, specific or temporary objectives. SPVs were often used by firms to isolate a transaction for the benefit of a client and so, in theory, they would not bear risk of default of that firm.

Standard deviation   A measure used to characterise the variability of a random variable.

Stress testing   Simulating different financial market conditions and assessing their potential effects on a portfolio of financial instruments.

Strike price   The price at which an option holder can buy or sell the underlying asset. Also called **exercise price**.

Time value   The amount by which the value of an option exceeds the intrinsic value. It represents the potential gain from an increasing option premium in the future.

Total return swap (TRS)   A financial contract which allows synthetic transfer of both the credit and market risk of an underlying asset.

Unexpected loss   A term commonly used to give an indication of the volatility of losses around the expected loss. The unexpected loss will be defined as a worst case loss at some confidence level. The expected loss may or may not be subtracted from this value.

Value-at-risk (VAR)   For a given confidence level and time horizon, VAR is defined as a value such that the probability that the loss on a portfolio exceeds this value in the defined time horizon is one minus the confidence level. For example, a 99% VAR of $1m in 10 days means that the probability of having a loss of more than $1m in 10 days is 1%.

Variation margin   Additional margin required to bring an account up to the required level due to market fluctuations. Will normally correspond to the current exposure less any initial margin (independent amount) and previously posted margin but also accounting for minimum transfer amount and rounding.

Volatility   Standard deviation represented on an annualised basis.

Walkaway feature (or extinguisher)   Contractual feature that allows an institution to terminate (walk away from) a transaction in the event their counterparty defaults. In case the MtM value to the institution is negative then this represents a gain from their counterparty defaulting.

Yield curve   For a particular series of fixed income instruments such as government bonds, the graph of the yields to maturity of the series plotted by maturity.

References

Altman, E. (1968) "Financial ratios, discriminant analysis and the prediction of corporate bankruptcy," *Journal of Finance*, **23**, 589–609.

Altman, E. and V. Kishore (1996) "Almost everything you wanted to know about recoveries on defaulted bonds," *Financial Analysts Journal*, November/December.

Andersen, L., J. Sidenius and S. Basu (2003) "All your hedges in one basket," *Risk Magazine*, November.

Arvanitis, A. and J. Gregory (2001) *Credit: The Complete Guide to Pricing, Hedging and Risk Management*, Risk Books

Arvanitis, A., J. Gregory and J-P Laurent (1999) "Building models for credit spreads," *Journal of Derivatives*, **6**(3), Spring, 27–43.

Baird, D.G. (2001) *Elements of Bankruptcy*, Third Edition, Foundation Press, New York.

Basurto, M.S. and M. Singh (2008) *Counterparty Risk in the Over-the-Counter Derivatives Market*, IMF Working Paper, November, pp. 1–19. Available at SSRN: *http://ssrn.com/abstract=1316726*

Bates, D. and R. Craine (1999) "Valuing the Futures Market Clearinghouse's default exposure during the 1987 crash," *Journal of Money, Credit & Banking*, **31**(2) (May), 248–272.

BCBS (2004) *An Explanatory Note on the Basel II IRB Risk Weight Functions*, Basel Committee on Banking Supervision, October. Available at *www.bis.org*

BCBS (2005) *The Application of Basel II to Trading Activities and the Treatment of Double Default*, Basel Committee on Banking Supervision. Available at *www.bis.org*

BCBS (2006) *International Convergence of Capital Measurement and Capital Standards, A Revised Framework – Comprehensive Version*, Basel Committee on Banking Supervision, June. Available at *www.bis.org*

Black, F. and J. Cox (1976) "Valuing corporate securities: Some effects of bond indenture provisions," *Journal of Finance*, **31**, 351–367.

Black, F. and M. Scholes (1973) "The pricing of options and corporate liabilities," *Journal of Political Economy*, **81**(3), 637–654.

Bliss, R.R. and G.G. Kaufman (2005) *Derivatives and Systemic Risk: Netting, Collateral, and Closeout*, FRB of Chicago Working Paper No. 2005-03, May 10. Available at SSRN: *http://ssrn.com/abstract=730648*

Bluhm, C., L. Overbeck and C. Wagner (2003) *An Introduction to Credit Risk Modeling*, Chapman & Hall.

Brady, N. (1988) *Report of the Presidential Task Force on Market Mechanisms*, US Government Printing Office, Washington, DC.

Brigo, D. and M. Masetti (2005a) "Risk-neutral pricing of counterparty risk," in M. Pykhtin (Ed.), *Counterparty Credit Risk Modelling*, Risk Books.

Brigo, D. and M. Masetti (2005b) *A Formula for Interest Rate Swaps Valuation under Counterparty Risk in Presence of Netting Agreements*. Available at *www.damianobrigo.it*

Brigo, D., K. Chourdakis and I. Bakkar (2008) *Counterparty Risk Valuation for Energy-Commodities Swaps: Impact of Volatilities and Correlation*, June 24. Available at SSRN: *http://ssrn.com/abstract=1150818*

Canabarro, E. and D. Duffie (2003) "Measuring and marking counterparty risk," in L. Tilman (Ed.), *Asset/Liability Management for Financial Institutions*, Institutional Investor Books.

Canabarro, E., E. Picoult, and T. Wilde (2003) "Analyzing counterparty risk," *Risk*, **16**(9), 117–122.

Collin-Dufresne, P., R.S. Goldstein and J.S. Martin (2001) "The determinants of credit spread changes," *Journal of Finance*, **56**, 2177–2207.

Cooper, I.A. and A.S. Mello (1991) "The default risk of swaps," *Journal of Finance*, **46**, 597–620.

Das, S. (2008) *The Credit Default Swap (CDS) Market – Will It Unravel?*, February 2. Available at *http://www.eurointelligence.com/Article3.1018+M583ca062a10.0.html*

Das, S. and R. Sundaram (1999) "Of smiles and smirks, a term structure perspective," *Journal of Financial and Quantitative Analysis*, **34**, 211–239.

De Prisco, B. and D. Rosen (2005) "Modelling stochastic counterparty credit exposures for derivatives portfolios," in M. Pykhtin (Ed.), *Counterparty Credit Risk Modelling*, Risk Books.

Downing, C., S. Underwood and Y. Xing (2005) *Is Liquidity Risk Priced in the Corporate Bond Market?*, Working Paper, Rice University.

Duffie, D. and M. Huang (1996) "Swap rates and credit quality," *Journal of Finance*, **51**, 921–950.

Duffie, D. and K.J. Singleton (2003) *Credit Risk: Pricing, Measurement, and Management* (Princeton Series in Finance), Princeton University Press.

Duffie, D. and H. Zhu (2009) "Swap rates and credit quality," *Journal of Finance*, **51**, 921–950.

Duffee, G. R. (1996a) "Idiosyncratic variation of Treasury Bill yields," *Journal of Finance*, **51**, 527–551.

Duffee, G. R. (1996b) "On measuring credit risks of derivative instruments," *Journal of Banking and Finance*, **20**(5), 805–833.

Engelmann, B. and R. Rauhmeier (Eds.) (2006) *The Basel II Risk Parameters: Estimation, Validation, and Stress Testing*, Springer-Verlag.

Figlewski, S. (1984) "Margins and market integrity: Margin setting for stock index futures and options," *Journal of Futures Markets*, **13**(4), 389–408.

Financial Times (2008) "Banks face $10bn monolines charges," June 10.

Finger, C. (1999) "Conditional approaches for CreditMetrics portfolio distributions," *CreditMetrics Monitor*, April.

Finger, C., V. Finkelstein, G. Pan, J-P. Lardy and J. Tiemey (2002) *CreditGrades Technical Document*, RiskMetrics Group.

Fitzpatrick, K. (2002) "Spotlight on counterparty risk," *International Financial Review*, **99**, November 30.

Fleck, M. and A. Schmidt (2005) "Analysis of Basel II treatment of counterparty risk," in M. Pykhtin (Ed.), *Counterparty Credit Risk Modelling*, Risk Books,

Geman, H. (2005) *Commodities and Commodity Derivatives*, John Wiley & Co.

Geman, H. and V.N. Nguyen (2005) "Soy bean inventory and forward curve dynamics," *Management Science*, **51**(7), July, 1076–1091.

Gemmill, G. (1994) "Margins and the safety of clearing houses," *Journal of Banking and Finance*, **18**(5), 979–996.

Ghosh, A., G. Rennison, A. Soulier, P. Sharma and M. Malinowska (2008) *Counterparty Risk in Credit Markets*, Barclays Capital Research Report.

Gibson, M.S. (2005) "Measuring counterparty credit risk exposure to a margined counterparty," in M. Pykhtin (Ed.), *Counterparty Credit Risk Modelling*, Risk Books.

Glasserman, P. and J. Li (2005) "Importance sampling for portfolio credit risk," *Management Science*, **51**(11), November, 1643–1656.

Glasserman, P. and B. Yu (2002) "Pricing American options by simulation: Regression now or regression later?", in H. Niederreiter (Ed.), *Monte Carlo and Quasi-Monte Carlo Methods*, Springer-Verlag, Berlin.

Gordy, M. (2002) "Saddlepoint approximation of credit risk+," *Journal of Banking and Finance*, **26**, 1335–1353.

Gordy, M. (2004) "Granularity adjustment in portfolio credit risk management," in G.P. Szegö (Ed.), *Risk Measures for the 21st Century*, John Wiley & Sons.

Gordy, M. and B. Howells (2006) "Procyclicality in Basel II: Can we treat the disease without killing the patient?" *Journal of Financial Intermediation*, **15**, 395–417.

Gordy, M. and S. Juneja (2008) *Nested Simulation in Portfolio Risk Measurement*, Working Paper.

Gregory, J. (2008a) "A trick of the credit tail," *Risk*, March, 88–92.

Gregory, J. (2008b) "A free lunch and the credit crunch," *Risk*, August, 74–77.

Gregory, J. (2009) "Being two-faced over counterparty credit risk," *Risk*, **22**(2), 86–90.

Gregory, J. and J-P. Laurent (2003) "I will survive," *Risk*, June, 103–107.

Gregory, J. and J-P. Laurent (2004) "In the core of correlation," *Risk*, October, 87–91.

Gupton, G.M., C.C. Finger and M. Bhatia (1997) *CreditMetrics Technical Document*, Morgan Guaranty Trust Company, New York.

Hamilton, D.T., G.M. Gupton and A. Berthault (2001) *Default and Recovery Rates of Corporate Bond Issuers: 2000*, Moody's Investors Service, February.

Hardouvelis, G. and D. Kim (1995) "Margin requirements: Price fluctuations, and market participation in metal futures," *Journal of Money, Credit and Banking*, **27**(3), 659–671.

Hartzmark, M. (1986) "The effects of changing margin levels on futures market activity, the composition of traders in the market, and price performance," *Journal of Business*, **59**(2), S147–S180.

Hille, C.T., J. Ring and H. Shimanmoto (2005) "Modelling counterparty credit exposure for credit default swaps," in M. Pykhtin (Ed.), *Counterparty Credit Risk Modelling*, Risk Books.

Hills, B., D. Rule, S. Parkinson and C. Young (1999) "Central counterparty clearing houses and financial stability," *Bank of England Financial Stability Review*, June, 122–133.

Hughston, L.P. and S.M. Turnbull (2001) "Credit risk: Constructing the basic building block," *Economic Notes*, **30**(2), 257–279.

Hull, J. and A. White (1990) "Pricing interest rate derivative securities," *Review of Financial Studies*, **3**(4), 573–592.

Hull, J. and A. White (2004) *Valuation of a CDO and an nth to Default CDS without Monte Carlo Simulation*, Working Paper, September.

Hull, J., M. Predescu and A. White (2004) "The relationship between credit default swap spreads, bond yields, and credit rating announcements," *Journal of Banking and Finance*, **28**(11), November, 2789–2811.

Hull, J., M. Predescu and A. White (2005) *The Valuation of Correlation-dependent Credit Derivatives Using a Structural Model*. Available at SSRN: *http://ssrn.com/abstract=686481*

Jamshidian, F. and Y. Zhu (1997) "Scenario simulation: Theory and methodology," *Finance and Stochastics*, **1**, 43–67.

Jarrow, R.A. and S.M. Turnbull (1992) "Drawing the analogy," *Risk*, **5**(10), 63–70.

Jarrow, R.A. and S.M. Turnbull (1995) "Pricing options on financial securities subject to default risk," *Journal of Finance*, **50**, 53–86.

Jarrow, R. and S.M. Turnbull (1997) "When swaps are dropped," *Risk*, **10**(5), 70–75.

Jarrow, R.A. and F. Yu (2001) "Counterparty risk and the pricing of defaultable securities," *Journal of Finance*, **56**, 1765–1799.

Johnson, H. and R. Stulz (1987) "The pricing of options with default risk," *Journal of Finance*, **42**, 267–280.

Jorion, P. (2007) *Value-at-Risk: The new benchmark for managing financial risk*, Third Edition, McGraw-Hill.

Kealhofer, S. (1995) "Managing default risk in derivative portfolios," in *Derivative Credit Risk: Advances in Measurement and Management*, Renaissance Risk Publications, London.

Kealhofer, S. (2003) "Quantifying credit risk, I: Default prediction," *Financial Analysts Journal*, January/February, 30–44.

Kealhofer, S. and M. Kurbat (2002) *The Default Prediction Power of the Merton Approach, Relative to Debt Ratings and Accounting Variables*, KMV LLC, Mimeo.

KMV Corporation (1993) *Portfolio Management of Default Risk*, KMV Corporation, San Francisco.

Kolb, R.W. and J.A. Overdahl (2006) *Understanding Futures Markets*, Wiley/Blackwell.

Laurent, J-P. and J. Gregory (2005) "Basket default swaps, CDOs and factor copulas," *Journal of Risk*, **7**(4), 103–122.

Leland, H. (1994) "Corporate debt value, bond covenants, and optimal capital structure," *Journal of Finance*, **49**, 1213–1252.

Levy, A. and R. Levin (1999) "Wrong-way exposure," *Risk*, July.

Li, D.X (1998) "Constructing a credit curve," in *Credit Risk: A RISK Special Report*, November, pp. 40–44.

Li, D.X. (2000) "On default correlation: A copula function approach," *Journal of Fixed Income*, **9**(4), March, 43–54.

Lomibao, D. and S. Zhu (2005) "A conditional valuation approach for path-dependent instruments," in M. Pykhtin (Ed.), *Counterparty Credit Risk Modelling*, Risk Books.

Longstaff, F.A. and S.E. Schwartz (2001) "Valuing American options by simulation: A simple least squares approach," *Review of Financial Studies*, **14**(1), 113–147.

Matthews, R.A.J. (1995) "Tumbling toast, Murphy's law and the fundamental constants," *European Journal of Physics*, **16**, 172–176.

Martin, R., K. Thompson and C. Browne (2001) "Taking to the saddle," *Risk*, June, 91–94.

Mashal, R. and M. Naldi (2005) "Pricing multiname default swaps with counterparty risk," *Journal of Fixed Income*, **14**(4), 3–16.

MacKenzie, D. (2006) *An Engine, Not a Camera: How Financial Models Shape Markets*, MIT Press.

Meese, R. and K. Rogoff (1983) "Empirical exchange rate models of the seventies," *Journal of International Economics*, **14**, 3–24.

Merton, R.C. (1974) "On the pricing of corporate debt: The risk structure of interest rates," *Journal of Finance*, **29**, 449–470.

Moody's Investors Service (2007) *Corporate Default and Recovery Rates: 1920-2006*, Moody's Special Report, New York, February.

O'Kane, D. (2007) *Approximating Independent Loss Distributions with an Adjusted Binomial Distribution*, EDHEC Working Paper.

O'Kane, D. (2008) *Pricing Single-name and Portfolio Credit Derivatives*, Wiley Finance.

Ong, M.K. (Ed.) (2006) *The Basel Handbook: A Guide for Financial Practitioners*, Second Edition, Risk Books.

Picoult, E. (2002) "Quantifying the risks of trading," in M.A.H. Dempster (Ed.), *Risk Management: Value at Risk and Beyond*, Cambridge University Press.

Picoult, E. (2005) "Calculating and hedging exposure, credit value adjustment and economic capital for counterparty credit risk," in M. Pykhtin (Ed.), *Counterparty Credit Risk Modelling*, Risk Books.

Pindyck, R. (2001) "The dynamics of commodity spot and futures markets: A primer," *Energy Journal*, **22**(3), 1–29.

Pirrong, C. (2009) *The Economics of Clearing in Derivatives Markets: Netting, Asymmetric Information, and the Sharing of Default Risks through a Central Counterparty*. Available at SSRN: *http://ssrn.com/abstract = 1340660*

Polizu, C., F.L. Neilson and N. Khakee (2006) *Criteria for Rating Global Credit Derivative Product Companies*, Standard and Poor's Working Paper.

Press, W.H., S.A. Teukolsky, W.T. Vetterling and B.P. Flannery (2007) *Numerical Recipes: The Art of Scientific Computing*, Third Edition, Cambridge University Press.

Pugachevsky, D. (2005) "Pricing counterparty risk in unfunded synthetic CDO tranches" in M. Pykhtin (Ed.), *Counterparty Credit Risk Modelling*, Risk Books.

Pykhtin, M. (2003) "Unexpected recovery risk," *Risk*, **16**(8), 74–78.

Rebonato, R. (1998) *Interest Rate Options Models*, Second Edition, John Wiley & Sons.

Reimers, M. and M. Zerbs (1999) "A multi-factor statistical model for interest rates," *Algo Research Quarterly*, **2**(3), 53–64.

Remeza, A. (2007) *Credit Derivative Product Companies Poised to Open for Business*, Moody's Investor Services Special Report.

Rowe, D. (1995) "Aggregating credit exposures: The primary risk source approach," in *Derivative Credit Risk*, Risk Books, pp. 13–21.

Rowe, D. and M. Mulholland (1999) "Aggregating market-driven credit exposures: A multiple risk source approach," in *Derivative Credit Risk*, Second Edition, Risk Books, pp. 141–147.

Sarno, L. (2005) "Viewpoint: Towards a solution to the puzzles in exchange rate economics: Where do we stand?" *Canadian Journal of Economics*, **38**, 673–708.

Sarno, L. and M.P. Taylor (2002) *The Economics of Exchange Rates*, Cambridge University Press.

Segoviano Basurto, M. and M. Singh (2008) *Counterparty Risk in the Over-the-counter Derivatives Market*, IMF Working Papers, pp. 1–19. Available at SSRN: *http://ssrn.com/abstract = 1316726*

Shadab, H.B. (2009) "Guilty by association? Regulating credit default swaps," *Entrepreneurial Business Law Journal*, August 19. Available at SSRN: *http://ssrn.com/abstract = 1368026*

Shelton, D. (2004) *Back to Normal, Proxy Integration: A Fast Accurate Method for CDO and CDO-squared Pricing*, Citigroup Structured Credit Research, August.

Singh, M. and J. Aitken (2009) *Deleveraging after Lehman: Evidence from Reduced Rehypothecation*, IMF Working Paper, March, pp. 1–11. Available at SSRN: *http://ssrn.com/abstract = 1366171*

Sorensen, E.H. and T.F. Bollier (1994) "Pricing swap default risk," *Financial Analysts Journal*, **50**(3), May/June, 23–33.

Soros, G. (2009) "My three steps to financial reform," *Financial Times*, June 17.

Standard & Poor's (2007) *Ratings Performance 2006: Stability and Transition*, S&P, New York, February 16.

Standard & Poor's (2008) *Default, Transition, and Recovery: 2008 Annual Global Corporate Default Study and Rating Transitions*, April 2.

Tavakoli, J.M. (2008) *Structured Finance and Collateralized Debt Obligations: New Developments in Cash and Synthetic Securitization*, John Wiley & Sons.

Thompson, J.R. (2009) *Counterparty Risk in Financial Contracts: Should the Insured Worry about the Insurer?* Available at SSRN: *http://ssrn.com/abstract = 1278084*

Turnbull, S. (2005) "The pricing implications of counterparty risk for non-linear credit products," in M. Pykhtin (Ed.), *Counterparty Credit Risk Modelling*, Risk Books.

Tzani, R. and J. J. Chen (2006) *Credit Derivative Product Companies*, Moody's Investor Services, March.

Vasicek, O. (1997) *The Loan Loss Distribution*, KMV Corporation.

Wilde, T. (2001) *ISDA's Response to the Basel Committee on Banking Supervision's Consultation on the New Capital Accord*, May, Annex 1.

Wilde, T. (2005) "Analytic methods for portfolio counterparty risk," in M. Pykhtin (Ed.), *Counterparty Credit Risk Modelling*, Risk Books.

Index